PENGUIN  CLASSICS

THE PHILOKALIA

Andrew Louth is Emeritus Professor of Patristic and Byzantine Studies in the Department of Theology and Religion at Durham University.

Jonathan L. Zecher is a Senior Research Fellow in the Institute for Religion and Critical Inquiry at the Australian Catholic University.

The Philokalia

A Selection

Translated by JONATHAN L. ZECHER
and ANDREW LOUTH
with an Introduction by ANDREW LOUTH

PENGUIN BOOKS

PENGUIN CLASSICS

UK | USA | Canada | Ireland | Australia
India | New Zealand | South Africa

Penguin Classics is part of the Penguin Random House group of companies
whose addresses can be found at global.penguinrandomhouse.com

Penguin Random House UK
One Embassy Gardens, 8 Viaduct Gardens, London SW11 7BW

penguin.co.uk

Penguin
Random House
UK

First published in Penguin Classics 2025
002

Set in 10.25/12.25pt Sabon LT Pro
Typeset by Six Red Marbles UK, Thetford, Norfolk
Printed and bound in Great Britain by Clays Ltd, Elcograf S.p.A.

The authorized representative in the EEA is Penguin Random House Ireland,
Morrison Chambers, 32 Nassau Street, Dublin D02 YH68

A CIP catalogue record for this book is available from the British Library

ISBN: 978-0-241-20137-4

Penguin Random House is committed to a sustainable future
for our business, our readers and our planet. This book is made from
Forest Stewardship Council® certified paper.

MIX
Paper | Supporting
responsible forestry
FSC
www.fsc.org   FSC® C018179

Contents

SELECTIONS FROM THE PHILOKALIA OF THE HOLY ASCETIC FATHERS

Introduction

In 1782 there was published in Venice the *Philokalia of the Holy Ascetic Fathers*. It appeared in two folio volumes, continuously paginated and usually bound together, consisting of an anthology (which is what *philokalia* means in Greek, though etymology suggests 'love of the beautiful') of works of ascetical and mystical theology from the fourth to the fifteenth century – more than a millennium of monastic literature. The only names mentioned on the title page of the book are John Mavrogordatos, a wealthy Greek philanthropist who provided the funds for the publication of the collection, and Antonio Bortoli, the Venetian printer and publisher. Nevertheless the *Philokalia* is indelibly associated with two other names: Nikodemos, a native of Naxos and for most of his life a monk of the Holy Mountain of Athos until his death in 1809 (and thus called Nikodemos the Hagiorite, or Nikodemos of the Holy Mountain), declared a saint in 1955, and Makarios, a native of Corinth, briefly its bishop, a position he lost as a result of the Russo-Turkish war of 1768, after which he was confirmed in 1773 as a bishop, with a stipend but without a see, by the Sultan, and spent the rest of his life in various islands of the Aegean, much sought after as a teacher, and canonized by popular acclaim by his fellow Corinthians shortly after his death in 1805.

Both men, Nikodemos and Makarios, were associated with revival movements in Greece, as the Greeks started to flex their muscles and move towards independence from the Ottoman Empire, which they achieved (or, rather, began to achieve) in 1821. These movements involved the emergence of a national consciousness, the encouragement of Hellenism through teaching and the establishment of schools, as well as a religious revival, which sought to restore authenticity to the practice of Orthodox Christianity, especially Orthodox monasticism, which had been damaged during the years from 1453 of the *Tourkokratia*, the 'Turkish Yoke'. Orthodox Christianity, or 'Orthodoxy', is the version of Christianity practised for centuries in Greek, Arab and Slavic lands, and now globally. But it traces its roots to the earliest Christians via the history and Christian culture of the Eastern Roman – 'Byzantine' – Empire. It was within that world that Christian monasticism began and all of the authors of the *Philokalia* lived, prayed and died. The movement to restoring and purifying Orthodoxy in the nineteenth century meant recovering its roots in early and Byzantine Christian life, available through the long memory of liturgy and communal life, and, in this case, in the written monuments of unageing intellect.

The *Philokalia* is a shining beacon of this religious revival. But it does not stand alone: Nikodemos was tireless in preparing the ground for the renewal of Orthodoxy in Greece, to be independent of the political and religious authority of the Ottoman Empire; he put together a work called the *Pedalion* (the 'Rudder'), a compilation of the Holy Canons (the legal code of the Orthodox Church) together with his own commentary; expositions of the meaning of the festal hymns of the Orthodox services; and a host of works of spiritual theology – guidance for the Christian life, especially the importance of frequent communion. Although his purpose was a kind of harvest of the Greek Orthodox tradition, he also drew on the spirituality of the Catholic Counter-Reformation, not least the Jesuits.

The contribution of the two men to the *Philokalia* remains unclear: the work itself is anonymous and, though the names of both men are associated with the work, what role each one played is a matter of conjecture – conjecture apparently affected by the rise and fall of the esteem in which they were individually held. After the canonization of St Nikodemos in 1955, modern scholars, writing in response to and celebration of this event, tended to attribute at least the scholarship displayed in the work to Nikodemos, but in the celebrations following the second centenary in 2005/6 of Makarios's death and canonization it is

Makarios's role that has been in the ascendant. It looks likely that Makarios provided the support for the project, eliciting from John Mavrogordatos the funds necessary for the publication of the final work in Venice (there, since in the Ottoman Empire there were no presses authorized to publish religious works in Greek script), and may well have had a say in the selection of the texts included in the *Philokalia*, while Nikodemos was involved in putting them together, providing introductions to each of the writers included, as well as the introduction to the volumes as a whole. Mavrogordatos is a rather shadowy figure, though a member of a prominent Greek family in Constantinople, with a long history of intellectual and cultural patronage. He was a lay-person (not a monk or priest) and devoted to Orthodoxy.

Presenting the texts of the *Philokalia* in chronological sequence has the effect – surely intended – of demonstrating the traditional character of hesychast spirituality, as it emerged from the controversies of the fourteenth century. 'Hesychast' spirituality is a way of life – especially the monastic life – that sets great store on the acquisition of quiet and tranquillity (for which the Greek is *hesychia*) in which prayer might become possible. The use of the term *hesychia* goes back to the beginnings of Christian (and indeed non-Christian) attempts to live a life centred on prayer. By the beginning of the second Christian millennium, there had grown up a considerable body of advice on living such a life of prayer and quiet (many such texts are included in the *Philokalia*), and also claims for the efficacy of this way of life: claims that monks who persisted in their solitary prayer could come to see the uncreated light of the Godhead, and in beholding that light be irradiated by it and transfigured – claims dismissed by the opponents of hesychasm, in the controversy that arose in the first part of the fourteenth century, as self-deluding hallucination. In this sense, the *Philokalia* might be understood as a monumental statement of what tradition is and how one finds one's place in it.

Many of the monks who pursued hesychast prayer in this way belonged to the monastic republic settled on a narrow peninsula, reaching out south-east of Thessaloniki into the Aegean, and dominated by Mount Athos; they found their champion in

St Gregory Palamas (c.1296–1359), himself for a time an Athonite monk, and later Archbishop of Thessaloniki, to the diocese of which the Athonite peninsula belonged, who defended transfiguration into the uncreated light of the Godhead as the final end of a process of deification or divinization, in which the human person was restored to the original state in which God had created him in the image and likeness of God (cf. Gen. 1:26–7). Furthermore, Palamas's defence of hesychasm went beyond simply establishing the legitimacy of hesychasm as a devotional practice; for him it meant seeing prayer as a life-transforming engagement with God, in which the human is transfigured into the divine ('deification') without breaching the utter transcendence of the uncreated God over his creation, including the human creation, brought into being out of nothing. This theological vision was seen as entailing a distinction within the uncreated Godhead between his essence and his activities or operations (between his *ousia* and his *energeiai*), as well as seeing the human person and the created cosmos as mutually informing each other in the ultimate reality of the Incarnate Christ – something manifest in the way in which the reality of every creature, its *logos* or principle, is grounded in the *Logos* or Word of God, incarnate in Christ. The lineaments of this vision of the ultimate coinherence of God and his creation were first traced by the great seventh-century theologian St Maximos the Confessor, who – after Palamas – is granted most space in the selections that make up the *Philokalia*.

This amazing vision of the ramifications of Christian belief in a God who creates all that is out of love, and who also, out of love, identifies himself with his creation through the Incarnation of the Word of God to the point of experiencing death on the Cross, is worked out by St Maximos in a way that draws on all the resources of patristic or Byzantine theology – Scriptural exegesis, liturgical experience growing out of the centrality of the Eucharist or divine Liturgy, the experience of prayer, the philosophical insights of the Greek tradition, beginning with Plato and Aristotle and reaching its speculative heights in Neoplatonism, an understanding of what it is to be human implicit in ascetical and mystical experience – and Maximos's vision is lent even greater power by the cumulative experience of Byzantine monasticism.

The selection of treatises, made by Sts Nikodemos and Makarios, traces adumbrations of this vision in early writers of the fourth and fifth centuries, such as Evagrios of Pontos, Diadochos of Photiki and Mark the Monk, leading quickly to a series of treatises by Maximos the Confessor, then to monks associated with the Monastery of the Burning Bush (now the Monastery of St Catherine) at the foot of Mount Sinai, with whom is associated a remarkable but otherwise unknown thinker, Elias Ekdikos. Then there follows a single long work by Peter of Damascus, itself a kind of *philokalia* or anthology of notable texts. He is followed by Symeon the New Theologian, represented by a short homily, an inauthentic popular work on three 'methods' of prayer, and a composition in the form of 153 chapters drawn from Symeon the New Theologian and his mentor, Symeon the Elder (or, 'the Pious'): a brief interlude, overshadowed by the three *Gnostic Chapters* of the one to whom Symeon the New Theologian had entrusted his spiritual legacy as his biographer and editor, Nikitas Stithatos. We then enter into the heart of the hesychast controversy with writings by Gregory Palamas himself, preceded by his mentors, Theoliptos of Philadelphia and – at greater length – Gregory of Sinai. The works of Palamas in the *Philokalia* mostly display his skill as a spiritual father and guide; nevertheless they include the *Hagioretic Tome*, a statement and defence of the hesychast position, and Palamas's summary of the philosophical basis of hesychasm in *One Hundred and Fifty Philosophical Chapters*. After Palamas we find a collection of works composed, no longer in the heat of the hesychast controversy, but in the decades following, when the assured doctrine of hesychasm could be 'recollected in tranquillity' – mostly, and confusingly, by authors called 'Kallistos'.

Anthologies are curious creations, and it is not always clear how to approach them, especially one so massive and apparently (though not actually) comprehensive as the *Philokalia*. How did Makarios and Nikodemos expect it to be read? Their title suggests a highly aspirational aim: *Philokalia of the*

Watchful Elders, Gathered from Our Holy and God-Bearing Fathers, in which the Intellect is Purified, Enlightened, and Perfected through Moral Philosophy in Action and Contemplation. This lengthy description is not unusual for an early modern title, and it tells us how its compilers hoped it would be read: as a resource and mirror for readers' own progress in prayer, contemplation and, as we will see below, deification. Yet they cannot have imagined that people would sit down and read the *Philokalia* cover to cover, all one thousand, two hundred and six double-columned pages. Probably, it was intended – as is this selection – for more limited, thoughtful forays. Readers might choose one author or another and read, pray, meditate, ponder, slowly, and without hastening to the next thing. There is no right order, no single method, for reading the *Philokalia*, and we hope that readers will find their own way into this anthology.

A thread that becomes increasingly manifest with the passage of time is a way of praying based on the use of the Jesus Prayer: 'Lord Jesus Christ, Son of God, have mercy on me, a sinner'. The earliest references are tantalizing in their allusiveness – the prayer 'Lord Jesus', mentioned by Diadochos, for example – but gradually there emerges the prayer in its recognizable form, accompanied by breathing techniques to hold the one praying in the presence of God. The *Philokalia* itself, then, ranges from simple practical instruction in the Prayer of the Heart through the use of the Jesus Prayer – several of the most concise and practical works, including the *Three Methods of Prayer*, attributed to Symeon the New Theologian, and Mark of Ephesos's brief commentary on the Jesus Prayer, are contained in a kind of appendix, outside the chronological sequence of works in Byzantine Greek, in a more accessible modern Greek ('demotic') translation – to works of real philosophical density, such as the works of Maximos the Confessor, and indeed Gregory Palamas himself. Both simple practical instruction in prayer and some indication of the philosophical complexities that underlie such prayer (but which the one praying does not himself need to understand) are to be found in the *Philokalia* – or at least in the Greek *Philokalia* of 1782, for the selection of texts found in translation into Church Slavonic (by St Paisy Velichkovsky) and later into Russian (by St Theophan the Recluse), called the *Dobrotolyubie*, fights shy of the more intellectually demanding texts: the Church Slavonic version including nothing by either Maximos or Palamas, while the Russian version includes only the shorter pieces by Palamas.

Although this volume draws only on the Greek *Philokalia*, a word is necessary about the Slavonic and Russian versions called the *Dobrotolyubie*, a kind of chiastic calque of *philoka-lia* (with no independent meaning in the Slav languages, unlike *philokalia*, which means, we have already noted, an 'an-thology'): that is, *dobro* = *kalos*, meaning 'good', while *lyubie* = *phil-*, meaning 'love' or 'affection'. The natural inference is that the *Dobrotolyubie* is a translation of the *Philokalia*, but the truth is more complicated. Indeed, the project of seeking out authentic monastic texts and translating them into Slavonic (and Romanian) began quite independently of the similar har-vesting of monastic texts that culminated in the *Philokalia* of 1782, and is to be associated with the name of a Moldavian monk, St Vasile of Poiana Mărului. One of St Vasile's disci-ples was St Paisy Velichkovsky, whose collection of monastic texts, called the *Dobrotolyubie*, is to be regarded as parallel with, rather than dependent on, the texts that came to form the *Philokalia* (the use of the calque *Dobrotolyubie* as its title was deliberate and probably an attempt to claim the authority of the Greek collection, published eleven years ahead of St Paisy's *Dobrotolyubie*, to meet Paisy's reluctance to publish a printed version of such texts at all). Furthermore, when we come to consider the influence of the *Philokalia*, this was not direct – the second edition of the Greek *Philokalia* did not appear for over a century, when it was published in an edition of five vol-umes in Athens in 1893; rather, the influence of the *Philokalia* was spearheaded by the Slavonic and Russian versions, which formed part of a monastic revival, as well as the revival of spir-itual fatherhood (*starchestvo*), in the course of the nineteenth century, assisted by a popular work that has come to be known as *The Way of a Pilgrim*, which achieved enormous popularity in the twentieth century – indeed through its figuring as the 'small pea-green clothbound book' carried by Franny in her handbag in J. D. Salinger's *Franny and Zooey*, it acquired something of a cult status in the 1960s.[1]

The relationship between the Greek *Philokalia* of 1782 and the Slavonic and Russian versions of 1793 and 1877–89 is perhaps better expressed as a family resemblance rather than a simple dependence through translation – and the same is true, in an analogous way, of the relationship between the 1782 *Philokalia* and the later Greek editions of 1893 and 1957–63, the modern Greek translation of 1984–7, the Romanian version of 1946–91, the French (complete versions, 1979–91, reprinted in 1995, though an earlier *Petite philocalie* of 1953), the English (complete 1979–2023, though earlier selections from Theophan's Russian, 1951–4), and the Italian of 1982–7. The Romanian version differs perhaps most radically from the 1782 *Philokalia* in that it includes many 'Philokalic' works not found in the Nikodemos and Makarios 'original': the correspondence of the Fathers of the Gaza desert, Barsanouphios and John, as well as Dorotheos of Gaza, *The Ladder of Divine Ascent* by John of Sinai, Isaac the Syrian and many works of Romanian hesychasm – Vasile of Poiana Mărului, George of Cernica and others. The text of 1782 was not regarded as sacrosanct: modern critical editions are often substituted for the 1782 texts, a process that began with the second Greek edition of 1893, which added 'missing texts' to Patriarch Kallistos's *Fourteen Chapters on Prayer* and included further texts by Kallistos Angelikoudis (in the 1782 volume called *Tilikoudis*, and probably identical with Kallistos Kataphygiotis).

This Penguin *Philokalia* is by design no more than a selection, intended to introduce the 'Philokalic literature' to the reader. The selection has been made on grounds of interest, but to reduce the work to a single volume it was necessary to omit many texts that might be regarded as 'secondary', notably the whole work compiled by Peter of Damascus, and the 'made-up' centuries attributed to Maximos the Confessor, added to the two authentic *Centuries on Theology and the Divine Economy* to form a series of seven *Centuries*. *Centuries* 3–7 are mostly drawn from Maximos's *Questions to Thalassios*,

the Confessor's major work of Scriptural exegesis, more illuminating for how monks of later generations tempered the
complexity of Maximos's thought. The enormous, and enormously valuable, *Exact Method and Rule* of the Xanthopouloi,
Kallistos and Ignatios, has, with regret, been omitted, as have
the *Three Centuries on Knowledge* of Nikitas Stithatos, as we
were concerned to include not extracts, but whole treatises,
and the addition of these, admittedly fascinating and important
treatises, would, in our view, have unbalanced the selection.

We have, however, in contrast to the 'complete text' of the
Philokalia published by Faber & Faber (all five volumes of
which have now, after a long delay, been published), included
a translation of the preface, written for the 1782 volume by,
presumably, St Nikodemos. For this preface is important for
understanding the intentions of the original editors. On the
one hand, Nikodemos makes much of the rediscovery of long-
forgotten and disregarded monastic texts to be found in the
Philokalia:

> Because of their great antiquity and their scarcity – not to men-
> tion the fact that they have never yet been printed – they have
> all but vanished. And even if some few have somehow survived,
> they are moth-eaten and in a state of decay, and remembered
> about as well as if they had never existed.

And his lament continues:

> For behold, writings never ever published in earlier times!
> Behold, works which lay about in corners and holes and dark-
> ness, unknown and moth-eaten, and here and there cast aside
> and in a state of decay! Behold, texts conducive to purification
> of the heart, watchfulness of the intellect, and the dwelling in us
> of grace; and in addition scientifically guiding us to deification!

Nikodemos is certainly exaggerating. The earlier work in restoring authentic monastic texts associated with the circles of Vasile
of Poiana Mărului and Paisy Velichkovsky makes it clear that
Nikodemos was entering into an attempt to recover texts about

the core of the monastic, indeed, of the Christian life, already well advanced. Nevertheless, on the other hand, his sense of the need to restore the spiritual kernel of monasticism is certainly heartfelt: speaking of the neglect of the heart of monastic prayer, Nikodemos laments that 'There is a real danger that such efficient and exceedingly sweet practice may, in the end, fail utterly, that grace itself be darkened and quenched in this world, and with it our union with God and divinization shattered.'

It is deification, divinization, becoming God, that Nikodemos sets at the heart of the Christian, the monastic, life. His preface begins with an address to God that recalls the opening of Dionysios the Areopagite's *Mystical Theology*:

> God, the blessed Nature, the perfection beyond perfection, Principle beyond the good and the beautiful that fashions everything good and beautiful – from eternity he determined, in accordance with his divine plan, to deify humankind.

Deification is the work of God; it is beyond human achievement:

> ultimately to bear fruit and become through grace children of God [John 1:12] and to be deified, having attained to perfect manhood, unto the measure of the fullness of the stature of Christ [Eph. 4:13]. For this was, as in summary, the whole end and goal of the economy of the Word concerning us.

An unfailing way of laying hold on what the Incarnate Word has secured for us is to be found in the Jesus Prayer:

> to *pray without ceasing* [1 Thess. 5:17] to our Lord Jesus Christ, the Son of God – not simply, I say, in our mind or only with our lips, for verbal prayer is obvious to all those who choose to worship God, and easy for the one who tries it.

And it is this that Nikodemos brings out by his careful choice of words. Alongside speaking in terms of *theosis*, a process of assimilation to God, he speaks of *theourgesai*, related to the word *theourgia*, which for Dionysios, Nikodemos's source here, means God's work or activity, his working within us – primarily through the sacraments of the Church.

The *Philokalia* can, in short, be regarded as an epitome of theology, understood less as a learned discipline, and more as drawing out the entailments of the practice of prayer, leading to union with God.

Andrew Louth

Preface to the Translation

The principles of this, like those of any modern translation really, are a balance of fidelity to the original (Greek) and readability in English. We have differed from previous translators in precisely how we achieve those ends, though we have aimed at as strict a fidelity as modern English allows. The *Philokalia* presents several unique challenges in this balancing act, which require some explanation.

1. **Technical terminology.** Technical terminology presents two challenges. First, philosophical and theological Greek is replete with terms like *nous*, *dianoia*, *ennoia*, *logismos*, all of which refer to rational mental faculties, processes and products. In some instances these can be synonymous, in others they can be fitted to subtle distinctions, and some of them are particularly prone to negative moral connotations. For example, *ennoia* is a thought or concept, and so is *logismos*, but in some cases *logismos* means one's rational capacity generally, and often it means a sinful or impassioned train of thought. It is difficult to tease out these distinctions without resorting to pleonastic constructions and cumbersome notes. We have aimed at consistency, which, in context, will hopefully give readers a sense of the connotative difference a given author is aiming for in a given moment.

Then there are load-bearing philosophical categories passed down from Plato and Aristotle all the way to Nikodemos, like *dunamis* and *energeia*, or *nous* and *hêgemonikon*. These carry rich intellectual histories and yet are the common stock of educated Greek-speakers. Words like *nous* and *energeia* are badly served by exoticisms like 'noetic' and 'energy', which have been popular with previous translators. I confess, 'energy' has always made me think of batteries and aerobics rather than 'that activity which is possible and appropriate to an entity by virtue of its nature and constitution'. However, this latter phrase, while more accurate, is a little unwieldy, and so we have simply translated *energeia* as 'activity'. In this regard, we have generally opted for commonplace English terms, in keeping with current conventions in translations of wider Greek literature. We have let context determine connotation, as it usually does, and have avoided terms that suggest authors in the *Philokalia* were running a trade in exotic words. They were not. They were using the language available to them, which gradually came to be shaded with theological meanings thanks to the efforts of authors contained in this very collection. Thus, Gregory Palamas uses words and phrases learned from Gregory of Sinai, and both were deeply influenced by Maximos and Diadochos, among others. Maximos and Diadochos read deeply in Evagrios, and all of them in Aristotle and the Neoplatonic traditions. If you read Aristotle in English, you'll see *energeia* rendered as 'activity', and the same should be true for Gregory Palamas, as he deploys this age-old category to distinguish the experience of divine light in prayer from an impossible cognition of God's infinite and unknowable 'essence' (*ousia*).

And then there is *logos*. How do you solve a problem like *logos*? We have sometimes included it in brackets where we felt the wordplay demanded clarification. As, for example, when Gregory of Sinai uses *logos* to mean Word of God, teaching, account, spoken word and discursive reason, all in the same paragraph. A further, perhaps even more pressing, example is the frequent use of the noun *gnosis*, and its adjective, *gnostikos*, the latter translated 'gnostic'. In English, 'gnostic' and related words have acquired an esoteric ambiance, and in scholarship on the early Christian centuries tend to be narrowed down to refer to second-century dualistic 'gnosticism', the archetypal heresy for those, like Irenaeus, later regarded as champions of Orthodoxy. However, in Byzantine ascetic literature, of which the *Philokalia* is a prime example, 'gnostic' is a common term for one who has begun to experience knowledge (*gnosis*) of God and union with Him, and it should perhaps be reclaimed for this purpose.

For interested readers, we have included a short glossary at the back of some of the more commonly used technical terms.

2. **Language conventions and authorial style.** Over the millennium of culture from which Philokalic texts were culled, changes in language, developments in technical terminology, not to mention a wide variety of individual styles, were all inevitable. Indeed, by Nikodemos's day 'Classical' Greek had long given way to modern forms far closer to what is spoken today than what Plato wrote. Generally, Philokalic authors wrote in something like 'Classical' Greek, although the complete collection contains a few demotic texts and versions from the fifteenth and sixteenth centuries. More generally, our authors are writing in genres like the 'gnomic century' that encourage elliptic, not to say cryptic, aphorisms marked by terseness and allusion. In those cases, we have tried to clarify the sense without adding too much to the text. Thus, we have frequently reinserted the noun where Elias Ekdikos or Gregory of Sinai has only a definite article. We have not aimed for uniformity among the pieces translated here, and readers will readily discover that some authors, like Diadochos, are dense but beautiful writers, while others, like Maximos, are simply dense. By and large, we have happily sacrificed Greek syntax on the altar of readability. In some cases, this has meant splitting up sentences into two or more. In Maximos's case, it has meant splitting sentences into two or more paragraphs and, in one case, pages. We hope, however, that such choices help clarify the meaning for readers without sacrificing the flow of argument.

3. **Gender.** Greek defaults to a masculine pronoun and so the implied reader or 'someone' of so many illustrations and exhortations is coded masculine. Moreover, almost all of our writers originally wrote for all-male communities, whether in monasteries or elite settings. However, we have taken seriously Symeon of Thessaloniki's reminder that the Jesus Prayer is for everyone, and Nikodemos's claim that the *Philokalia* is likewise for all. In the interest of inclusivity, we have used a mix,

then, of masculine, feminine and the increasingly common singular 'they', and likewise used 'humankind' or 'human', rather than 'mankind', for the Greek *anthrôpos*. In some cases, where it is clear that a male or female individual is implied (as in Gregory Palamas's *To Xenia*), we have retained exclusively masculine or feminine pronouns as seemed appropriate.

It is, of course, impossible to translate any part of the *Philokalia* into English without paying tribute to the monumental translation undertaken by Gerald Palmer, Philip Sherrard and Metropolitan Kallistos Ware over several decades, and only recently and post-humously completed. This present volume is, to repeat, a fresh translation of selected treatises from the *Philokalia*, fulfilling a rather different purpose from that full translation of the *Philokalia* by offering an introduction and overview, a sampler platter representative of the banquet that awaits with further reading.

The *Philokalia* abounds in biblical quotations, allusions and citations. We have translated these as they appear in our authors, which is usually (but not always) the same text as underlies English Bibles. However, all quotations from the Old Testament are from the Septuagint version (abbreviated herein as LXX, but only noted to alert the reader to significant differences), which differs in several ways from the Hebrew text as it is translated in modern Bibles. There are three to be aware of:

1. The numbering of the Psalms and, in some cases, their verses is different. Because the Psalms are quoted more than any other biblical book in the *Philokalia*, it is worth keeping in mind that the numbering differs somewhat from the Hebrew text trans-lated in most modern Bibles. For most psalms, the Septuagint number is one less than the Hebrew. However, what follows is a complete table of correspondences:

Septuagint Psalm	Hebrew Psalm
1–8	1–8
9	9–10
10–112	11–113

113	114–15
114	116:1–9
115	116:10–16
116–45	117–46
146	147:1–11
147	147:12–20
148–50	148–50
151	—

2. Content, especially in poetic texts like Isaiah or Job, is frequently obscure and not always traceable to the Hebrew. However, Christian writers frequently make much of semantic nuances in the Septuagint text, so it is essential to preserve what might otherwise be thought of as mistranslation.

3. The Septuagint contains a number of books not included in the Protestant canon of Scripture, though these are found in Eastern Orthodox and Roman Catholic Bibles. Several such texts – referred to frequently as 'apocrypha' or 'deuterocanonical' books – are very important to our writers, such as the Wisdom of Jesus Ben Sirach (sometimes called Ecclesiasticus, cited throughout as 'Sirach'). Some books of the Septuagint Old Testament bear a different name from those given in the Hebrew Bible. So the books of Samuel and Kings are grouped together as four books of Kingdoms (1 and 2 Samuel – 1 and 2 Kingdoms (Kgds); 1 and 2 Kings – 3 and 4 Kgds). 1 and 2 chronicles are called 1 and 2 Paralipomena (meaning supplements, as they supplement, rather than continue, 1–4 Kgds).

Outside Scripture, our authors regularly quote or allude to non-biblical texts, both Christian and, more infrequently, Greek philosophical ones. While all translations of these are our own, we have noted them in the endnotes and, where possible, directed readers to accessible English translations. Where English translations do not exist, we have referred instead to available editions.

Liturgical Hours and Offices

Over the millennium of Christian history behind the Philokalic texts, Christian rites and rituals (liturgies) developed and regularized around set patterns of daily, weekly and yearly cycles. Our authors do not discuss these very often. Rather, they presume the rhythms of prayer, hymns and sacraments as the warp and woof of Christian life. All services include prayers, psalms and hymns. Psalms are sung in every service, in groups that, over the course of a week, comprise the entire Psalter. At the same time, some services always include certain psalms. Thus, Psalm 50 ('Have mercy on me, O God . . .') is sung at almost every service, while Orthros (or, Matins, 'morning prayer') begins with the 'Six Psalms': 3, 37, 62, 87, 102 and 142, and Hesperinos (or, Vespers, 'evening prayer') with Ps. 103.

Byzantine services are also peppered with other hymns, concerning the life of Christ, his Passion and Resurrection, the Cross, Mary, and the saints being commemorated that day. These are determined by the hour of the day, the day of the week, the day of the year, the festal seasons and so on. The day itself was divided not by clocks but by sunrise and sunset. The time of daylight was divided into twelve parts, called hours; and the time of darkness likewise. Liturgical offices came to be celebrated, especially in monasteries, at the first, third, sixth and ninth hours. The offices associated with these hours are relatively short, though the first was preceded by Orthros, and the ninth followed by Vespers, sung at sunset. Compline was sung after sunset. One thing to keep in mind is that these hours necessarily vary over the course of the year, and our authors sometimes account for seasonal differences in daytime and night-time.

The Eucharist came to be celebrated daily in monasteries, but more ancient practice had it only once or twice per week, on Saturday and Sunday, as part of a service known generally as the divine Liturgy, though sometimes just called the Synaxis. Each day of the week would eventually have its particular commemoration – angels, apostles and so on – in addition to the saint of the calendar day, and whatever fast or feast was being observed. Since Easter (in Greek, *Pascha*) was, and is, reckoned according to a lunar calendar, the fast of Great Lent and feast of Pascha to Pentecost fall at different times in the spring. Depending on their era, Philokalic authors may presume either pattern or name, but in every era their lives were defined by interlocking rhythms of day and night, week and calendar, season and feast.

SELECTIONS FROM THE PHILOKALIA OF THE HOLY ASCETIC FATHERS

St Nikodemos of Athos,
Introduction to This Book

ST NIKODEMOS OF ATHOS,
'THE HAGIORITE' (1749–1809)

In his *Prologue* to the *Philokalia*, Nikodemos sets out both the purpose and scope of the anthology, and its genesis. Of this latter, the account he gives, of neglected manuscripts unknown and unread, is a stock device among premodern historians. It seems clear from comparison with other ascetic miscellanies copied between the fifteenth and eighteenth centuries, that the range of authors and works gathered in the *Philokalia* is rooted in Athonite reading and scribal practices going back centuries. Nikodemos, though, is not satisfied with exposing these texts to a wider monastic audience. Rather, he sees in them a way of prayer incumbent on all Christians, ever since Paul admonished the Thessalonians to 'pray without ceasing'. Moreover, Nikodemos takes seriously the claims among authors that the 'Jesus Prayer' and its repetition, the cultivation of interior prayer, is the means of salvation and even deification. He presents the *Philokalia* as a practical manual, a source of inspiration, a guide and ever-present voice of conscience for readers who take its words seriously.

Sources

Text: *PHILOKALIA* (1782): 1–8; *Philokalia* (1893/1982): vol. 1, 19–24
For Nikodemos's biography, please refer to our Introduction.

Introduction to This Book

God, the blessed Nature, the perfection beyond perfection, Principle beyond the good and the beautiful that fashions everything good and beautiful – from eternity he determined, in accordance with his divine plan, to deify humankind. Having pre-eminently set himself this goal from the beginning, at the time when it pleased him to do so, he created humankind. Taking the body from matter, he placed in it a soul from himself, which he established as a sort of world in miniature, though great in the multitude and pre-eminence of its faculties. This creature he made overseer of sensible Creation and initiate of the intelligible according to Gregory who is great in theology.[1] And what else is man than God's true portrait and image made by Himself, filled with every gift of grace? So then, having established the law of his command for man as a sort of trial of his liberty, God knew that he had to leave the rest to man. For, as Ben Sirach says, God left man to his own devices [Sirach 15:14], to choose to do whatever he was resolved on, with the prize that, if he kept the command he had received, he would obtain the genuine grace of deification, becoming God and blazing with the most pure light forever. But in fact – oh the wicked knavery of envy! – the original author of evil did not allow all this to happen. Rather, he conceived envy against both the Creator and his creation, as Holy Maximos says: envy of the Creator, lest the active power of the all-hymned Goodness that divinely works in humanity be manifest; envy of creation, lest it be revealed a partaker of such supernatural glory as deified.[2] Cunningly did the deceiver outwit wretched man, and, indeed, he convinced them with plausible-sounding arguments to transgress the God-given command. Having drawn man away from divine glory – alas! – the usurper fancied himself some kind of Olympian, because he had been able to thwart the fulfilment of God's pre-eternal plan.

Since according to the divine oracles, God's plan for the deification of human nature endures forever, and the thoughts of his heart to generation and generation [Ps. 32:10], the principles of providence and judgement, which alike drive towards this goal, operate unalterably both in this present age and in the age to come – according to the explanation of the Holy Maximos.[3] So in these last days [Heb. 1:2], because of his tender mercy [Luke 1:78], the supremely divine Word of the Father was pleased to topple the plans of the rulers of darkness, to accomplish and bring into action what he established as his ancient and true plan. Therefore, by the good pleasure of the Father and the cooperation of the Holy Spirit the Word became incarnate and took to himself our whole nature and deified it. First, he gave us his salvific and deifying commands and the perfect grace of the All-Holy Spirit through Baptism – as though he were sowing divine seed in our hearts. Then he gave to us, according to the divine Evangelist, authority – provided we live according to his life-giving commands, maturing in the Spirit and through their operation preserve unquenched the grace in us – ultimately to bear fruit and become through grace children of God [John 1:12] and to be deified, having attained to perfect manhood, unto the measure of the fullness of the stature of Christ [Eph. 4:13]. For this was, as in summary, the whole end and goal of the economy of the Word concerning us.

But, alas! *It is good to weep bitterly at this point*, to quote the divine Chrysostom.[4] For we were enjoying such grace and made worthy of such nobility, that our soul shone more than the Sun, by the Spirit in Baptism. Since as children we received such a most godlike radiance, we have been blinded to this by ignorance, but mostly by the darkness of worries about this life, and have buried grace under the passions so deeply that we are in real danger of quenching the Spirit of God within us. We are in danger even of suffering nearly the same things as those who replied to Paul saying, *But we have not heard whether*

there is a Holy Spirit [Acts 19:2]. We are risking even reverting back to where we were in the beginning when, according
to the Prophet, grace did not rule us. Alas, our infirmity! That
wickedness and our unnecessary attachment to sensible things
should destroy us! And this is indeed a marvel, that even if we
should sometimes hear that grace is actively working in others,
we become envious and slander them – and do not even believe that grace is active in the present age! What, then? The
Holy Spirit instructs our divinely wise Fathers and, through
their unbroken watchfulness, their constant attentiveness and
guarding of the intellect, reveals to them the way to find grace
anew, a way truly marvellous and absolutely scientific. This
way is: to *pray without ceasing* [1 Thess. 5:17] to our Lord
Jesus Christ, the Son of God – not simply, I say, in our mind
or only with our lips, for verbal prayer is obvious to all those
who choose to worship God, and easy for the one who tries
it. Rather, having our whole mind turned towards *the inner
man* [2 Cor. 4:16] – which is also a marvel! – inwardly and in
the very depths of our heart to call upon the all-holy Name of
the Lord and seek out his mercy, paying attention only to the
simple words of the prayer, admitting nothing else from within
or without, so as to guard our mind wholly from anything of
form and colour.

The means of this practice and, if I may put it thus, its
matter I have from our Lord's own teaching, when he said,
The kingdom of God is within you [Luke 17:21]. And then,
*Hypocrite! First cleanse the inside of the cup and dish and then
their outside will be clean* [Matt. 23:26]. These statements are
understood not as pertaining to matters of the sensory world,
but to our *inner man*. And from the Apostle Paul writing to
the Ephesians, we have this: *For this reason I bend my knees to
the Father* of our Lord Jesus Christ, *that he may give it to you
to be strengthened with power through his Spirit in your inner
man, so that Christ will dwell in your hearts through the Spirit*
[Eph. 3:14–17]. What could be clearer than this witness? And
elsewhere he writes, *Praising and singing psalms to the Lord
in our heart* [Eph. 5:19]. Do you hear? *In our heart*, he says!
Moreover, Peter, the leader of the apostles, further confirms

this, saying, *until the day dawns and the morning star rises in your hearts* [2 Pet. 1:19]. The Holy Spirit teaches in these and how many myriad other pages in the New Testament that this practice is necessary for everyone practising piety, as can be seen by those who inquire carefully in these places. Alongside the more accessible practice of the commandments and the rest of the moral virtues, this practice, since it is both spiritual and scientific, utterly consumes the passions through the fervency which emerges in the heart from the invocation of the all-holy Name, and through the spiritual activity appropriate to that fervency. *For our God is* fire and *a fire which consumes* wickedness [Heb. 12:29]. As our intellect and heart are purified gradually, they come to be united one with another, and then the salvific commands are accomplished more easily. Thereafter the fruits of the Spirit make their appearance in the soul and the whole heap of good things sprouts up. Finally, to keep things brief, we will be able to return more swiftly to the perfect grace of the Spirit which was given to us in Baptism, which, though it is in us, has been buried under the passions like a spark in soot. Kindling this spark to flame we will see far and wide: we will be intelligibly enlightened, then perfected and, in due order, deified.

Most of the Fathers mention this activity here and there in their writings, crafting their argument for those who understand. Some of them, perhaps envisaging our generation's ignorance and carelessness regarding this salvific practice, and having expressed its practical manner in detail through certain physical methods, did not shrink from handing this down to us their children as a kind of family inheritance. These men also extolled this practice under many names and addressed it as the principle of every other God-loving activity, the heaping-up of good things, the purest token of repentance, and the intellective act which leads to true contemplation. Extolling and addressing it thus, they exhorted everyone to this profitable activity.

But now I must mourn, and grief cuts short my account! For I speak of all the books which philosophize about such purifying, illuminating and perfecting activity (to speak like the Areopagite) – and not only these but others as well – as many as are popularly called 'Watchful', because they expound in detail attentiveness and watchfulness. All of these alike are the necessary means and tools for attaining the same purpose, having the one goal of achieving divinization in humankind. Because of their great antiquity and their scarcity – not to mention the fact that they have never yet been printed – they have all but vanished. And even if some few have somehow survived, they are moth-eaten and in a state of decay, and remembered about as well as if they had never existed. I will add that most of our monks are disposed to be careless, and *troubled about many things* [Luke 10:41] – that is, bodily matters and the practice of virtues, or, to speak more accurately, only the tools of virtue, in which they spend their whole life. But as to the *one thing* – clearly, guarding the intellect and pure prayer – I do not understand how they stupidly neglect it. There is a real danger that such efficient and exceedingly sweet practice may, in the end, fail utterly, that grace itself be darkened and quenched in this world, and with it our union with God and divinization be shattered.

This very thing – our divinization – was, as has been said, planned from the beginning and, *according to* his *good pleasure, the will of God* [Eph. 1:4]. For this, indeed, as for a goal most suited to his purpose, we have been both brought into being and, through the economy of his Word concerning us, are being brought to well-being and eternal well-being and, to be blunt, all that has been accomplished in a manner befitting God in both the old and the new dispensations.

Once many even of those who were in the world – Kings themselves, and those who lived in palaces and exerted themselves in myriad thoughts and cares of this life – all had one and the same work: praying unceasingly in their heart. We find them often in our histories. But now, from carelessness and ignorance, not only among those in the world but even among monks and those who live as solitaries in stillness, this work is extremely rare and – what a tremendous loss! – hard to find. Deprived of what is needed, though they struggle each according to his own ability, and endure labours for the sake of virtue, none actually reaps any fruit. For, without unceasing mindfulness of the Lord, which gives rise to purity, free from every evil, in the heart as well as in the intellect, it is impossible to bear fruit: *Without me*, it says, *you can do nothing*. And again, *Who abides in me bears much fruit* [John 15:5].

Right now, I can see no other reason why those eminent in holiness (both while living and after death) have been so forsaken, and so *those being saved are so few* [Luke 13:23] in our present time, than this, that clearly we have abandoned the work that leads to deification. And, someone says, apart from the deification of the intellect, it is not possible for the human to be sanctified or saved – which, even but to hear is exceedingly horrible, for being saved and being deified are the same thing according to the revelation of those wise in God. But the decisive issue is that we are robbed of the books which would guide us to our salvation and deification. Without these, it is absolutely impossible to attain our goal.

Behold, the ever noble and good Lord John Mavrogordatos, a true lover of Christ! One second to none, even among those of the highest rank, in the principles of liberality, of love for the poor and the stranger, and of the whole chorus of virtues. Behold one who ever glows with divinely inspired zeal for public beneficence! This man, yes, this very man, inspired by the grace of Christ *who wills all people to be saved* [1 Tim. 2:4] and deified, transforms my lament into joy as he resolves my perplexity! For having displayed the means of deification to the public with all his soul he works together in his turn in every way – indeed, if I may be so bold, with his hands and feet runs together – with the pre-eternal will of God. What glory! What magnificence! For behold, writings never ever published in earlier times. Behold, works which lay about in corners and holes and darkness, unknown and moth-eaten, and here and there cast aside and in a state of decay. Behold, texts conducive to purification of the heart, watchfulness of the intellect, and the dwelling in us of grace; and in addition scientifically guiding us to deification. Gathering these into a single whole without caring a whit about cost, he hands them over now to the glorious, shining light of the printed word. (For it was necessary, it was indeed necessary, that things which speak in detail about divine illumination be deemed worthy of the light of printing!) And through this he frees the erudite from the labours of transcription while rousing the neophyte to the desire of its acquisition, and, I think, to putting this learning into practice.

So, dearest reader, you have without further labour easily procured this spiritual book, thanks to John, a man best in every way: a book which is a treasury of watchfulness, a guard-house for the intellect, a mystical schoolhouse of intellectual prayer; a book which is an excellent outline of the practical life, an unerring guide in contemplation, the Paradise of the Fathers, a golden chain of virtues; a book which is intimate converse with Jesus, the sounding trumpet of grace, and – to speak briefly – the very tool of deification. It is a possession longed for ten thousand times more than any other, for many years pursued and sought after, but not found. For this reason an inescapable debt is imposed upon you, owed according to every principle of justice, that you beseech the Divinity with fervent prayers for your benefactor and his fellow-workers, that they may attain to the same measure of deification and that, since they have laboured on this, they may be the first to enjoy its fruits.

But at this point someone might perhaps find fault with what we have said, saying that it is not lawful to publish some of the things in this book and thus bring them to the ears of the public, because of their strangeness. They might add that a certain danger accompanies these things. We will briefly lodge our counter-objections. First of all, beloved companion, we did not come to such an undertaking contenting ourselves with our own thoughts; rather, we followed exemplars. First, we see in the sacred Scriptures that it is commanded to absolutely all the faithful without distinction *to pray without ceasing* [1 Thess. 5:17], and always to have the Lord before our eyes. And, according to Basil the Great, it is impious to say that something hinders the precepts of the Spirit or that they are impossible to follow.[5] Moreover, we see the same also in the written tradition of the Fathers. For Gregory the Theologian commands absolutely all the laity under him to be mindful of God rather than even to breathe.[6] The divine Chrysostom dedicates three whole sermons to unceasing and intellectual prayer, and in ten thousand places in the rest of his works, he exhorts everyone to pray always. And that marvellous man, Gregory of Sinai, travelled through various cities teaching precisely this salvific practice. But even God himself, having by a miracle sent an angel from above, set his seal on such truth when he silenced the monk who spoke against it, as is seen in the end of this book! And what else should I say? Where those who are in the world, even living in palaces, have such meditation as their unbroken work (as we have said), they confirm our account by their actions, and are themselves sufficient to silence any critics.

If some went astray after a little while, why is that so strange? In most cases, according to Gregory of Sinai, they have suffered their fall out of self-conceit. But I consider the cause of this wandering to be especially and properly this: that they do not carefully submit to the teaching of the Fathers concerning this activity. It is nothing against the activity itself. Stop that nonsense! For the activity is holy and we pray to be delivered from all error through it. And though unceasing prayer is a *command* according to the law of God, guiding us *to life* – in some, says Paul, *it is found* to be *unto death* [Rom. 7:10]. But this has not happened because of the command. How could it, when the command is *holy, just, and true*? [Rom. 7:12]. Rather, it is because of the depravity of those *sold under sin* [Rom. 7:14]. Why, then, because of this? Must we condemn the divine command because of the sin of some? Must we set at naught such salvific activity because of the apostasy of some? In no way! We should do neither the one nor the other. Rather, having confidence in the one who said, *I am the way and the truth* [John 14:6], we must undertake the work with all humility and a sorrowful disposition. For, according to the teaching of the Fathers, even if every wicked phalanx of demons should attack him, they will not be able to come near one who has been delivered from self-conceit and the desire to please people.

Since these matters stand thus, and on all sides Scripture proposes always and in every way blameless perfection (of which some passages have been quoted), it would be most opportune, finally, to take in our hands that invitation to the banquet of Wisdom, and with a sublime proclamation to call all to the spiritual feast of this book. All of you – you are no despisers of the divine banquet, nor ones to offer excuses about *fields* and *oxen* and *wives*, like those in the Gospel [Luke 14:18–20] – all of you, then, come, come! Eat the gnostic bread of wisdom found in this book, and drink the *wine which gladdens the heart* [Ps. 103:15] intelligibly, abandoning everything, both sensible and intelligible, for the sake of ecstatic deification, and be drunk with a drunkenness truly sober! Come all, as many as are partakers of an orthodox calling, both laypeople and monks together, who have endeavoured to find the *Kingdom of God* that *is within you* [Luke 17:21], and *the treasure hidden in the field* of your heart [Matt. 13:44], which is our sweet Jesus Christ, so that with your intellect freed from the captivity and whirlwind of things below, and your heart purified from all passions, through the unceasing, fearsome invocation of our Lord Jesus Christ, with the cooperation of the other virtues which are taught in this book, you may be united to yourselves, and through yourselves to God. So did our Lord beseech his Father *that they may be one, as we are one* [John 17:11]. Finally, having been united to God and wholly transformed by the inspiration and ecstasy of divine *eros*, may you be most richly deified, in your intellectual sense and unwavering assurance, and return at last to God's first purpose, glorifying Father, Son and Holy Spirit, the one, most thearchic Godhead, to whom is due all glory, honour and worship to the ages of ages. Amen.

Evagrios Pontikos, *One Hundred and Fifty-Three Chapters on Prayer*

EVAGRIOS PONTIKOS (*c*.345–99)

Evagrios hailed from Pontos, on the south coast of the Black Sea, in what is now Turkey. He was ordained a reader by St Basil of Caesarea ('the Great', 330–79) in 371 and a decade later went to Constantinople with St Gregory Nazianzen, whom he impressed with his learning and theological acumen, and whom Evagrios would call 'our wise teacher'. After an unhappy love affair, he fled Constantinople for Jerusalem and the monastic community led by a noblewoman named Melania, who eventually persuaded him to seek Egypt. Evagrios settled in Nitria, and spent the rest of his life there. He was already a renowned and controversial figure when he died in 399. In the sixth century, he would be implicated in attacks on the legacy of Origen of Alexandria and decried as a heretic. Many of his works survive only in Syriac, while others, like *On Prayer*, passed under the name of Neilos. So it is found in the 1782 edition of the *Philokalia*. Under this guise Evagrios's works influenced traditions of prayer in Byzantine and Eastern Christianity, as the inclusion of *On Prayer* in the *Philokalia* demonstrates.

Evagrios was a prolific and profound writer, who leveraged philosophical concepts and ideas onto an educational programme for Christian ascetics. In this programme, the monk engages first in unlearning old affective and cognitive habits and developing new ones defined by tranquillity, humility and love (the life of 'practical' or 'active' virtue). They can turn then to contemplation, first of the created world, and then of its creator (the 'contemplative' life). Prayer runs as a golden thread through these stages of life, though its content and practice develop with the Christian, from supplication to conversation with God. This text, *On Prayer*, was intended for Christians in the final stages of development, and presumes a life of careful discipline within the rhythms of monastic life. In it Evagrios describes the conditions and experience of 'pure prayer' as a way of communion between the intellect and the infinite God, unmediated by any imagined form or idea that would place limitations on the Deity.

Sources

Text: Paul Géhin (ed.), *Évagre le Pontique: Chapitres sur la prière*, Sources Chrétiennes 589 (Paris: Éditions du Cerf, 2017): 208–368
Alternative text: *PHILOKALIA* (1782):155–65; *Philokalia* (1893/1982): vol. 1, 176–89

One Hundred and Fifty-Three Chapters on Prayer

Prologue to the One Hundred and Fifty-Three Chapters on Prayer

You always refresh me when I burn with the fire of unclean passions, by the touch of your pious words, having imitated our great guide and teacher, Makarios.[1] You have soothed my intellect, which flounders in the most shameful things. And no wonder! The speckled sheep have ever been your lot, as they were for the blessed Jacob [Gen. 30:42]. Like him, too, you served well for the sake of Rachel and, having received Lea [Gen. 29:25], you still seek the woman you desired, since for her too you have completed your seven years' labour. But I would not deny that, having laboured the whole night, I have caught nothing. Nevertheless, having let down my net at your command, I have caught a multitude *of fish*. While I do not consider them very *large*, there are altogether *one hundred and fifty-three* [John 21:11]. Having sent these in a basket of love, through an equal number of short chapters, I have fulfilled the requisition.

I marvel at you and I greatly envy your desire for the excellent prospect of chapters on prayer. For you do not simply want such as are handy and which exist merely in ink on the page, but, rather, inscribed in your intellect, through love and absence of malice. But since *All things are twofold, one opposite the other*, according to the wise Jesus [ben Sirach] [Sirach 42:24], receive the spirit along with the letter. You know that understanding [*nous*] always precedes the letter – for where there is no understanding, there is certainly no letter! And so, therefore, the way of prayer is also twofold. The first is practical, the second theoretical. So too about the number of chapters: its quantity is a handy mnemonic aid; its quality is significant.

Having divided our discourse on prayer into one hundred and fifty-three parts, we have sent you an evangelical wage, that you may find delight in the symbolic number, with regard to its triangular[2] and hexagonal forms.[3] The former reveals a pious knowledge of the Trinity; the second, a pattern of this world. But, in addition, the number one hundred is itself a square number. And fifty-three is both triangular and spherical: you get it by adding twenty-eight to twenty-five, and while twenty-eight is triangular, twenty-five is spherical, since five times five is twenty-five.[4] Then, you have the square form:[5] for not only do you have the tetrad of the virtues, but also the wise knowledge of the present age – as with the number twenty-five, on account of the recurrent nature of time. For week moves into week and month into month, and time revolves from year to year and moment to moment, as we behold in the motion of sun and moon, spring and summer, and the seasons. But the triangular form could signify to you the knowledge of the Holy Trinity. Otherwise, preserving through multitude the number one hundred and fifty-three, which is triangular, consider it as practical, natural and theological knowledge; or, perhaps, as *faith, hope and love* [1 Cor. 13:13]; or even *gold, silver* and *precious stones* [1 Cor. 3:12]. There you have the number.

But do not mock the humility of these short chapters, since you *have known* how *to be filled* and how *to go hungry* [Phil. 4:12], especially since you remember that the widow's two mites were not rejected, but received more than the wealth of many others [Mark 12:42]. So then, having known how to guard the fruit of goodwill and love with your neighbouring brothers, pray for one who is unwell that he may become healthy, and, having *taken up* his *pallet*, he may *walk* by the grace of Christ [John 5:8]. Amen.

On Prayer: One Hundred and Fifty-Three Chapters

1. Should someone wish to prepare fragrant incense, he will mix in equal measure translucent frankincense, cassia bark, onyx and oil of myrrh, as it prescribes in the Law [Exod. 30:34–7]. These four ingredients represent the tetrad of virtues, for if those are mixed in completely full and equal measure, the intellect will not be betrayed.

2. A soul purified through the fullness of the virtues prepares a stable arrangement for the intellect and so makes it receptive to the state that is sought.

3. Prayer is the intellect's conversation with God. What sort of state must the intellect need such that it can be unstintingly drawn out towards its rightful master and, without need of any mediator, intimately converse with him?

4. If, when he attempted to approach the burning bush on earth, Moses was prevented until he *loosed the sandals from his feet* [Exod. 3:5], how will you – who wish to see the one beyond all perception and thought, and to be his confidant – how will you not remove from yourself every notion marked by passion?

5. First, pray concerning the acquisition of tears, that through mourning you may be enabled to sooth the savagery that indwells your soul, and, having *confessed your transgression to the Lord* [Ps. 31.5], you may find forgiveness with him.

6. Make use of tears for the success of every petition. For your master rejoices exceedingly when he receives tear-stained prayers.

7. Even if you pour out whole fountains of tears in your prayers, do not be exalted in yourself, as though you were better than the common crowd. For your prayer received additional aid, that you might be able to confess your sins eagerly, and propitiate your master with tears. So do not turn this defence against passions into a passion itself, lest you anger all the more the one who has given you this grace.

8. Many who weep for sins have forgotten the goal of tears and so they have fallen away in their madness.

9. Stand diligently, pray vigorously, and turn away all pre-occupation with present concerns and calculations, for those trouble and confuse you to slacken your vigour.

10. When the demons see you exerting yourself to pray truly, then they will suggest notions of certain seemingly necessary matters. After a little while, they will take from you the memory of those same matters, and they will move your intellect to search for them – so that, when it does not find them, it will be greatly grieved and discouraged. At other times, when you are standing in prayer, they will remind your intellect of things sought after and recalled, so that your intellect will relax into the knowledge of those matters and so utterly lose its fruitful prayer.

11. Strive to make your intellect deaf and dumb during the time of prayer, and you will be able to pray.

12. Whenever temptation or contradiction come upon you or provoke you to be moved, for the sake of revenge on some opponent, to anger or to break into cries with an unseemly voice – remember your prayer and judge in accord with it, and immediately the disorderly movement within you will come to rest

13. Whatever you do to get revenge on a brother who has wronged you will become a stumbling block for you in the time of prayer.

14. Prayer is the flower of meekness and freedom from anger.

15. Prayer is the product of joy and thanksgiving.

16. Prayer is the remedy for sadness and discouragement.

17. Going away, *sell your goods and give to the poor* [Matt. 19:21] and, having taken up the cross, *deny yourself* [Matt. 16:24], that you may be able to pray without being distracted.

18. If you wish to pray praiseworthily, deny yourself hour by hour, and even if you suffer numerous terrible things, bear them philosophically for the sake of prayer.

19. You will find at the time of prayer the fruit of whatever difficulty that you endure philosophically.

20. If you desire to pray as you should, do not grieve a single soul – if you do, you will run in vain.

21. *Leave your gift*, it says, *before the altar* and, going away, first *be reconciled with your brother* [Matt. 5:24]. Then, on

return, you will pray without disturbance. For the remembrance of wrongs blinds the soul's leading faculty in one who prays and darkens his prayers.

22. Those who heap griefs and grudges on themselves and yet imagine they are praying are like people who draw water and pour it into a sieve.[6]

23. If you are a patient sort of person, you will always pray with joy.

24. When you are praying as you should, matters will occur to you that you imagine justify anger. But there is no such thing as justifiable anger against your neighbour. If you seek, you will find that it is possible to resolve the matter without resorting to anger. Therefore, use every possible means to avoid breaking out in anger.

25. Watch out, lest, imagining that you are healing someone else, you put yourself beyond healing and, in fact, give a fatal blow to your prayer.

26. Be sparing with anger and you will find yourself spared; show yourself prudent and be among those who pray.

27. Armed against anger, you will never give in to desire. For desire gives fuel to anger, and anger *troubles* the *eye* of the intellect [Ps. 6:7], ruining the state of prayer.

28. Do not pray in outward forms alone, but, rather, with much fear, turn your intellect to the conscious experience of spiritual prayer.

29. Sometimes when you stand for prayer all at once you pray well. Sometimes, however, after long labour you still do not achieve your goal, so that you will go on seeking and, having received it, you will clutch your success tightly.

30. When an angel stands over you, suddenly all those who would trouble you stand back, and as you pray healthily your intellect will be relaxed. But, when they wage their customary war against you, your intellect fights and is not permitted to relax, for it has already been affected by various passions. Still, if you *seek* all the more *you will find*, and *to the one who knocks* vigorously *it will be opened* [Matt. 7:8].

31. Do not pray that your wishes be fulfilled, for these do not accord entirely with God's will. Instead, pray just as you have been taught, saying, *Let your will be done* in me [Matt. 6:10]. Petition God thus in every matter, that his will be done. For he desires what is good and beneficial for your soul, but you do not always seek that.

32. Often when I have prayed, I sought that what I thought good would come to pass for me, and I persisted, irrationally trying to constrain God's will instead of yielding to it so that he might dispense what he knows to be beneficial. When I received exactly what I had asked for, I was then greatly grieved because I had not, instead, asked that his will be done – for the matter did not turn out as I had expected.

33. What is good but God? Let us, therefore, yield everything that concerns us to him, and it will be well with us. For he is entirely good and the giver of good gifts.

34. Do not fall into doubt when God does not immediately grant your request. For he wants to do you far more good if you *persist in prayer* before him [Acts 1:14]. For what could be nobler than to converse intimately with God and to be drawn into union with him?

35. Prayer without distraction is the supreme intellection of the intellect.

36. Prayer is the ascent of the intellect to God.

37. If you long to pray, renounce everything that you may inherit the whole.

38. Pray first to be purified from passions; secondly to be delivered from ignorance and forgetfulness; and thirdly to be delivered from all temptation and dereliction.

39. In your prayer, *seek* only *righteousness and the kingdom* – that is, virtue and knowledge – *and all* the rest *will be added to you* [Matt. 6:33].

40. It is right to pray not only for your own purification, but also for the whole human race, that you may imitate the way of the angels.

41. Look and see whether you have truly presented yourself to God in your prayer or are instead overcome by human praise and hastening to chase after it, so that you are using the appearance of prayer as a screen.

42. Whether you pray with your brothers or by yourself, force yourself to pray not by habit but with feeling.

43. Feeling in prayer means meditation with reverence, compunction, and pain in the soul as it confesses its failing with silent groans.

44. If your intellect is still looking around in the time of prayer, it does not yet know that it is a monk praying; rather, it is still a worldling decorating its outer tabernacle [cf. 2 Cor. 5:14].

45. When you pray, guard your memory with all your might, so that, instead of its presenting you with your own concerns, it moves you to attentive knowledge. For the intellect is quite naturally prone to be carried off by the memory at the time of prayer.

46. When you pray, your memory brings you the imaginings of old deeds, or new cares, or the face of someone who has grieved you.

47. The demon begrudges a person who prays and will use every trick to wreck their pursuit. Therefore, he does not cease from rousing the concepts of things through the memory, or from raising up as many passions as he can through the flesh, so that he can impede their excellent course and pilgrimage to God.

48. When that most wicked demon, after many attempts, cannot impede the zealous one's prayer, he relaxes a little and thereafter revenges himself on the one who prays. For either, having kindled them to anger, he causes the excellent state that was formed in them from their prayer to vanish. Or, having provoked some irrational pleasure, he insults their intellect.

49. When you are praying as you should, watch out for what should not be, and stand boldly, guarding your fruit. For you were given this command right from the beginning: *to work and to guard* [Gen. 2:15]. So then, when you have worked, do not leave the fruits of your labour unattended, otherwise, for all your praying, you will gain nothing.

50. All war contrived between us and the impure demons is over nothing else than spiritual prayer, for it is exceedingly hostile and grievous to them, while to us it is salvific and supremely pleasant.

51. What does it mean for the demons to rouse in us gluttony, lust, greed, anger, resentment and the other passions? It is so that the intellect, having been fattened up on these passions, cannot pray as it should. For as the passions of the irrational part of the soul take control, they do not permit the intellect to be moved rationally and to seek after God the Word.

52. We pursue the virtues for the sake of the natural principles [*logoi*] of created things, and we pursue those inner principles for the sake of the substantial Word [*Logos*] – but this last is accustomed to appear in the state of prayer.

53. The state of prayer is a dispassionate disposition which by a love most supreme finally enables the philosophical, spiritual intellect to attain the intelligible summit.

54. The person who wishes to pray truly must not only rule over anger and desire, but must pass beyond impassioned thought.

55. One who loves God will always converse with him as with a father, provided he turns away from every impassioned thought.

56. One who has already attained dispassion does not thereby pray truly. For it is possible to be among simple thoughts yet distracted by relating them, and so be far off from God.

57. It is not merely when the intellect does not linger among bare thoughts of things that it thereby finds the place of prayer. For it is possible to be in contemplation of things and meditate on their principles [*logoi*]; for, even though they are mere words, they are nevertheless contemplations of things, which form and shape the intellect, and so lead it away from God.

58. Even if the intellect surpasses the contemplation of bodily nature, it has not yet seen the perfect place of God. For it is possible to come to the knowledge of intelligible things and still partake in their diversity.

59. If you wish to pray, you need God who *gives prayer to the one who prays* [1 Kgds 2:9]. Therefore, you must call upon him, saying, *Hallowed be your name*, that is, your only-begotten Son; *Your kingdom come*, that is, your Holy Spirit

[Matt. 6:9–10]. So Jesus taught, when he spoke of *worshipping the Father in spirit and truth* [John 4:23–4].

60. One who prays *in spirit and in truth* no longer honours the creator on account of his creations, but praises him on his own account.

61. If you are a theologian, you will pray truly. And if you pray truly, you will be a theologian.

62. When by its great longing for God your intellect withdraws (as it were) for a little while from the flesh and turns away from all thoughts of sense, memory and temperament, and has been filled with reverence and joy simultaneously, only then consider that you are drawing near to the frontier of prayer.

63. *The* Holy *Spirit* that suffers *with our infirmity* [Rom. 8:26] also visits us, impure beings that we are. And should he find the intellect praying solely to him with love of truth, he comes upon it and causes the whole encircling phalanx of trains of thought and concepts to vanish, turning it to love for spiritual prayer.

64. Everything else stamps trains of thoughts, concepts and contemplations on the intellect through alteration of the body. But God does the opposite: coming upon the intellect itself he places therein the knowledge of the things that he wants, and, through the intellect, stills the body's disorder.

65. No one who yearns for true prayer and yet gets angry or bears grudges will escape madness. For they are like someone who wants to be sharp-sighted but keeps irritating their own eyes.

66. If you long to pray, do none of the things that oppose prayer, so that God will *draw near and walk with you* [Luke 24:15].

67. When you pray, do not picture the divine in yourself or even permit your intellect to be stamped by any form. Rather, approach the immaterial as one immaterial, and you will understand.

68. Keep guard against your opponents' traps. For it happens, when you are praying purely and without disturbance, that suddenly a strange and alien form stands before you to lead you into self-conceit as you imagine that the godhead

stands in a place, just before you – so that you believe that the magnitude suddenly revealed to you actually is the godhead. But remember – the godhead is without magnitude or shape.

69. When the envious demon cannot activate your memory in prayer, then he exploits the body's temperament to form some strange imagination in the intellect. Being accustomed to dwelling among concepts, it easily gives way, and so one who is striving for immaterial and formless knowledge is deceived, and lays hold on smoke instead of light.

70. *Stand on your guard* [Heb. 2:1]: that is, guarding your intellect from concepts during the time of prayer, and standing in your own proper tranquillity so that [the Holy Spirit] who suffers *with the ignorant* [Heb. 5:2] will also visit you. Then will you receive the all-glorious gift of prayer.

71. You cannot pray purely while you are tangled up in material things and whirled about by constant worries. For prayer is the rejection of concepts.

72. A person bound with ropes cannot run. Nor can an intellect enslaved to passions behold the place of spiritual prayer. For it is dragged and carried about hither and thither by impassioned thoughts, and so will have no stable place of rest.

73. When, finally, the intellect prays purely and dispassionately, then the demons no longer attack from the left hand, but from the right, that is, they suggest to it the glory of God in a certain form pleasing to the senses, to make the intellect think that it has already perfectly attained the goal of prayer. A man well versed in practical virtue said that this happens because of the passion of vainglory and is accomplished by the demon touching the place in the brain that pulsates in the veins.

74. I think that the demon, having touched the aforementioned place, actually bends light around the intellect however he wishes. Thus, he can move the passion of vainglory into a train of thought which moulds the intellect thoughtlessly to localize divine and substantial knowledge. The sort of person who is no longer troubled by fleshly and impure passions, and, rather, now thinks to hold himself purely, reckons that no opposing activity any longer arises within him. Whence he takes for the divine what is really a manifestation aroused in him by

the demon's singular cunning in altering and shaping, by means of the brain, the adjoining light, just as we have described.

75. When the angel of God stands over us, with a single word he makes all opposing activity to cease in us and moves the light of the intellect to operate unerringly.

76. I take the saying in *Revelation*, that the angel received *incense, that he* might *give it* for *the prayers of the holy ones* [Rev. 8:3],[7] to mean by *incense* the grace that is made active through the angel. For grace implants knowledge of true prayer, so that the intellect may thereafter stand outside of all turmoil, despondency and negligence.

77. *The bowls of incense* are said to be *the prayers of the saints*, which *the twenty-four elders* offer [Rev. 5:8]. But *bowl* [*phiale*] must be understood as *friendship* [*philia*] with God, that is, perfect and spiritual love, in which prayer is made active, *in spirit and truth* [John 4:24].

78. When you think that you no longer need tears in your prayer on account of sin, then consider how far from God you have stood, when you ought always to be in him – then you will shed more fervent tears.

79. Yes indeed, as you recognize the limits of your life, you will gladly weep, deeming yourself unhappy, as Isaiah did: How, *impure* as you are, and *in the midst of* so *impure a people* – that is, our opponents – do you dare to stand before *the Lord Sabaoth* [Isa. 6:5]?

80. If you are praying truly you will find much assurance, and angels will accompany you as they did Daniel [Dan. 6], and those angels will enlighten you about the inner principles of created beings.

81. Know that the holy angels urge us to prayer and they stand with us, rejoicing even as they pray for us. So, if we are careless and accept contrary thoughts, we greatly irritate them since they strive so much on our behalf while we hold their ministrations in contempt, and abandoning our mutual master and God, we fall in with impure demons.

82. Pray continuously and without disturbance, *chant with understanding* [Ps. 46:8] and a measured rhythm, and you will be like an eaglet borne upon the heights.

83. Psalmody soothes the passions and brings the body's disorder to peace; prayer prepares the mind to operate in its own proper activity.

84. Prayer is an activity befitting the dignity of the intellect. Indeed, prayer is its better and more unadulterated activity and use.

85. Psalmody belongs to *manifold wisdom* [Eph. 3:10]; prayer is a prelude to immaterial and unvarying knowledge.

86. Knowledge is supremely excellent, for it cooperates with prayer in rousing the intellectual power of the intellect to contemplation of divine knowledge.

87. If you have not yet received the spiritual gift of prayer or psalmody, wait patiently, and you will receive.

88. *He also told them a parable*, it says, *to show that they must pray always, and not lose heart* [Luke 18:1]. So then, do not *lose heart* or grow despondent when you have not received, for you will receive later. For he added at the end of the parable: *Even though I neither fear God nor regard man, since that woman gives me so much trouble, I will vindicate her cause* [Luke 18:4–5]. So too, then, *God will execute vindication for those who cry out to him day and night with haste* [Luke 18:7–8]. Take heart, therefore, and persist vigorously in holy prayer.

89. Do not want your affairs to turn out as seems good to you, but as it pleases God, and you will be undisturbed and grateful in your prayer.

90. Even if you think you are with God, guard against the demon of fornication. He is exceedingly deceptive and envious, and he aims to be swifter than the movement and vigilance of your intellect, to remove you far from God, even when you stand before him with piety and fear.

91. If you are diligently engaged in prayer, then be ready for the demons' onslaught, and bear up patiently under their blows. For they will come upon you like wild beasts and distress your whole body.

92. Prepare yourself like an experienced wrestler, then if you suddenly see an apparition, do not be disturbed. If you see a *sword drawn* against you [Num. 22:23] or a lamp crossing your line of sight, do not be troubled. If you see some hideous and bloody form, do not lose heart at all. Rather, stand *confessing with a good confession* [1 Tim. 6:12] and *you will* easily *look down upon your enemies* [Ps. 117:7].

93. Whoever endures miseries will find delights, and whoever persists through unpleasant things will not miss out on pleasant ones.

94. Watch, lest the wicked demons deceive you through some vision. Instead, be thoughtful as you go to prayer, and call upon God, so that, if the thought comes from him, he will enlighten you. If not, he will swiftly drive the error from you. Take courage! Those dogs will not stay near, if you swing out with the fiery rod of entreaty to God! Beaten invisibly and silently by God's power, they will straightway be driven off.

95. It is right that you are not ignorant of this deception too: at times the demons divide themselves up. Then, if you think you are calling in aid against some of them, the others show up in angelic forms to drive the first group away, to deceive you into thinking thereafter that they are holy angels.

96. Take care to acquire much humility and courage, and the demons' abuse will not leave its impression on your soul. *And a scourge will not draw near your tent, because* God *has commanded his angels about you, that they guard you* [Ps. 90: 10–11]: the angels will invisibly chase all opposing activity from you.

97. Someone engaged diligently in pure prayer will hear crashes, bangs, voices, and cries of torment from the demons. But he will not fail in or abandon his train of thought, as he says to God, *I will fear no evil, for you are with me* [Ps. 22:4] and similar things.

98. During such trials make use of brief, intense prayer.

99. If the demons threaten to appear suddenly to you out of the air, or to terrify you and snatch up your intellect, or if they threaten to ravage your flesh like wild beasts, do not be terrified of them, nor give any heed to their threats. For they are frightening you to test whether you will pay attention to them or utterly despise them.

100. If in your prayer you are present with God, the ruler,

creator and provider of all, why on earth have you disposed yourself so irrationally as to forgo the unsurpassable fear of God and instead be terrified at gnats and beetles? Or have you not heard him say, *Fear the Lord your God* [Deut. 10:20] and *All things shudder and tremble before the face of his might* [Pr. of Man. 4 LXX], and so on?

101. As bread is nourishment for the body and virtue nourishment for the soul, so too is spiritual prayer nourishment for the intellect.

102. In the holy place of prayer do not pray in the manner of the Pharisee, but in the fashion of the tax collector, that you too may be justified by God [Luke 18:9–14].

103. Strive not to pray against anyone in your prayer, lest, making your prayer abhorrent, you tear down what you are building up [cf. Gal. 2:18].

104. Let the servant who owed ten thousand talents [Matt. 18:23–35] instruct you: unless you forgive your debtor, you will not find forgiveness yourself [cf. Matt. 6:12, 15]. For *He was handed over*, it says, *to the jailers* [Matt. 18:34].

105. Dismiss the body's needs during your service of prayer, lest, being troubled by a flea or a louse, by a mosquito or some fly, you be deprived of the great profit of prayer.

106. It came to our attention that the evil one once resisted one of the holy ones in his prayer so much that, as that man stretched out his arms, the evil one was transfigured into a lion. He rose up on his rear paws and drove his front claws into the wrestler's flanks, on both sides, and did not let go until that man lowered his hands – but he never did let his arms down until he had completed his customary prayer.

107. We knew such a man to have lived a solitary life in the lake – I mean John the Short, that monastic giant – he remained unmoved from his union with God, while a demon in dragon's form wound itself round him, chewed his flesh, and vomited in his face.

108. You are surely not ignorant of the lives of the Tabennesi-ote monks.[8] They say that when Abba Theodore[9] was giving a sermon to the brethren, two vipers slithered up to his feet. But he, untroubled, turned his feet to form a little vault, and sheltered

them there while he finished his sermon. Then he presented the vipers to the brethren and explained what had happened.

109. Again, we are not ignorant of another spiritual brother: as he was praying, a viper slithered up and fastened on to his foot. But he did not lower his arms until he completed his customary prayer. And no harm came to that brother who loved God more than himself.

110. Keep your eyes unmoving in your prayer, and, having denied your flesh and your soul, live in accordance with the intellect.

111. It happened to another holy one, who was vigorously praying as he lived in solitude in the desert, that demons appeared before him. For two weeks they threw him like a ball; they would bounce him into the air and catch him in a basket. But never in all that time, not even for a short while, could they draw his intellect down from his fiery prayer.

112. To another lover of God who was walking in the desert and devoting all his thought to prayer, two angels stood beside him and they walked on together, with him in the middle. But as for the monk, he paid them no heed at all, lest he be robbed of the better portion. For he remembered the apostolic saying that runs, *Neither angels nor principalities nor powers will be able to separate us from the love of God* [Rom. 8:38–9].

113. *Equal to an angel* – that is what a monk becomes through true prayer, for he yearns greatly to see *the face of his Father in heaven* [Luke 20:36].

114. Seek not to accept any form, shape or colour in the time of prayer.

115. Do not desire to see with your senses either angels or powers or Christ, lest you become utterly deranged as you accept a wolf instead of the shepherd and worship your enemies the demons.

116. Vainglory is the origin of the intellect's error. The intellect moved by this strives to circumscribe divinity in shapes and forms.

117. I will tell you my own advice, which I have given to neophytes: Blessed is the intellect which during the time of prayer acquires a perfect formlessness.

118. Blessed is the intellect which, as it prays undistractedly, receives ever more desire for God.

119. Blessed is the intellect which during the time of prayer becomes immaterial and detached from all.

120. Blessed is the intellect which during the time of prayer acquires perfect insensibility.

121. Blessed is the monk who regards himself as *the off-scouring of all* [1 Cor. 4:13].

122. Blessed is the monk who regards all humans as god after God.

123. Blessed is the monk who happily and with all joy beholds the salvation and progress of all as his own.

124. The monk is one who is separated from all and united with all.

125. The monk is one who regards himself as one with all because he seems to see himself in each, without exception.

126. He prays who always *offers the fruit* of every first thought *to God* [Rom. 7:4].

127. As a monk and one who wishes to pray, shun every lie and every oath. If you do not, you do nothing but vainly put on a show with what is not yours.

128. If you wish to pray in spirit, hate no one. Then you will have no cloud darkening you in time of prayer.

129. Entrust God with your body's needs and clearly you will be entrusting him with your spirit's needs as well.

130. If you *obtain the promises* [Heb. 11:33], you will reign. So then, if you always look to the promises, you will happily bear with your present poverty.

131. Do not repudiate poverty and affliction – they are the fuel for prayer that rises as if weightless.

132. Let the virtues of the body be your pledge for those of the soul, and those of the soul for those of the spirit – and let these last be your pledge for that immaterial and substantial knowledge.

133. As you pray earnestly, observe your thoughts: whether they abate easily and why this happens, lest you suffer ambush and, having been deceived, surrender yourself.

134. Sometimes the demons suggest thoughts to you, and

then incite you to pray against those thoughts, or to rebut them, at which they willingly depart. They do this so that in your delusion you will think you are actually beginning to conquer your thoughts and terrify the demons.

135. If you are praying against the passion or demon that troubles you, remember the saying: *I will pursue my enemies and overtake them, and not relent until they are annihilated; I will crush them and they will not be able to stand; they shall fall beneath my feet* [Ps. 17:38–9], and so on. These are timely sayings for you, as with humility you arm yourself against your opponents.

136. Do not imagine you have obtained virtue before you have battled for it *unto blood*. For you must *fight against sin* without reproach *until* death [Heb. 12:4], according to the divine Apostle.

137. If you help one person, you will suffer harm from another, so that, feeling aggrieved, you may say or do something out of place; so you will wickedly scatter what you gathered so well. This is the aim of the wicked demons, so pay careful attention!

138. Always accept the demons' grievous assaults, thinking instead how to escape servitude to them.

139. At night the wicked demons importune the spiritual teacher so as to trouble him about themselves. By day they attack him through humans, surrounding him with crises, calumnies and dangers.

140. Do not despise the wool workers, for even if they beat you, treading and stretching as they pull the comb through, still, it is thanks to them that your garment becomes resplendent.

141. However much you have renounced the passions, if your intellect remains opposed to virtue and truth, you will not find a *fragrant incense* [cf. Exod. 30:34–7] in your breast.

142. He yearns to pray, who has left things here below, always having his *citizenship in heaven* [Phil. 3:20], not in words alone, but with angelic action and more divine knowledge.

143. If you only remember the judge when you misbehave, he will appear terrifying and severe, for you have not yet learned *to serve the Lord in fear and rejoice in him with trembling* [Ps.

2:11]. For you know that even in times of spiritual relaxation and feasting, you must, rather, *worship* him *with reverence and awe* [Heb. 12:28].

144. Before coming to perfect repentance, the man of understanding will not keep himself from painful recollection of his own sins and their just punishment in eternal fire.

145. One who is caught up in sins and provocations, and yet shamelessly dares to stretch out towards knowledge of more divine matters, or who embarks upon immaterial prayer: let such a one receive the apostolic rebuke, that it is not without danger for him *to pray with his head uncovered* and bare [1 Cor. 11:5]. For it says, such a soul *ought to have a symbol of authority upon its head, for the sake of the angels* who stand over it [1 Cor. 11:10]. That is, it should be covered round with fitting shame and humility.

146. The unveiled, direct sight of the sun, at high noon, at the height of its brilliance, is of no benefit to someone suffering from eye troubles. Neither will the impression of that fearsome and overflowing prayer *in spirit and truth* [John 4:24] benefit someone who is impure and beset by passion. Rather, quite the opposite! He will rouse the divinity to indignation with him.

147. He who is self-sufficient and impartial did not receive the one who approached his altar with his gift until he had been reconciled with his neighbour who was grieved at him [Matt. 5:23–4]. Therefore, observe the need for such vigilance and discernment that we may offer incense acceptable to God upon his intelligible altar.

148. Do not rejoice in matter or in glory. If you fail in this, *sinners* will no longer *carve furrows on your back* but on your very face [Ps. 128:3]. Then, at the time of prayer, you will be their plaything, *being hooked and enticed* in alien thoughts by them [James 1:14].

149. Attentiveness that seeks diligently after prayer will find prayer. For prayer, though it is something different, follows on attentiveness, to which we must ever apply ourselves.

150. As sight is the best of all the senses, so prayer is the highest of all virtues.

151. Prayer's praiseworthiness lies not simply in its quantity,

but in its quality. Those who *have ascended to the mountain* reveal this [Luke 18:10], as does the saying, *When you pray, do not babble* [Matt. 6:7], etc.

152. So long as you devote yourself to the elegance of your body, and your intellect is concerned with adornments to your tent [cf. 2 Cor. 5:1], you have not yet beheld the place of prayer, but it is still far from you, the blessed way that leads there.

153. When standing in prayer comes to surpass every other joy, then you have truly found prayer.

St Mark the Solitary,
Letter to Nicholas

ST MARK THE SOLITARY (fl. *c*.430–*c*.480)

St Mark was once reputed to have been a disciple of St John Chrysostom, but this was not so. On the basis of his Christo-logical language, it is clear that St Mark knew the later thought of St Cyril of Alexandria (post-430), and so lived in at least the later fifth century. His works were translated into Syriac by 534 and quoted by Gazan monastics in the 550s. Probably he was long dead by this point, so scholars have hypothesized that Mark most likely flourished between the 430s and the 480s. He was, therefore, roughly contemporary with St Diadochos of Photiki, in this collection. We do not know where he lived, though his popularity among Syrian and Palestinian monastic writers, as well as the apocryphal connection to Chrysostom, has led scholars to suggest a connection with Antioch. All that is proffered with any certainty is that the group of writings circulating under his name are, probably, by the same author. However, the text here translated, *Letter to Nicholas*, while re-plete with tantalizing biographical details of its addressee, is of disputed authorship.

Whether or not *Letter to Nicholas* is by Mark himself, and whatever historical basis the details about Nicholas have, this short work offers psychological and spiritual insight paired with careful advice. It deals with practices (descending in thought into one's breast) and concepts (the three 'giants' of laziness, forgetfulness and ignorance) that appear again in later Philokalic texts, and helped shape the hesychast tradition of prayer and attentiveness.

Sources

Text: Georges-Matthieu de Durand (ed.), *Marc le moine: Traités II*, Sources Chrétiennes 455 (Paris: Éditions du Cerf, 2000): 106–54

Alternative text: *PHILOKALIA* (1782): 113–23; *Philokalia* (1893/1982): vol. 1, 127–38

Letter to Nicholas

To my beloved child, Nicholas:

1. Since you have recently been thinking a lot about your salvation and are much concerned about the godly life, you wrote to us, telling us about yourself. You described with what labours and eager desire you would henceforth cleave to the Lord through a strict way of life, self-control, every mortification, struggling in great watchfulness and concentrated prayer. You related how many battles and swarms of fleshly passions are enkindled in your bodily nature and aroused against your soul thanks to that *law of sin* which wages war against the *law of our intellect* [Rom. 7:23]. You were loudly lamenting that you were troubled by the passions of anger and desire. You sought from us some plan of action and words of encouragement, and how to use such labours and combats so as to overcome the destructive passions mentioned above. Now, at that time, so far as we could, we encouraged you face to face, out of love for you, with love in person, and suggested thoughts and mental attitudes that would benefit the soul. We also demonstrated to you how with such labours and hard discipline, undertaken with understanding and enlightened rational wisdom in accordance with the Gospel, a soul might live, helped through grace by faith, and prevail over the evils teeming within the heart, especially those of anger and desire.

The soul, exceedingly troubled and quickly dragged down by those passions which have become a habit through predisposition and even more by custom, ought very earnestly to take up unceasing combat against them, until it subdue the fleshly and irrational operations of the heart, by which it was formerly subdued and dragged down; for the soul was taken captive through inward assent to notions aroused by continual dwelling on trains of thought and by evil meditations.

But we have been bodily separated from you for a little while – from your face, at least, though not your heart. For we have gone into the desert to Christ's true workers and athletes, contending in some small way and struggling together with our brother athletes, who wrestle against hostile operations and so nobly withstand the passions, so that we ourselves may lay aside laziness, shake off indifference, cast away carelessness, and take up all zeal and diligence, urged on to be well-pleasing to God. Therefore, I have eagerly written a letter to your sincerity – a brief, encouraging message, a beneficial admonition – so that, as you carefully peruse our brief and humble letter of exhortation, you will learn about the very matters we spoke of in person and reap spiritual profit, as though we were present.

2. You ought, my child, to make the present moment the beginning of your godly profit. You must consider – without ever forgetting, always remembering, in ceaseless meditation – all the blessings and dispensations God, in his love for humankind, has brought about, and continues to bring about, for the salvation of your soul. And you must not, by forgetfulness of evil – which is the hidden cause of indifference – ever forget his many and great blessings, and, because of forgetfulness, pass the rest of your days with neither profit nor joy. For such unceasing memories, piercing the heart like a goad, rouse it always to confession, to humility, to thanksgiving *with a contrite soul* [Dan. 3:39 Theod.; cf. Ps. 50:19], to all good eagerness, and to the fashioning of useful ways, habits and every godly virtue, as you meditate with conscientious resolve on the prophetic saying, *What shall I render to the Lord for all he has rendered to me?* [Ps. 115:3].

Let a soul reckon up the benefits it has received from God's loving kindness from its very birth, let it count from how many dangers it has often been delivered, or let it remember that, despite having fallen into so many evils and often willingly slipped into offences, it has not been justly handed over to the deceitful spirits for destruction and death. Rather, our kind and loving Master, patiently overlooking the soul's sins [cf. Wis. Sol. 11:23] has guarded it, receiving its conversion [cf. Ezek. 33:11], and he has nourished it, though it was willingly enslaved through passions to the hostile and wicked spirits. Sheltering it and in all sorts of ways providing for it, he has by his good command led the soul into the perfect way of salvation. He implanted in the heart the love charm of the ascetic life. He has given the soul strength to abandon the world and all its illusions of fleshly pleasures joyfully. He has adorned it with the angelic garb of the ascetic order. He has prepared it readily to be enrolled among the holy men in the band of the brotherhood.

Who, conscientiously reckoning up all these things, will not persist always in contrition of heart, since he has such pledges of blessings to come, even though he has done nothing good before? Will he not always seize the *sure hope* [2 Cor. 1:6] and make the following resolve? – Despite the fact that I have done nothing good and, in fact, have often sinned right in God's face, and have been caught in impurity of flesh and many other evils, yet God *has not acted according to my sins, nor has he requited me according to my transgressions* [Ps. 102:10]. Rather, he has dispensed so many gifts and graces for my salvation! If then, for the rest of my life I give myself completely to serving him in *all* pure *conduct* [1 Pet. 1:15] and in the accomplishment of virtues, will he not grant me so many good and *spiritual gifts* [Rom. 1:10], and enable me in every good work, guiding and prospering me?

So, one who always preserves this line of thought, who does not lapse into forgetfulness of such blessings, will persuade, guide and urge himself towards every good discipline of virtue, and towards every activity of righteousness, being ever eager, ever ready for the will of God.

3. So then, my beloved child, since by God's grace you possess natural understanding, always guard within yourself this study, this good meditation. Do not be smothered by baleful forgetfulness, or be impeded by an indifference which frustrates and turns the intellect away from life, or darkened in your thought by ignorance – that cause of every wickedness. Do not

be caught by utterly wicked carelessness, or dragged down by the flesh's pleasure, or defeated by gluttony, or weighed down by sleep [cf. Mark 14:40], neither let your intellect be taken captive by desire and so by assent to lustful thoughts engender within yourself pollution. Do not be conquered by rage, that progenitor of fratricidal hatred. Neither, therefore, grieve another or be grieved on account of some petty and execrable pretext, nor, amassing memories of evil thoughts against your neighbour, be shut out from pure prayer to God, your intellect reduced to utter slavery, eyeing your brother – who is endowed with the same soul as you! – with a savage thought, your conscience chained by the irrational mode of fleshly thinking. If you do, then finally, for a time and for your education, you will be given over to the wicked spirits to whom you have yielded. For how long? Until your intellect, utterly confused, devoured whole by sadness and indifference, and having lost its godly progress thanks to the foregoing causes, comes again to find the beginning of the way of salvation through deep humility.

By labouring long in prayers and night-long vigils, you will dissolve the hold of these issues through humility and through confession to God and to your neighbour, and so your intellect will begin to return to sobriety [cf. 2 Tim. 2:26], and illuminated by the radiance of the knowledge of the Gospel by divine grace, it will know that – unless it gives itself entirely to the Cross in a mental attitude of humility and setting itself at naught, having cast itself beneath all to be trampled, derided, injured, mocked and scorned; unless it endures all these things with joy for Christ's sake; unless it refrains entirely from pursuing human interests, glory, honour, praise, pleasures of food, drink and raiment – it is impossible to become a true Christian.

4. So then, with such toils, struggles and crowns laid out for us, how long will we be fooled by the pious appearance we have assumed, serving the Lord with deceit? For how we are reckoned by humans and how we appear to the one who knows *hidden things* [cf. Rom. 2:16, 1 Cor. 4:5] are very different matters. Truly, many think us sanctified, but in fact our habits are utterly savage: they *have the appearance of piety, but* not *its power* before God [2 Tim. 3:5]. We are reckoned pure

virgins by many, but by the one who considers *hidden things*
we are known to be polluted within by the impurities of assent
to lustful thoughts and muddied with the activities of the passions. Because of our pretended discipline we are even puffed
up with the praises of men, while our intellect is blinded. How
long, therefore, shall we *wander in the vanity of the intellect*
[Eph. 4:17], not taking to heart the mind of the Gospel? Shall
we take no notice of the way of life that follows conscience, so
as to pursue it earnestly, and thus find the confidence that goes
with a pure conscience, still establishing ourselves on righteousness as judged by the outer man [cf. 2 Cor. 4:16] through lack
of true knowledge, and through concern for exterior behaviour
only, lead ourselves astray, wanting to please men and seeking
out *glory, honours and praise* [cf. 1 Pet. 1:7] from them?

Certainly, he will come, who reveals *the hidden things of
darkness and manifests the counsels of hearts* [1 Cor. 4:5],
the undeceivable judge who neither favours the rich man nor
pities the beggar. No, he peels away the appearance and reveals
the truth hidden within. At the coming of the angels, in the
presence of his own Father he crowns those who have lived
in accordance with conscience as true contestants and athletes
[cf. Matt. 25:31–45]. As for all those who have fashioned and
clothed themselves in a show of piety, who have shown to men
a life which only appeared to be ascetic, and who have vainly
established themselves on this and so deceived themselves – he
parades them before the Church of the Saints above and all the
host of heaven. They will be fearfully shamed and condemned
to the *outer darkness* [Matt. 8:11, 22:13, 25:29] like the *foolish
virgins* [Matt. 25:1–12]. These guarded an outward virginity
of the body – they are not accused about that! And, yes, they
also had some oil, at least, in their vessels – that is, they par-
took of some virtues, exterior merits and some divine gifts – so
their lamps burned for a while. But because of carelessness,
ignorance and indifference, they took no care in advance and
so they did not clearly recognize the swarm of passions hidden
within and roused by the wicked spirits. Rather, their thoughts
were utterly corrupted by opposing activities. They whored
themselves out in their assent to thoughts. They were dragged

down and defeated secretly by: wickedest envy, beauty-hating rivalry, strife, hatred, contention, wrath, bitterness, harbouring of grudges, hypocrisy, anger, pride, vainglory, people-pleasing, self-pleasing, greed, fleshly desires (as they fashion delights in their thoughts), faithlessness, temerity before God, coward-ice in all else, *acedia*, despondency, contradiction, relaxation, sleep, self-righteousness, pomp, arrogance, insatiate greed, profligacy, oppression, despair – most difficult of all to deal with – and the rest of the subtle machinations of evil.

The *foolish virgins* thought the activity of good – I mean a sober way of life – something to be done before men, and they expected to reap praises from others. If, indeed, they had a share in divine gifts, they bartered them away to the spirits of vainglory and people-pleasing, and, sharing in the rest of the passions, they mixed good habits with wicked and fleshly thinking. Therefore, their good habits are rendered unaccept-able and impure, like the sacrifice of Cain [Gen. 4:5]. And so the foolish virgins met a terrible end, deprived of the bride-groom's joy and shut out of the heavenly bridal chamber.

5. Considering these things, discerning them, scrutinizing them, let us recognize and understand whose company we keep, so that we may correct ourselves while we still have time for repentance and conversion. Let us do so that our good deeds accomplished purely may really be true and good, unmixed with fleshly thinking, lest they be rejected as a blemished sac-rifice because of some temerity before God, carelessness, or a failure of true knowledge. Lest we somehow wear out our days enduring the toil of virginity, self-control, fasting, vigil and suffering, but, because of the above-mentioned passions, our seemingly righteous acts become like a blemished sacrifice – unacceptable to Christ our heavenly priest.

My child, you must first and foremost take great care for knowledge and understanding, who would *take up his cross and follow Christ* [Matt. 16:24]: through unceasing inquiry of the thoughts in himself, through much care for salvation, much eagerness for God, through understanding and inquiring of like-minded and similar-souled servants of God who strug-gle in the same contest – lest, being ignorant where and how he walks in darkness [cf. John 12:35, Prov. 4:19], he make his way without even lamplight [cf. Ps. 118:105]. The man who keeps his own rule, without knowledge of the Gospel, without discernment and someone to guide him, stumbles often as he makes his way. He falls into many pits and snares of the Evil One [cf. Ps. 56:6, Sirach 27:25], frequently gets lost and runs foul of numerous dangers – and he does not know what his end will be. For many have traversed numerous toils and ascetic labours, and have endured sufferings and many hardships, as though for God, but their insistence on following their own rule, combined with their lack of discernment and self-reliance in the face of a neighbour's assistance – all these have nullified their many labours and troubles.

6. You, therefore, beloved child, just as I said at the beginning of this letter of encouragement, do not overlook the benefits of God, whom we worship and who loves us, by being dragged down by the thievery of evil and laziness. Rather, bringing before your eyes these benefits, whether bodily or spiritual, from your conception to the present moment, meditate and reflect on them: as it says, *Do not forget all his benefits* [Ps. 102:2]. So may your heart be moved readily to alacrity and to love of God, to render to him according to your ability a careful life, virtuous conduct, a pious conscience, a harmonious account; and to offer your whole self as a gift to God, abashed by the memory of such benefits as you have received from our good God who loves humankind, so that, as it were spontaneously, through such memory of his benefits, or rather, by a certain influence from above working together with you, your heart is wounded with love and longing. Why? Because he has not done these things for others – who are much more deserving than you – but he has performed a marvel for you by his own ineffable love for humankind. So make sure that all those acts of kindness sent to you from God remain constantly in your memory.

Especially recall without ceasing that great and marvellous grace and benefit which he offered you as you sailed from the Holy Land to Constantinople, together with your mother! You related the tale to us thus: a fearsome gusting squall, with a surging sea, developed during the night, and everyone in the boat – the sailors, and your mother herself – were lost in the abyss, but you alone, on account of a strange and divine power, having been thrown overboard, were saved with two others. You told us how it was ordained that you come to Ankyra in the heart of your ancestral lands, having been taken in by a freeborn man and yoked in disposition with my most pious child, Epiphanios. And so both of you were led by a holy man to come to the way of salvation and to be welcomed, as *legitimate children* [cf. 1 Tim. 1:2, Tit. 1:4], among the holy slaves of God.

7. What worthy recompense can you make, for all these good things bestowed on you by God, to the one who called your soul to eternal life? You ought, as is only just, *no longer to live for yourself but for the one who died and rose for you* [2 Cor. 5:15], unto every virtue of righteousness, unto every fulfilment of the commands, always seeking out *what is the will of God, his good and perfect and pleasing will* [Rom. 12.2], and you ought to strive to pursue it with all your strength. Despite your youth, my child, I have subjected you to the word of God, as the Word himself demands, to *present your body as a living sacrifice, holy, pleasing to God, this your rational worship* [Rom. 12:1] – cooling and drying every drop of fleshly desire through contentedness with little, moderation in drinking, and night-long vigils, that you may say on account of your condition, *I have become like a wineskin in smoke, but I have not forgotten your statutes* [Ps. 118:83]. And, knowing that you belong to Christ, *Crucify your flesh*, according to the apostolic saying, *along with its passions and desires* [Gal. 5:24]. And *mortify your members upon the earth* [Col. 3:5], not only with regard to the practice of fornication, but also the impurity roused in your flesh by the wicked spirits.

In addition, he does not simply stand in combat expecting to receive the crown of true, undefiled, and all-perfect virginity, but, following the apostolic teaching, he fights to *mortify* even the symptoms and movements of his passion. Neither does he feel assurance, while he waits with the utmost love for angelic and immaculate virginity to settle in his own body. Rather, he prays that even the idea contained in the merest thought of bare desire, which rises up without the motion or activity of bodily passion, in a momentary disturbance of the intellect will vanish utterly. This can be accomplished through the strength, aid and provision of the Spirit alone. If then some are vouchsafed this grace, so also he who awaits the crown of pure and immaculate virginity ought to *crucify his flesh* [Gal. 5:24] through ascetic labours and to *mortify his members upon the earth* [Col. 3:5], *wearing away his outward nature* [2 Cor. 4:16] with both the intensity and obduracy of self-control. He ought to thin down his flesh, shrivel it up, and reduce himself to a skeleton, so that he may through faith and struggles and by the activity of grace *renew his inner nature,* progressing *day by day* towards what is better [2 Cor. 4:16]: that he may be increased in love, magnified in hope, adorned with meekness, made joyous in exultation of spirit, guarded by goodness, encompassed with fear of God, enlightened with understanding and knowledge, made resplendent with wisdom, guided by humility. The intellect renewed by the Spirit with these and similar virtues recognizes the stamp of the deiform *image* in itself, perceives the intelligible and indescribable beauty of its masterly *likeness* [cf. Gen. 1:26], and comprehends the wealth of the self-taught and self-learned wisdom of the law established in it [cf. Rom. 2:14].

So, my child, trim down your youthful flesh and fatten up your immortal soul with the aforementioned labours. Renew your intellect by the virtues already mentioned, working together with the Spirit. For youth's flesh, fattened on a variety of foods and draughts of wine, is like a pig prepared for slaughter. Thus, by the burning of the body's pleasures, the soul is slaughtered, and by the boiling of wicked desire the intellect is led captive, being unable to endure the flesh's pleasures. For an inflow of blood brings about an outflow of spirit. Most especially, do not let your youth sniff out chances for taking wine, lest you be kindled by a twofold fire (I mean youth's natural effervescence and the drinking which pours fire from without), because of which fleshly pleasure boils over and chases out the spiritual pleasure of the labour of compunction, and produces confusion and fever in your heart. Rather, because of its spiritual desire, let your youth not accept even surfeit of water. For want of water greatly contributes to the assistance of continence. As you test this in action, you will gain assurance by the experience itself. For we do not lay this down as a law or define it as a yoke of necessity; rather, we lovingly advise and recommend that you adopt it as a plan and good method for helping to achieve true virginity and exacting continence, leaving it to your own free choice to do what seems best

8. But come then and let us uncover a few things about the irrational passion of wrath, which desolates the whole soul, confounds it and darkens it, and renders a person like wild beasts during the time of its movement and activity – especially someone who, faced with this passion, easily slips and succumbs to it. Wrath is supported, strengthened and rendered indissoluble especially by pride. To put it differently, the devilish root of bitterness, wrath and anger is watered with the swamp water of pride, until it flowers, blooms and bears much fruit – of lawlessness. Thus arises the indestructible edifice of the Evil One in the soul, having the foundations of pride for its support and strength.

So, therefore, you want the root of lawlessness (I mean the passion of bitterness, wrath and anger) to be withered and rendered fruitless, so that the axe of the Spirit, having come, may *chop it down and cast it into the fire* [Matt. 3:10] – according to the apostolic proclamation – and root it out along with every evil. Then there is the house of lawlessness, which the Evil One builds wickedly in your soul, gathering together its building stones from various excuses for anger, whether rational or irrational; he gathers them together through deeds and words of material gain in your thoughts; he creates a structure of evil in your soul, having laid down first the thoughts of pride as its support and strength. Do you want this structure to be destroyed utterly and razed to the ground? Then keep the Lord's humility unfailingly present in your heart. Think of who he was, what he became for us, and from what a height, light, Divinity – revealed in proportion to the strength of the beings above, glorified in the heavens by every rational nature: angels, archangels, thrones, dominions, rulers, authorities, cherubim and seraphim, and the nameless intelligible powers whose names have not reached us [cf. Eph. 1:21, Col. 1:16], according to the apostolic riddle. Consider that he came from all that to such depth of humiliation among men because of his unspeakable goodness, in everything made like us [cf. Heb. 4:15] *who are seated in darkness and the shadow of death* [Luke 1:79] – who have been born in captivity thanks to Adam's transgression; who have been tyrannized by the enemy thanks to the activity of the passions [cf. Heb. 2:14–15].

9. So then, we were in such captivity, ruled by unseen, bitter death, and the Master of all creation visible and invisible was not ashamed at us! Rather, having humbled himself and taken to himself humanity bound under the *dishonourable passions* [Rom. 1:26] and sentence of their master, he became *in all ways like us except sin* [Heb. 4:15] – that is, *except for* the *dishonourable passions*. For the Master took to himself those very passions added at his own command to humanity as penalties on account of Adam's sin of transgression: death, fatigue, hunger, thirst and the like. So he became in all respects what we are, that we might become what he is. *The Word became flesh* [John 1:14] that the flesh might become Word. *Being wealthy he became poor for us, that we might be made rich by his poverty* [2 Cor. 8:9]. He became like us because of his great love for humanity, so that we might become like him through every virtue.

Truly, from the moment Christ visited us, the *new human* [Eph. 2:15, 4:22] *according to the image and likeness* [Gen. 1:26] has been undergoing renewal through the grace and power of the Holy Spirit, attaining *to the measure* [Eph. 4:13] of *perfect love which casts out fear* [1 John 4:18], no longer capable of subjection to the Fall. *For love never fails* [1 Cor. 13:8]. For *Love*, says John, *is God, and whoever abides in love abides in God* [1 John 4:16]. The apostles were deemed worthy of this measure; so too those who, like the apostles, practised virtue and presented themselves perfect to God, and followed the Saviour with perfect yearning for their whole life.

Such, then, is the humility which the Lord, out of his love for us, assumed in his indescribable love for humankind, and which you should always consider and never forget: that is, the dwelling of God the Word in a womb; his assumption of humanity; being born of woman; his growing in bodily stature; the rebukes, insults, reproaches, mockery, abuse, blows, being spat upon, being laughed to ridicule, the derision, the scarlet cloak, the crown of thorns; his condemnation by the rulers; the crying out against him of the lawless Jews, his kinsmen: *Away, away, crucify him!* [John 19:15]; the cross, the nails, the lance, the bitter draught of vinegar; the jeering of the peoples, the jokes of those who passed by and said, *If you are the Son of God, descend now from the cross and we will believe you* [Matt. 27:40, 42]; and all the rest of the sufferings which he endured for our sake: crucifixion, death, burial in the tomb for three days and the descent into Hades. Then there is the crop he harvested from his sufferings, such as these: that is, the resurrection from the dead; the plundering of Hades and Death of the souls that gathered to their Lord; the assumption into the heavens; the sitting at the right hand of the Father, honour and glory *above every ruler and authority and every name that is named* (Eph. 1:21); the worship of all the angels for the *firstborn from the dead* [Col. 1:18] by reason of his suffering, according to the Apostle's word, which says, *Let this mind be in you which was in Christ Jesus, who, being in the form of God, did not reckon it robbery to be equal to God; but emptied himself, having taken the form of a slave, and being found in human likeness he humbled himself, becoming obedient unto death – even death on a cross. Therefore, also God exalted him and gave him the name above every name, so that at the name of Jesus Christ every knee might bow, whether in heaven or on the earth or beneath the earth* [Phil. 2:5–10], and the rest. See the reasons already given, why, in accordance with God's just judgement, the Lord's humanity has ascended to such glory and exaltation!

10. If, therefore, you preserve these recollections in your heart, by yearning and disposition never to forget, then the passion of bitterness, wrath and anger will not lord it over you. When the foundations of the passion of pride collapse through your pondering the humility of Christ, then the whole edifice of

lawlessness – rage and anger – is razed easily, almost spontaneously. What sort of hard and stony heart can constantly bear
in mind the profound humiliation of the divinity of the only-
begotten for our sake and can take inventory of the foregoing
sufferings in its memory, and yet not be wounded, driven to
compunction and humbled? Would it not rather become *earth
and ashes* [Gen. 19:27] and be trampled on willingly beneath
men's feet? When the soul is humbled and afflicted, gazing
upon the Lord's humility, what sort of anger could possibly
master it? What sort of wrath, what bitterness could possibly
encompass it?

But it seems that forgetfulness of these useful thoughts, that
give us life, with its sister laziness and their fellow-worker in
the same habit, ignorance, are the deeper and more inward passions of the soul, hard to find and harder to set right, which
veil and darken the soul with their terrible meddling. They prepare the way for all other passions to act and to lurk in the
soul, such as temerity before God and carelessness about good
things, and easily and freely present an entrance and activity for each passion. For since the soul has been veiled [cf. 2
Cor. 3:15] by all-wicked forgetfulness, destructive laziness and
ignorance, that mother and nursemaid of all evils, the intellect,
afflicted and blind, is easily bound to anything seen, thought
of or heard. If, for example, someone sees a woman's beauty,
his soul is immediately wounded with fleshly desire. Then, his
memory will have taken in what was beheld, heard or felt with
passion and pleasure. Then those memories vividly paint the
pictures of what is desired, through the figuration of thoughts
and a wicked interior meditation. So, finally, they pollute the
impassioned and miserable intellect through the activity of the
spirits of fornication.

11. Then the flesh too, if it is fat, youthful and moist, and
therefore readily aroused by such memories, brings its own
members into action by this passion, moving them to desire,
producing impurity, sometimes while waking, sometimes while
sleeping. Continuing the example, if someone has not openly
coupled with a woman, he is reckoned wise, virgin and pure
by people, and can even have a reputation for holiness. But

this same man is adjudged profane, adulterer and incontinent by the one who regards hidden things. He will justly be condemned *on that day* [Matt. 7:21, etc.], unless he mourns and weeps, having melted down his flesh with tears, fasts, vigils and ceaseless prayers. Then, having healed and corrected his intellect with holy memories and meditations on the word of God, let him offer worthy repentance to the God in whose presence he contemplated or accomplished wicked acts. For the living voice speaks no lie when it says, *But I say to you: Everyone who looks on a woman so as to desire her has already committed adultery with her in his heart* [Matt. 5:28]. On this account it is recommended to young men especially that, if at all possible, they completely avoid meeting women, if they would be accounted holy.

But, if it be possible to live far from all people, you will fight his war more nimbly and understand more clearly, especially if you pay careful attention to yourself and, as you fight, maintain your conduct with contentment with little, moderation in water and much wakefulness in prayer. Especially, too, if you are diligent in living with, associating with and being guided by those experienced in spiritual matters. For the solitary life, according to one's own rule, without witnesses, or with people inexperienced in spiritual combat, is very dangerous. Such people are caught in various modes of warfare, for many are the machinations of evil, while hidden pits and the various traps of the Enemy have been dug everywhere. On this account, if it be possible, instead, always to be together, you must hasten and struggle to meet up with knowledgeable men, so that, even if you yourself do not possess the lamp of true knowledge – since you are still an infant and have not reached intellectual manhood – you will not *walk in darkness* [1 John 5:3] since you travel with someone who does possess that lamp. You will run no risk of *snares* and *traps* [cf. Prov. 6:4] and will not fall among intellectual beasts, who range about in the darkness, and who snatch and destroy those who walk in it without the intellectual lamp of the divine Word.

12. So, you wish, my child, to procure your very own lamp, to shine the intelligible light of spiritual knowledge within you,

so that you can walk without stumbling in the deepest night of this age [cf. John 11:9]? You wish for your *steps to be prospered by the Lord* and you greatly *desire the way* of his Gospel [cf. Ps. 36:23], in accordance with the prophetic saying – that is, you desire to be compassed about with fiery faith in the more perfect evangelical commandments, and to become a communicant of the Lord's sufferings through desire and prayer? If you desire all this, well then, I will show you a marvellous method and design, which requires a spiritual way of life – not requiring bodily toil or struggle, but discovering instead labour of soul and intellect, and attentive thoughts. It works together with fear and love of God. Through this plan you can easily turn aside the whole enemy phalanx, just as the blessed David destroyed the single giant, Goliath of the aliens, and through faith and assurance in God with his own people easily turned thousands of enemies to flight [1 Kgds 17:40–54].[10]

The keys to our plan are three vigorous and powerful giants from among the aliens, in whom every opposing power, belonging to the intellectual Holophernes [cf. Judith 2:4–14:19], is constituted. If these are destroyed and put to death, then every power of the wicked spirits quickly grows powerless and is destroyed. Who are those reckoned the three mighty giants of the Evil One? They are the three we have already mentioned: *ignorance*, mother of all evils; *forgetfulness*, her sister, colleague and helpmate; and *laziness*, which weaves the inky cloak and veil of a black cloud in the soul. Laziness, indeed, makes fast and strengthens both the others; she provides a kind of union to them, while she effects enduring evil in the most careless souls. For the supports of the other passions are strengthened and enlarged by laziness, forgetfulness and ignorance. These three, being one another's helpers and unable to last without each other, are shown to be mighty powers of the adversary, and strong princes of the Evil One. Through them every army of the spirits of wickedness infiltrates, encamps and accomplishes its designs. Without them, the aforementioned passions cannot last.

13. If, therefore, you wish to claim victory against the passions just mentioned, and easily put the intellectual aliens' phalanx

to flight, then, having retreated into yourself through prayer and working together with God, and having plunged into the depths of your heart, hunt down these three strong giants of the Devil. I mean, to repeat, forgetfulness, laziness and ignorance, the mainstays of the intellectual aliens, through which the rest of the passions sneak in, operate, live, and grow strong in the souls of the uneducated and lovers of pleasure. Then, through much attentiveness and mental control, together with a helping push from above, you will have discovered evils unknown to many – imagined, even, not to exist! – which are more destructive than all the rest. Take up the weapons of righteousness which oppose those three. First, there is the good memory of the cause of all goods. Secondly, enlightened knowledge, through which the soul, waking up, chases from itself the darkness of ignorance. Thirdly, the finest desire for salvation which readies the soul and urges it on. Being clothed, then, in these arms of virtue, in the power of the Holy Spirit, by every prayer and supplication, nobly and manfully will you prevail against the three giants, already mentioned, of the intellectual aliens.

Always considering *whatever things are true, whatever honourable, whatever righteous, pure, lovely, if there is any excellence, any praiseworthiness* [Phil. 4:8], chase all-wicked forgetfulness right out of yourself with a good and godly memory. By an enlightened and heavenly knowledge scatter the destructive darkness of ignorance. With an all-virtuous and most beautiful desire expel the godless indifference which works evil in your soul. When you gain these three virtues – not from mere resolve but, rather, from the power of God and working together with the Holy Spirit in great attentiveness and prayer – you can in this way be delivered from the three mighty giants of the Evil One. The tracks of forgetfulness, ignorance and laziness fade entirely in the soul, and are wiped out of existence by the concord of true knowledge, memory of God's word, and good desire, operating through grace in the soul which works diligently to unite them, and zealously guards them.

Then will grace rule within you, *in Christ Jesus our Lord* [Rom. 8:39], to whom be glory to the ages of ages. Amen.

St Diadochos of Photiki,
One Hundred Gnostic Chapters

ST DIADOCHOS OF PHOTIKI
(*fl.* 451–*c*.486)

We know very little about St Diadochos, which is a pity, because it would be nice to know better the author of such a
luminous work as the *One Hundred Gnostic Chapters*, translated here. We do know that Diadochos was Bishop of Epiros,
the mountainous region of western Greece that tumbles down
to the Ionian Sea. He could not have been bishop until after the
Council of Chalcedon in 451 (since the Bishop of Epiros then
was named John). He co-signed a letter with several fellow
bishops to Emperor Leo I in 457, and is referred to as one of
the blessed dead in 486. Everything else is speculation gleaned
from hints in his writings – which are few. His *One Hundred
Gnostic Chapters* refers to 'brothers', and distinguishes at
points between those living in monastic communities ('coen-
obia') and those living solitary lives, so perhaps Diadochos
lived as a monastic before being consecrated bishop.

The *One Hundred Gnostic Chapters*, sometimes called *An
Ascetic Treatise*, is simply that: a set of one hundred (relatively)
short chapters. These deal with numerous aspects of human
psychology treated within a general – but deliberately loose –
outline of creation, fall and restoration. Diadochos moves
fluidly through a range of concerns, including an extended
reflection on the effects of baptism. This section suggests at
least an interest in the 'Messalian Controversy' over the efficacy of sacraments and the centrality of prayer. The question is

whether baptism alters the human being ontologically or only symbolically – if the former, how can people sin after baptism? If the latter, then when and how is the Holy Spirit received? Diadochos offers subtle responses to these questions as part of his fuller meditation on the restoration of appropriate sense-perception, memory and desire, and the reintegration of body, soul and intellect in quest of God. Diadochos describes this, rather unusually, in terms of *taste*, rather than sight or hearing. Diadochos is also the first witness to devotion to the name of Jesus (or, more precisely, use of a prayer addressed to Jesus by name), a key component in what would mature into hesychast practices of the Jesus Prayer.

Sources

Text: Édouard des Places (ed.), *Diadoque de Photicé: Œuvres spir-ituelles*, Sources Chrétiennes 5 (3rd edn, Paris: Éditions du Cerf, 1966): 84–163

Alternative text: *PHILOKALIA* (1782): 205–37; *Philokalia* (1893/1982): vol. 1, 236–72

One Hundred Gnostic Chapters

Ten Preliminary Definitions

Faith: a dispassionate conception of God.

Hope: a departure of the intellect in love towards *things hoped for* [Heb. 11:1].

Endurance: to persevere ceaselessly in seeing the unseen as seen with the mind's eye.

Freedom from avarice: to desire not having things as much as someone else desires having them.

Knowledge: being ignorant of oneself in reaching out towards God.

Humility: the attentive forgetfulness of one's achievements.

Freedom from anger: a great desire not to lose one's temper.

Purity: a felt sense of always cleaving to God.

Love: an increasing affection for those who insult us.

Perfect transformation: through delight in God to count as joy the horror of death.

Discourses on judgement and spiritual discernment by Diadochos, Bishop of Photiki, in Epiros.

With the Lord showing us the way, we must arrive through such knowledge at the perfection which has been shown to us in advance, so that each of us in keeping with the plan of that liberating parable may cause the seed of the Word to bear fruit [Matt. 13:1–23].

1. Let faith, hope, love take the lead in every spiritual contemplation, but especially love. For these teach us well to

disdain visible goods, but love joins the soul together with the very virtues of God, hunting out the invisible by an intellectual sense.

2. God alone is good by nature [cf. Luke 18:19]. But a human, by taking care of his ways, becomes good through the one who is truly good, being changed into what he is not when through care for the good his soul comes to be in God, as much as he is able to will. For he says, *Be good and merciful as your Father in heaven* [cf. Luke 6:36].

3. There is no evil in nature, nor is anyone evil by nature: for God did not make anything evil. But when in his heart's desire someone gives form to what has no essential being, then the very thing which the one doing it wants begins to exist. Therefore, we must always, in our concern for the recollection of God, avoid any concern for an evil disposition. For the nature of good is stronger than the evil disposition, since the former actually exists, while the latter does not, save only in action.

4. All of us humans are *in the image of God*. But being *in the likeness* [Gen. 1:26] pertains only to those who, through much love, have enslaved their own freedom to God. For when we are not our own [cf. 1 Cor. 6:19], then are we like the one who through love reconciled us to himself [cf. 2 Cor. 5:18]: him to whom no one will attain, unless they persuade their own soul not to be stirred by the glittering glory of this life.

5. Self-determination belonging to a rational soul is a faculty of willing readily moved to whatever it wills. Let us prevail upon it to head readily towards the good alone, so that we may always starve out the memory of evil by good thoughts.

6. The light of true knowledge is unerring discernment of good from evil. For then the *way of righteousness* [Prov. 21:21], which leads the intellect up towards the *sun of righteousness* [Mal. 4:2], introduces it to an unbounded illumination of knowledge as thereafter it seeks out love with confidence. It is necessary, therefore, to seize with wrathless anger what is right from those who dare to insult it. For the zeal of piety reveals the victory not by hatred but by conviction.

7. The spiritual word confirms our intellectual sense, for it is borne from God by the activity of love. Our intellect remains,

therefore, unbothered in the movements of theology. For it does not suffer want that leads to anxiety, since it is broadened in contemplations as much as the activity of love wills. It is always good, then, by means of faith made active through love, to await the enlightenment of speech. For nothing is more impoverished than a mind outside of God philosophizing about the things of God.

8. Neither should one who is unenlightened devote himself to spiritual contemplations, nor indeed should one who has been richly enlightened by the exceeding goodness of the Holy Spirit rush to speech. For poverty of illumination brings ignorance, but a wealth of it does not permit speech, for then the soul drunk on the love of God desires to delight with silent voice in the glory of the Lord. Thus, it belongs to one keeping the mean of activity to embark on theological speech. For this measure is favoured with a form, as it were, of glorious speech, and the costliness of enlightenment nourishes the faith of the one speaking in faith, so that the teacher first tastes the fruit of knowledge through love. For, it says, *The farmer who toils should first have a share of the fruits* [2 Tim. 2:6].

9. Wisdom and knowledge are gifts of the one Holy Spirit, as are all the divine gifts, but each individually has its own proper activity. Thus, *to one is given wisdom, to another knowledge, according to the same Spirit*, as the Apostle testifies [1 Cor. 12:8]. For knowledge unites a human to God by experience, but does not move their soul to speak about things. This is why some of those who live the solitary life through philosophy are enlightened by knowledge in their perception, but do not attain to divine speech. Wisdom, if indeed it has been given to someone along with knowledge in fear – and this is rare – lays bare the very activities of knowledge. This is because knowledge generally enlightens by activity, and wisdom by word. Now, prayer and much stillness in total freedom from anxiety bring knowledge, while wisdom is borne by humble meditation upon the sayings of God and is, first and foremost, the gracious gift of God who gives it.

10. When the irascible part of the soul is roused against the passions we should know that then is the time for silence, for

this is a period of struggle. But when someone sees that agitation coming to calmness through prayer or almsgiving, let him be stirred to motion by a loving yearning for divine sayings, securing the wings of the intellect firmly with the chain of humility. For unless someone in deep humility regards himself as nothing, he cannot discuss the greatness of God.

11. The spiritual word always keeps a soul free from vainglory. For, benefitting all of the soul's parts by a sensation of light, it causes it to have no need of the honour that comes from people [cf. John 5:41]. Thus also this word carefully preserves the mind free of images, since it transforms the whole intellect into the love of God. Conversely, the word of *worldly wisdom* [1 Cor. 3.19] always urges a person on to love of glory. For since it can offer no benefit by the experience of sensation, it offers to its devotees affection for praise, being, as it is, a forgery made by vainglorious humans. We will, therefore, recognize unerringly the disposition of the divine word, if by an unanxious silence we use up the hours dedicated to silence in fervent remembrance of God.

12. Whoever loves himself cannot love God; whoever does not love himself, on account of the *exceeding riches of the love of God* [Eph. 2:7], loves God. Thus, such a one never seeks his own glory, but, rather, the glory of God. For one who loves himself seeks only his own glory, but one who loves God loves the glory of the one who made him. For it belongs to a perceptive soul enamoured of God always to seek God's glory in all the commands it keeps, and to take delight in its own humility. For glory befits God because of his grandeur, but humility befits a human, that through it he may be assimilated to God. If, indeed, we do this, then we too, rejoicing in the glory of the Lord, will start saying ceaselessly with John the Baptist, *He must increase, but* we *must decrease* [John 3:30].

13. I know one such person, who loves God and yet mourns that he does not love God as he wishes: so that his soul is in such inexhaustibly fervent desire for God, as to be glorified in him, while he himself is as nothing [cf. Gal. 1:24]. But this person does not know what he is, even in the words of those who praise him, for in his great yearning for humility he does not know his

worth. Rather, while he ministers to God as the law ordains for priests, he still manages by some great disposition of piety to conceal the memory of his worth somewhere in the depth of his love of God while he hides the boasting which might come from this in a spirit of humility. Thus, he constantly appears to his own mind as a *worthless slave* [Luke 17:10]. It is as though his desire for humility alienates him from his own worth. Wherefore it is necessary also for us, in everything we do, to flee far from honour and glory for the sake of the abundance of *the riches of the love of* the Lord [Eph. 2:7] who loved us so.

14. One who loves God with felt perception in his heart will be known by God [cf. 1 Cor. 8:3]. For inasmuch as someone receives the love of God in his soul's felt perception, so does he come to be in the love of God. Therefore, then, such a one ever reaches out in an exceeding great love for the illumination of knowledge until he perceives it in his very bones and no longer knows himself, but is transformed wholly by the love of God. Such a one is at once present in this life and not present: still dwelling in his own body he goes out, through love, by his soul's movement, ceaselessly towards God. For the rest, then, unyieldingly enkindling his heart with the fire of love, he has been joined to God by a certain necessity of desire, as he stands altogether outside of any affection for himself in the love of God. *For if we are out of our minds*, says the Apostle, *it is for God; and if we are wise, it is for you* [2 Cor. 5:13].

15. When someone begins richly to sense the love of God, then he begins also to love his neighbour with a spiritual perception. For this is the love of which all the Scriptures speak. Fleshly affection is too easily dissolved when some shallow cause has been discovered since it is not bound by spiritual perception. On the other hand, even if some kind of earthquake should strike the soul moved by God, the bond of love remains unbroken by it. For, rekindling itself from the heat of the love of God, the soul is swiftly recalled to the good and to the love of neighbour with much joy, even if it has been greatly insulted or abused by that same neighbour. In the sweetness of God the bitterness of strife entirely disappears.

16. No one can love God with his whole heart unless he

fears God in his heart's perception. For through the activity of
fear the soul is cleansed and softened, and so comes to love in
action. For no one can come wholly to fear God in the manner
just described, unless he stands apart from all the cares of this
life. For when the intellect comes to be in much stillness and
freedom from care, then the fear of God troubles it, purifying it from all earthly density [cf. Ps. 141:7] with a powerful
feeling, so as to lead it into a great love of God's goodness.
And so, on the one hand, fear accompanied by a middling love
belongs to those being purified. But love, perfect love, belongs
to those already purified, in whom there is no longer any fear.
For, it says, *perfect love casts out fear* [1 John 4:18]. Of course,
both belong only to the righteous, who, by the activity of the
Holy Spirit, keep the commandments. And for this reason, the
divine Scriptures say in one place, *Fear the Lord, all you his
holy ones* [Ps. 33:10]; and in another, *Love the Lord, all you
his holy ones* [Ps. 30:24]. This is so that we may learn precisely
that while fear belongs (with what we have called a middling
love) to those yet being purified, perfect love belongs to those
already purified, in whom there is no longer even any notion of
fear, but only ceaseless kindling and joining of the soul to God
through the activity of the Holy Spirit. So it is said, *My soul has
been united to you, let your right hand uphold me* [Ps. 62:9].

17. We know how it is with bodily wounds: if left scabbed
and untended they do not respond to the drugs applied by
doctors; when cleaned out they feel the drug's action moving
within them to swift healing. So it is with the soul: as long
as it is untended, all scabbed over by the sores of the love of
pleasure, it is unable to perceive the fear of God, even if someone were constantly to describe for it the terrifying and mighty
judgement of God. But when it begins to be purified through
much attentiveness, then it senses divine fear as some life-saving
cure burning it, as by the activity of reproaches, in the fire of
dispassion. For which reason, being purified bit by bit, the soul
presses forward to the completion of purification, increasing
in love as much as it is degraded by fear. In this way it comes
upon perfect love, in which, as we have said, there is no fear,
but, rather, total dispassion made active through the glory of

God. Let the fear of God first be our endless boast of all boasts, and then love, which is the fullness of the law of perfection in Christ [cf. Rom. 13:10].

18. A soul that has not been delivered from worldly cares neither genuinely loves God nor abhors the Devil worthily, for it has its anxiety about life as a heavy veil. For which reason the intellect cannot recognize its own tribunal concerning such matters, so as to count up the tally of judgement accurately by itself. For all these reasons, then, retreat from the world is beneficial.

19. The properties of a pure soul are: an unenvying reason [*logos*], irreproachable zeal and ceaseless love of the *Lord of Glory* [1 Cor. 2:8]. Then, indeed, the intellect accurately calibrates its own scales, as though present with its own mind in the flawless tribunal.

20. Faith without works and works without faith are scrupulously to be rejected in the same way. For a faithful person must offer up to the Lord his faith revealed in actions. For not even to our father Abraham was faith *reckoned as righteousness* without his offering up his son as its fruit [cf. Gen. 15:6/ Rom. 4:22].

21. The one who loves God both genuinely believes and venerably completes the works of faith. But the one who believes only and is not in love lacks even the faith he thinks he has. For he believes only with some lightness of mind, and not as being roused by the *weight of* love's *glory* [cf. 2 Cor. 4:17]. Faith, then, being roused to action through love is the greatness of the virtues.

22. When scrutinized, the depths of faith roll like the sea, but, when contemplated with a simple disposition, become calm. The abyss of faith, being the water of forgetfulness of evils, cannot bear to be contemplated by merely curious thoughts. Let us, then, sail the waters of faith in simplicity of mind, that we may finally arrive at the *safe harbour of* God's *will* [Ps. 106:30].

23. No one can love or believe properly unless he no longer has himself as his own accuser. For when our conscience stirs itself up with reproaches, it prevents the intellect from

perceiving the savour of goods beyond this world. The intellect is immediately divided in doubt: it reaches out with a fervent motion for the sake of its prior experience of faith, but can no longer grasp this experience through love in the heart's perception, because of the frequent irritations of the reproach of the conscience, as I've said. However, we will attain what we desire when we have purified ourselves with more fervent attentiveness along with further experience in God.

24. Our bodily senses urge us almost violently towards things which seem beautiful. So too our intellectual sense-perception is accustomed to lead us by the hand towards invisible good things once it has tasted divine goodness. For each always yearns for its kin: the soul, being incorporeal, yearns for heavenly beauties; the body, being dust, yearns for earthly food. We shall come unerringly to experience immaterial perception only if we lighten our material by toil.

25. The activity of holy knowledge teaches us that the soul has a single, natural[1] felt perception, which was later split into two activities because of Adam's disobedience. There is also a single, simple perception that comes about in the soul from the Holy Spirit, which none can know save those gladly freed from the beauties of life through hope of the good things to come, who have caused every longing for bodily sensations to wither through self-control. For in such matters only an intellect which moves firmly, thanks to its freedom from anxiety, can silently taste divine goodness. Therefore, the intellect then confers on the body a share of joy, according to the measure of its own progress, rejoicing beyond all measure in love for its confession. *For in him*, it says, *my heart has hoped and been helped, and my flesh has been revived, and I will confess him from my whole will* [Ps. 27:7]. For then truly the joy which has sprung up in both soul and body is an unerring reminder of the incorruptible life.

26. Those labouring in the contest must always keep their minds unruffled, so that the intellect, discerning the thoughts that rush upon it, may store the good ones sent by God in the treasuries of memory, but cast the dark and demonic ones somewhere outside its natural storehouses. For the sea, too,

when peaceful, can be seen by men out fishing even to the movements of its depths, since nothing hides the movements of the creatures swimming about therein. But when the sea is troubled by the winds, it hides in the gloom of its turbulence the same things which it loved to disclose in the smile of its calm. Then we see how ineffective is the art of those who devise cunning fishing baits. So it is always with the contemplative intellect, especially when the depths of the soul are troubled by unjust anger.

27. To recognize accurately all one's own faults is given to very few, only those whose intellect is never wrested away from the recollection of God. For just as our bodily eyes see in such a way that, when healthy, they can see everything, even mosquitoes and gnats buzzing about the air, but when they are covered by cataracts or discharge, then, even if they run into something massive, they see it indistinctly, while they do not perceive small things by the sense of sight at all. So also our soul, if by attention it attenuates the blindness which comes about from love of the world and regards its slightest faults as very great, then it ceaselessly offers tears upon tears in profound gratitude. For *the just*, it says, *will confess your name* [Ps. 139:14]. If, on the other hand, it stays in a worldly disposition, then, even if it should do something murderous or worthy of terrible punishment, it feels this only slightly, and cannot discern its other faults at all. Rather, it even often takes them to be some kind of achievement, and so this wretched soul is unashamed even when hotly defending its actions.

28. It is the Holy Spirit's task alone to cleanse the intellect. For unless the strong man enters and despoils the robber, in no way will the stolen goods be released [cf. Mark 3:27]. It is necessary, therefore, by all means and especially by the peace of the soul to cause the Holy Spirit to rest there, that we may have the light of knowledge shining in us always. With its ceaseless shining in the treasuries of the soul not only are all those vindictive and shadowy assaults of the demons revealed to the intellect, but their being exposed by that holy and glorious light utterly weakens them. *Do not quench the Spirit* [1 Thess. 5:19]: that is, do not grieve the goodness of the Holy Spirit by

doing or speaking evil, lest you douse that champion's torch. For the eternal and life-giving [Spirit] is not quenched, but its being grieved [cf. Eph. 4:30] – that is, its departure – leaves the mind gloomy, bereft of the light of knowledge.

29. As I said, the Holy Spirit of God, in his love for humankind, teaches us that the soul's natural sense is unitary, for the five senses differ only in respect of the body's needs. But because of the slipperiness which has come to characterize the intellect thanks to Adam's disobedience this sense is divided according to the movements of the soul itself. Thus, on the one hand, it follows the passionate part of the soul, and so we perceive earthly goods with pleasure; while, on the other, it frequently delights in its rational and intellectual [νοερά] movement, and so (when we are sober-minded) our intellect longs to run towards heavenly beauties. If, therefore, we come to a state of despising the beauties of this world, we will be able to join the earthy yearning of our soul to its rational disposition, as the communion of the Holy Spirit apportions this to us. For unless the Spirit's divinity efficaciously illuminates the treasuries of our heart, we will not be able to taste true goodness with an undivided sense, that is, with a whole and healthy disposition.

30. The sense of the intellect is an accurate taste of things discerned. It is much the same way with our bodily sense of taste, in that, when we are healthy and can unerringly discern nutritious things from nasty ones, we desire good foods. So too our intellect, when it begins to move vigorously without anxiety, is able richly to sense divine comfort and never to be dragged away by its opposite. For as the body has an infallible experience of sensation in tasting earthly delicacies, so also the mind, when it glories over the fleshly tendency, is able to taste unerringly the comfort of the Holy Spirit – for *Taste*, it says, *and see that the Lord is good* [Ps. 33:9]! – and to hold enduringly the memory of that taste through the activity of love in *approving what things are excellent*. As the holy [Paul] says, *And this I pray, that your love abound yet more and more in knowledge and every perception, that you approve what is excellent* [Phil. 1:9–10].

31. When our intellect begins to sense the comfort of the

Holy Spirit, then Satan comforts the soul with a seemingly sweet sensation in the stillness of the night, when it succumbs to a moment of light sleep. If, instead, the intellect be discovered holding fast to the holy name of Jesus with fiery recollection, wielding that holy and glorious name like a weapon against Satan's fraud, then the error of cunning departs, and Satan engages in open warfare against the soul. Therefore, the intellect that recognizes precisely the deception of the evil one progresses all the more towards the experience of discernment.

32. Good comfort manifests itself whether the body is awake or even about to fall asleep, when someone is in some sense united to the love of God by fervent recollection of him. But deceptive comfort always comes when the combatant with a middling recollection of God is falling into a light sleep, as I have said. For good comfort, coming manifestly from God, aims to exhort the souls of combatants in piety towards love in a great outpouring of their souls. The other sort, since it generally shakes the soul with a gale of deceit, attempts through bodily sleep to steal the experience of the healthy intellect's sense of the memory of God. If at that moment, as I have said, the intellect is found attentively remembering the Lord Jesus, it scatters that seemingly sweet breeze of the enemy. It is roused joyously to battle against the enemy, having the exultation of experience as a second weapon alongside grace.

33. If the soul is aflame with the love of God by an unequivocal and imageless movement, dragging the body, so to speak, to the depth of that inexpressible love – whether waking or, as I just described, falling asleep – by the holy grace at work in it, and if it thinks of nothing but that towards which it moves, then we should recognize this as the activity of the Holy Spirit. For, since the whole soul has been delighted by that unutterable sweetness, it cannot think of anything else while leaping with unflagging joy. But if the intellect in its activity conceives some dubious or wholly defiled thought, and if it has used the holy name for warding off evil and not yet for the love of God only, we must know that whatever comfort comes in such moments is from the deceiver, and only the semblance of joy, since the joy of the enemy who desires to murder souls

is wholly without order or quality. For when he sees the intellect exulting correctly in the experience of its own sense, then he comforts the soul with some seemingly good comforts, as I have said, so that, having been dissipated without knowing it by that damp spongy pleasure, its joy is mixed unawares with treachery. From this, then, we will know the *spirit of truth and the spirit of deception* [1 John 4:6]. It is impossible, of course, to taste either the divine goodness with one's sense or to experience sensibly the bitterness of the demons, unless one is fully assured that grace has settled in the depth of the intellect, while the wicked spirits only linger around the members of his heart. For this reason the demons never want humans to believe in them, lest the intellect, seeing this clearly, take up arms against them by the recollection of God.

34. The soul's natural love is one thing and the love which comes to it from the Holy Spirit is another. For natural love is moved by our willing, to the extent that we will it. It is, therefore, easily snatched away by the wicked spirits so long as we do not hold fast to our choice. The other, though, so inflames the soul to the love of God that all its parts are fixed unutterably on the goodness of divine yearning in a boundless simplicity of disposition. For then the intellect, in a sense pregnant by this spiritual activity, wells up as a fountain of love and joy.

35. Just as the sea, when oil is poured over it when it is rough, naturally yields to the fattiness of the oil and the squall is overcome, so also our soul, when it grows fat on the goodness of the Holy Spirit, gladly grows calm. It is joyously bested by his overshadowing, dispassionate and unspeakable goodness, according to the word of the Saint: *Let my soul submit to God* [cf. Ps. 61:6]. For this reason, then, however many provocations may be attempted against the soul by the demons, it endures them all without anger and full of every joy. No one can enter into or abide in such a state, unless he unceasingly sweetens his soul in the fear of God. Indeed the fear of the Lord Jesus brings a certain form of purification to spiritual athletes, for *the fear of the Lord remains pure to the ages of ages* [Ps. 18.10].

36. Let no one who hears 'sense of the intellect' hope that the glory of God would visibly appear to him. For, while we call it 'perceiving' when one purifies the soul in an unutterable taste of divine comfort, we do not mean that some invisible reality appears to it, since we now 'walk by faith, and not by sight', as the blessed Paul says [cf. 2 Cor. 5:7]. If, therefore, either light or fiery shape appear to some spiritual athlete, let him in no wise accept such a vision. For it is a clear deceit of the enemy. Many, victims out of ignorance, have wandered from the way of truth. But we know that, so long as we remain in this corruptible body, we dwell far from God [cf. 2 Cor. 5:6], that is, unable to see visibly either him or his heavenly wonders.

37. Dreams which display the love of God to the soul are, in a way, unerring indicators of a healthy soul. Therefore, they do not shift about from one shape to another, nor do they terrify the sense, nor do they cause laughter or sudden gloominess. But in all gentleness they approach the soul, filling it with spiritual gladness. Then also after the body's waking, the soul eagerly seeks the joy of the dream. But the fantasies of the demons work in every way contrary. That is, they do not remain in the same shape; nor do they show a form untroubled for long. For what they do not have by choice, but only lease out of their congenital deceit, cannot satisfy them for long. They say great things and promise numerous ones, often shaping themselves into the form of soldiers. Sometimes they even sing uproariously to the soul! Thus, the intellect that is pure, since it recognizes these, wakes the body during the dream; sometimes it rejoices that it was able to recognize the demons' deceit. Often, therefore, when the intellect exposes the demons in the dream it rouses them to terrible rage. Of course, it also happens that good dreams do not bring the soul joy, but produce in it a sweet sadness and painless weeping. This comes about in those progressing towards profound humility.

38. We have described, as we have heard it from those who have experience, the discernment of good and bad dreams. Let this suffice for us, as a primary virtue: never to trust imagining in any way. For dreams, for the most part, are nothing but side effects of deceptive trains of thought; or, again, as I have said,

the delusions of demons. Even were a vision to be sent down to us from the goodness of God, and we did not accept it, still our much-desired Lord would not be angry on that account. For he knows that we have come to this decision because of the trickeries of the demons. For, while the discriminatory criteria described above are accurate, it happens that the soul, having been polluted by some unperceived plundering – from which, I think, no one is exempt – loses the trail of accurate diagnosis and believes things good which are not.

39. Let our model for action be a slave, called at night by a long-absent master from outside the outbuildings of the household. The house-slave totally refused to open any of the doors – for he had been afraid lest, having been fooled by a similar voice, he become a betrayer of the property entrusted to him. When day dawns, not only would his master not be angry with him, but would heap praises on him, because in his desire not to lose any of the master's property, the slave deemed even his master's voice a deception.

40. It cannot be denied that when the intellect begins to be roused frequently by the divine light, it too becomes wholly transparent so as richly to see its own light. This is what happens, at least, when the soul is able to prevail over the passions. On the other hand, the divine-speaking Paul teaches us clearly that everything visible to the mind in a shape, be it light or fire, comes from the Enemy's evil arts, when he says that [our enemy] transforms himself into an angel of light [2 Cor. 11:14]. No one should undertake the ascetic life in this hope, lest Satan find his soul inwardly open to plunder; but, rather, strive only to love God with full feeling and assurance of the heart, which is to say, *with all our heart and all our soul and all our mind* [Luke 10:27]. For the mind roused by God's grace departs from the world, even if it be in the world.

41. In the case of all the introductory virtues, it is to be recognized that obedience is the chief good, for, to begin with, it rejects self-conceit, and gives birth in us to humility. In this way it becomes the gateway to the love of God for those who cleave to it gladly. Now Adam, when he rejected obedience, slipped down into the abyss of Tartarus. But the Lord, having

loved obedience according to the plan of the [divine] economy, was obedient to his Father, even to the cross and death [Phil. 2:6–8], though he is in no way inferior to his Father's majesty. The Lord did this so that, having voided the charge of human transgression through his own obedience, he might lead those who would live in obedience to the blessed and ever-enduring life. Those taking up the contest against the Devil's conceit must pursue obedience first of all, since it will unerringly reveal all the practices of the virtues to those of us who are making progress.

42. Self-control is a common factor in all the virtues. One, therefore, who exercises self-control must do so in all things. Just as the whole human being is disfigured if even the tiniest parts be removed, even if their figure lacks just a little, so it is with a man who disregards a single virtue: though he does not realize it, the whole comeliness of self-control disappears. He should, then, have laboured diligently not only for bodily virtues, but also for those that can purify *our inward self* [2 Cor. 4:16]. For what benefit will there be for a person who keeps his body virgin but his soul is drawn into adultery by the demon of disobedience? Or how will he be crowned who, having been thrifty with gluttonous hunger and every bodily desire, neither took care against self-conceit and his love of glory nor could endure a little affliction. Affliction, after all, is the scale that compensates in the light of the righteousness to come those who have practised works of righteousness in a spirit of humility [cf. Rom. 8:17].

43. Thus, those who are engaged in struggle must diligently despise all irrational desires, so as to make hatred for them into a habitual disposition. However, one should preserve self-control with regard to foods so as never actually to end up loathing some one of them, for that is accursed and utterly demonic. For we do not refrain from foods as being themselves evil – perish the thought! – but, rather, we abstain from many good foods that we may moderately discipline the *members of our* flesh [cf. Col. 3:5] that are prone to inflammation; and then too that our superfluity may be dispensed to help the poor, which is, after all, the token of sincere love.

44. Eating whatever is set out and drinking whatever has been mixed for us, while giving thanks to God, certainly does not war against the law of knowledge, for *all things are exceedingly good* [Gen. 1:31]. However, happily refraining from many pleasures is supremely discerning and more in keeping with knowledge. We would not happily despise present pleasures unless we tasted the sweetness of God with full feeling and assurance.

45. In the manner in which the body, being weighed down by abundance of foods, produces a cowardly and sluggish intellect, so that the contemplative part of the soul, worn out by overmuch self-control, ends up gloomy and averse to reason. It is necessary, therefore, to adapt foods to the motions of the body, so that when healthy it may be appropriately disciplined, and moderately fattened when sick. For the combatant must not exhaust his body, but nourish it enough to be ready for the struggle, that the soul be fittingly purified by bodily labours.

46. When vainglory is greatly inflamed against us, taking the visit of some brothers or even random strangers as pretext for its wickedness, then it is good to offer a measured relaxation to our accustomed way of life. For thus we will send the demon off unsuccessful and bewailing his attempt on us. We will also acceptably fulfil the ordinance of love, and through our condescension preserve hidden the mystery of our self-control.

47. Fasting has reason for boasting, *but not before God* [cf. 1 Cor. 1:29]. For it is a tool for the training of those seeking after temperance. Those, therefore, engaged in the struggle of piety must not think too much of fasting, but use it only with faith in God to reach the end we are aiming for. For no one skilled in any craft would ever boast of the finished product of their profession merely on account of their tools! But, rather, each of these awaits the final form of his production, that the precision of his art be proven from that.

48. The earth, being watered in due measure, sprouts the pure seed which was sown in it with great increase. Yet if it is made drunk by many storms, it bears only *thorns and thistles* [Gen. 3:18 LXX]. In like manner the earth of our heart, provided we work it with wine in proper measure, will sprout its natural seeds and what was sown in it by the Holy Spirit will blossom and bear fruit. But if it be soaked by excessive drinking, it will produce thoughts which are indeed *thorns and thistles*.

49. When our intellect swims on the waves of excessive drink, not only does it behold in dreams the impassioned phantom images shaped by demons, but also, fashioning comely faces in itself, it feverishly uses its own imaginings as sexual partners. For, when the organs of sexual desire are brought to boiling by the heat of wine, the intellect inevitably displays for itself a delectable shadow of the passion. We, therefore, must flee from the damage of excess by using moderation. For when the intellect does not have pleasure dragging it down to the portrait painted by sin, it remains without fantasy and, what is better, without becoming effeminate.

50. Those mixed drinks which bartenders call aperitifs (because, it seems, they prepare the stomach for a large meal) are hardly to be sought out by those who wish to discipline their sexual organs. For not only is their quality harmful for athletic bodies, but also their very irrational mixture quite overpowers the God-bearing conscience. What, indeed, is it that wine lacks, that its usually invigorating effect should be mollified by the admixture of various condiments?

51. Our Lord and teacher of this sacred way of life, Jesus Christ, was given vinegar to drink during his passion, by those serving the diabolical commands, so that he might, it seems to me, leave behind for us a vivid lesson as to how to dispose ourselves in sacred struggles. It is as though he were saying that those competing against sin ought not take pleasing food and drink, but, rather, they must accept with patience the bitterness of battle. Let the hyssop be added to that insulting sponge, that the form of our purification might reach perfection by the example [John 19:29; cf. Ps. 50:7]. For just as bitterness belongs to struggles, so too certainly does purification to perfection.

52. Going to the bath does not demonstrate that someone is irrational or a sinner, but refraining from it because of self-control I would call manly and exceedingly wise. For the pleasure we take in bathing is not to mollify our body, nor are

we to come to recall Adam's inglorious nakedness, so as to find a secondary pretext for our shame by covering ourselves with leaves; all the more in our case who have only a little while ago departed from the utter destruction of this life and ought to be being united to the beauty of chastity by the purity of our body.

53. Nothing stops one calling on physicians in time of sickness. Since remedies naturally exist in nature, it has been possible for the art of healing to be developed from human experience. Nevertheless one should not put one's hope for healing in these, but in our true Saviour and physician, Jesus Christ. I say these things to those who seek to practise their self-control in monastic communities or cities, because, owing to their attendant circumstances, they cannot maintain unceasingly their activity of faith through love, but, above all, lest they fall into vainglory and temptation by the Devil, which has led some to claim publicly that they have not needed physicians for years. But if someone takes up the anachoretic life in desert places, with two or three like-minded brothers, let him apply himself in faith to the Lord alone, who heals our every disease and infirmity [Matt. 4:23], whatever sufferings might have befallen him. For, besides the Lord, he has in the desert sufficient consolation for his ailments. For this reason such a person never lacks the activity of faith, not least because he can find no chance to display the fine quality of his patience, since the desert provides a splendid protection. That is why the Lord *makes the solitaries to dwell in a house* [Ps. 67:7].

54. When we are annoyed by the ups and downs of our bodily condition, we need to realize that our soul is still enslaved to the body's desires – for which reason, yearning after material comforts, our soul does not want to depart from the goods of this life; rather, it regards as terrible boredom its inability to enjoy the fine things of life because of disease. But if a soul gratefully accepts the troubles of illnesses, it shows that it is not far from the *frontiers of dispassion*,[2] and even comes to embrace with joy death as the occasion, rather, of true life.

55. The soul will not wish to be separated from the body until it becomes indifferent towards the air which we breathe.

For all the body's senses are opposed to faith since, while they emerge from things present, faith proclaims only the supreme worth of the good things to come. The contestant ought never to ruminate on fine foliage and thickly shaded trees, lovely flowing springs, the play of light on meadows, pleasant homes, kinsmen or companions – nor even to recall solemn public honours, should he have received them – but, rather, to make do with necessities gratefully, and to consider this life as a strange road, devoid of every fleshly attachment. Only by constraining our mind thus will we return it to the track of the eternal road.

56. Eve, the first woman, shows us that seeing and tasting and the other senses dissipate our heart's memory when we make use of them beyond measure. For so long as she did not gaze with pleasure on the forbidden tree, she carefully remembered the divine commandment. Thus, she took shelter under the wings of divine love [cf. Ps. 90:4], where she was ignorant of her own nudity. But after she saw the tree with pleasure and touched it with much desire, and then tasted of its fruit with a certain intense pleasure – first, she was immediately coaxed to bodily intercourse, as a naked woman now united with passion; secondly, she bestowed her whole desire on the enjoyment of things present, having entangled Adam in her fall for the sake of the fruit's sweet sheen. For the human intellect can only remember God or his commandments with difficulty. We, therefore, always look to the depth of our heart with the ceaseless memory of God and spend our days in this sweetly deceiving life as if blind to its sights. For it is a genuine characteristic of spiritual philosophy always to clip the wings of one's love for sights. And this also the sorely tried Job teaches us, saying, *If also my heart has pursued my eye* [Job 31:7]. Thus, our firm purpose remains the surest sign of most exacting self-control.

57. Whoever dwells always in his own heart lives far from the pleasures of life, for, walking by the Spirit, he cannot see the desires of the flesh [cf. Gal. 5:24–5]. Such a one walks within the citadel of the virtues and possesses these virtues as gatekeepers to the central keep of purity. Therefore, indeed, the machinations of the demons are, in the end, impotent against

him, even should the darts of vulgar *eros* fly somehow to the very windows of nature.

58. When our soul begins to desire no more the pleasures of this life, then most commonly a sense of despondency slyly invades it, which neither allows it to serve with delight the *ministry of the word* [Acts 6:4], nor allows any clear desire of the good things to come. Rather, it thoroughly devalues this passing life as capable of no deed worthy of virtue while setting knowledge itself at naught, suggesting either that it has already been given to many others or that it signifies to us no promise of perfection. But we will escape this lukewarm, sluggardly passion [cf. Rev. 3:16] only if we establish very narrow limits for our mind and direct our attention towards the memory of God alone. Only thus can the intellect, having returned to its own fervour, escape irrational dissipation.

59. When we have blocked off these concerns by calling God to mind, the intellect is bound to demand work that can satisfy its natural industriousness. It is necessary, therefore, to give it the prayer 'Lord Jesus!' alone as fulfilling its purpose. For *no one says Lord Jesus, except by the Holy Spirit* [1 Cor. 12:3]. But let the intellect always contemplate that saying in its own depths, concentrating on it so much that it cannot turn to any fantasies. For as many as unceasingly contemplate this holy and glorious name in the depth of their heart will eventually be able to see the light of their own intellect. For this name, held fast by the close care of the mind, is felt to be burning up all the overflowing filth in the soul. For *Our God*, it says, *is a consuming fire* [Heb. 12:29], and thus the Lord calls the soul unto a great love of his own glory. For over time that glorious and much longed-for name creates in us, through the intellect's memory by means of the heart's fervour, a habitual disposition to love its goodness in every way, with nothing to oppose it any longer. For this is the pearl of great price, which someone, having sold all his property, could procure and so have inexpressible joy at its discovery [Matt. 13:46].

60. Introductory joy is one thing and another is the joy which makes perfect. For the former is not without imagination, but the latter has the power of humility. Between these

lie God-beloved grief and painless weeping. For truly *in a mul-titude of wisdom is a multitude of knowledge* and *the one who adds to himself knowledge adds also pain* [Eccles. 1:18]. Thus, our soul must be summoned to the contests by means of intro-ductory joy, and thereafter be tried and proven by the truth of the Holy Spirit, concerning what evils it has done and what delays it yet makes. For it says, *You have disciplined a person with reproofs for lawlessness, and melted his soul like a spider's web* [Ps. 38:12], so that, divine reproof having tested the soul's activity as in a smelting-furnace, it might receive joy without imaginings in the fervent memory of God.

61. When the soul is stirred by wrath or muddied by intox-ication, or is troubled by harsh despair, the intellect cannot (however much one constrain it) come to possession of the memory of the Lord Jesus. For the intellect, entirely blinded by the terrible intensity of the passions, is utterly alienated from its proper perception. And so, since the mind's memory has been hardened by the crudity of the passions, desire has nowhere to imprint its own seal so that the intellect might bear the form of meditation without it fading. But, if the in-tellect is free from these passions, even if its object of desire is briefly lost through forgetfulness, straightway by means of its natural industriousness the intellect fervently seizes its prey, much longed for and bringing salvation. For then the soul has this grace which exercises with it and strengthens its cry of the 'Lord Jesus!', just as a mother might teach and then prac-tise with her little darling the name 'father', until she can get him into the habit of calling clearly for his father (even when sleeping!) instead of any other baby-talk names. Therefore, the Apostle says, *So also the Spirit helps our weakness, for we do not know what we will pray for, as we should, but the Spirit himself intercedes for us with groans unutterable* [Rom. 8:26]. For since we are childish with regard to the perfection of the virtue of expressing prayer, we require the Spirit's aid in every way, so that, with all our thoughts gathered together and delighted by its unutterable sweetness, our whole dis-position may be moved to remember and love our God and Father. Therefore, when taught by it to call on God our father

unceasingly, it is in it, as the divine Paul himself says, that we cry out: *Abba, Father!* [Rom. 8:15].

62. Anger, more than any of the other passions, is accustomed to stir up and to confuse the soul, but sometimes it offers the greatest benefits. For when we use anger (without ourselves being stirred up) against the impious, that they be saved, or against the licentious, that they be ashamed, we procure gentleness for our soul. For we always race together to the finishing line of God's righteousness and goodness, but often need to harden the soul's softness with a vehement anger at sin. It is beyond question that when we are in great despondency, we disdain proud death by raging at the demon of corruption. To teach us exactly this, the Lord twice was *deeply moved in spirit* against Hades and troubled in himself [John 11:33, 38], while doing all that he wanted in an untroubled way by a simple wish, so that he restored Lazarus's soul to the body. I take from this that the God who created us furnished our nature with prudent anger rather as a weapon, so that, if Eve had used it in this way against the serpent, she would not have succumbed to that impassioned pleasure. Really, it appears to me that the intellect that wisely makes use of anger through zeal for piety will always be esteemed more highly on the scales of virtue than the intellect never moved to anger at all, owing to its inertia. For the latter appears to have a charioteer untrained in human experience, but while the former is ready for the contest and drives the horses of virtue through the midst of the demonic mob, steering its four-horsed chariot of self-control in the fear of God. The Scriptures call this the 'chariot of Israel', as we find in the divine Elias's [Elijah] being taken up into heaven; since it was first to the Jews, it seems, that God spoke clearly about the four virtues. For this reason such a nursling of Wisdom [as Elias] was taken up on a chariot of fire – for, it seems to me, that in his chastity he used his own virtues as horses – when the Spirit caught him up in a breath of fire [4 Kgds 2:11].

63. One who partakes of holy knowledge and has tasted the sweetness of God ought neither to prosecute nor even to initiate prosecution against someone, even if someone has taken the very shirt from off his back. For the righteousness of the rulers

of this world is always inferior to the righteousness of God, or, rather, it is nothing in comparison with God's justice. What sort of difference, then, would there be between the adopted children of God and the people of this age, save that the rights of the latter appear so deficient in comparison to the righteousness of the former, that we speak of human rights, but of divine righteousness? So too our Lord Jesus *did not reproach when he was reproached, and did not threaten when he suffered* [1 Pet. 2:23]. Rather, he endured in silence even the theft of his clothing [Matt. 27:28], and – what I would say is even greater – he petitioned his Father for the salvation of those who maltreated him [Luke 23:34]. But the people of the world never cease from litigating against one another, unless sometimes they recover with interest the goods that are in dispute, especially when they collect interest before calling in the debt, in which cases their purported justice becomes the source of great injustice.

64. I once heard some pious people saying that we ought not yield to those who come to plunder the resources which we have for our own dwelling or for the poor, especially if we suffer this at the hands of Christians, lest, through the outrages we patiently suffer, we become enablers of sin for our malefactors. But this kind of thinking is nothing other than using an irrational pretext for wanting to keep my goods to myself. For if I abandon both praying and attending to my own heart in order to plead my cause against those who try to abuse me, and begin frequenting the lobbies of the courts, it is clear, then, that court judgments matter more to me than my own salvation, to say nothing of the command of the Saviour himself. For how, doing such things, could I ever follow the Gospel command which is given to me – that is, *Do not demand your goods back from the one who takes them* [Matt. 5:40] – if I do not endure with joy (according to the apostolic saying) the theft of things belonging to me, especially since usually, despite my prosecuting and seizing whatever I wanted, the greedy man is not freed from his sin? So the corruptible courts are unable to determine the incorruptible judgement of God, for the culprit only needs to defend himself in respect of those laws invoked against him. Thus, it is good to bear the violence of those who wish to wrong

us and to pray for them, that through repentance – not just through returning what they took from us! – they may be freed from the charge of greed. For the Lord's justice wants this: that we receive, not the things taken greedily, but the greedy one himself, once set free from sin through repentance.

65. If we truly recognize the way of piety, it is exceedingly appropriate and above all useful straight away to sell our goods and distribute the proceeds in accordance with the Lord's command [Matt. 19:21], and not, on pretext of desiring to keep all the commandments, to disregard the Saviour's summons. From this action we will have, first, a wonderful freedom from anxiety, and second, an unassailable interior poverty, which disdains every outrage and prosecution alike because we no longer have the material which kindles the fires of greed. Humility warms us round more than all the other virtues and since we are naked it will give us rest in its own bosom [cf. Luke 16:22], just as a mother, enfolding her child in her arms, warms him, when because of his childish simplicity he takes off his clothes and throws them away (because, I should note, of his great guilelessness rather than simply wanting to change outfits). For *the Lord guards children*, it says, and *I was humbled and he saved me* [Ps. 114:6].

66. The Lord will only ever demand an accounting of our acts of charity in accordance with what we have, not what we have not. If, then, out of fear of God I give away at his command in a short time what I might have given away over many years, of what could I, with nothing, be accused? But someone will ask, 'From where will the poor, accustomed to receive little by little from our measures, receive mercy later on?' Let such a man learn not to reproach God on the pretext of his own love of property! For the God who has from the beginning ordered well his own creation will not fail to do so now! For beggars hardly lacked food and raiment until someone or another turned up to show pity. It is good, therefore, for us who hate our own desires – that is, *hate our own soul* [Luke 14:26] – to throw away the irrational boastfulness that comes with wealth, so that, no longer delighting in distributing goods ourselves, we may thoroughly set our own soul at naught, as

doing nothing good. For while we have abundance of any kind, we rejoice greatly – if indeed it is for us a good activity – when distributing our goods, as joyfully serving the divine command. But then, after we have thoroughly drained ourselves dry, there steals into us a boundless sadness and humility, as to those who practise nothing worthy of righteousness. Whence, finally, our soul returns to itself in great humility, so that it acquires for itself through laborious prayer, endurance and humility the very thing which it no longer has to acquire daily through almsgiving. For, it says, *The beggar and the poor man praise your name, O Lord* [Ps. 73:21]. For no one is ready for the gift of theology prepared by the Lord, save the one who makes himself ready by ridding himself of all his possessions for the sake of the glory of the Gospel of God, so that in God-beloved poverty he may preach the wealth of the Kingdom of God. For the one who said, *You have prepared in your kindness for the poor, O God*, and also added, *The Lord will give a word to those who preach the Gospel with great power* [Ps. 67:11–12], expresses this clearly.

67. While all the gifts of our God are *exceedingly good* [Gen. 1:31] and productive of every goodness, nothing so ignites and moves our heart to love of his goodness as theology. For as theology is the early child of God's grace, it always bestows the first gifts upon the soul. How so? First, it prepares us to rejoice in despising every love of this life, since we have in place of corruptible desires an indescribable wealth – *the utterances of God* [Ps. 106:11]. Next, it illuminates our intellect with the fire of transformation, and makes it a fellow of the *ministering spirits* [Heb. 1:14]. Beloved, we who have been prepared beforehand for this process properly desire this virtue: well-fitting, all-seeing, procuring freedom from all anxiety, nourishing the intellect with *the utterances of God* in the radiance of unspeakable light. In short, with the holy prophets' aid it unites the rational soul with God the Word in indissoluble communion, so that among humans – o great marvel! – theology, that divine conductor of the bridal chorus, may bring deified voices into harmony, as they sing clearly of the mighty acts of God.

68. Often our intellect can hardly bear to pray, owing to the

extreme narrowness and constraint imposed by petition, but it rejoices as it gives itself to theology, because of the broad vistas of divine contemplations. Lest we give way to our intellect's desiring to say many things or grant that it take wing beyond due measure in its joy, let us devote our time mostly to prayer, psalmody and interpretation of the Holy Scriptures, not overlooking the readings of skilled men, whose faith is known through their words. So far from contriving our own statements to mingle with the words of grace or permitting our intellect to be scattered in its joy and prolixity and so be dragged down by vainglory, by such activity we will even keep our intellect free from every imagining during the time of contemplation and from this we will even make nearly all its conceptions tearful ones. For, being refreshed in times of stillness and gratified by the exceeding sweetness of prayer, not only will our intellect escape the aforementioned causes of trouble, but more and more be renewed to devote itself keenly and without toil to divine contemplations, while progressing in much humility towards the contemplation of discernment. But it is necessary to know that there is prayer that transcends any level – but it belongs only to those who are filled with holy grace in all feeling and assurance.

69. At the beginning of ascetic struggle, grace is accustomed to illuminate the soul with a felt sense of its own light. As struggle proceeds, grace works its own mysteries for the most part in an unfelt way in the soul that reaches out towards theology, so that we then rejoice at setting out on the track of divine contemplations, being called as from ignorance to knowledge, while our knowledge is guarded, in the midst of our struggles, from vainglory. It is necessary to be plunged in grief, within measure, as if quite abandoned, so that we may be humbled all the more and submit to the glory of the Lord, taking wing to rejoice in timely fashion in our good hope. For just as a great grief gnarls the soul in hopelessness and faithlessness, so also a great joy invites it to self-conceit – I mean, for those who are still childish. For experience is the middle ground between illumination and abandonment, hope the middle ground between grief and joy. For, it says, *Patiently, I waited for the Lord and*

he attended to me [Ps. 39:2], and again, *According to the multitude of pains in my heart your consolations have caused my
soul to rejoice* [Ps. 93:19].

70. When the doors of the baths are continually left open,
they quickly let the heat inside escape. So too the soul, when
it desires to engage in much conversation (even if it says good
things), scatters its own memory through the gate of speech.
Thus, it is ultimately robbed of timely thoughts, and instead
speaks with those it meets in a crowded jostle of thoughts,
since it no longer has the Holy Spirit to keep its mind free from
imagining. For goodness, being a stranger to every disturbance and imagining, always flees excessive speech. Therefore,
a timely silence is good, being none other than the mother of
wisest thoughts.

71. The *word of knowledge* [1 Cor. 12:8] teaches us that
at the beginning many passions annoy the soul engaged in
theology – but anger and hatred more than all others. But our
soul suffers this not so much because demons cause them as
because of its own progress. For so long as a soul is misled by
what the world calls good sense, even if it sometimes sees justice being trampled underfoot by people, it remains unmoved
and untroubled. For it takes thought for its own desires and
so gives no heed to the justice of God. But when, thanks to its
disdain for present things and its love of God, the soul begins
to rise above its own passions it cannot bear to see justice cast
aside, even in a dream. Rather, it is angered at the wrongdoers
and troubled until it sees the insulters of righteousness making
proper amends through reverent thoughts. On this account,
therefore, while this soul hates the unjust, it loves and even
cherishes the righteous. For the eyes of the soul will never be
distracted, when it has woven its veil – I mean the body – to
great fineness through self-control. Of course, it is still much
better to bewail their insensitivity than actually to hate the
unrighteous. For even if those people are deserving of hatred,
still reason does not want the God-loving soul to be troubled
by hatred, since knowledge is paralysed when hatred is present
in the soul.

72. The theologian, whose soul is delighted and enflamed

by the very sayings of God, in due time breaks through to the broad spaces of dispassion. For, it says, *The sayings of the Lord are pure sayings, silver tested in fire, pure of anything earthly* [Ps. 11:7]. Likewise, the man of knowledge, strengthened by his active experience, rises above the passions. The theologian, provided he makes himself humbler, tastes the experience of knowledge; while the man of knowledge, provided the soul's faculty of discernment is unfailing, tastes contemplative virtue a little. For the two gifts do not accrue completely to one person, so that, each marvelling at that in which the other surpasses, humility along with zeal for righteousness may abound in both. Because of this the Apostle says, *To one the word of wisdom will be given through the Holy Spirit, and to another the word of knowledge, according to the same Spirit* [1 Cor. 12:8].

73. When the soul is in an abundance of its natural fruits, it sings psalms with a louder voice and desires to pray out loud too. But, when it is roused by the Holy Spirit, it sings with total abandon and delight, and prays in the heart alone. An imagined joy follows the first disposition, but spiritual tears follow the second, and after these comes a gladness that loves silence. For thanks to the good measure of the voice the memory remains fervent, and prepares the heart to bear certain tearful, but mild, conceptions. So there can truly be seen the seeds of prayer sown with tears in the earth of the heart in hope of the joy of the harvest. But – when we are weighed down by much discouragement, we must chant our psalmody with a voice a little stronger, using the joy of hope to motivate the voices of the soul until that weighty cloud is dispersed by the breezes of the melody.

74. When the soul comes to recognize itself, it draws from itself a kind of God-loving fervour. For, not being confounded by the cares of this life, it gives birth to an *eros* for peace, seeking in a measured way the *God of peace* [Rom. 15:33; Heb. 13:20, etc.]. However, the soul is quickly robbed of this peace, either because its memory is betrayed by the senses or because through poverty its nature soon wastes its own beauty. That is why the wise among the Greeks did not attain what they thought they had through self-control, because their intellect was not roused by ever-flowing, all-true wisdom. On the other

hand, the fervour borne by the Holy Spirit to the heart is, first of all, totally peaceful and unflinching, summoning all the parts of the soul to yearning for God. Nor is this fervour kindled outside the heart, but, rather, through the heart it causes the whole person to rejoice in boundless love and joy. It is necessary that those who recognize the soul's fervour attain also that of the Holy Spirit. For, though natural love is a sign of a nature kept healthy through self-control, it can never bring the intellect to dispassion as spiritual love can.

75. The air that surrounds us remains pure when the north wind blows over creation, because of the wind's light and clarifying nature. But, when the south wind blows, the whole air is thickened by the darkening nature of this wind, which, through a certain affinity, draws clouds from its own regions and covers the whole world with them. It is the same with the soul: when it is roused by the inspiration of the true and Holy Spirit it finds itself well clear of any demonic mist. But, when it is roughly blown upon by the *spirit of error* [1 John 4:6], it is covered entirely by the clouds of sin. It is necessary, therefore, for us with all our strength to turn our intention back to the lifegiving and purifying breeze of the Holy Spirit – that is, towards the wind which Ezekiel, in the light of knowledge, saw coming from the north [Ezek. 1:4] – that the contemplative part of our soul especially might remain clear, so that we are drawn unerringly to divine contemplations, *seeing* the things of *light in* the air of *light* [Ps. 35:10]. For this is the light of true knowledge.

76. Some imagine grace and sin – that is, the *spirit of truth* and *the spirit of error* [1 John 4:6] – to be hidden together in the intellect, even of those who have been baptized. And so they say that one of these spirits exhorts the intellect to good things, but the other immediately exhorts it to the opposite. I, however, have learned from the divine Scriptures and from the intellect's perception itself that prior to holy baptism grace exhorts the soul to good things from the outside, while Satan lurks in its depths scrambling to block up all the intellect's avenues to goodness. But, from the very hour in which we are born again, the demon is outside us and grace within. Whence we find that, as before error was lording it over our soul, so after

baptism truth reigns. Of course, even after baptism Satan still works many nasty things in the soul, just as before; not coexisting in it with grace – God forbid! – but stifling the mind, as it were, with the sweet smoke of irrational pleasures, through the body's humours. But this comes about by God's withdrawal, so that, having passed through the storm and fire of testing, one may come, if he wishes, into the enjoyment of goodness. For *We have passed*, it says, *through fire and water and you have led us to refreshment* [Ps. 65:12].

77. Grace, as I have said, from the very moment of our baptism is hidden deep in the depth of our intellect, concealing its own coming even from the intellect's perception itself. But when someone begins with full resolve to love God then, by an ineffable word, grace communicates to the soul, through the intellect's perception, some portion of its own good things. Thereafter, one who wants to possess what has been discovered with full assurance comes, by joyfully desiring to renounce all present goods, truly to procure the field in which he will find buried the treasure of life [Matt. 13:44]. For when anyone renounces everything that passes for wealth in this life, then he finds the place in which God's grace has been concealed. For the divine gift manifests its own goodness to the intellect in accord with the soul's progress. But then the Lord may allow the soul to be troubled by the demons, in order to teach the soul discernment of good and evil and render it more humble through the deep shame it will feel when it is purified because of the obscenity of the demonic thoughts that came to it.

78. We are *in the image of God* [Gen. 1:27] in the intellectual movement of our soul, for the body is, as it were, its dwelling-place. Since, then, through Adam's transgression not only were the features of the image imprinted on the soul made filthy, but our body succumbed more and more to corruption. For this reason the holy Word of God was made flesh, granting us the water of salvation for rebirth through his own baptism as God. We are reborn through the water by the activity of the Holy and Life-giving Spirit. Whence we are immediately thereafter purified in both soul and body, if we approach God with a whole and single disposition, by the Holy Spirit who

overshadows us and by him sin is banished. For, since the image
imprinted on the soul is one and simple, it is impossible for two
opposing tendencies to coexist in it, as some would imagine.
For since divine grace adapts itself through holy baptism and
a certain boundless affection to the traits of one who is *in the
image* as a pledge of *the likeness* [Gen. 1:26], where could the
countenance of the Evil One find space, especially since there
is no *fellowship of light with darkness* [2 Cor. 6:14]? We, who
are runners in the sacred games, trust that the many-shaped
serpent is banished from the treasuries of the intellect through
the 'bath of incorruption', and so let us not be surprised at
those instances when, even after baptism, we think nasty things
along with good ones. For the bath of holiness strips off from
us the filth of sin, but it does not alter the double nature of our
will let alone stop the demons from warring on us or prevent
them whispering deceptive words to us. This is so that, what
we did not guard when we were merely *natural* [cf. 1 Cor. 2:14,
15:44], we will keep safe, as we take up the weapons of righteousness in the power of God.

79. As I said, while Satan is cast out of the soul through holy
baptism, he is permitted, because of the reasons already given,
to be active in it through the body. For the grace of God set-
tles in the very depth of the soul – that is, in the intellect. For it
says, '*All the glory of the daughter of the king is within her*, not
revealing itself to the demons' [Ps. 44:14]. That is why we sense
God from the very depth of our heart, like desire springing up,
when we remember God fervently. But the wicked spirits then
ambush our bodily senses and lurk therein, operating through
the pliability of the flesh on those who are still children in their
soul. Thus, therefore, while our intellect, in accordance with
the Apostle's words [Rom. 7:22], ever delights in the laws of
the Spirit, the senses of the flesh wish to consort with silky
pleasures. Whence, on the one hand, grace gladdens the body
through our intellectual sense to an ineffable rejoicing for those
who are making progress in wisdom. However, the demons,
through our bodily senses – especially when they find us neg-
ligently pursuing the path of piety – capture the soul by force;
they are murderers provoking it to act against its will.

80. Some justify their claim that two spirits of grace and sin coexist simultaneously in the hearts of the faithful from something the Evangelist [John] said: *And the light shines in the darkness and the darkness has not comprehended it* [John 1:5]. They seek to support their opinion by saying that the divine radiance is in no way defiled by its association with evil, however close the divine light in the soul is to the demonic darkness. Yet they are convicted by the same Gospel passage of thought alien to the Holy Scriptures! For the Word of God, the *true light* [John 1:4], deigned to reveal himself to his own creation in the flesh [John 1:14], having, with boundless love for humankind, kindled the light of his holy knowledge among us. However, the mind of the world [cf. 1 Cor. 2:12] *did not comprehend* the counsel of God – that is, it *did not know* it [1 Cor. 1:10] since *the mind of the flesh is hostile to God* [Rom. 8:7] – this is why the theologian [John] used such a saying. At any rate, having said a few words between, the divine one continues: *This was the true light, which enlightens everyone who comes into the world* – meaning by this that he 'guides' and 'makes alive' – *He was in the world and the world came to be through him, and the world did not know him. He came unto his own and his own did not receive him. But as many as received him, to those who believed in his name, he gave authority to become children of God* [Rom. 1:9–12]. Now, by way of interpreting the *did not comprehend*, the supremely wise Paul says, *Not that I have already received or already been perfected, but I pursue it that I may comprehend it, because I have been comprehended by Christ Jesus* [Phil. 3:12]. Note, the Evangelist does not say that Satan has not comprehended the *true light*, for from the beginning he has been alien to it, since it does not shine in him. Rather, in this passage he is rightly reproaching those people who heard the mighty acts and marvels of the Son of God, but did not wish to draw near, because their heart was darkened to the light of his knowledge.

81. The *word of knowledge* teaches us that there are two races, as it were, of evil spirits. Some are finer and subtler; the others more earthy and almost material. The subtler ones war against the soul while the more earthy ones are accustomed

to capture the flesh through certain slippery-smooth consolations. They are, therefore, always directly opposed to one
another, the demons who wrestle with the soul and those who
wrestle with the body, even if they share the purpose of hurting
humans. So, when grace does not dwell in a person, truly these
demons lurk like serpents would in the depths of his heart, and
in no wise permit the soul to see clearly its desire for goodness.
However, when grace is hidden in the intellect, they wander
through the regions of the heart like shadowy clouds, taking
the shapes of sinful passions and various vain imaginings so
that disturbing the intellect's memory they sunder it from its
converse with grace. When, therefore, we are enflamed with
passions of the soul (and especially self-conceit, the mother of
all evils) by the demons who trouble the soul, we can put the
swelling pretension of the love of glory to shame by considering
the dissolution of our body. We must do the same when the
demons who wrestle with the body cause our heart to boil over
with shameful desires. For this consideration can itself abol-
ish all the manifold strategy of the wicked spirits, thanks to
the memory of God. Now, if on the basis of our meditation
on mortality, the demons of the soul induce in us a boundless
contempt for our human nature, as possessing no value at all
because of the flesh (for they love to do this when someone
wishes to torment them by such a thought), then let us recall
the honour and glory of the heavenly kingdom, not overlooking the bitterness and gloom of judgement, so that by the first
we may bolster our failing spirit, and by the second deflate the
contentment of our heart.

82. The Lord teaches us in the Gospels that when Satan
returns and finds his *house* – that is, a fruitless heart – *swept
and vacant, then he invites seven spirits* and they enter into
the heart and they lurk there, making *the latter days of that
person worse than the first* [Matt. 12:44–5]. From this we need
to understand that, insofar as the Holy Spirit dwells in us, although Satan may have entered into the depths of our soul,
he cannot remain. The divine Paul teaches us quite clearly the
meaning of this contemplation, for, having reflected on this
proposal from the knowledge gained by ascetic struggle, he

says, *For I rejoice in the law of God according to the outward person. But I see another law in my members warring against the law of my intellect and leading me captive by the law of sin which is in my members* [Rom. 7:22–3]. But as one who has achieved perfection, he says, *Now, therefore, there is no condemnation for those in Christ Jesus. For the law of the Spirit of life has freed me from the law of sin and death* [Rom. 8:1–2]. To teach us again that Satan uses the body to war on the soul which participates in the Holy Spirit, he says elsewhere, *Stand, therefore, having girded your loins with truth, and having put on the breastplate of righteousness, and having shod your feet with the preparation of the gospel of peace, above all taking up the shield of faith, with which you can quench the flaming arrows of the enemy. And take the helmet of salvation and the sword of the Spirit, which is the Word of God* [Eph. 6:14–17]. But 'captivity' is one thing and 'battle' another – for the former denotes 'violent seizure' but the latter indicates an 'equally balanced contest'. Therefore, the Apostle says that the Devil comes upon Christ-bearing souls with *flaming arrows*. One who is not able to overcome his opponent certainly uses arrows against him, so that he may, with his feathered shafts, hunt the one who would fight him from a safe distance. So it is with Satan. Thanks to the grace which dwells there, he is unable to lurk in the intellect of those who contend with him as he did formerly. So, he slips in through the humours and lurks in the body, that by its pliancy he may catch the soul. Therefore, we must allow our body to waste away moderately lest through its pliability the intellect slip into the sleekness of pleasures. We ought to be persuaded by the apostolic word, first, that the intellect of those who compete is roused by the divine light, and therefore serves and *rejoices in the law of God*; secondly, however, the flesh readily gives entrance to the wicked spirits because of its own pliancy, and is therefore eventually drawn by them to serve evil. From this it is clear that the intellect cannot be a shared dwelling place for God and the Devil. How, then, can *I serve the law of God with my intellect but with my flesh the law of sin* [Rom. 7:25], unless my intellect stands in perfect freedom to fight the demons, happily serving the goodness of grace, while my body readily admits the perfume of irrational pleasures? Only because, as I have said, the wicked spirits of error are allowed to lurk in the bodies of those engaged in competition. *For I know*, it says, *that goodness does not dwell in me – that is, in my flesh* [Rom. 7:18] – this refers to those resisting sin in a kind of midway struggle. For the Apostle does not say this *on his own account* [John 12:49]: while the demons openly war against the intellect, they endeavour to draw the flesh down into the softness of pleasures by oily consolations. For they are permitted once for all, according to God's just judgement, to dwell around the depths of the body and upon those earnestly struggling against sin, because the self-governance of human mentality is forever subject to testing. But if someone were to die through toils while yet living, he would then become solely a dwelling of the Holy Spirit. For before such a man has died, he rises again, just as the blessed Paul did, as well as all those who struggled perfectly or even now struggle against sin.

83. From itself the heart brings forth chains of thought both good and not good [cf. Luke 6:45]. It does not bear the fruit of bad notions by its nature, but only insofar as, following the original delusion, it retains the memory of evil as a habitual state. However, it receives most wicked thoughts from the demons' bitterness. Yet we perceive all such thoughts as coming from our heart, which leads some to suggest that sin is present in the intellect together with grace. Therefore, they quote what the Lord said, *What comes out of the mouth proceeds from the heart, and this defiles a person, for out of the heart come wicked thoughts, murders*, and the like [Matt. 15:18–19]. But they do not know that our intellect, having a faculty of extremely subtle perception, assimilates the thoughts suggested to it by the wicked spirits, as it were, on account of the activity of the flesh, the body's pliancy carrying the soul into this all the more through their commixture, though how, we do not know. Moreover, the flesh always has an immoderate love of being caressed by deceit, and for this reason too the thoughts sown by the demons in the soul seem to emerge from the heart. And we really make them our own, whenever we want to find pleasure in them. It is this that the Lord blamed, as the divine

saying itself makes clear, when he used the expression cited above. For when a man delights in the thoughts suggested to him by the wickedness of Satan and, as it were, inscribes the memory of them in his heart, it is no secret that thereafter he trots them out as the fruit of his own reflection.

84. The Lord says in the Gospels that it is impossible for a strong man to be thrown out of his own home, unless someone even stronger binds and strips him first [cf. Matt. 12:29]. How, then, can someone who has so ignominiously been cast out enter again and dwell there with the true master of the house, who resides at his leisure in his own house? Neither will a king who has cast down the tyrant who once opposed him consider allowing that foe to dwell with him in the royal apartments. Rather, he either cuts his throat immediately or, having bound his foe, gives him over to his own soldiers for prolonged torment and a most pitiable death.

85. If someone believes that because we can think both good and bad things the Holy Spirit and the Devil dwell together in the mind, let them learn that this happens because we have ceased to *taste and see that the Lord is good* [Ps. 33:9]. For, as I said above, at first grace hides its presence in those who are baptized while it awaits the soul's intention. When someone turns wholly towards the Lord, then by a certain ineffable feeling grace manifests its presence in the heart and now awaits the soul's movement, while nevertheless permitting demonic arrows to fly in even to the soul's deep feeling, that it might seek out God with a more fervent intention and humble disposition. Should anyone then begin to make progress in keeping the commandments and ceaselessly to call upon the Lord Jesus, then the fire of holy grace will spread to the outer senses of the heart and burn up the weeds of the human earth completely. Then the demonic designs will fall far short of those places, and scarcely prick the passible part of the soul. Now, when someone engaged in ascetic struggle has bound himself with all the virtues and especially perfect poverty, then grace irradiates his whole nature with an even deeper feeling, warming him all over with a great love of God. At that point, therefore, all demonic arrows are quenched before they even reach

the body's sense-perception. For the gentle breeze of the Holy
Spirit, which rouses the heart to peaceful gusts, quenches the
arrows of the fire-bearing demon while they fly through the
air. Nevertheless God sometimes abandons to the wickedness
of the demons even someone who attains this measure, leaving
his intellect unillumined, so that our self-governance may not
be completely bound by the chains of grace – not only because
we conquer sin through struggle, but also because it benefits
those still progressing towards spiritual experience. For what
is held to be perfect in those who are being educated – even if
they could climb the ladder shown to Jacob [Gen. 28:12] by
progress in toils – remains still imperfect in comparison with
the wealth of the God who educates us through his utterly
generous love.

86. The Lord himself says that Satan fell *from the heavens as
lightning* [Luke 10:18], that the ugly one might not gaze upon
the dwelling places of the angels. How, then, could one deemed
unworthy of fellowship even with God's good servants dwell in
a human intellect together with God himself? But they will say
that this takes place when God withdraws. But that is to say
nothing. For an educative withdrawal in no way robs the soul
of divine light. It is only that, as I have already said, grace often
hides its presence from the intellect. Why? That it may propel
the soul, as it were, by the demons' bitterness, that it may seek
God's assistance with much fear and great humility, thus little
by little learning to recognize the evil of its enemy. In much
the same way if an infant refuses to nurse properly, his mother
will push him from her lap for a moment, so that, terrified
by whatever scary men or beasts are standing about, he will,
thoroughly frightened, tearfully return to his mother's bosom.
Contrariwise, the withdrawal of rejection actually hands the
soul that rejects God over to the demons as their captive. However, *we are not* children *who shrink back* [Heb. 10:39] – God
forbid! – but believe ourselves to be genuine nurslings of God's
grace, being milk-fed by it with little abandonments and frequent consolations, that through its goodness we may come *to
maturity, to the fullness of growth* [Eph. 4:13].

87. Educative withdrawal brings the soul much sadness,

humility and even a measure of despair, so that its part that loves glory and is easily frightened may fittingly come to humility. Meanwhile, it immediately brings to the heart fear of God, tears of confession, and a great desire for supremely beautiful silence. But the withdrawal which comes about through God's rejection permits the soul to be filled with despair together with faithlessness, wrath and vanity. It is, therefore, necessary for us who have known the experience of both kinds of withdrawal to draw near to God in a manner appropriate to each. As regards the former, we owe our thanks to God, along with our excuses, as to one who chastens our mindset's lack of discipline by ceasing his consolation so that, as a good father, he may teach us the difference between virtue and vice. But as to the latter, we ought to make ceaseless confession of our sins, shed endless tears, and undertake a greater withdrawal from the world, so that with the addition of such toils we may importune God to cast his gaze upon our hearts as he did before. Nevertheless we must know that, when the battle between soul and Satan takes place for real – I refer to educative withdrawal – grace, as I have said above, hides itself but still works together with the soul with invisible assistance, to show the soul's enemies that the victory belongs to the soul only.

88. When someone stands in an open place on a wintry day at daybreak and gazes directly east, his front is well warmed by the sun, but his back is not, because the sun is not overhead. In just the same way those at the beginning of spiritual activity have their heart warmed only partially by holy grace. At this point, then, their intellect also begins to bear the fruit of spiritual thoughts, but the more superficial parts of the heart continue to *think according to the flesh* [Rom. 8:5], because not all the members of the heart have yet been illuminated in deep feeling by the light of holy grace. Those who do not consider this fact imagine that there are two persons, as though standing opposite one another, present in the intellect of those engaged in spiritual struggle. Thus, it happens that, in the same moment, the soul thinks things both good and not good, in the same way as the man in our example is both warm and cold at the same touch of the sun. For from the moment our intellect

slipped into duality in its knowing, it must, even if it wishes otherwise, produce in the very same moment beautiful and nasty notions alike. This is especially so for those approaching the subtlety of discernment: for as their intellect strives to think always of goodness, it immediately remembers evil, since human memory has been split into a certain dual thought ever since Adam's disobedience. If, therefore, we begin to really keep God's commandments with fervent zeal, then grace illuminates all our senses with a certain deep feeling and incinerates, as it were, our ruminations, as it delights our heart with the peace of unbending affection and prepares us to think spiritual things and no longer *according to the flesh*. But this happens almost continuously to those drawing near to perfection, who ceaselessly hold the memory of the Lord Jesus in their heart.

89. Through the baptism of rebirth holy grace accomplishes two good things for us, one of which boundlessly surpasses the other. The lesser good is given immediately: right there in the water baptism renews us and polishes the features of the soul – that is, what is *according to the image* – rubbing us clean from every smudge of sin. The other, which is the *according to the likeness* [Gen. 1:26], looks for our cooperation. When, therefore, our intellect starts to taste the goodness of the Holy Spirit with much feeling, then we need to know that grace is then beginning to paint, as it were, the *likeness* within the features of the *image*. It is just like painting: painters first sketch their model's portrait with just one colour, and then add colour by colour to their picture, a little at a time, so as to bring out the likeness of their model, even down to their hair. God's grace is the same: first through baptism it brings what is *in the image* into what it was before when humans came to be. But when grace beholds us desiring with all our will the beauty of *the likeness* and sees us standing naked and unafraid in its workshop, then God's grace adorns our soul virtue by virtue and lifts its form *from glory to glory* [2 Cor. 3:18], and so produces the impress of *the likeness* in it. So then, while we feel ourselves being formed *in the likeness*, we come to know the perfection of *the likeness* from illumination. For our intellect receives all the virtues through its feeling, making progress in accordance with a certain measure and rhythm that are very difficult to describe. But the only way of possessing spiritual love is through being enlightened in full assurance by the Holy Spirit. For unless the intellect fully receives what is *according to the likeness* through divine light, it can hardly have all the other virtues and remains without a share in perfect love. For when our intellect is assimilated to God's virtue – I mean, so far as the human can be assimilated to God – then also it bears *the likeness* of divine love. In portraits, when the brilliant shades of colour are applied to the image they preserve the likeness of the model even down to the smile. So also with those being restored by divine grace to the divine likeness, when the illumination of love is added, it shows what is *according to the image* now totally in accord with the majesty of *the likeness*. For no other virtue acquires dispassion for the soul, save love alone. For *love is the fullness of the law* [Rom. 13:10], and so *our inner self is being renewed day by day* [2 Cor. 4:16] in the taste of love, and is filled with love's perfection.

90. During the first stages of progress (if, indeed, we are fervently in love with the virtue of God), the Holy Spirit gives the soul a taste of the sweetness of God with full feeling and assurance, so that the intellect can with precise recognition know the perfect prize of toils that please God. For the most part, though, the Spirit hides the costliness of this life-giving gift, lest we imagine ourselves to be something special, since, although we are active in all other virtues, we still do not have holy love as a habitual state. Then the demon of hatred annoys the souls engaged in spiritual struggle all the more, so as to draw them into hateful strife with those who love them, and he brings the lethal activity of hatred even into the kiss. For this reason, then, the soul which bears the memory of spiritual love is even more pained because it cannot keep that love in its feeling, because it has still to undergo the most perfect toils. It is therefore necessary to force the memory for a while, so that we may advance unseen in full feeling and assurance to the taste of spiritual love. For no one can gain love's perfection while still in the flesh, save only the saints who come even to martyrdom and perfect confession, since whoever comes to it is wholly altered

and no longer yearns for ordinary sustenance. For what sort of desire could one nourished on divine love even have for the good things of this world? Therefore, the wisest Paul, the great vessel of knowledge, who from his own assurance proclaims to us the delight that is to come for the first among the saints, says, *The kingdom of heaven is not food and drink, but justice and peace and joy in the Holy Spirit*, which are the fruit of perfect love [Rom. 14:17]. So then, those who are making progress to perfection are able to taste divine love continuously here and now, but no one can obtain it perfectly, until *what is mortal is perfectly swallowed up by life* [2 Cor. 5:4].

91. One of those who love the Lord with an insatiable resolution told me this: 'While I yearned to know the love of God at the level of knowledge, the good one presented me instead in much feeling and assurance a sense of such inner activity as to urge my soul to go out of my body with a kind of inexpressible joy and love and depart *to the Lord* [2 Cor. 5:8], having no longer any sense, as it were, of this passing life. One who has become experienced in this love, even if he is insulted or punished in myriad ways by another – since something of the sort will happen to a hard worker – is not made angry against the other, but continues, I might say, to be attached to the soul of the one who is insulting or punishing him. He is kindled to wrath only against those who come against the poor or, as the Scripture says, *speak iniquity against God* [Ps. 74:6], or who otherwise live wickedly. For the one who loves God much more than himself (rather, he no longer loves himself at all, but God alone) does not avenge his own honour, but desires only the honouring of the righteousness of the one who honours him with an eternal honour. However, no longer does he have this attitude in momentary acts of will only; rather, it has become a habitual state because of his great experience of God's love. We need to know that one roused to such love by God comes to transcend even faith while such activity lasts, since through great love he possesses in the feeling of the heart the one honoured by faith. The holy Apostle clearly indicates this very idea when he says, *But now remain these three, faith, hope, love; but the greatest of these is love* [1 Cor. 13:13]. For the one who

seizes God in a wealth of love (as I said) is much greater then than his own faith, because he is rapt in his longing [for God].'

92. The middle state of the activity of holy knowledge causes us to be not a little saddened when we make someone our enemy by insulting him in a fit of outrage. Therefore, it never ever stops stinging our conscience until we draw the one we insulted back to his previous disposition with a full apology. Its most stinging compunction is this: when some worldling is unjustly enraged against us, it makes us meditate and worry greatly, since we have in some way become an offence to those whose conversation belongs to *this present age* [1 Cor. 2:6]. When this happens the intellect lies fallow in contemplation, for the principle [*logos*] of knowledge belongs wholly to love, and so it does not permit the discursive mind to open wide to receive divine contemplations, unless we have first reconciled in love anyone who is – even unjustly – angry with us. If he refuses this or avoids us, then this knowledge drives us to stamp the impress of his countenance on our own disposition in an undiminished largesse of soul, *and so fulfil the law of love* [Gal. 6:2] in the depths of our heart. That man continued: 'For we who desire to have knowledge of God must imagine in our discursive mind the faces of those who are angry with us without cause, but with a regard devoid of anger. When this happens, the intellect will not only be moved unfailingly in theology, but will also ascend with great confidence to the love of God, as it passes unhindered from the second rank to the first.'

93. The way of virtue appears bleak and dismal when someone first falls in love with piety, not because it actually is, but because human nature is turned towards the broad plain of pleasures right from the womb. Now, to those able to ascend to virtue's middle state, its way appears rather pleasant and open. For wickedness, having been subdued through the activity of goodness by good habits, is destroyed along with the memory of irrational pleasures. Therefore, the soul traverses all the ways of the virtues happily thereafter. Because of this the Lord, leading into the way of salvation, says, *Narrow and constricted is the way which leads to the kingdom and few enter through it* [Matt. 7:14]. But, to those who are fully determined to keep his

holy commands, he says, *For my yoke is good and my burden light* [Matt. 11:30]. Therefore, in our initial struggles we must undertake the holy commands of God, forcing our will, so that our good Lord, having seen our purpose and toil, will send down to us a will fully prepared to serve with pleasure his own glorious desires. For *the will is prepared by the Lord* [Prov. 8:35], so that we unceasingly accomplish goodness in much joy. For then we will truly feel that God is *at work in us both to will and to accomplish his good will* [Phil. 2:13].

94. Wax cannot long retain the seal set on it unless it is first heated or otherwise softened. So too a human cannot accept the seal of God's virtue unless tested with pains and infirmities. On this account, then, the Lord says to the divine Paul, *My grace is sufficient for you. For my power is perfected in weakness.* But the same Apostle immediately boasts, saying, *Therefore, I will boast all the more gladly in my infirmity, that the power of Christ may visit me* [2 Cor. 12:9]. But it is also written in Proverbs, *Whom the Lord loves he chastises; everyone whom he receives as a son he flogs* [Prov. 3:12; or Heb. 12:6]. Now, by 'infirmities' the Apostle means those uprisings of the enemies of the Cross which back then continually befell him and all the saints, lest they exalt themselves by the pre-eminence of their revelations [2 Cor. 12:9]. Rather, those saints through humility stayed true to the form of perfection, guarding in holiness the divine gift by frequent humiliations. We, however, intend by 'weakness' wicked trains of thought and bodily perturbations. For in those days, when the bodies of the saints who contended against sin were handed over to murderous tortures and other different afflictions, they were well beyond reach of the passions which have entered human nature thanks to sin. But now since, thanks to our Lord, *peace is multiplied* [2 Pet. 1:2] in the Churches, it is therefore necessary that those who contend in piety be tested – their body by frequent perturbations and their souls by wicked thoughts – especially those among whom knowledge is active in full feeling and assurance, so that they may escape all vainglory and distraction, and, as I said, receive the seal of divine beauty in their hearts through great humility. This is just as the holy Scripture says: *The light of*

your countenance has been sealed upon us, Lord [Ps. 4:7]. We
must, therefore, endure the Lord's will with gratitude, for then
the frequency of our illnesses and our battle against demonic
thoughts *will be reckoned to* us as a second martyrdom [Rom.
2:26, 4:9–10]. Back then [the Devil] said to the holy martyrs
through their wicked rulers: 'Deny Christ! Desire the glories
of this life!' Now, however, he suggests these same things in
person, speaking ceaselessly to the servants of God. Then he
tormented the bodies of righteous men and inflicted the most
extreme insults on the teachers of honour through men who
served diabolical ways of thinking. Now with many insults
and outrages he brings upon the confessors of piety various
different passions, especially when with great strength they
assist others crushed in poverty, for the sake of the glory of the
Lord. For this reason we ought to undertake the *testimony* [or,
martyrdom] *of our conscience* [2 Cor. 1:12]³ before God with
steadfastness and endurance: for *patiently*, it says, *I waited for
the Lord, and he heard me* [Ps. 39:2].

95. Humility is a difficult matter: it is achieved through struggles whose difficulty is proportionate to its greatness. It accrues
to partakers of holy knowledge in two ways. First, when the
contestant of piety has come to the middle state of spiritual
experience, his thinking becomes somewhat humbler thanks
either to bodily infirmity, to people hostilely importuning those
concerned with justice or to wicked thoughts generally. Secondly, when the intellect is illuminated by holy grace with deep
feeling and assurance, then the soul finds humility natural, as
it were. For being fattened by divine goodness, it can no longer
be roused to the swelling of vainglory, and even if it should
ceaselessly fulfil God's commandments, it would regard itself as
lower than all because of communion in divine clemency. While
the first humility very often brings grief and even despondency,
the second brings joy with all-wise reverence. Thus, the first
accrues to those in the midst of their labours, as I have said,
but the second is sent down to those nearing perfection. Thus,
while the first is often eaten away by worldly successes, the
latter – even if someone should parade *all the kingdoms of the
world* before it [Matt. 4:8] – would neither be terrified nor even

perceive the dreadful arrows of sin [cf. Eph. 6:16]. For this humility is entirely spiritual and thus totally impervious to bodily
glory. However, the one engaged in struggle needs in every way
by traversing the first to come to the second. For unless grace
first softens our self-governance through the first humility, by
the application of educative passions – for testing, that is, and
not by necessity – the profound perfection of the second will
not be given to us.

96. Those who are fond of the pleasures of this life go from
thinking about them to outright falls. For, carried along by
their undiscerning frame of mind, almost all the notions they
entertain are full of passion, which they yearn to express in
unruly speech and unholy deeds. Contrariwise, those who take
up ascetic practice to rectify their life go from outright falls
to wicked thoughts or certain wicked and harmful words. For
if the demons see such people listening to reproaches with a
smile, discussing some idle and inappropriate matter, laughing
as they should not, becoming immoderately angry, or desiring vain and empty glory – immediately the demons take up
arms against them. Taking love of glory as pretext for their
own wickedness, they leap through it like a dark window and
plunder their souls. Those who desire to make the multitude
of virtues their cellmates ought not to aim at glory, meet with
many people, make frequent public appearances, reproach
others (even if those being reproached ought to be!) or talk
about many things, even if they can say only good things. For
talkativeness immoderately dissipates the intellect and not only
makes it idle with regard to its spiritual activity, but even hands
it over to the demon of acedia; this demon first weakens the
intellect immoderately and then hands it over to the demons
of sadness and anger. Our intellect, therefore, must be thoroughly occupied with the keeping of the holy commandments
and a profound memory of the Lord of glory. For, it is said, *one
who keeps the commandment will not know a wicked word*
[Eccles. 8:5]: meaning, they will not turn aside to evil thoughts
or words.

97. When our heart receives the demons' arrows with such
blistering pain that their victim imagines they are physical

arrow wounds, then with painful labour the soul hates the passions, since it is at the beginning of its purification. For unless it agonizes at the shamelessness of sin, it cannot rejoice richly in the goodness of righteousness. So then, let the one who desires to purify his own heart always set fire to it with the memory of the Lord Jesus, having this as his constant meditation and task. For those who wish to expel their putrefaction cannot sometimes pray and sometimes not. Rather, they must always engage in prayer in the guarding of their intellect, even if they are staying somewhere outside usual houses of prayer. When someone wants to purify gold, if he neglects the fire of the crucible even for a moment, then the material he is purifying will harden again. So it is when someone sometimes practises memory of God and sometimes not: what he thinks to procure through prayer he loses through neglect. For it belongs to one who loves virtue to burn up what is earthy in his heart by constant memory of God, so that, as evil is gradually consumed by the fire of the memory of goodness, his soul will return to its own natural radiance with greater glory.

98. Dispassion does not mean the cessation of demonic warfare, since in that case *we would have to have departed from the world*, as the Apostle says [1 Cor. 5:10]. Rather, it means that those attacked by the demons remain invincible. For soldiers in heavy armour are shot at by opposing archers and they hear the sound of the arrows and also see almost all these same darts fired at them – but they are not struck, thanks to the solidity of their armour. Those who are clothed in iron are invincible in the fighting. As for us, armed as we are by all our good works with the *armour* of holy light and *the helmet of salvation* [Eph. 6:17], we will cut our way through the shadowy battle lines of demons. For the fact that we no longer do evil deeds does not confer purity, but, rather, that we utterly reject them by pursuing good deeds with all our might.

99. When the *man of God* [3 Kgds 13:1, 1 Tim. 6:11] conquers nearly all the passions, two demons stay behind, wrestling with him. One of them annoys the soul, dragging it from a great love of God to an inappropriate zeal, so that it does not wish anyone else to please God as it does. The other annoys the body, arousing in it through a kind of fiery activity a yearning for sex. This befalls the body first, because this pleasure is a property of nature for the sake of procreation, and so through it the soul is easily defeated. Of course it can also happen through God's permission. For when the Lord sees one of his contestants blossoming with a multitude of virtues, he then allows the contestant to be soiled by such a demon, that he learn to see himself as more worthless than everyone else in this world. Doubtless, the annoyance of passion either follows after successes or it pre-empts them, so that by either the predisposition to or visitation of the passion the soul may appear worthless, however great its successes may be. But let us fight the first demon with much humility and love, and the second with self-control, lack of anger and a profound awareness of death, so that, as we constantly perceive the activity of the Holy Spirit here and now, we may transcend these passions in the Lord.

100. As many of us as have become partakers of holy knowledge will give an account of every instance of involuntary inattention. *You have marked it*, says Job, *if I have transgressed, even unwillingly* [Job 14:17] – and justly so! For if someone did not neglect to remember God and did not disregard his holy commandments, then he would not fall into sin willingly or unwillingly. We must, therefore, immediately offer up to the Master an earnest confession of our involuntary sins – that is, regarding our keeping of the customary rule (for no human avoids all failure) – until our conscience receives in the tears of love assurance of its forgiveness for these sins. 'For if,' it says, '*we will confess our sins, God is faithful and just to forgive us our sins and cleanse us from all unrighteousness*' [1 John 1:9]. We must constantly attend to our feeling of confession lest perchance our conscience deceive itself, imagining that it is fully confessing to God, for the judgement of God is much greater than our own conscience, even if someone is quite certain that he knows of nothing against himself. Thus, the wisest Paul teaches us, saying, *But I do not examine myself. For I am aware of nothing against me, but I have not been justified by this fact; rather, the Lord is the one who examines me* [1 Cor. 4:

3–4]. For unless we confess properly and about our own selves, we will discover in ourselves an indistinct fear at the time of death. We who love the Lord ought to pray that we be found then beyond all fear. For the one who is found afraid then will not pass the Tartarean rulers as a free man, since they have as their ally, as it were, our soul's terror at their wickedness. But the soul transformed in the love of God is borne with the angels of peace above all those shadowy ranks at the hour of its death. That soul is given wings by spiritual love since it unfailingly bears love, the *fullness of the law* [Rom. 13:10]. Therefore, also at *the Lord's coming with all his saints* [1 Thess. 3:13] those who depart this life with such confidence *will be snatched up* [1 Thess. 4:17]. But, if they are terrified even for a moment at the time of death, they will be left behind in the crowd with all the others because they are *under judgement* [James 5:12]. This is so that *being tested in the fire* of judgement [1 Pet. 1:7, cf. 1 Cor. 3:13] they may yet receive the inheritance owed them in accordance with their deeds from our good God and King Jesus Christ. For he is the God of righteousness and to us who love him he gives the *wealth of the goodness* [Rom. 2:4] of his kingdom to the age of the age. Amen.

St Maximos the Confessor, *Four Hundred Chapters on Love*

ST MAXIMOS THE CONFESSOR (*c.*580–662)

If we lack a biography for many of the authors here, we have almost too much for St Maximos: that is, one version of his life is preserved in Greek and a wildly different one in Syriac. According to the Greek he was wealthy, highly educated, a fixture at the imperial court, before retiring to monasticism in Palestine and then North Africa. According to the Syriac he was the bastard son of a Samaritan slave-woman, and things get worse from there. The Greek *Life* is pious fan-fiction, the Syriac pure invective, and neither is reliable. We can say with certainty that Maximos spent about a decade in a monastery in North Africa, where he acquired a reputation as a theologian and spiritual teacher whose correspondents ranged from imperial officials to bishops to other monks. The pieces here translated – the *Four Hundred Chapters on Love* and the *Commentary on the Lord's Prayer* – belong to that period. In the 630s, Maximos would involve himself in controversies over the finer points of Christ's natures, which would lead him to Rome and Constantinople, to papal protection and imperial condemnation, and, eventually, to exile to Lazica (western modern Georgia), Byzantium's 'Siberia', and death in 662. He would eventually be recognized as the finest theologian of his era – indeed, the finest Byzantium would ever see.

The two pieces that follow reflect Maximos's holistic incorporation of spiritual themes and ascetic concerns into a cosmic vision of human restoration and deification through the work of Christ and the power of prayer. Maximos incorporates ideas from Evagrios, Diadochos and Mark the Solitary (not to mention Aristotle and the Platonic tradition) into that vision. The *Four Hundred Chapters on Love* explore numerous themes around prayer, meditation and community within an understanding of being human that regards the habit, character, and cultivation of God-like love as the one enduring and defining trait of the Christian. Note, though, that while we have noted explicit quotations, we have not marked the numerous uncited quotations from and allusions to Evagrios's works. The *Commentary on the Lord's Prayer*, by contrast, uses Jesus' prayer in Matthew 6:9–13 as a model and springboard for exploring salvation on the individual, the corporate and the cosmic level, each conceived in terms of seven movements which Maximos discerns in the Lord's Prayer itself. Please note that, in this text, we have not generally attempted to translate the Greek word *logos*, because Maximos plays so frequently on the numerous possible meanings it can have, for which there is no good English equivalent. For more on the word *logos*, please see the Glossary.

Sources

Text (*Four Hundred Chapters on Love*): A. Ceresa-Gastaldo (ed.), *Massimo confessore: Capitoli sulla carità* (Rome: Editrice Studium, 1963): 48–238

Alternative text: PHILOKALIA (1782): 291–330; *Philokalia* (1893/1982): vol. 2, 4–51

Text (*On the Lord's Prayer*): Peter van Deun, *Maximi confessoris opuscula exegetica duo*, Corpus Christianorum. Series Graeca 23 (Turnhout: Brepols, 1991): 27–73

Alternative Text: PHILOKALIA (1782): 440–53; *Philokalia* (1893/1982): vol. 2, 187–204

Four Hundred Chapters on Love

Prologue to Elpidios

See, in addition to the treatment of ascetic life, I have also sent a treatise on love to your holiness, Father Elpidios, in chapters equal in number to the four Gospels multiplied one hundred-fold. Probably none of it lives up to your expectations, but it is the best that I can do. Nevertheless your holiness should know that these chapters are none of them the tillage of our own intellect. Rather, I have gone through the writings of the holy Fathers and collected from them an understanding of the theme of love. I condensed many things into a few words, so that they may be read at a glance, and easily remembered. And having done all this, I have sent it to your holiness, encouraging you to read them thoughtfully and to hunt out only what is beneficial in them – to ignore the infelicity of my prose, and to pray for my mediocrity, bereft of all spiritual benefit.

I also ask you not to consider these chapters an annoyance, for I have only fulfilled your command. I say this, since there are many of us today who cause annoyance with our words. But they are very few indeed who teach or are taught by deeds. Rather, I beg you to attend carefully to each chapter. For, as I see it, not all things are easy for all to apprehend; but instead, many things demand close scrutiny by many readers – even if they seem to be spoken rather simply. For perhaps something hidden in these chapters may appear useful to the soul. Well, it will always be revealed by the grace of God to one who reads, not out of curiosity, but with fear of God and love. Of course, if someone happens upon either this treatise or whatever else and does not approach for the sake of spiritual benefit, but, instead, to hunt out its style for the purpose of belittling the treatise – doing so, I suppose, out of self-conceit, to set himself up as wiser than the author – well, he will never get any benefit from anything!

First century

1. Love is a good disposition of the soul, according to which it prefers none of the things which are to the knowledge of God. It is impossible for one who maintains attachment to any earthly thing to come to this state.

2. Dispassion brings forth love; hope in God brings forth dispassion; endurance and patience bring forth hope; all-encompassing self-control brings forth these two; fear of God brings forth self-control; and faith in the Lord brings forth fear.

3. One who has faith in the Lord fears punishment, and one who fears punishment keeps himself from passions. One who keeps himself from passions endures afflictions, and one who endures afflictions will have hope in God. One who has hope in God distances himself from every earthly attachment. And the mind which is distanced from this attachment will have love for God.

4. One who loves God prefers knowledge of him to all things which have come to be through him [John 1:3], and unstintingly devotes himself to it through yearning.

5. If all beings have come to be through God and because of God, God is greater than what has come to be through him. One who abandons the greater and devotes himself to lesser things shows that he prefers to God the things which have come to be through God.

6. One who keeps his mind nailed to the love of God despises all visible things and even his own body as alien.

7. If the soul is greater than the body, and God who made the world is immeasurably greater than it, then one who prefers his body over his soul and the world created by God over God differs in no respect from idolaters.

8. One who has separated his intellect from its love and close attention to God, and has it bound to some sensible object: this is the one who prefers body to soul and things created by God to the God who created them.

9. If the life of the intellect is the enlightenment of knowledge, love for God brings it forth. Well has it been said that nothing is greater than divine love [1 Cor. 13:13].

10. When the intellect goes out of itself in the intensity of its *eros* for God, then it does not perceive in any way either itself or any other being. For by being illumined by a divine and boundless light, it becomes insensible to everything made by God, just as the physical eye is unable to perceive the stars when the sun has risen

11. All the virtues cooperate with the intellect towards divine *eros*, but pure prayer more than all. Through this the intellect is raised on wings towards God and so comes to be outside everything that has being.

12. When through love the mind is ravished by divine knowledge and finds itself outside all that has being, it becomes aware of divine infinity – then, according to the divine Isaiah, amazement brings it to a consciousness of its own humility, and it says with conviction the words of the prophet: *Wretched man that I am, for I have been wounded. For being human and having impure lips, I dwell in the midst of a people with impure lips, and I have seen with my eyes the king, the Lord Sabaoth* [Isa. 6:5].

13. It is impossible for one who loves God not to love every human as himself, even if he is disgusted at the passions of those who are not yet purified. Thus, when he sees their return and correction, he rejoices with boundless and unspeakable joy.

14. The soul overrun by passion is impure, filled as it is with thoughts of desire and hatred.

15. One who sees a trace of hatred in his heart, on account of whatever fault, or with regard to anyone whatever, will find himself utterly estranged from love for God, since love for God cannot bear in any way hatred towards another.

16. *One who loves me*, says the Lord, *will keep my commandments: this is my commandment, that you love one*

another [John 14:15, 15:12]. One, therefore, who does not love his neighbour does not keep the commandment. But if he does not keep the commandment, neither can he love the Lord.

17. Blessed is the one who can love everyone equally.

18. Blessed is the one who is involved in no corrupt or transient deed.

19. Blessed is the intellect that has passed beyond all beings and unceasingly delights in divine beauty.

20. One who *takes thought for the desires of the flesh* [Rom. 13:14] and bears a grudge against his neighbour because of passing things – such a one *worships the creature rather than the creator* [Rom. 1:25].

21. One who keeps his body free from pleasure and sickness has it as a fellow servant in the service of better things.

22. One who flees all worldly desires sets himself above every *worldly sorrow* [2 Cor. 7:10].

23. One who loves God certainly loves his neighbour too. Such a one cannot keep guard over his possessions, but dispenses them as God pleases, providing for each of those in need.

24. One who gives alms in imitation of God does not differentiate between wicked and good or just and unjust so far as bodily necessities are concerned. Rather, he distributes to each equally according to their need, even if he prefers the virtuous to the bad because of their good intention.

25. God, being good by nature and dispassionate, loves all equally as his creatures, but glorifies the virtuous as those who want to be his friend; and in his goodness is merciful towards the wicked, chastising them in this age to turn them back to him. In the same way, one who is by intention good and dispassionate loves all equally but loves the virtuous because of nature and their good intention, and the wicked because of nature and out of sympathy, pitying them as foolish and wandering about in the dark.

26. The disposition of love is made known not only by the distribution of goods, but much more by making known the Word of God and serving the bodily needs of others.

27. One who has genuinely renounced the things of the world and sincerely serves his neighbour in love will quickly be freed

from every passion and come to partake of divine love and knowledge.

28. One who has acquired divine love in himself does not *grow weary in following after* the Lord his God, according to the divine Jeremiah [Jer. 17:16 LXX]. Rather, he endures all toil, every reproach and every insult nobly, thinking evil of no one at all [1 Cor. 13:5].

29. When you are insulted by someone, or despised in something, then take care not to entertain the thoughts of wrath, lest, depriving you of love through dejection, they place you in the region of hatred.

30. When you suffer much toil because of an insult or dishonour, then realize how greatly you have benefitted, since, by God's dispensation, vainglory has been cast out of you through dishonour.

31. Just as the memory of fire does not heat one's body, so also faith without love does not kindle the illumination of knowledge in the soul.

32. Just as the sun's light draws a healthy eye towards itself, so also the knowledge of God naturally attracts to itself the pure intellect through love.

33. An intellect is pure which has been separated from ignorance and illumined by divine light.

34. A soul is pure which has been freed from passions and ceaselessly cheered by divine love.

35. A passion is a blameworthy movement of the soul contrary to nature.

36. Dispassion is a peaceful condition of the soul, making it hard to be moved to evil.

37. One who has gained the fruits of love through diligence is not to be dislodged from this, even if he suffers innumerable troubles. And let Stephen persuade you, that disciple of Christ, and those like him who pray for their murderers, and beg the Heavenly Father for their forgiveness, because they did not know what they were doing [Acts 7:60, Luke 23:34].

38. If being *patient* and *kind* belong to love [1 Cor. 13:4], then one who loses his temper and acts wickedly has clearly become a stranger to love; but a stranger to love is a stranger to God, since *God is love* [1 John 4:8].

39. *Do not say*, says the divine Jeremiah, *that the temple is the Lord's* [Jer. 7:4]. And you should not say that mere faith in our Lord Jesus Christ can save me. For this is futile, unless you also procure love for God through works. As for merely believing, well, *even the demons believe and tremble* [James 2:19].

40. The work of love is to do good to one's neighbour out of a genuine desire; it is patience and endurance and making use of everything with right reason.

41. One who loves God does not grieve another, nor is he grieved with another because of transient things. He only grieves another or is grieved with another in a saving way, just as the blessed Paul was grieved by, and himself grieved, the Corinthians [2 Cor. 7:8–10].

42. One who loves God lives the angelic life on earth: fasting, keeping vigil, singing psalms, praying and always thinking good things about everyone.

43. If someone desires something, he strives to attain it. But divinity is better and incomparably more desirable than any good that might be desired. How much zeal ought we to show in order to attain that which is by nature good and desirable!

44. Do not stain your flesh with shameful practices, and do not defile your soul with evil thoughts, and the peace of God *will come upon you*, bearing love.

45. Torture your flesh with want of food and sleeplessness, and resolutely pursue psalmody and prayer, and the sanctification of temperance *will come upon you*, bearing love.

46. One who has been deemed worthy of divine knowledge and has gained the illumination of knowledge through love will never be shaken by the spirit of vainglory. But one who has not yet been deemed worthy of divine knowledge is easily borne about by this spirit. If, then, such a man looks to God in everything he does, as doing everything for him, he will easily escape it with God's help.

47. One who has not yet attained divine knowledge made active through love thinks highly of the godly things he has done. But one who has been deemed worthy to attain this knowledge says with conviction the words of the patriarch Abraham, which he himself said when counted worthy of God's manifestation: *I am dust and ashes* [Gen. 18:27].

48. One who fears the Lord always has humble-mindedness as his companion and through thoughts inspired by this comes to divine love and thanksgiving. For he remembers his former way of life in the world [Eph. 4:22] and his various falls and the temptations which beset him from his youth, and how the Lord delivered him from all of them and brought him from a life mired in passion to a godly life. So, with fear he receives, too, love, giving thanks always with deep humility to the benefactor and pilot of our life.

49. Do not defile your intellect, clinging to thoughts of desire and anger, lest, having fallen away from pure prayer, you meet with the spirit of despondency.

50. The moment the intellect becomes a companion to evil or defiled thoughts, it falls away from its confident intimacy with God.

51. A fool is moved by the passions. When he is troubled, being roused by anger, he has an irrational urge to flee his brothers, but when he is again inflamed by desire, he changes his mind and is eager to meet them. But the prudent man does the opposite in both cases. For, in the case of anger, he cuts off the causes of trouble and stops himself causing grief to his brothers; while with regard to desire, he controls the irrational impulse and chance encounter.

52. In the time of temptations do not abandon your monastery, but, rather, bear the waves of thoughts nobly – especially those of dejection and despondency. For having thus been providentially tested through afflictions, you will gain a firm hope in God. But if you abandon your monastery, you will be found a reprobate, unmanly and unstable.

53. If you desire not to fall away from godly love, never allow your brother to go to sleep grieved with you, or yourself to go to sleep grieved with him. But *go, be reconciled with your brother and, returning, offer* to Christ *your gift* of love [Matt. 5:24] with a pure conscience through fervent prayer.

54. If someone has all the gifts of the Spirit, but lacks love, it is of no value, according to the divine Apostle [1 Cor. 13:1–3]. We must go to any length to obtain this love.

55. If *love does no evil to its neighbour* [Rom. 13:10], then one who envies his brother, or is grieved by his good reputation, or slanders his character with jests, or plots against him by some evil craft – how does such a man not make himself a stranger to love, and *liable to* eternal *judgement* [Matt. 5:22]?

56. If *love is the fullness of the law* [Rom. 13:10], then one who bears malice towards his brother and devises schemes against him, praying against him and exulting over his fall – how is he not a transgressor and worthy of eternal punishment?

57. If *one who speaks against his brother or judges him insults and judges the law* [James 4:11] – and remember the law of Christ is love – how does such a slanderer not fall away from the love of Christ and become the cause of his own eternal punishment?

58. Never pay attention to slanderous talk or gossip in the hearing of those who love to find fault – whether readily speaking or listening to things against your neighbour, lest you fall from divine love and find yourself an alien to eternal life.

59. Accept no reproach against your father, and do not encourage one who dishonours him, lest the Lord be angered at your works [Ps. 103:31; Jer. 38:16 LXX] and utterly erase you *from the land of the living* [Jer. 11:19 LXX].

60. Stop the mouth of one who speaks against others in your hearing, lest you commit a double sin with him [Isa. 40:2], at once accustoming yourself to destructive passion and not preventing him from babbling against your neighbour.

61. *I say to you*, says the Lord: *Love your enemies, do well by those who hate you, pray for those who abuse you* [Luke 6:27–8]. Why did he command these things? So that he might free you from hatred, dejection, wrath and remembrance of wrongs, and make you worthy of the greatest possession – perfect love. It is impossible for someone to have perfect love who does not love all humans equally in imitation of God who loves all equally and *desires that* they *be saved and come to knowledge of the truth* [1 Tim. 2:4].

62. *I say to you not to resist evil. Rather, if someone strikes you on your right cheek, turn to him the other. If someone wants to sue you and take your shirt, give him your cloak. And if someone compels you to go for one mile, go with him two* [Matt. 5:39–41]. Why? So that he might preserve you free from anger and dejection, educate the other through your forbearance, and, good as he is, bring you both under the yoke of love.

63. Anything we have previously experienced can be the source of impassioned imaginings that we now bear. One, therefore, who conquers his impassioned imaginings will completely disregard the things that are the cause of these imaginings. For the struggle with memories of things is that much harder than the struggle against the things themselves, just as sinning in thought is so much easier than to sin in outward action.

64. Of the passions, some pertain to the body and others to the soul. Those of the body originate in the body. Those of the soul come from outside. Love and self-control intercept both kinds: love the passions of the soul, and self-control those of the body.

65. Of the passions, some pertain to the irascible part, others to the desiring part of the soul. Both are set in motion through the senses: they are moved, that is, when the soul finds itself bereft of love and self-control.

66. The passions of the soul's irascible part are much harder to fight than those of its desiring part. For this reason, the command of love was given by the Lord as a stronger remedy for it.

67. All other passions of the soul affect either its irascible part or its desiring part only, or they touch its rational part as well – as with forgetfulness and ignorance. But despondency lays hold of all the soul's faculties at once and moves all together the remaining passions, for it is the heaviest of all the passions. Rightly, then, the Lord has given us a remedy for despondency: *By your endurance*, he says, *gain your souls* [Luke 21:19].

68. Never strike a brother, especially without reason, lest he depart, because he cannot bear the affliction, and you will then never escape the reproof of your conscience, which will always

bring you sadness in the time of prayer and will drive your intellect far from divine intimacy.

69. Have nothing to do with suspicions or with humans that cause you to stumble. For those who entertain in any way whatever occasions of stumbling whether willingly or against their will do not know the way of peace which bears lovers of the knowledge of God to it through love.

70. One does not yet possess perfect love who is still disposed to human considerations. For example, loving one and hating another for whatever reason; or sometimes loving and at other times hating someone for the same reasons.

71. Perfect love does not divide up the single nature of humans according to diverse individual considerations; rather, always attentive to this nature it loves all people equally, loving the zealous as friends and the wicked as enemies, doing good, being patient and putting up with whatever they do. It *reckons no evil* at all [1 Cor. 13:5], but, rather, suffering on their behalf, if the occasion arises, so that, if possible, they become friends. And if not, love does not desert its own intention of always equally displaying the fruits of love towards all humans. Therefore, also, our Lord and God Jesus Christ, showing us his love, suffered for the whole of humanity and gave to all equally the hope of resurrection, even though it lies with each one to become worthy of either glory or punishment.

72. If you do not scorn glory and dishonour, wealth and penury, pleasure and sadness, you have not yet procured perfect love. For perfect love not only scorns these, but even this passing life and death itself!

73. Hear the kind of things they say who have been counted worthy of perfect love: *Who will separate us from the love of Christ? Will affliction, constraint, persecution, hunger, nakedness, danger or sword? Just as it is written: 'For your sake we are killed all day long; we are reckoned as sheep for the slaughter'* [Ps. 43:23]. *But in all these things we are more than conquerors through him who has loved us. For I have become convinced that neither death nor life, neither angels nor rulers nor powers, neither things present nor those to come, neither height nor depth, nor any other creature, will be able*

to separate us from the love of God in Christ Jesus our Lord [Rom. 8:35–9]. And all the Saints say and do such things about their love for God.

74. Regarding love for our neighbour, hear again the kind of things they say: *I speak the truth in Christ, I do not lie, as my conscience in the Holy Spirit testifies with me, that I am deeply sad and suffer ceaseless pain in my heart. For I prayed to be anathema from Christ for my brothers, my kinsmen by blood, the Israelites* [Rom. 9:1–3], etc. So also Moses and the rest of the saints [Exod. 32:31–5, etc.].

75. If you do not scorn glory and pleasure, as well as the avarice which they introduce and which nourishes their growth, you cannot cut off the suggestions of anger. And if you do not, you cannot attain perfect love.

76. Humility and suffering free a human from every sin, the former cutting away sins of the soul, the latter sins of the body. For the blessed David makes this clear, too, when he prays to God, saying, *See my humility and my toil and forgive all my sins* [Ps. 24:18].

77. Through the commandments the Lord renders those who do them dispassionate. Through the divine doctrines he grants them the enlightenment of knowledge.

78. All doctrines concern either God, things visible and invisible, or the principles of providence and judgement in them.

79. Almsgiving heals the irascible part of the soul; fasting withers desire. Prayer purifies the intellect and prepares it for the contemplation of beings. For the Lord has given us his commandments for the faculties of our soul.

80. *Learn from me*, he says, *for I am meek and humble in heart*, etc. [Matt. 11:29]. For meekness keeps the irascible faculty undisturbed; and humility frees the intellect from delusion and vainglory.

81. The fear of God is twofold. The first is born in us from the threats of punishment, because of which accrue to us self-control, endurance [1 Pet. 1:6], hope in God, and dispassion, from which comes love, all in their right order. The second has been yoked with love itself, and always forms piety in our soul lest through the familiarity of love it come to contempt for God.

82. *Perfect love casts out* the first *fear* from a soul which has procured it [1 John 4:18], because it no longer fears punishment. But the second love always has fear as her yoke-mate, as said above. Sayings that refer to the first kind of fear are these: *By the fear of the Lord is everyone turned from evil* [Prov. 15:27a LXX]; and *The fear of the Lord is the beginning of wisdom* [Prov. 1:7]. And to the second kind: *The fear of the Lord is pure, enduring from age to age* [Ps. 18:10]; and *There is nothing lacking in those who fear him* [Ps. 33:10].

83. *Put to death, therefore, your members upon the earth: fornication, impurity, passion, wicked desire, wanting more*, and the rest [Col. 3:5]. He calls the *mind of the flesh* [Rom. 8:6] 'earth'. By 'fornication' he means sin in action. He calls assent 'impurity'; and passion refers to impassioned thought. 'Wicked desire' means the merest acceptance of a thought of desire. By 'wanting more' he means material that engenders and nourishes passion. All of these together, constituting the 'members' of the *mind of the flesh*, the divine Apostle commanded us to *put to death*.

84. First, our memory calls a mere thought into the intellect, and, when this has stayed for a while, it arouses passion; if this is not removed, it turns the mind to assent; and when this happens, one comes to sin in action. Thus, the all-wise Apostle, writing to people among the gentiles, first commands them to remove the final act of sin, and then, to go step by step in due order until they finish off its cause. But, as has been said, the cause that generates and nourishes passion is wanting more. I think that here he means that gluttony is the mother and nurse of fornication. For wanting more is not only evil with regard to possessions, but with regard to food, just as self-control is not only good for food, but also concerns property.

85. If a sparrow, bound by its claw, begins to fly, it falls to the ground, being pulled down by the string. In the same way, if an intellect has not attained dispassion and begins to fly towards knowledge of heavenly things, it will fall to the ground, dragged down by the passions.

86. When the intellect has been completely freed from the passions, then it journeys without looking back towards the contemplation of beings, making its way to knowledge of the Holy Trinity.

87. An intellect that is pure, when it takes up intellectual perceptions of realities, is moved to spiritual contemplation of them. An intellect, impure through carelessness, imagines mere conceptions of other things, while, in receiving thoughts about human beings, it turns them into shameful or wicked trains of thought.

88. When during the time of prayer no conceptions of the world ever trouble the intellect, then know that you are not outside the frontiers of dispassion.

89. When your soul begins to feel its own healthiness, then it will begin to see even images in dreams as calm and untroubling.

90. Just as the beauty of things visible attracts our physical eye, so too the knowledge of things invisible draws the pure intellect to itself – by things invisible I mean the bodiless powers.

91. It is a great thing not to be affected by things, but far greater to remain dispassionate when imagining them. Because the war the demons wage against us through thoughts is more severe than their war through things.

92. One who has achieved the virtues and grown rich in knowledge, since he then clearly discerns things naturally, does and thinks everything in accordance with right reason, being entirely free from delusion. For it is by our well-reasoned or irrational use of things that we become either virtuous or wicked.

93. A sign of utmost dispassion is that only bare conceptions of things ever ascend into the heart, both when the body is awake and in dreams.

94. Through the performance of commandments, the intellect strips off the passions: through the spiritual contemplation of things visible it strips off impassioned conceptions of things; through the knowledge of things invisible, it strips off the contemplation of things visible; and, finally, it strips off even this last, through knowledge of the Holy Trinity.

95. The sun, when it rises and enlightens the world, reveals

itself as well as the things illuminated by its light. So also the *sun of righteousness* [Mal. 4:2], rising in a pure intellect, reveals himself and the natural principles of everything which has come to be and will come to be through him [John 1:3].

96. We do not know God from his being, but from the grandeur of his works and his providence for all that is. For through these as through mirrors we contemplate his boundless goodness, wisdom and power.

97. The pure intellect is to be found either among bare conceptions of human things, or in the natural contemplation of visible or invisible beings, or in the light of the Holy Trinity.

98. The intellect which has come to the contemplation of visible things either explores their natural principles or what is signified by them or else it seeks out the cause itself.

99. Dwelling among invisible things, the intellect seeks out their natural principles, as well as the cause of their coming to be and what follows from these, as well as how providence and judgement relate to them.

100. Being in God, finally, the intellect, set aflame by yearning, seeks first the principles about his being, but finds no consolation from these principles that concern him. For this is impossible and denied equally to every nature that has come into being. But the intellect finds consolation in the principles that are about him, I mean those that concern eternity, boundlessness and infinitude, or his goodness, wisdom and power, with which he fashions beings, provides for them and judges them. And this alone is fully comprehensible: God's boundlessness. For to know nothing is knowledge surpassing the intellect, as those theologians Gregory and Dionysios have said somewhere.[1]

Second century

1. One who genuinely loves God always prays without distraction; and one who always prays without distraction loves God truly. But one whose intellect is still nailed to anything earthly does not pray without distraction. Therefore, one whose intellect is bound to anything earthly does not love God.

2. The intellect which lingers over something perceived by sense will always have a passion for it, whether that passion be of desire, grief, anger or resentment. And unless the mind disregards that thing, it cannot be free of the passion.

3. The passions of the intellect chain one mastered by them to material things, and separate it from God, making it to be occupied with such material things. But once the love of God gains control, it frees the intellect from bonds, persuading it to despise not only things perceived by sense, but even our transient life itself.

4. The work of God's commandments is to free intellectual conceptions of things from passion. The work of spiritual reading and contemplation is to render the intellect immaterial and formless. And from this comes undistracted prayer.

5. The way of practical virtue is not enough to free the intellect completely from its passions, so that it may pray without distraction – unless followed by various spiritual contemplations. For the way of practical virtue only frees the intellect from incontinence and hatred, whereas spiritual contemplations deliver it from forgetfulness and ignorance; and thus the intellect will be able to pray as it ought.

6. The highest states of pure prayer are twofold: one is for those engaged only in the practice of virtue, the other for those engaged in contemplation. The first comes about in the soul from fear of God and good hope; the second from divine *eros* and utmost purification. Signs of the first state are that the intellect concentrating all conceptions of the world within itself, and, as it were, standing in God's presence – as indeed it is – makes its prayers without distraction or disturbance. Signs of the second state are that, at the very inception of prayer, the intellect is snatched up by the divine and boundless light and perceives neither itself nor any other being whatsoever – save only the one who through love brings about such radiance in it. Then, also being occupied with the natural principles concerning God, it receives pure and limpid impressions about him.

7. One who loves always cleaves to this and scorns everything which gets in his way, lest he be deprived of it. And one

who loves God takes great care over pure prayer and casts from himself every passion that gets in the way of prayer.

8. One who rejects self-love, the mother of the passions, will easily put aside the rest with God's help, such as wrath, grief, resentment, and the rest. But one who is ruled by self-love, will be wounded by the others, even against his will. Self-love is an impassioned attachment to the body.

9. There are five reasons why people love each other, whether in a praiseworthy or blameworthy way. First, because of God, as the virtuous man loves all and one not yet virtuous loves a virtuous man. Secondly, by nature, as parents love their children and vice versa. Thirdly, through vainglory, as one praised loves the one who praises him. Fourthly, through avarice, as one might love a rich man for what one can get from him. Fifthly, through love of pleasure, as one might care for the stomach and the sexual organs. Of these, the first cause is to be praised; the second in between; the rest are the results of passion.

10. If there are some you hate, others you neither love nor hate, others you love moderately and others you love exceedingly, then know, from this inequality, that you are far from perfect love, which presupposes that you love all equally.

11. *Turn from evil and do good* [Ps. 36:27]. That is, fight your enemies that you may diminish the passions. Then, be watchful lest they increase. And again, fight, that you may obtain the virtues and then again be vigilant, that you may keep them. And this is what *till it* and *keep it* signify [Gen. 2:15].

12. Those who tempt us with God's permission either heat up the desiring faculty of our soul, trouble its irascible faculty, darken its rational faculty, encompass the body with pain or deprive it of its necessities.

13. Either the demons tempt us themselves or they arm against us those who do not fear the Lord: themselves, when we are on our own away from others, just as the Lord was tempted in the desert [Matt. 4:1–13]; through others, when we pass our time among them, just as the Lord did with the Pharisees [Matt. 19:3]. However they attack us, let us shake them off, by gazing steadfastly on our Lord's example.

14. When the intellect begins to progress in the love of God,

then also the demon of blasphemy begins to tempt it and suggest to it thoughts such as no human, but only the Devil, the
father of demons, could possibly invent. For the Devil envies
the lover of God and wants him to despair for having entertained such thoughts, and so no longer dare to be united to
God through habitual prayer. Of course, the destroyer gets no
nearer his own goal, but, rather, makes us all the firmer. For,
as we war against him and fight back, we find ourselves more
thoroughly tested and more genuine in the love of God: his
sword will enter his *own heart and* his *bow will be shattered*
[Ps. 36:15].

15. An intellect which turns to visible things considers them
naturally through the medium of the senses. And neither is the
intellect evil, nor thinking naturally, nor things themselves, nor
sense-perception – for these are works of God. What, then,
is evil? Manifestly, it is the passion that accompanies natural
thinking, which need not occur in entertaining concepts, provided the intellect is vigilant.

16. A passion is a movement of soul contrary to nature,
involving irrational love or indiscriminate hatred, either of
someone or of something perceived by the senses. Irrational
affection could be for food or a woman or possessions or fading
glory or something else perceived by the senses, or because
of them; indiscriminate hatred could be of any of the things
already mentioned, or for someone, because of them.

17. Again, evil is the mistaken use of concepts, leading to
the abuse of things themselves. For example, the correct use
of intercourse with a woman is with a view to procreation. If
you are looking for pleasure you are mistaken in what you are
doing, pursuing as good what is not good. In such a case you
are abusing intercourse with a woman. And it is the same with
other things and concepts alike.

18. When the demons deprive the intellect of soberness of
mind and encircle it with lustful thoughts, then say with tears
to our Master: *Having cast me out they now encircle me; O my
Joy, save me from those who surround me!* [Ps. 16:11, 31:7]
and he will save you.

19. Terrible is the demon of fornication: he violently attacks

those who are struggling against passion, especially those who are careless about their way of life, or in meeting women. For secretly, with the oiliness of pleasure, this demon beguiles the intellect, and then makes his way through the memory to one practising stillness, at once setting the body on fire and presenting various forms to the intellect, thus enticing him to consent to sin. If you do not wish these forms to linger in you, return to fasting, toil, vigil, and the beauty of stillness with fervent prayer.

20. *Those who are always seeking after* our *soul* [Ps. 34:4] seek it through impassioned thoughts, that they may cast it into sin, whether in thought or action. When, therefore, they find the intellect unwilling to receive them, they will *be ashamed* and humiliated. But when they find it engaged in spiritual contemplation, then *they shall be quickly turned back and exceedingly put to shame* [Ps. 6:11].

21. One who anoints his intellect for sacred combat and drives impassioned thoughts far from it holds fast the principle of the diaconate. One who illuminates his intellect for knowledge of beings and dispels false knowledge holds fast the principle of the priesthood. One who perfects with holy chrism the knowledge of the adorable and holy Trinity holds fast the principle of the episcopate.

22. The demons grow weak when through the Lord's commandments the passions diminish within us. But they perish when they are finally utterly destroyed by the soul's dispassion, since they no longer find in us those ways through which they entered the soul and made war against it. And this could be what is meant by *they will grow weak and perish before your face* [Ps. 9:4].

23. Some people abstain from the passions through human fear, others through vainglory, still others through self-control. Different again is being freed from passions through divine judgements.

24. All the words of the Lord embrace these four divisions: commandments, doctrines, threats and promises. And because of them we endure every austerity, such as fasting, vigil, sleeping on the ground, labours, toil in service of others, insults, dishonour, tortures, deaths, and the like [Heb. 11:37–8]. For

Because of the words of your lips, it says, *I have kept hard ways* [Ps. 16:4].

25. Reward for self-control: dispassion; for faith: knowledge. While dispassion gives birth to discernment, knowledge gives birth to love for God.

26. The intellect engaged in ascetic struggle advances towards sobriety. The intellect engaged in the contemplative life advances towards knowledge. Ascetic struggle yields discernment of virtue and vice; the contemplative way leads to participation in the principles of bodiless and embodied beings. But, as soon as one is deemed worthy of the grace of theology, at that very moment, having been carried beyond the two stages just mentioned on the wings of love and come within God, he will examine through the Spirit the principle of what surrounds God, so far as is possible for a human intellect.

27. When you come to the realm of theology, do not seek the principles that belong to God, for no human intellect will ever find them, nor will any other of those after God. But the intellect may examine the principles that surround him, as it were, such as those concerned with eternity, boundlessness and infinitude, or his goodness, wisdom, and the power which fashions, provides for and judges beings. For this is what it is to be a great theologian among humans: to seek out these principles, even if only to a small extent.

28. To be powerful is to yoke knowledge to practice. For with the latter he quenches his desiring faculty and tames his irascible one; with the former he gives wings to his intellect and departs towards God [cf. 2 Cor. 5:8].

29. When the Lord says, *I and the Father are one* [John 10:30], he signifies the identity of being. When he says again, *I am in the Father and the Father in me* [John 14:11], he shows the inseparability of persons. Thus, those tritheists who separate the Son from the Father fall into a crevasse. For either they say that the Son is co-eternal with the Father, but separating one from the other, they are forced to say that the Son is not begotten from the Father, and so fall into speaking of three gods and three beginnings or principles. Or else, saying that the Son is begotten of the Father, but separating them, they are forced

to say that the Son is not co-eternal with the Father, and they subject to time the Lord of time. For one must, with the great Gregory, at once *maintain one God and confess three Persons, each with his particular properties.* For as he says, God *is divided* but *in an undivided way,* and *is united,* but *separately.* And because of this there is a *paradox of division and union*[2] – but in what would this paradox consist if the Son and Father were joined or separated in the same way as humans?

30. One who is perfect in love and has come to the utmost dispassion does not know the difference between his own and another's, or between a believer and an unbeliever, or between *slave and free,* or even *male and female* [Gal. 3:28]. Rather, raised above the tyranny of the passions and looking steadfastly at the single nature of humans, he beholds all equally and is equally disposed to all. For in such a one there is *neither Greek and Jew, nor male and female, nor slave and free* [cf. Gal. 3:28] – but Christ is *all and in all* [1 Cor. 15:28].

31. The demons take from the passions lying deep down in the soul occasions for arousing impassioned thoughts within us. Then, warring on the intellect through these, they violently compel it to give assent to sin. Having defeated it, they lead it to sin in thought. When this has been accomplished, they drag it captive to sin in action. Finally, having laid waste the mind through thoughts, the demons withdraw, taking the thoughts with them, leaving in the intellect nothing more than the idol of sin, about which the Lord says, *When you see the abomination of desolation set up in the holy place, let the reader understand* [Matt. 24:15]. The *holy place* and *temple of God* is the human intellect, in which the demons have laid waste the soul through impassioned thoughts and have set up the idol of sin. That these things have happened in history none would doubt, I think, who has read Josephus's works.[3] Although some say that these things are also going to happen at the time of the Antichrist.

32. There are three things which move us to good deeds: natural seeds, holy powers and good choice. The natural seeds move us, as when we do to others what we would have them do for us, or when we see someone in poverty and constraint

and naturally feel pity. The holy powers move us, as when roused to do a fine work we find good assistance and guidance. Good choice moves us as when we discern good from evil and choose the good.

33. There are likewise three things which move us to evil deeds: the passions, the demons and bad choice. The passions move us, as when we desire something contrary to reason, such as between-meal snacks and unnecessary foods, or a woman who is not our wife and not with the intention of procreation. Or again, when we are angered or grieved unreasonably, for example, against someone who has dishonoured or harmed us. The demons move us, as when they catch us out in our carelessness and suddenly set upon us with violence, stirring up the passions already mentioned and other similar ones. And bad choice, as when in full knowledge of the good, we choose evil instead.

34. The recompense of virtue's labours is dispassion and knowledge. For these become harbingers of the Kingdom of Heaven just as the passions and ignorance are harbingers of eternal punishment. Anyone, therefore, who seeks these for the sake of human glory and not for the good itself hears from the Scripture: *You ask and do not receive, because you ask badly* [James 4:3].

35. There are many things done by people that are by nature good, but again are not good for some reason: such as fasting and vigil, prayer and psalmody, almsgiving and hospitality – these are by nature good works, but when done for the sake of vainglory are no longer good.

36. God seeks out the intention of everything we do: whether we do it for his sake or some other reason.

37. When you hear the Scripture saying that *You will render to each according to his deeds* [Ps. 61:13], do not think that deeds done without a right intention, so long as they seem to be good, will be rewarded by God, but evidently what is done with a right intention. For God's judgement looks not simply at what has taken place, but at what lies behind it.

38. The demon of pride has a double wickedness. For either he persuades a monk to ascribe his accomplishments to himself

and not God, the giver of good things and helper of those who do them; or, if that monk is not persuaded by this, he suggests that he despise his brothers who are not yet perfect. The monk who acts like this does not realize that the demon is persuading him to deny God's help. For if he despises his brothers as being unable to attain virtue, then clearly he puts himself forward as one whose success is down to him. Which is impossible, as the Lord says, *Apart from me you can do nothing* [John 15:5]; since our own weakness, even when moved to good deeds, cannot bring them about without the giver of good things.

39. One who has known the weakness of human nature has gained experience of divine power, and such a one – having accomplished things through that power and hastening to accomplish more – never despises anyone. For he knows that, just as he was helped and set free from many passions and difficulties, everyone can be helped, when God wishes, and especially those engaged in spiritual struggle for his sake. And if, for certain reasons, he does not deliver everyone all at once from the passions, but, rather, in his good time, as a good physician who loves humankind, he heals each one of those who strive for spiritual progress.

40. Pride follows upon the inactivity of the passions, whether that comes from their causes being cut off or through the treacherous withdrawal of the demons.

41. Nearly every sin happens because of pleasure and its removal through suffering and grief, whether voluntary or involuntary, through repentance or divine providential visitation. For, *if we were our own judges, we would not be judged; being judged by the Lord we are disciplined, so that we may not be judged along with the world* [1 Cor. 11:31–2].

42. When a temptation comes to you from an unexpected direction, do not blame the one through whom it has come, but, rather, *seek* why *and you will find* correction [Matt. 7:7], since one way or another you will always have to drink the wormwood of God's judgements.

43. As long as you have bad habits, do not reject suffering, so that, being humbled by it, you may vomit out your pride.

44. Some temptations introduce pleasure, others sadness and

still others bodily pleasures, to humans. For it is in accordance with the indwelling cause of passions in the soul that the physician of souls prescribes medicine, according to his own judgements.

45. Attacks of temptations come to some for the removal of sins already committed, to others for the removal of sins now being committed, and to still others for the avoidance of sins yet to be committed. Different again are those that come to test you, as in the case of Job.

46. Someone sensible, considering the healing art of divine judgements, bears with thanksgiving the misfortunes which befall him through these judgements, and reckons no other cause for them than his own sins. On the other hand, a fool, ignorant of God's supremely wise providence, when he sins and is disciplined reckons that either God or other people are the source of his sufferings.

47. Some things stop the passions and do not permit them to increase; others diminish them and make them decrease. For example, fasting, labour and vigil do not let the desiring faculty grow. Flight from the world, contemplation, prayer and love for God actually lessen desire and make it disappear. And the same with the irascible faculty: for example, patience, forgetting wrongs, and meekness stop it and do not let it grow, while love, almsgiving, kindness and service to others make it diminish.

48. In someone whose intellect is always with God, the desiring faculty increases to overflowing with divine *eros* and the irascible faculty is wholly changed into divine love. For by prolonged participation in divine illumination the intellect has become entirely radiant, and its passible part bound to itself, and it has turned to an incalculable divine *eros*, as has been said, and unceasing love, wholly transported from earthly things to the divine.

49. If you have neither envy, nor anger, nor resentment for someone who has grieved you, it does not mean that you already possess love for him. For while you can, without yet loving someone, *not return evil for evil*, according to the commandment [Rom. 12:17], you certainly cannot return good for evil spontaneously. For to be disposed to do good to those who hate you only comes from spiritual, perfect love.

50. If you do not love another, you do not always hate him, or again, if you do not hate, you do not always already love him. For one can be, as it were, in between about someone, neither loving nor hating them. For there are only five ways of forming a loving disposition, which are given in the ninth chapter of this century, whether praiseworthy, or blameworthy or in between.

51. When you notice that your intellect is easily engrossed in material things and fond of dwelling among concepts of them, then know that you love these things instead of God. *For where your treasure is*, says the Lord, *there will your heart be also* [Matt. 6:21].

52. An intellect that has been joined to God and spends time with him through prayer and love becomes wise, good, powerful, philanthropic, merciful and patient. In a word, it bears within itself nearly all the divine qualities. However, if it departs from this state and cleaves to material things, then either it becomes bestial, from its fondness for pleasure, or it becomes savage, from fighting with others over material goods.

53. The Scripture calls material things *the world* and it calls *worldlings* those whose intellect is engrossed with them. To these people Scripture says to their shame: *Do not love the world or the things in the world: the desire of the flesh, the desire of the eyes, and the pride of life are not from God, but from the world*, etc. [1 John 2:15–16].

54. A monk is one who has separated his intellect from material things and, through self-control, love, psalmody and prayer, cleaves to God.

55. Someone practising the virtues is spiritually a *keeper of cattle*: for cattle signify moral achievements. Therefore, Jacob says, *Your children are keepers of cattle* [Gen. 46:34]. But one engaged in knowledge is a *shepherd of sheep*. For trains of thoughts are designated by sheep, being shepherded by the intellect upon the mountains of contemplation. For this reason Jacob also said, *Every shepherd of sheep is an abomination to*

the Egyptians [Gen. 46:34] – by which he meant the powers opposed to us.

56. A vitiated intellect, when the body is roused by the senses to its own desires and pleasures, follows and assents to the imaginings and impulses of this arousal. But a virtuous intellect controls and keeps itself from impassioned imaginings and impulses, and instead, like a good philosopher, considers how to make such movements better.

57. Of the virtues, some pertain to the body, others to the soul. The body's virtues are, for example, fasting, vigil, sleeping on the ground, service to others, doing handiwork so as not to burden another or to give to others, and the like. The soul's virtues are such as love, patience, meekness, self-control [Gal. 5:22–3], prayer, and the like. So then, if it happens, because of some constraint or bodily crisis – whether sickness or something similar – that we cannot accomplish the bodily virtues, just mentioned, we will be pardoned by the one who has seen the reasons. But, if we do not accomplish the soul's virtues, we have no defence, for these are not subject to necessity.

58. Love for God persuades one who shares in it to disregard every passing pleasure, every toil and every grief. Let all the Saints persuade you of the truth of this, those who have suffered such things with joy for Christ's sake.

59. Guard yourself from the mother of evils, self-love, which is an irrational affection for the body. For from self-love are born, on specious pretexts, the first three most generic impassioned trains of thought – I mean the thoughts of gluttony, avarice and vainglory, which find their occasion, I think, in the necessary needs of the body. From these three is born the whole catalogue of evils. We must, as has been said, necessarily guard ourselves and fight against self-love with much vigilance. For when self-love has been taken away, then with it all evils are taken away too.

60. The passion of self-love suggests to the monk that he should have mercy on his body and indulge it with unnecessary foods, for the sake of caring for it and guiding it, so that, dragged little by little, he will fall into the pit of the love of pleasure. To a worldling, however, self-love prompts him to care for himself by slaking his desires here and now.

61. They say that the highest state of prayer is this: that the intellect find itself outside both flesh and world, and entirely immaterial and formless during prayer. One, therefore, who maintains this state unblemished truly *prays without ceasing* [1 Thess. 5:17].

62. Just as, when the body dies, it is separated from all things of this world, so also the intellect that dies while in the highest state of prayer is separated from all concepts of the world. For unless it dies such a death as this it cannot live and be found with God.

63. Let no one deceive you, monk, that you will be saved while enslaved to even one pleasure or any vainglory.

64. The body sins through things and has bodily virtues for its education, that it may become temperate. In the same way the intellect sins through impassioned concepts and has its corresponding virtues of the soul for its education, so that it too may be temperate as it beholds things purely and dispassionately.

65. Just as night follows day and winter follows summer, so grief and pain follow vainglory and pleasure, either in this present age or in the age to come.

66. It is not possible for a sinner to flee the judgement to come [Luke 3:7] without voluntary toils now, or unchosen afflictions.

67. They say that we are allowed by God to be attacked by the demons for five reasons. First, they say, that by being attacked and fighting back, we come to the discernment of virtue from vice. Secondly, that acquiring virtue by struggle and toil, we have it as a sure and enduring possession. Thirdly, so that, as we make progress towards virtue, we do not become high-minded, but, rather, learn to be humble. Fourthly, that, having been tested by vice, we hate it with perfect hatred. And fifthly, above all the foregoing, so that, when we attain dispassion, we do not forget our own weakness and the power of the one who helped us.

68. The intellect of one who is starving imagines bread, and one dying of thirst, water. In the same way, too, a glutton's intellect imagines different kinds of foods; one who loves pleasure, the shapes of women; the vainglorious, human honour; the avaricious, profit; the resentful, vengeance against the one who grieved him; the envious, misfortune for the one envied, and so for the rest of the passions. For the intellect troubled by the passions entertains impassioned concepts, both when the body is awake and during sleep.

69. When our desiring faculty swells, the intellect conjures up in dreams the materials that make for pleasures. But when our irascible faculty surges, the intellect sees things that terrify it. And so the impure demons amplify the passions, taking as their partner our own carelessness and stirring up the passions. But the holy angels diminish the passions, moving us instead towards practice of the virtues.

70. When the desiring faculty of our soul is frequently roused, it introduces to our soul a habit of pleasure-loving which is hard to break. But when our irascible faculty is continuously provoked, it renders the intellect cowardly and feeble. The desiring faculty is healed by a discipline consisting of fasting, vigil and prayer; the irascible by kindness, care for others, love and mercy.

71. The demons make war on us either through things or through impassioned concepts of things: through things with those who are occupied by things, through concepts with those who are detached from things.

72. As much as it is easier to sin in thought than in deed, so much more pressing is the warfare that comes through concepts of things than through things themselves.

73. Though things themselves are outside the intellect, concepts of things are fashioned within it. It lies with the intellect whether it uses these concepts well or badly, for the abuse of things follows upon the mistaken use of their concepts.

74. Our intellect receives impassioned concepts in three ways: through sense-perception, through temperament and through memory: through sense-perception when things presented to it, to which it is already passionately attached, move the intellect to impassioned trains of thought; through the temperament, when through undisciplined diet, or demonic activity, or some sickness the body's temperament is changed, and it moves the intellect, again, to impassioned trains of thought or thoughts

contrary to providence; through memory, when our memory calls up the concepts of things to which we had once been attached, and it then moves the intellect likewise to impassioned trains of thought.

75. Among things given us by God for our use, some are found in the soul, others in the body, and yet others concern the body. Those in the soul include, for example, its faculties; those in the body the organs of sense and other members; those that concern the body include foods, goods, possessions and the rest. How we use these things, whether well or badly, and the things that depend on them, manifests us as either virtuous or bad.

76. As to what depends on things, some are in the soul, some in the body, and some things that concern the body: in the soul, knowledge and ignorance, forgetfulness and memory, love and hate, fear and courage, sadness and joy, and the rest; in the body, pleasure and pain, feeling and numbness, health and disease, life and death, and such like; concerning the body, the blessing of children and childlessness, wealth and poverty, glory and disgrace, and the rest. Some of these are commonly reckoned as good and some bad, but none of them is intrinsically bad. Rather, it is the way they are used that determines whether they are actually bad or good.

77. Knowledge is good by nature, so is health; but many have profited from their opposites more than from these themselves. For knowledge may not be good for those who are bad, even if, as has been said, it is by nature good. Similarly with health, wealth or joy, for they may not use them appropriately. Instead, their opposites may be more use to such people. For none of these is bad in itself, even though it may seem to be bad.

78. Do not abuse concepts of things, lest you find yourself forced to abuse the things themselves. For unless someone sins first in thought, he will never sin in action.

79. The principal vices exist as an *image of the earthly* – such as folly, cowardice, intemperance, injustice. The principal virtues, on the other hand, are an *image of the heavenly* – such as moral wisdom, courage, moderation, justice. But *just as we bore the image of the earthly, so we shall also bear the image of the heavenly* [1 Cor. 15:49].

80. If you wish to find *the way that leads to life* [Matt. 7:14], seek it in the Way who said, *I am the way, and truth and life* [John 14:6], and there you will find it. But seek it with exceeding diligence, for *there are few who find it* [Matt. 7:14], and maybe you, having been left out of the few, will find yourself among the *many* [Matt. 7:13].

81. The soul is restrained from sinning in these five ways: through fear of what people will think, through fear of judgement, through future reward, through love of God or, finally, because its conscience strikes it.

82. Some say that there would be no evil among beings unless there was some other power drawing us towards it. But this power is none other than the neglect of the natural activities of the intellect. Therefore, those who attend to these activities always do good things and never bad ones. If, therefore, you want to, put away neglect and drive off wickedness – which is, after all, the mistaken use of concepts upon which follows the abuse of things

83. It is natural for our rational part to submit to the divine word and to govern our irrational part. Let this order be guarded in all things and neither will there be evil among beings, nor will there be found anything drawing us towards evil.

84. Some thoughts are simple, others compound. Simple thoughts are without passion; compound ones are impassioned, since they are made up of a passion and a concept. Since things are thus, it is possible to see many simple thoughts follow in the train of compound ones, when they start to be moved to sinning in thought. For example – gold. An impassioned train of thought about gold arose in someone's memory and urged him mentally to theft and he committed the sin in his intellect. Then the memory of gold is joined by the memory of a purse, a money box, a bed chamber and the rest. So the memory of gold was compound, for it had passion. But the memories of the purse, the money box and the rest were simple, for the intellect had no passion for them. And it is the same with every train of thought, whether of vainglory, or a woman, or whatever else. For not all thoughts that follow after an impassioned one are themselves impassioned, as this example has shown.

From these examples we can know what sort of concepts are impassioned and what simple.

85. Some say that the demons touch the genitals during dreams and arouse the passion of fornication. Then the passion, being moved, calls up the shape of a woman from the memory into the intellect. Others say that the demons present themselves to the intellect in the shape of a woman and then, touching the genitals, stir up desire and so sexual fantasies come about. Still others say that the passion that predominates in the approaching demon stirs up the same passion and so the soul is set on flame with thoughts that call up their shapes by means of the memory. Likewise for other impassioned imaginings, some say that it happens in one way, and some in another. Nevertheless, if love and self-control are present to the soul, the demons have no strength to rouse any passion at all by any of the methods discussed, whether the body is awake, or during dreams.

86. Some commandments of the Law must be kept both bodily and spiritually, others only spiritually. *Do not commit adultery, do not murder, do not lie*, and suchlike [Exod. 20: 13–15], such commandments we must keep both bodily and spiritually, and spiritually in a threefold way. But circumcision [Gen. 17:12], keeping the Sabbath [Exod. 20:10], sacrificing lambs [Exod. 12:5], eating *unleavened bread with bitter herbs* [Exod. 12:8] and suchlike: these commandments we only keep spiritually.

87. Among monks there are three general moral states: the first is not to sin in action; the second, not to let impassioned thoughts linger in the soul; the third, to behold dispassionately with the mind the shapes of women and those who have grieved us.

88. Someone without possessions has renounced everything belonging to him and possesses absolutely nothing on earth apart from the body, and if he breaks his attachment even to this, he has entrusted the care of his life to God and the devout.

89. Among those with possessions, some possess dispassionately and, when deprived of them, are not grieved, but are like

those who *cheerfully accept the plundering of their possessions* [Heb. 10:34]. Others possess with passion and, at the prospect of being deprived, are deeply grieved, like the rich young ruler in the Gospel who *went away grieving* [Matt. 19:22]. If they are actually deprived, they are like to die of grief. Deprivation, then, demonstrates the disposition of both the dispassionate and the impassioned.

90. The demons wage war on those who pray perfectly, so that they may not preserve their concepts of things perceived by sense simple. They attack those with knowledge so that impassioned thoughts may linger in them. And they attack those engaged in ascetic struggle so as to persuade them to sin in action. But the demons struggle against all in every way possible, so that – sorry wretches that they are! – they might separate humans from God.

91. Those who by divine providence exercise themselves in this life for the sake of piety are tested by means of three temptations: through the gift of pleasant things, like health, beauty, the blessing of children, goods, glory and the like; through bearing with grievous affliction, such as the loss of children, goods and glory; through things that cause pain to the body, such as diseases and tortures, etc. To the first group the Lord says, *If anyone does not renounce all his possessions, he cannot be my disciple* [Luke 14:33]; to the second and third, he says, *By your endurance you will gain your souls* [Luke 21:19].

92. They say there are four things that alter the body's temperament and give the intellect thoughts either impassioned or dispassionate: angels, demons, the weather and diet. They say, too, that the angels alter the temperament by a word; the demons, by touch; the weather, by the way it changes; and diet, by the quality of food and drink, and when it is too much or too little. Not to mention alterations which happen to it through memory, hearing and sight, since the soul is primarily affected by the griefs and joys that come to it by these means. Suffering in these ways as well, the soul brings about changes in the body's temperament, which, being altered in this way, furnishes the intellect with trains of thought.

93. Death is, properly speaking, separation from God, for *the sting of death is sin* [1 Cor. 15:56]. Adam, receiving the sting, found himself at once excluded from the tree of life and paradise and from God [Gen. 3:22–4], and upon this there followed, of necessity, the death of the body. Life, properly speaking, is the One who says, *I am life* [John 14:6]: this One, entering into death, again led the one who was dead back to life.

94. A treatise is put together either to aid its author's memory or for the benefit of others, or both; or to harm others, to prove something, or out of necessity.

95. *A place of green pasture* refers to practical virtue; *water of refreshment* to the knowledge of what has come into being [Ps. 22:2].

96. *The shadow of death* is human life. If, then, someone is with God and God is with him, such a one can say clearly, *Though I walk in the midst of the shadow of death, I will fear no evil, for you are with me* [Ps. 22:4].

97. A pure intellect sees things correctly; trained reason brings what is seen to clarity; keen hearing grasps what is heard. But one deprived of all three thinks evil of the one who speaks.

98. One who knows the Holy Trinity and its work in creation and providence, who also possesses serenity in the passible part of his soul: such a one is with God.

99. The *rod* is said to signify the judgement of God; the *staff* his providence. One who has participated in true knowledge of both can say, *Your rod and your staff, they comfort me* [Ps. 22:4].

100. When the intellect has been stripped of passions and made radiant by the contemplation of beings, then it is able to come to be in God, and to pray as it ought.

Third century

1. The reasonable use of concepts and of things is productive of moderation, love and knowledge. Their irrational use, however, is productive of intemperance, hatred and ignorance.

2. *You have prepared a table before me*, etc. [Ps. 22.5–6]. The *table* here signifies practical virtue, for this has been prepared by Christ for us *in the presence of those who afflict us*. The *oil* signifies anointing the mind – that is, the contemplation of what has come into being. The *cup* of God signifies knowledge of God, and his *mercy* the Word of God and God. For the Word, through his incarnation, pursues us *all our days*, until he gathers in all those who will be saved, as Paul affirms [Phil. 3:12]. The *house* signifies the kingdom in which all the Saints are established; and *length of days* eternal life.

3. Vices of the soul's faculties come about through misuse of either the desiring, the irascible, or the rational faculty. Misuse of the rational entails ignorance and folly; of the irascible and desiring hatred and intemperance. The right use of these leads the rational to knowledge and sagacity; the others to love and temperance. If this is so, then none of those things created by God and brought into being is evil.

4. Foods are not evil, but gluttony is. Procreation is not evil, but fornication is. Nor are possessions evil, but avarice is; nor glory, but vainglory is. If this is so, then there is nothing evil among what exists, save their misuse – which comes about from the intellect's neglect in cultivating its natural powers.

5. The blessed Dionysios says that what is evil in the demons is: irrational anger, mindless desire and unconsidered imagining.[4] But irrationality, mindlessness and rashness are, for rational beings, effectively deprivations of reason, mind and consideration. Deprivations, however, come second to states, so at one point reason, mind and pious consideration existed in the demons. If so, then not even the demons are evil by nature. Rather, they became evil from the misuse of their natural faculties.

6. Some passions cause intemperance; some hatred; and some both intemperance and hatred.

7. Overeating and indulgent eating are the causes of intemperance; avarice and vainglory the causes of hatred for one's neighbour. But the mother of these passions, self-love, is the cause of both intemperance and hatred.

8. Self-love is an impassioned and irrational affection for the

body, opposed to which are love and self-control. One who has self-love has all the passions.

9. *No one*, says the Apostle, *hated his own flesh* [Eph. 5:29], *but* manifestly he *maltreats it and leads it captive* [1 Cor. 9:27], offering it no more than *nutrition and clothing* [1 Tim. 6:8] – and of these, even, only what are necessary for life. In this way, then, someone can love his flesh dispassionately as a servant of divine things and *nourish and comfort it* [Eph. 5:29] with only what it needs.

10. Whomever a person loves he is always keen to serve. If, therefore, someone loves God, he is always eager to please him. If he loves his flesh, he hastens to gratify it.

11. Things pleasing to God: are love, temperance, contemplation and prayer; to the flesh: gluttony, intemperance, and whatever increases them. For this reason, *Those who are in the flesh cannot please God* [Rom. 8:8]; *but those who belong to Christ have crucified the flesh with its passions and desires* [Gal. 5:24].

12. If the intellect inclines to God, it holds the body as a slave and provides it with nothing more than is necessary for life. But if the intellect inclines to the flesh, it is enslaved to the passions, and always takes care to fulfil its desires.

13. If you wish to prevail over your thoughts, take great care over the passions and you will easily drive them from the intellect. So with lust, take care to fast, keep vigil, labour and be alone; with wrath and grief, despise glory, dishonour and material things; with resentment, pray for the one who grieved you and you will be delivered.

14. Do not measure yourself by weaker people, but, rather, strive to fulfil the command of love. For when you measure yourself by those who are weaker, you fall into the pit of self-conceit. But when you strive to fulfil the command, you make progress towards the summit of humble-mindedness.

15. If you are on your guard completely to fulfil the command to love your neighbour [Matt. 22:39], how could you ever be grieved with him or feel bitterness towards him? Otherwise, clearly you fight against your brother, preferring what is transient to love and clinging to it?

16. Human envy of gold is not so much because of need as because through it many cultivate pleasures.

17. There are three causes of love for things: love of pleasure, vainglory and lack of faith. Lack of faith is more dangerous than the others.

18. The lover of pleasure loves money to find delight; one who is vainglorious loves it to be honoured. But one without faith loves it in order to hide and conceal it, fearing famine or old age, sickness or exile, putting his hope rather in money than in God who fashions and provides for the whole creation, even the least and smallest of living things.

19. There are four types of people who acquire things: the three just mentioned, and the one who acts as steward. Clearly, only this last acquires things rightly, so that he may never fail anyone in need.

20. All impassioned thoughts either arouse the soul's desiring faculty, stir up its irascible faculty or darken its rational faculty. From this it happens that the intellect grows blind to spiritual contemplation and the flight of prayer. Because of this, the monk – and especially the one practising stillness – must pay careful attention to his thoughts and come to know their causes and cut them off. What is meant by such knowing is this: for example, the impassioned memories of women arouse the soul's desiring faculty; the causes of these memories are intemperance in food and drink, and frequent and senseless converse with women: they are cut off by hunger, thirst, vigil and withdrawal from others. Again, impassioned memories of those who have grieved us stir up the irascible faculty: they are caused by love of pleasure, vainglory and love of material things – because of them an impassioned man is grieved, either as if deprived of something, or failing to attain something. But disdain and contempt suffered for the love of God cut off these causes.

21. God knows himself, and he knows what he has brought into being. The holy powers know God, and they know, too, what God has brought into being. But the holy powers do not know God and what he has brought into being as God knows himself and what he has brought into being.

22. God knows himself from his own blessed essence; but what he has brought into being, he knows by his own wisdom, through which and in which he made all things [Prov. 3:19]. The holy powers, however, know by participation God who is beyond participation, and they know the things that have come to be by coming to know spiritual contemplations of what is in those things.

23. Although the intellect receives within itself contemplation of things that have come to be, they are in fact outside the intellect. This is not so with God the eternal, the boundless, the infinite, who grants to beings their being, well-being, and eternal being.

24. Beings endowed with reason and intellect participate in the holy God by their very being and by their capacity for well-being – I mean their goodness and wisdom – and by the grace that grants them eternal being. In this way, they know God. But what God has brought into being, they know by acquisition, as has been said, of a fashioning wisdom contemplated in what has come to be – which subsists in the intellect in a simple and impersonal form.

25. There are four divine properties, which hold together, guard and preserve beings, and which God has made common to all through his supreme goodness, as he leads each rational and intellectual essence into being – being, eternal being, goodness and wisdom. Of these God presented two to the essence itself and two to the deliberative capacity. To the essence he gave being and eternal being; to the deliberative capacity, goodness and wisdom – so that what God is by essence, the creature might become by participation. Because of this, he is said to have come into being *in the image and likeness of God*. On the one hand, humans are then, as being, *in the image* of God's being; as being eternal, images of God's eternal being – save that they are not without beginning, though they are without end. They are *in the likeness* as good, in the likeness of the good God; as wise, of the wise God, so that they are by grace, what God is by nature. Now, every rational nature is *in the image of God*, but only the good and wise are *in the likeness* [Gen. 1:26–7].

26. All essences endowed with reason and intellect are div-ided into two: that is, into the angelic and the human nature. The whole angelic nature is divided again by their settled inten-tions into two groups, holy and cursed: that is, into holy powers and impure demons. And the whole human nature is divided into two intentions only: I mean, the pious and the impious.

27. God, as existence itself, goodness itself and wisdom itself – or, rather, to speak more accurately, beyond all these qualities – has absolutely no quality contrary to these. But crea-tures, who all have their existence by participation and grace, and, as endowed with reason and intellect, a capacity for good-ness and wisdom too – also have their contraries: contrary to existence, non-existence; contrary to the capacity for good-ness and wisdom, evil and ignorance. Whether creatures exist always or not is in the power of their Maker; whether rational beings participate in God's goodness and wisdom lies in their own will.

28. The Greeks who say that the essence of beings co-exists with God from eternity and that they only derive their qualities from him, say then that there is nothing contrary to essence, and that it is only in qualities that there is any contra-riety. But we say that it is only the divine essence that has no contrary, since it is eternal, unbounded, and bestows eternity on other beings; and that non-being is contrary to the essence of beings, and that whether beings exist eternally or not lies in the power of the one who alone exists, properly speak-ing [Exod. 3:14 LXX]. But God's *gifts are irrevocable* [Rom. 11:29], therefore they are and will be eternally, sustained by God's almighty power, even if they have, as has been said, non-being as a contrary, since they have been brought by God from non-being into being and whether they exist or not lies in God's will.

29. Just as evil is privation of good, and ignorance is priva-tion of knowledge, so also non-being is privation of being – not of being, properly speaking, since that has no contrary – but of being by participation in what is properly being. The privation of good and knowledge follows from the inclination of those beings that have come to be. But the privation of being lies

in the will of the Maker, in his goodness, who always wants beings to exist, and always shows kindness to them.

30. Everything that has come to be is either rational, intellectual and receptive of their contraries – such as virtue and vice or knowledge and ignorance – or they are composite bodies consisting of contraries, that is, earth, air, fire and water. The former are in every way bodiless and immaterial, even if some of them have been joined to bodies. The latter have only come into being from matter and form.

31. All bodies by nature lack the capacity for motion. They are moved by the soul, whether by a rational soul, or by an irrational soul, or by a soul without sense or feeling.

32. Of the soul's faculties, one is concerned with nourishment and growth; one with imagination and impulse; and one is rational and intellectual. Plants partake of the first alone; irrational animals of the second and the first; and humans of all three. While the first two faculties are corruptible, the third is manifest as incorruptible and immortal.

33. While the holy powers share illumination among themselves, they also share with human nature their virtue or the knowledge that they possess in themselves. In the case of virtue, this is the goodness that imitates God, in accordance with which they bestow blessings on themselves, each other and their inferiors, thus making them God-like. In the case of knowledge, they share either loftier ideas of God – for *You*, it is said, *are most high forever, Lord* [Ps. 91:9] – or deeper understanding of bodies, something more precise concerning bodiless beings, something clearer concerning providence, or something more distinct concerning judgement.

34. The first impurity of intellect is to possess false knowledge; the second is to be ignorant of some universal – I am speaking with regard to a human intellect; for it belongs to the angelic not to be ignorant even of any particular – the third is to have impassioned thoughts; and the fourth is to give assent to sin.

35. Impurity of soul is to fail to act in accordance with nature, for, from this are impassioned thoughts born in the intellect. For, when the soul operates naturally, then its passible

faculties – I mean the irascible and appetitive – remain dispassionate before the assault of things and concepts bound up
with them.

36. Impurity of the body is sin in action.

37. One unaffected by the things of the world loves stillness;
one who loves nothing merely human loves all human beings;
and one who is not scandalized with another either because of
his transgressions or by thoughts born of suspicion possesses
knowledge of God and things divine.

38. It is a great thing not to be attached to things. Far greater
than this is to remain unmoved before conceptions of these
things.

39. Love and self-control preserve the mind dispassionate
towards both things and concepts of them.

40. The intellect of one who loves God does not wage war
against things or even against concepts of them, but against the
passions that are linked to those concepts. For example, his
intellect does not wage war against a woman or someone who
grieves him or even against his imaginings of these, but against
the passions bound up with those imaginings.

41. The whole struggle of the monk is against the demons,
that he may separate the passions from concepts. For otherwise
it is impossible to behold things dispassionately.

42. There are things, and concepts and passions, all different. A thing may be a man, woman, gold or something else. A
concept is, for example, the bare memory of one or another of
these. But a passion is, for example, an irrational affection or
confused hatred for one of them. The monk's battle, therefore,
is with passion.

43. An impassioned concept is a thought composed of passion and concept. Let us separate the passion from the concept,
and a mere thought will remain. And, if we wish, we make the
separation through spiritual love and self-control.

44. The virtues separate the intellect from the passions; spiritual contemplations separate it even from mere concepts. But
pure prayer sets the intellect before God himself.

45. Virtues are for the sake of knowledge of things that have
come to be; knowledge for the sake of the knower; the knower

for the sake of the one who is known unknowably and who knows beyond knowledge.

46. It is not as if it was because he needed anything that God – who is more than overflowing – brought what has come to be into being, but that these beings, participating in him by analogy, might know enjoyment, and that he might *rejoice in his works* [Ps. 103:31], as he sees them rejoicing and forever taking their fill without feeling full of the one whose being is inexhaustible.

47. The world has many who are *poor in spirit*, but not in the proper way. It has many who *mourn*, but for damage to their possessions or loss of their children. It has many *meek*, but meek only to the impure passions. It has many who *hunger and thirst*, but only to seize others' goods and profit from injustice. It has many who are *merciful*, but only to their body and bodily things. And it has those *pure in heart*, but for vainglory; *peacemakers*, but who subject soul to body. It has many who are *persecuted*, for being disorderly. It has many who are *reviled*, for their shameful sins. But *blessed* are only those few who do and suffer these things for Christ and in accordance with Christ. Why? *For theirs is the Kingdom of Heaven* and *they shall see God*, etc. So it is not because they do and suffer these things that they are *blessed*, for those already mentioned do the same. Rather, it is because they do and suffer these things for Christ and in accordance with Christ [Matt. 5:3–11].

48. In everything we do, as has often been said, God scrutinizes our purpose, whether we are acting for his sake or for some other reason. If, then, we are to do something good, let us make sure our intention is not to please people, but God, so that, always looking to him, we do everything for his sake, lest we endure the toil but miss the reward.

49. Cast out of your intellect during the time of prayer both the mere conceiving of human affairs and any notion of anything that has come to be, lest, imagining lesser things, you fall away from the one who is incomparably greater than all beings.

50. If we genuinely love God, let us cast off the passions through this very love. And love for God means preferring him to the world, and the soul to the flesh. It consists in despising worldly things and always devoting ourselves to God through self-control, love, prayer, psalmody and the rest.

51. If, devoting ourselves to God for a long time, we carefully manage the passible part of our soul, then we shall no longer drift into being assaulted by thoughts. But also, by careful scrutiny of the causes of these assaults and by cutting them off, we become more clear-sighted, so that the saying is fulfilled in us: *And my eye looked down among my enemies, and my ear will hear among those who rise up against me and plot evil* [Ps. 91:12].

52. When you see your intellect engaging piously and righteously with worldly concepts, know, too, that your body remains pure and sinless. But when you see your intellect lingering among sins to consider them and not cutting them off, know also that your body will not delay long in falling in with them.

53. Just as things constitute the body's world, so concepts form the world of the intellect. And just as the body fornicates with a woman's body, so the intellect fornicates with its image of that woman through imagining its own body. For the intellect sees in thought the form of its own body in intercourse with the woman's form. In the same way, in thought it exacts vengeance on the form of someone who grieved it through the form of its own body. The same holds true for the other sins too. Thus, the very things which the body does actively in the world of things, the intellect does in the world of concepts.

54. There is no reason for us to tremble, panic and be astonished at the thought that our God and Father *judges no one but has given all judgement to the Son* [John 5:22]. Now the Son commands, *Judge not, lest you be judged; condemn not, lest you be condemned* [Matt. 7:1, Luke 6:37]. And the Apostle says likewise, *Judge no one before the Lord comes* [1 Cor. 4:5] and *By the judgement with which you judge another, you condemn yourself* [Rom. 2:1]. Those who have forgone weeping for their own sins have taken judgement from the Son and, as if they were sinless, judge and condemn one another. *Heaven was*

astonished at this, and the earth *trembled* [Jer. 2:12], but such people, now insensible, are not ashamed of themselves.

55. One who busies himself with the sins of others, or judges his brother out of suspicion, has neither yet made a beginning of repentance, nor begun to search out and know his own sins – which are, in truth, weightier than many talents of lead. Nor does he know how it comes about that someone is heavy of heart, loving vanity and seeking for lies. Because of this he wanders about like a fool in darkness: passing over his own sins, he imagines those of others, either real or conjured up from suspicion.

56. Self-love, as has been said many times already, constitutes the cause of all impassioned trains of thought. For from it are born the three most general thoughts of desire: gluttony, avarice and vainglory. Now, from gluttony is born the thought of lust; from greed the thought of wanting more; and from vainglory the thought of pride. All the remaining thoughts follow one or other of these three: that is, thoughts of wrath, grief, resentment, despondency, envy, slander and the rest. These passions, then, chain the intellect to material things and drag it down to the earth, placed on it like a terribly heavy stone, though it is by nature more limpid and acute than fire.

57. The beginning of all the passions is self-love, and their end, pride. Self-love is irrational affection for the body. To cut this off is to cut off with it all the passions which spring from it.

58. Just as bodily parents are attached to the children they have begotten, so also the intellect is naturally disposed to its own reasons. And just as children, even if they are ridiculous in every way, seem to their indulgent parents to be the most sensible and lovely of all, so too, to the witless intellect, its own thoughts, even if they are quite unsound, seem to be more intelligent than most. The wise man does not regard his own thoughts like this. When he seems most convinced that they are true and good, then most of all he does not trust his own judgement, but makes other wise men judges of his own thoughts, lest he be *running or have run in vain* [Gal. 2:2]; and from them it gets assurance.

59. When you conquer one of the dishonourable passions,

such as gluttony, lust, anger or wanting more, straight away the thought of vainglory will alight upon you. And if you conquer this, the thought of pride will follow.

60. All the dishonourable passions which master our soul drive the thought of vainglory far from it. And when all the aforementioned passions are bested, they release this thought upon it.

61. Vainglory, whether done away with or remaining, gives birth to pride; if done away with, it introduces self-conceit; if remaining, arrogance.

62. The hidden exercise of virtue does away with vainglory; ascribing our achievements to God does away with pride.

63. One counted worthy of the knowledge of God and the abundant enjoyment of the pleasure that comes from this despises all pleasures that arise from the desiring faculty.

64. One who desires earthly things desires food, or things that nurture his sexual urges, or human glory, or goods, or something else associated with these. Unless his intellect finds something better than these, to which to transfer his desire, he will never be persuaded finally to despise them. The knowledge of God and of divine things is incomparably better than these earthly things.

65. Those who despise pleasures do so either from fear, or hope, or out of knowledge and love for God.

66. Knowing things divine without feeling does not ultimately persuade the intellect to despise what is material, but is, rather, like a mere thought of something perceived by sense. So there are to be found many who have a good deal of knowledge and yet wallow in fleshly passions like pigs in mud. Those who purify themselves with great care for a little while and acquire knowledge, but later grow careless, are like Saul: who, having been counted worthy to reign, but having ruled unworthily, was cast down from his kingship with fearful wrath [1Kgds. 15–31].

67. Just as a mere thought of things human does not compel the mind to despise things divine, neither does the mere knowledge of divine things finally persuade the mind to despise things human, for truth now dwells in shadows and conjectures. For this reason there is need of the blessed passion of

holy love, which binds the intellect to spiritual contemplations and persuades it to prefer the immaterial to the material, and spiritual things perceived by the intellect to those perceived by the senses.

68. Not everyone who has cut off the passions and occupied himself with mere thoughts has already turned to things divine themselves, for it is possible to have no feeling either for things human or for things divine, which indeed is what happens to those occupied with practical virtue alone and have not yet been counted worthy of knowledge, who abstain from passions either through fear of punishment or through hope of the Kingdom.

69. *We walk by faith, not by sight* [2 Cor. 5:7] and have knowledge in *mirrors* and *riddles* [1 Cor. 13:12]. Therefore, we need much diligence in these matters, that by long meditation on them and study we may form a habit of contemplation from which it is hard to be dragged away.

70. If we cut off the causes of passions for a little while, and come to occupy ourselves with spiritual contemplations, then, unless we devote all our time to this work of contemplation, we shall easily be turned back again to the passions of the flesh, and gain nothing from our effort except mere knowledge together with self-conceit. The result will be little by little the darkening of this knowledge itself and a complete turning away of our intellect to material things.

71. A blameworthy passion of love engages our mind in material matters. But a praiseworthy passion of love binds it to things divine. For the intellect is accustomed to develop and expand among those things in which it spends time. And where the intellect develops, among those things it directs its desire and love, whether among divine and intellectual things, where it belongs, or among matters of the flesh and its passions.

72. God created the invisible world and the visible one, and clearly he made the soul and the body. And if the visible world is so beautiful, how much more the invisible one? And if the invisible is finer than the visible, how much greater than both must be God who made them? If, then, the Fashioner of everything beautiful is greater than everything that has come into being, what possible reason could the intellect have for abandoning the one greater than all and becoming engrossed instead in things worse than all – I mean, the passions of the flesh? Or is it not obvious that, being associated with and accustomed to this flesh from birth, the intellect has not yet acquired perfect experience of the One greater than all and above all? If, therefore, by prolonged discipline in self-control of the pleasures and in meditation on things divine, we tear our intellect little by little away from such association, then it will develop and expand among things divine, advancing gradually, and come to recognize its own proper value, and, finally, it transfers its whole yearning to the divine.

73. One who speaks dispassionately of his brother's sin does so for one of two reasons: either to correct his brother, or to benefit someone else. If he speaks, either to himself or to another, for some other reason, then it is either to rebuke or to ridicule, and he will certainly not escape being abandoned by God. Rather, he will always fall into one sin or another and, accused and reproached by others, he will be put to shame.

74. There is no one reason why people commit the same sin; rather, there are several. For example, it is one thing to sin out of habit and another to sin on an impulse. In the latter case, he has no conception of it either before or after the sin, and feels terrible as soon as it has happened. But it is the opposite with the one who sins out of habit: beforehand, he had not ceased from sinning in thought, and after the deed he remains in the same disposition.

75. One who seeks out the virtues for the sake of vainglory is clearly going to seek out knowledge for the same reason. But clearly such a person neither does anything nor discusses it in order to edify, but, rather, is always fishing for glory from those who see or hear him. But his passion convicts him whenever some of these aforementioned bystanders blame him on account of his words or deeds. For he is exceedingly grieved at this, not because they were not edified – for that was never his aim – but because he has been set at naught.

76. The passion of avarice convicts us inwardly, when we find ourselves rejoicing to receive, but sharing with sorrow. Such a person cannot be a steward.

77. Someone endures suffering either for the love of God, or for the hope of reward, or for the fear of punishment, or out of fear of people, or because of nature, pleasure, profit, vainglory or necessity.

78. It is one thing to be delivered from thoughts and another to be freed from passions. Frequently one is free from thoughts, because of the absence of those things to which one is attached. But the passions lurk hidden in the soul and manifest themselves when those things appear. It is necessary, therefore, to guard the intellect from things, and know the kind of things to which we are attached.

79. A true friend is one who, during the time of trial, endures with his neighbour the ensuing afflictions, constraints and misfortunes, unperturbed and untroubled, as if they were his own.

80. Do not dishonour the conscience which always counsels what is best. For it suggests to you divine and angelic advice; it frees you from the hidden pollutions of the heart; and it gives you confidence before God at your death.

81. If you want to be prudent and moderate, and no longer to serve the passion of self-conceit, then always seek out among beings what is hidden from your knowledge. And as you discover the multitude and variety of things which you had no idea existed, marvel at your own ignorance and be unassuming in your thinking! Then, learning to know yourself you will understand many great and marvellous things, for reckoning that you already know prevents you from advancing towards knowledge.

82. One who really wants to be saved is not one to refuse healing treatment. Such treatment consists of the pains and griefs brought on in various misfortunes. One who refuses such treatment knows neither what it accomplishes here nor what he will gain from it when he departs this life.

83. Vainglory and avarice lead one to another. For the vainglorious are rich, and the rich are filled with vainglory – that is, for those living in the world. For the monk, it is possessing nothing that rather leads to vainglory, while one who has money hides it, ashamed of having something incongruous with the monastic habit.

84. It belongs to the vainglory of a monk to be puffed up by his own virtue and what follows from this. It belongs to his pride to be exalted at his own achievements and belittle others, ascribing his achievements to himself and not to God. It belongs to the vainglory and pride of someone in the world to be puffed up and exalted by beauty, wealth, power and arrogance.

85. The achievements of those in the world are failings in monks; and the achievements of monks are failings for those in the world. So, achievements in the world are wealth, reputation, power, luxury, good bodily health, the blessing of children and their consequences. All these would destroy a monk if he obtained them. Monastic achievements are lack of possessions, lack of reputation, lack of power, abstinence, mortification and their consequences. If a lover of the world encountered these unwillingly, he would think it a terrible misfortune and frequently be in danger of hanging himself. Indeed, some have done so.

86. Food was created for two reasons: for nourishment and healing. People, therefore, who eat for other reasons are condemned as gluttons, because they abuse things given by God for our use. Indeed, the misuse of anything is a sin.

87. Humble-mindedness is continual prayer with tears and toils. For this prayer, always calling on God for help, does not let us trust foolishly in our own strength and wisdom or to behave arrogantly towards others. These are grievous diseases of the passion of pride.

88. It is one thing to fight a mere thought, lest it stimulate a passion; and it is another to fight an impassioned thought, to prevent assent. Either way stops thoughts from lingering.

89. Grief is yoked to resentment. When, therefore, our intellect entertains with grief the face of a brother, clearly it harbours resentment towards him. *The ways of those who bear resentment lead to death*, therefore *everyone bearing resentment transgresses the law* [Prov. 12:28, 21:24].

90. If you bear resentment towards anyone, pray for him and you will stop the passion being aroused; through prayer you separate grief from the memory of the wrong he did to you. By becoming loving and kind to him, you make the passion vanish entirely from your soul. If another bears resentment towards you, be generous to him and humble, and associate kindly with him, and you will deliver him from this passion.

91. It is hard to quell the grief of one who envies you, for what he envies in you he regards as his misfortune, and this cannot be quelled, save by hiding it from him. If you are a blessing to many but you grieve just one, which will you ignore? You have to be of service to the many without, so far as possible, failing to care for the one, nor be led astray by the cunning of the passion itself, since you are not defending the passion but the one suffering from it. But in humility you must consider him as surpassing you, and, in every time and place and matter, you must prefer him. As for your own envy, you can quell that, if, in everything that the one you enjoy rejoices, you rejoice together with him, and grieve together with him in everything that grieves him, thus fulfilling what the Apostle says: *to rejoice with those who rejoice and grieve with those who grieve* [Rom. 12:15].

92. Our intellect is in the middle between angel and demon, each of which works in its own way, the one towards virtue, the other towards vice. But the intellect has authority and power to follow or resist, whichever it wills.

93. The holy powers exhort us to good things, while natural seeds and our freedom to choose good help us too. But the passions and our freedom to choose what is wrong are in league with the assaults of the demons.

94. When the intellect is pure, sometimes God himself approaches it and teaches it himself. Sometimes the holy powers, and sometimes the nature of things it contemplates, make good suggestions.

95. It is necessary for the intellect counted worthy of knowledge to keep its concepts of things passion-free, its contemplations unshaken, and its state of prayer untroubled. Nonetheless the intellect cannot always guard them from the exhalations of the flesh, when darkened by the smoke caused by the schemes of demons.

96. It is not simply the things that grieve us that we get angry about. For things that lead to grief are far more numerous than

those that lead to wrath. For example, this thing was broken, that was destroyed, so-and-so died: over such things we only grieve. But other things both grieve us and anger us, for we are in such an unphilosophical state of mind.

97. When the intellect attends to concepts of things, it is naturally assimilated to each concept. When it contemplates them spiritually, it is transformed in various ways in accordance with each object of contemplation. But, once in God, it becomes completely formless and without configuration; for, beholding the one simple of form, it becomes itself simple of form and entirely formed by light.

98. The soul is perfect when its passible faculty is entirely inclined towards God.

99. The intellect is perfect which through true faith has known beyond knowing in ways beyond knowing the One who is beyond knowing; and which has beheld the entirety of what has been fashioned by him; and has received from God the knowledge that comprehends in created things God's providence and judgement – so far as this is possible for human beings.

100. Time is divided threefold and, while faith extends over all three, hope covers only one, and love two. And while faith and hope extend only up to a certain moment, love persists into boundless ages, being united beyond union to the one beyond boundary, and always increasing beyond limit. And therefore *greater than all is love* [1 Cor. 13:13].

Fourth century

1. At first the intellect marvels as it considers the divine infinitude, that boundless and much longed-for ocean. Next, it is astonished at how God brought beings out of their nothingness into existence. But as *there is no limit to his greatness* [Ps. 144:3] neither is there any *searching out of his understanding* [Isa. 40:28].

2. How can he not marvel who contemplates that boundless, that utterly astonishing, sea of goodness? Or how can he not be perplexed, as he considers how and whence there came

to be rational and spiritual substance with the four elements, from which derive all bodies – when no matter whatsoever pre-existed their genesis? What sort of power is that which, moved to action, brought these things into being? But the children of the Hellenes do not accept this, being ignorant of this all-powerful goodness and its active knowledge and wisdom which pass understanding.

3. God (who exists as a creator from all eternity) created when he wished, by his consubstantial Word and Spirit, on account of his boundless goodness. And were you to say: for what reason did he create now, given that he is always good? Then, let me tell you, because the inscrutable wisdom of the boundless being does not fall within the range of human knowledge.

4. The Creator, when he wished, gave being to and brought forth the pre-existent knowledge of beings which he possessed within himself from all eternity. It is absurd to doubt that the almighty God could give being to anything when he wishes.

5. Seek out the reason why God created – for that constitutes knowledge. But do not seek how and why God created only recently – for such knowledge does not fall within the range of your intellect, for with matters divine some are comprehensible to humans, and some not. Unbridled contemplation pushes us over the edge of the abyss, as one of the Saints says.

6. Some say that created things coexist from eternity with God, which is impossible! For how could things that are bounded in every respect coexist from eternity with One who is utterly boundless? And how could they be properly called created if they are co-eternal with their Creator? But this is the account of the Greeks, who maintain that God is a fashioner only of properties and not of being at all. But we who have come to know the almighty God say that he is the fashioner not only of properties, but of beings as well. But if this is so, then created things cannot have been coexistent with God from eternity.

7. The divine and things divine are in one way knowable and in another way unknowable: knowable in the case of concepts about him, unknowable, concerning what he is himself.

8. Do not look for habits and propensities in the simple and boundless being of the Holy Trinity, lest you make it seem composite, like creatures. It is absurd, even blasphemous, to think of God like that.

9. The boundless and almighty being, creative of everything, is alone single, simple, without qualities, at peace and imperturbable. But every creature exists as a composite of being and accident, and ever in need of divine providence since it is not free from change.

10. Every substance, whether perceived by intellect or by senses, brought into being by God, has received powers, which enable it, in turn, to apprehend beings: the intellectual powers, by intellection (concepts), the sensible powers, by sense-perception.

11. God is only participated in, but a creature both participates in and passes something on. Moreover, it participates in both being and well-being, but communicates well-being alone. But differently with a bodily being than with a bodiless being.

12. A bodiless being communicates well-being by speaking, acting and being contemplated, but a bodily being only through being contemplated.

13. Whether a rational and intellectual being exists eternally or not depends on the wish of the Creator who made everything fine. But whether what has come into being is good or bad depends on the free choice of its will.

14. Evil is not to be seen in the being of creatures, but in their erroneous and senseless impulsion.

15. The soul moves rightly when its desiring power is subjected to self-control, its irascible power cleaves to love, rejecting hatred, and its rational power spends time with God through prayer and spiritual contemplation.

16. One who does not yet possess perfect love or any deep knowledge of divine providence, if in time of temptation he does not bear patiently with the miseries that befall him, but rather cuts himself off from the love of his spiritual brothers.

17. The goal of divine providence is to bring about unity through right faith and spiritual love in those who have been torn apart in manifold ways by evil, since this was

why our Saviour suffered *that he might gather into one the scattered children of God* [John 11:52]. Anyone, therefore, who cannot put up with annoyance or bear with miseries or endure his toils has strayed outside divine love and the purpose of providence.

18. If *love is patient and kind* [1 Cor. 13:4], then one who grows discouraged at the miseries which befall him, and for this reason acts wickedly towards those who have grieved him, and cuts himself off from love for them – how has he not alienated himself from the purpose of divine providence?

19. Pay attention to yourself, lest ever the evil that separates you from your brother be found not in him, but in you. And hasten to be reconciled to him, lest you be banished from the commandment of love.

20. Do not despise the commandment of love, for through it you will be a son of God; if you transgress it, you will be found to be a *son of Gehenna* [Matt. 23:15].

21. These are the things that separate us from the love of our friends: envying or being envied, punishing or being punished, dishonouring or being dishonoured, and the thoughts that come from suspicion. May you, then, having never done or suffered any of these, never be separated from the love of your friend.

22. Your brother became a trial to you and grief led you to hatred? Do not be conquered by hatred but conquer it in love. You will conquer it thus: either by praying genuinely to God for him and accepting his apology, or by healing him yourself by apologizing, reckoning yourself the cause of the trial, and bearing it patiently until the cloud passes.

23. A patient person is one who waits for the end of temptation and hopes to boast of having endured.

24. *A long-suffering man* is *great in moral wisdom* [Prov. 14:29], because he bears everything which befalls him until the end, and as he awaits that, he is content with his sufferings. *But the end is eternal life* [Rom. 6:22], according to the divine Apostle, *And this is eternal life, that they know you the only true God and Jesus Christ whom you have sent* [John 17:3].

25. Do not lightly accept the loss of spiritual love, because there is no other way of salvation left for humans.

26. Do not judge a brother as evil and wicked, who yesterday was spiritual and virtuous, simply because today hatred for him has arisen in you on account of the evil one's intrigue. Rather, by considering with long-suffering love what yesterday you reckoned good, cast out today's hatred from your soul.

27. Do not revile today as evil and wicked the brother you yesterday praised as good and spoke of publicly as virtuous, changing from love to hate, making his criticism of you an excuse for your evil hatred, but go on praising him, even though you have been overcome by grief, and you will swiftly regain this saving love.

28. Do not, in conversation with the other brothers, corrupt your customary praise of your brother by secretly mixing criticism in what you say because there still lurks within you a hidden grief towards him. Rather, use unmixed praise in conversation and genuinely pray for him as you would for yourself, and you will quickly be delivered from destructive hatred.

29. Do not say: I do not hate my brother, when all you are doing is turning aside any thought of him from your mind. Rather, listen to Moses, who says, *Do not hate your brother in your thought: but reproach your brother openly and you will not fall into sin on his account* [Lev. 19:17].

30. If by chance a brother, being tempted, persists in slandering you, do not let this deprive you of your state of love, nor allow yourself to be troubled in thought by this same wicked demon. You will not be deprived of this state, if, *when reviled, you bless* [1 Cor. 4:12], you speak well of those who slander you, and you think well of those who plot against you. This is the way of Christ's philosophy, and unless you follow it you will not be his companion.

31. Do not think that those who come with stories that work grief in you and hatred for your brother are well disposed towards you, even if they seem to tell the truth. But turn away from them as from venomous snakes, that you may check their slander and deliver your own soul from evil.

32. Do not irritate your brother with riddling words, lest, if he does the same to you, you drive away from both of you the disposition to love. Instead, go and rebuke him with loving candour, so that, having taken away the causes of grief, you may both be delivered from turmoil and grief.

33. Examine your conscience scrupulously, lest it be your fault that your brother is not reconciled to you. And do not cheat your conscience, for it knows your secrets and will both accuse you at the hour of death and in the time of prayer be a hindrance.

34. Do not, during a time of peace, call to mind what your brother said in a time of grief, whether grievous things spoken to your face or to another about you which you heard of later, lest, suffering from thoughts of resentment, you turn back to destructive hatred of your brother.

35. A rational soul which feeds on hatred for another cannot find peace with God, the giver of the Commandments. *For if*, it says, *you do not forgive people their failures, neither will your heavenly Father forgive you your failures* [Matt. 6:14–15]. So, even if someone does not wish to make peace, you at any rate should guard yourself from hatred, praying genuinely for him and not slandering him to anyone.

36. The indescribable peace of the holy angels has been maintained through these two dispositions: love for God and love for one another. The same is true of all the Saints from the beginning. Therefore, it was very well said by our Saviour that *on these two commandments hang all the law and the prophets* [Matt. 22:40].

37. Do not please yourself and you will not hate your brother. Do not love yourself and you will be a friend of God.

38. Once you have chosen to live together with spiritual brothers, leave your own wishes at the door. For in no other way will you be able to find peace either with God or with your companions.

39. One who has been able to procure perfect love and has brought his whole life into harmony with it: such a one says in the Holy Spirit, *Lord Jesus* [1 Cor. 12:3]. And vice versa.

40. Love for God always likes to wing the intellect to divine communion. Love for one's neighbour makes sure that it always thinks well of them.

41. Someone who still loves empty praise or is attached to material things is going to be grieved at people over matters transient, or resentful of them, or harbour hatred for them, or be enslaved to shameful thoughts. But to a soul that loves God all this is completely different.

42. When you no longer speak or do anything shameful, even in thought; and when you have no resentment over one who harms or slanders you; and when in the time of prayer you always keep your intellect immaterial and formless: then know that you have drawn near to the measure of dispassion and perfect love.

43. It is no small feat to be delivered from vainglory. A person is delivered from it through hidden practice of the virtues, and more extended prayer. A sign of deliverance is no longer bearing a grudge against anyone who slandered you or still slanders you.

44. If you want to be just, distribute to each part of you what it is due; I mean, to soul and body. To the rational faculty of the soul, assign spiritual readings and contemplations and prayer; to the irascible faculty, spiritual love, which is opposed to hatred; to the desiring faculty, give temperance and self-control – and to your fleshly portion, *sustenance and clothing* [1 Tim. 6:8], all that it really needs.

45. The intellect acts in accordance with nature when it keeps the passions subdued, contemplates the principles of beings and spends time with God.

46. As health and sickness are to the body of a living being, and light and dark to the eye, so too virtue and evil are to the soul, and knowledge and ignorance to the intellect.

47. There are three objects of Christian philosophy: the commandments, doctrines and faith. The commandments separate the intellect from the passions; doctrines lead it to the knowledge of beings; and faith to the contemplation of the Holy Trinity.

48. Some engaged in ascetic struggle only drive away impassioned thoughts; others cut off the passions themselves. Thoughts are driven away by either psalmody, or prayer, or raising the

mind to God or some other appropriate distraction. But one cuts off the passions by despising those things to which one has become attached.

49. Our passions are aroused by, for example, women, possessions, glory and the like. We can find detachment from women when, after withdrawing from the world, we wither the body, as we ought, through self-control; from possessions, by persuading ourselves to be frugal in everything; from glory, by coming to love the hidden practice of the virtues, manifest only to God; and so with other passions. One who has attained such detachment will never come to hate anyone.

50. Detachment from things – such as women, possessions and the rest – makes the *outer man* a monk, but not yet the *inner man* [2 Cor. 4:16]. Detachment from impassioned concepts of these things tonsures the *inner man*, which is the intellect. It is easy to make the *outer man* a monk, if only one wants it; but the struggle to make a monk of the *inner man* is no light matter.

51. Who, then, in this generation, has been delivered from all manner of impassioned concepts and been granted pure and immaterial prayer, which is the mark of the inner monk?

52. Many passions have been hidden in our souls, but they are exposed only when the objects of these passions are brought to light.

53. One can be untroubled by the passions when their objects are absent, and so attain a partial dispassion. But if those objects reappear, straightway the passions convulse the intellect.

54. Do not imagine that you have perfect dispassion when the objects of passions are not present. But when the object reappears and you remain unmoved by it and afterwards by the memory of it, then *know that you have reached the frontier of dispassion.*[5] Even so, do not take this lightly, for virtue takes a long time to kill the passions, and, when neglected, they will rise up again.

55. Anyone who loves Christ always imitates him so far as possible. For example, Christ never stopped doing good to his fellow humans; was patient, when they were ungrateful and

blasphemed him; endured it, when they beat him and even killed him; and never imputed evil to anyone at all. These are the three works of love for one's neighbour, without which anyone who claims to love Christ and to have attained his kingdom merely deceives himself. For he says, *Not everyone who says to me, 'Lord, Lord!', will enter into the kingdom of heaven, but those who do the will of my Father* [Matt. 7:21]; and again, *Whoever loves me will keep my commandments* [John 14:15], etc.

56. The whole purpose of the Saviour's commandments is to free the intellect from dissipation and hatred and lead it to love of God and neighbour. From these two is born the light of holy knowledge in action.

57. Having been granted partial knowledge by God, do not neglect love and self-control. For these thoroughly purify the passible part of the soul and make you always ready for the way to knowledge.

58. The way to knowledge is dispassion and humility, *without which no one will see the Lord* [Heb. 12:14].

59. Since *knowledge puffs up but loves builds up* [1 Cor. 8:1], yoke love to knowledge and you will be free from arrogance, and become a spiritual builder, building up yourself and everyone close to you.

60. Therefore, *love builds up*, since it neither envies nor is embittered by those who envy; nor does it ostentatiously display the object of envy; nor does it reckon that it has already attained its end, instead unblushingly confessing its ignorance of what it does not know. In this way, then, love frees the mind from arrogance and always prepares it to advance towards knowledge.

61. Somehow self-conceit and envy naturally accompany knowledge, especially in the early stages. While self-conceit comes only from within, envy comes both from within and from without: from within when it is envious of those who have knowledge, from without when those with knowledge are envious of us. Love, therefore, overturns all three: self-conceit, for *it is not puffed up*; envy from within, for it *is not envious*; and envy from outside, for it *is patient and kind* [1 Cor.

13:4]. It is necessary for one who has knowledge, therefore, to add love as well, so that he may always keep his intellect invulnerable.

62. One who has been granted the grace of knowledge, and yet harbours grief, resentment or hatred against his fellow human, is like someone who stabs his own eyes with *thistles and thorns* [Gen. 3:18]. Therefore, knowledge absolutely requires love.

63. Do not give all your attention to your flesh, but simply prescribe for it what discipline you can and turn your whole intellect to things within. For *bodily exercise is of some use, but piety is of use in every way* [1 Tim. 4:8], etc.

64. One who constantly occupies himself with things within is temperate, patient, kind, humble. Not only this, but he also contemplates, attains theology and prays. And this is what the Apostle means when he says, *Walk in the Spirit* [Gal. 5:16], etc.

65. Someone who does not know how to walk the spiritual way does not take care about impassioned concepts. Rather, he is wholly occupied with the flesh, and either he is greedy and licentious, grieved and angry and resentful, and therefore darkens his intellect, or he engages in immoderate asceticism and confuses his mind.

66. Scripture does not deny any of those things given to us by God for our use, but it does censure immoderation and corrects irrationality. For example, it does not forbid anyone from eating or having children or possessing wealth and administering it properly, but it does forbid gluttony, fornication, etc. Nor does Scripture forbid us from thinking about these things – since they were made for this reason – but it does forbid thinking about them with passion.

67. Some of the things done by us in godly fashion are done in accordance with a commandment; other things are not done in accordance with a commandment, but, rather, one might say, as a voluntary offering. For example, loving God and neighbour, loving enemies, not committing adultery, not killing and the rest: these are in accordance with commandments, and those who transgress them are condemned. But virginity, singleness, poverty, withdrawal from the world and the rest:

these are not commanded, but, rather, are like gifts, so that, if through weakness we cannot keep the commandments, we can propitiate our good Master through our gifts to him.

68. One who honours celibacy and virginity needs to have his *loins girded* and *lamp burning* [Luke 12:35]: loins girded through self-control, and the lamp burning through prayer, contemplation and spiritual love.

69. Some of our brothers reckon that they are beyond the gracious gifts of the Holy Spirit. For, because of their carelessness in keeping the commandments, they fail to understand that one who has pure faith in Christ has the divine graces all together in himself. For since because of our laziness we are far from active love for Christ – which reveals to us all the divine treasures within us – we understandably reckon that we are excluded from the divine graces.

70. If *Christ dwells in our hearts through faith* [Eph. 3:17], according to the divine Apostle, and *in him are hidden all the treasures of wisdom and knowledge* [Col. 2:3], then all the treasures of wisdom and knowledge are hidden in our hearts. These treasures appear in each one's heart in proportion to their purification through the commandments.

71. This is the *treasure hidden in the field* of your heart [Matt. 13:44], which you can no longer find thanks to laziness. For if you had found it you would have done all you could to procure this field. Now, having lost the field, you are concerned with the land around it, in which nothing is to be found but *thorns and thistles* [Gen. 3:18].

72. This is why the Saviour says, *Blessed are the pure in heart, for they shall see God* [Matt. 5:8]: since he is hidden in the heart of those who believe in him. Then will they see him and the treasures within him, when through faith and self-control they purify themselves; the more intense their purity, so much the more will they see him.

73. For this reason he says again, *Sell all your goods, give them as alms, and behold, all things will be pure for you* [Luke 12:33, 11:41], meaning no longer to devote ourselves to things of the body, but to hasten to purify the intellect (which the Lord calls 'heart') from hatred and dissipation. For these things

defile the intellect and do not allow it to see the Lord who dwells within through the grace of holy baptism.

74. Scripture calls virtues 'ways'. And love has taken its place as greater than all the virtues. Therefore, the Apostle says, *I will show you a still more excellent way* [1 Cor. 12:31] that persuades us to despise material things and to prefer nothing transient to things eternal.

75. Love for God is opposed to desire, for it persuades the intellect to exercise mastery over the pleasures. Love for neighbour is opposed to anger, for it makes us despise glory and goods. And these are the two denarii which the Saviour gave to the innkeeper that he might take care of you [Luke 10:35]. But do not show yourself foolish by mixing with thieves, lest you be wounded again and found this time not *half dead* [Luke 10:30] but altogether dead.

76. Purify your intellect from anger, resentment and shameful thoughts, and then you will be able to recognize Christ's indwelling.

77. Who illuminated you in faith in the holy, adorable and consubstantial Trinity? Or, who made known to you the incarnate dispensation of one of the holy Trinity? Or who taught you the natural principles [*logoi*] of the bodiless powers, or those concerning the coming into being and the consummation of the visible world, or concerning resurrection from the dead and eternal life, or the glory of the kingdom of heaven and the fearful judgement? Was it not the grace of Christ dwelling in you, which is *the pledge of the* Holy *Spirit* [2 Cor. 5:5]? What is better than this grace, or greater than this wisdom and knowledge? What is more exalted than these promises? If we are lazy and careless, and do not purify ourselves from the passions which defile us and utterly blind our intellect, so that we can see the inner meaning of all these things more clearly than the sun, then let us blame ourselves and not deny the indwelling of grace.

78. God, who promised you eternal good things and gave *the pledge of the Spirit* [2 Cor. 5:5] in your heart, commanded you to take thought for your life, so that your *inner man* [2 Cor. 4:16], having been freed from the passions, might from now on begin to enjoy these good things.

79. Having been granted divine and lofty contemplations, take exceeding care of love and self-control, so that, guarding your passible faculties undisturbed, you will keep unfailing your soul's splendour.

80. Bridle the irascible part of the soul with love, and quench its desiring portion with self-control, and give wings to its rational part in prayer. Then the light of the intellect will never be darkened.

81. Such things as these dissolve love: dishonour, punishment, calumny – whether against one's faith or one's way of life – beatings, wounds and the like; they dissolve love whether they befall oneself or one's relations or friends. Anyone, then, who loses his love for any of these reasons has not yet come to know the purpose of Christ's commandments.

82. Strive to love every human being as much as you can. If you cannot yet do this, at least do not hate anyone. But you cannot even do this unless you despise the things of the world.

83. Someone has uttered terrible blasphemies. Do not hate him, but hate his blasphemy and the demon which has led him to blaspheme. If you hate the one who blasphemes, you have hated a human being and so transgressed the commandment: what that person did in word, you have done in deed. If, however, you keep the commandment, you will show him something of love and, if you can, help to free him from evil.

84. Christ does not want you to harbour hatred, sadness, anger or resentment towards your fellow human in any way at all or on account of any kind of transient matter. The four Gospels proclaim this in every way.

85. There are many of us who talk, but few who do. So then, no one ought to corrupt the word of God out of his own carelessness, but, rather, confess his own infirmity and not hide the truth of God – lest we be convicted of transgressing the commandments and misrepresenting God.

86. Love and self-control free the soul from passions. Reading and contemplation deliver the intellect from ignorance. But the state of prayer brings it into the presence of God himself.

87. When the demons see us despising the things of this world, lest thanks to them we come to hate people and fall from love, then they stir up slanders against us, so that, unable to bear our grief, we come to hate our slanderers.

88. Nothing distresses the soul more than slander, whether regarding our faith or our way of life. And no one can take this lightly, unless, as Susanna did, he looks solely to God [cf. Sus. 35 LXX], who alone can deliver from dire necessities (as with her), give people assurance (as he did concerning her virtue) and through hope offer consolation to the soul.

89. The more you pray from your very soul for your slanderer, the more will God grant assurance to those who have been scandalized.

90. God alone is good by nature, and only God's imitator is good by intent. For the latter's intention is to unite the wicked to the one who is good by nature, so that they too become good. For this reason, *being cursed he blesses, being persecuted he endures* [1 Cor. 4:12], being blasphemed he encourages, being killed he prays for his killers [Luke 23:34]. He does everything that he may not fail to attain the goal of love – which is, after all, our God himself.

91. The Lord's commandments teach us to use indifferent things in a blessed fashion. The blessed use of morally neutral things purifies the soul's state. Its purified state gives birth to discernment. Discernment gives birth to dispassion, from which is born perfect love.

92. If, when temptation occurs, you cannot overlook your friend's failure, whether real or apparent, you are still lacking in dispassion. For when the passions that lurk in the soul are stirred up, they utterly blind the mind and prevent it from looking directly at the rays of truth or discerning the better from the worse. Such a one, therefore, certainly has not yet attained *perfect love* that *casts out* the *fear* of judgement [1 John 4:18].

93. *There is no substitute for a faithful friend* [Sirach 6:15], since he reckons a friend's misfortunes as his own, and supports him, suffering with him even to death.

94. Friends are plentiful – but only in fair weather. In time of testing, you will scarcely find one.

95. Every human being is to be loved from your very soul. But on God alone are you to put your hope and him alone to

serve *with your whole strength* [Mark 12.30]. For as long as he watches over us, all our friends honour us and all our enemies are powerless against us; but should he abandon us, all our friends will turn from us and all our enemies grow strong against us.

96. There are four kinds of abandonment. The first is providential, as with the Lord, so that through a seeming abandonment those who have been abandoned might be saved. The second is for testing, as with Job and Joseph [Gen. 39], so that they might shine forth as pillars – the former of courage, the latter of chastity. The third is for discipline, as with the Apostle, so that, being humbled, he might keep the abundance of grace [2 Cor. 12:7]. The fourth is according to rejection, as with the Jews, so that, being punished, they might be turned to repentance. All these ways bring about salvation and are full of divine goodness and wisdom.

97. Only those who keep the commandments strictly and are genuine initiates of the divine judgements will not abandon their friends when God permits them to be tempted. Those who sit lightly to the commandments and are uninitiated in divine judgements will also rejoice with their friends when things go well, but should they suffer in time of trial, they will abandon them and sometimes even side with their opponents.

98. Friends of Christ love everyone genuinely, though they are not loved by all. Friends of the world neither love all nor are loved by all. Friends of Christ maintain the continual practice of love until the end, friends of the world maintain it only until they take offence at one another for the sake of worldly things.

99. *A faithful friend is a strong defence* [Sirach 6:14], since when things are going well he is a good counsellor and a like-minded fellow worker; and when they are going badly he is a most genuine helper and most sympathetic defender.

100. Many people have said many things about love, but only among the disciples of Christ will you seek and find it, since they alone have true love itself as their teacher of love, concerning which it is said, *If I have prophecy and know all mysteries and all knowledge, but lack love I gain nothing* [1 Cor. 13:2–3]. Therefore, one who possesses love possesses God, since *God is love* [1 John 4:8]. To whom be glory to the ages. Amen.

St Maximos the Confessor,
Commentary on the Lord's Prayer

On the prayer, 'Our Father': A brief interpretation for one who loves Christ

In receiving your elegant letters, I have received my God-protected master himself. For you are always present in spirit and can never be entirely absent; in imitation of God, through the abundance of your virtue, you never fail to take advantage of the opportunities God gives to converse with your servants. Therefore, wondering at how much you have reached down to my level, I have mixed fear of you with desire, and made from both – my fear and my desire – a single love, consisting of reverence and goodwill together, lest fear denuded of desire become hatred, or desire contempt from lack of prudent fear. Thus, love may be shown as an inward law of tenderness, making its own everything naturally kin to it, mastering hatred through goodwill, and keeping contempt at bay through reverence. The blessed David recognized fear as best of all to preserve divine love, when he said, *The fear of the Lord is pure, enduring throughout the ages* [Ps. 18:10]. For he knew that this fear is quite different from terror at threats of punishment; indeed, that kind of fear is expelled, and quite vanishes at the presence of love, as the great evangelist John makes clear somewhere in his letters, saying, *Love casts out fear* [1 John 4:18]. Rather, such fear naturally characterizes the law of genuine tenderness, which through reverence preserves forever completely incorrupt among the Saints the ordinance and manner of love for God and for one another.

At any rate, having mixed fear of my lord with desire, I have established this as the law of love up to this very day: kept from writing by reverence, lest familiarity take hold; driven to write by goodwill, lest an absolute refusal to write be considered hatred. So I write – doing this under orders – not whatever comes to mind, since according to Scripture *human thoughts are cowardly* [Wisd. 9:14]; but whatever God counsels and confers by grace so that good may come of it. For, *The counsel of the Lord*, says David, *endures forever; and the thoughts of his heart to generation and generation* [Ps. 32:11]. By *counsel* David probably meant the indescribable self-emptying of the *only-begotten Son* [John 1:18] of our God and Father for the deification of our nature. God has circumscribed the boundary of all the ages in accordance with this counsel. By *thoughts of his heart*, David probably meant the principles [*logoi*] of providence and judgement. In accordance with these, God arranges both our present life and that to come like different generations, assigning to each the mode proper to its activity.

If, however, the deification of our nature is a work of divine counsel and the aim of divine thoughts is to provide what is needed for our lives to attain their end, then it is good to know the Lord's Prayer and to practise it, and thus suitably to describe its power – especially as my lord in writing to me his servant was moved by God to make mention of this prayer. I am bound, then, to make the Lord's Prayer the subject of my own words. I ask the Lord, as teacher of this prayer, *to open my intellect* [Luke 24:45] to grasp its mysteries and give me adequate words to make clear what I have understood. For mystically hidden it contains in outline the whole purpose of which we have just been speaking. Or, rather, to speak more precisely, it proclaims its meaning openly to those with sound intellects. For its inner principle [*logos*] is to contain a petition for all that the *Logos* of God achieved through his flesh in his self-emptying. It teaches us to strive for those good things whose sole provider is in truth the God and Father through the natural mediation of the Son in the Holy Spirit, since the *mediator between God and humankind* is, according to the divine Apostle, the Lord *Jesus* [1 Tim. 2:5], who through the flesh makes the unknown Father manifest to human beings, as he leads them, now reconciled in himself, to the Father through the Spirit. For it was on their behalf and for their sake that without change he became human, and has become the author and teacher of many new mysteries, of such multitude and magnitude that no account could ever encompass them. Of the many mysteries he has given to humans, seven, generative of the rest, have been revealed as particularly worthy of distinction, the power of which the prayer's account encompasses. They are: theology, adoption by grace, equality in honour with the angels, participation in eternal life, restoration of nature impassibly recalled to itself, dissolution of *the law of sin* [Rom. 8:2], and destruction of the wicked tyrant who ruled us through deceit [cf. Heb. 2:14–15].

The Logos of God, being incarnate, teaches theology since he reveals the Father and the Holy Spirit in himself. For the whole Father and whole Spirit were essentially and perfectly in the whole Son in the Incarnation, even though Father and Spirit themselves were not incarnate. Rather, the Father blesses the Incarnation and the Spirit works together with the Son who himself wrought his Incarnation, since indeed the Word remains intellectual and living, and shares in being with none save the Father and Spirit only, as he makes a hypostatic union with the flesh in his love for humankind.

The Logos gives adoption, in granting us through the Spirit supernatural *birth from above* [John 3:3], which is guarded and preserved in God by the free choice of those thus born. The grace thus bestowed is confirmed by their sincere disposition and the careful practice of the commandments makes radiant the beauty given them by grace. Furthermore, by emptying themselves of the passions, they are changed into the divine, to the same extent as the Logos of God, in accordance with the divine economy, by his own will emptied himself of his own pure glory, having truly become, as he is also called, human.

The Logos has made humans equal in honour to the angels. This is not simply because *he brought things in heaven and on earth to peace through the blood of his cross* [Col. 1:20] and brought to naught the opposing powers who filled the middle air between earth and heaven, and so established a festal assembly of earthly and heavenly powers for the distribution of divine gifts – at which human nature sings in rejoicing the glory of God with one and the same will as the powers above, but also because after the *fulfilment of his dispensation for us*,[1] when he was *taken up* together with the body he had assumed [Mark 16:19], he united heaven and earth in himself and joined sensible things with those intellectual, thus proclaiming created nature one, with its extremities bound together in himself in accordance with both virtue and knowledge of the first cause. He showed, I think, through what he accomplished mystically, that *logos* unites what is divided, and its absence divides what is united. And so let us learn to lay hold of *logos* through what we do, that we may be united not only to the angels in virtue but to God through spiritual knowledge in accordance with abstraction [or, detachment] from the realm of beings.

The Logos was made food, so that we might participate in the divine life – in a way he knows and also those who have received such an intellectual sense from him – in order to *taste* of this food and *see* truly in full awareness that *the Lord is good* [Ps. 33:9]. The divine quality of this food changes those who eat it, advancing them towards deification, and so the Logos clearly is and is called the *bread of life* and power [John 6:35].

He restored nature to itself. This is only in part because having become man he guarded his intention tranquil and unperturbed by nature, never wavering in the least from its own natural movement in the face of those who crucified him. On the contrary, instead of life, he chose, rather, death on their behalf, and thus showed the voluntary nature of the passion that he suffered through his steadfast love for humankind. But also he restored nature to itself because *he destroyed hostility* [Eph. 2:14–15], *having nailed the record* of sin *to the cross* [Col. 2:14], since our nature was implacably at war with itself. And, having called *those who were far off and those who were near* [Eph. 2:17] – which refers to *those under the law* [Gal. 4:5] and those outside the law [Rom. 2:14] – he *destroyed the middle wall of separation, the law* indeed *of commandments* revealed *in dogmas. He made the two into one new human being, making peace and reconciling* us through himself to the Father and to one another [Eph. 2:14–16], we who no longer have an intention opposed to the principle of our nature, but are unchangeable in our intention as in our nature.

He rendered our nature pure *of the law of sin* [Rom. 8:2] since he did not permit pleasure to be the occasion of his incarnation for our sake. For his conception was miraculous, being without seed, and his birth transcended nature, being incorrupt. Clearly, in being born from his mother, God held tight the bonds of virginity in her giving birth in a way that surpassed nature, and freed, in those who want it, their whole nature from the tyranny of the law which ruled them, insofar as they imitate his self-chosen death by mortification in their feeling *their members on the earth* [Col. 3:5]. For the mystery of salvation belongs to those who choose it, not those who are forced.

The Logos brought about the destruction of the wicked tyrant who ruled over us through deceit, by taking the flesh that had been conquered in Adam and wielding it as a weapon against that tyrant, conquering him, so that he might show the flesh, formerly overcome by death, now making prey of the predator and by his natural death utterly destroying the life of that tyrant. So, for the tyrant Christ's flesh was fatal, and caused the tyrant to vomit forth all whom he had *swallowed down, being mighty* [Isa. 25:8], since he *had the power of death* [Heb. 2:14]. And so he gave life to the human race, like yeast causing the whole of nature to rise in the *resurrection of life* [John 5:29], for which reasons especially the Logos, being God, became man – truly a strange and unheard-of deed! – and willed to accept the death of the flesh.

As I said, the *logos* of the Lord's prayer will be found to contain a petition for each of these.

First, it speaks of *Father*, the Father's *name* and his *kingdom*, and in turn presents the one who prays as son or daughter of this Father by grace. It also seeks for beings *in heaven* and *earth* to be of one *will*. It commands us to ask for our *daily bread*. It lays down reconciliation between one another and by *forgiving* and *being forgiven* unites our nature to itself, as it is no longer split apart by difference of intention and will. It teaches prayer against entering *into temptation*, for this is the *law of sin* [Rom. 7:23, 8:2] and exhorts us to *be delivered from the evil one*. For it was necessary that the author and giver of good things be also our teacher, offering the words of this prayer as precepts of true life for his disciples who believed in him and imitated his conduct in the flesh, through which he revealed the *hidden treasures of wisdom and knowledge* [Col. 2:3] that exist in him as pure form, awakening in those who make this prayer the enjoyment of both knowledge and wisdom.

Therefore, I think, the *Logos* has called this teaching *prayer* [cf. Luke 11:1], since it contains a request for the gifts given to humans from God by grace. So our God-inspired fathers have explained prayer by way of definition, saying that prayer [*proseuchê*] is a request for those things that God, as befits him, naturally gives to humans, whereas a vow [*euchê*] is an undertaking or promise of offerings made to God by those who genuinely worship him. They cite Scripture as frequently bearing witness to this difference – like *Make your vows and render them to the Lord our God* [Ps. 75:12] and *All that I have vowed I will repay you, my Lord, my Saviour* [Jonah 2:10] refer to a 'vow'; while concerning 'prayer' we have *And Anna prayed to the Lord, saying, 'Lord Adonai, Eloi Sabaoth, if only you will hearken to your handmaid, give me the fruit of the womb'* [1 Kgds 1:10–11]; and *Hezekias the king of Judah prayed to the Lord, and Isaias son of Amos the prophet too* [2 Paral. 32:20, 24]; and as the Lord said to his disciples, *When you pray, say, 'Our Father in heaven'* [Luke 11:2]. So, a 'vow' is keeping the commandments, confirmed by the deliberate putting into effect of what has been vowed. By contrast, 'prayer' is the petition by one who has kept the commandments to be transformed into the good things prayed for. Or, rather, a 'vow' is the contest for virtue, which God receives most gladly when it is offered to him. 'Prayer', on the other hand, is the reward of virtue, which God rejoices most of all to award.

Therefore, since prayer has been shown to be a request for the good things given by the Incarnate Logos himself, taking him as our teacher of the meaning of prayer. Let us take courage and carefully investigate the meaning of each phrase, laying it bare, as it were, by contemplation, as the Word himself is accustomed to lead us and give us the capacity to understand what he says.

Our Father in heaven, may your Name be hallowed; your Kingdom come.

It is appropriate, right at the beginning, that the Lord teaches those who pray to begin with theology and initiate them in how the creative cause of beings exists, since he is by essence the source of beings. For the words of the prayer hold the manifestation of the Father and the Father's name and his kingdom, so that from this beginning we may learn to reverence, call upon and worship the monadic triad. For the only-begotten Son is the God and Father's name, subsisting essentially, while the Holy Spirit is the God and Father's kingdom, subsisting essentially. For what Matthew here calls 'kingdom', elsewhere another evangelist has called 'Holy Spirit', saying, *Let your Holy Spirit come and purify us* [Luke 11:2]. For the Father has not acquired a name, nor indeed do we understand the kingdom as an aspect of his worth. For he did not begin to be, so that he might begin to be Father or King, but being eternally, he is eternally both Father and King, having in no wise begun to be or to be Father and King. If being eternally, he is eternally both Father and King, then equally eternally both the Son and the Holy Spirit have by essence coexisted with the Father, being always from him and naturally in him beyond cause and principle, but not having later come into being together with him for any reason. For the category of relation has the force of indicating jointly those related and said to be related, not allowing them to be considered one after another.

As we begin this prayer, then, we are led to celebrate the Triad, both of one being and beyond being, as the creative cause of our coming into being. Moreover, we are taught to proclaim the grace of adoption, given to us, as we are deemed worthy by grace to call Father the one who is by nature our fashioner, so that, holding in awe the title of our begetter by grace, we may strive to engrave in our lives the marks of our begetter, hallowing his name on earth, showing him to be our Father, and showing ourselves his children through our deeds and magnifying, through all we think or do, the Father's natural Son as the author of this our adoption.

We hallow the name of our Father in heaven by grace, when

we mortify our desire for material things and purify ourselves of the corrupting passions, since sanctification, or hallowing, is the complete stilling and mortification of sensuous desire. Once in this state we lull to sleep the unseemly howls of the irascible faculty and no longer have the desire that stirs it up and persuades it to fight hard for its own pleasures, for it has already been put to death by holy *logos*. For anger, by nature the advocate of desire, will naturally cease from raging as soon as it sees desire quelled.

It is natural, then, after the rejection of anger and desire, that in accordance with the prayer the rule of the kingdom of the God and Father should come upon those deemed worthy to say, *Your kingdom come* – that is, 'May the Holy Spirit come' – for, having put these aside, they have already been made temples for God through the Spirit by *logos* and practice of meekness or gentleness. For it says, *Upon whom shall I rest, save on the meek and humble one who fears my words?* [Isa. 66:2]. It says this to make clear that the kingdom of the God and Father belongs to the meek and gentle. For it says, *Blessed are the meek, for they shall inherit the earth* [Matt. 5:5].

For it is not this earth, which naturally occupies the middle place in the universe, that God promised as an inheritance to those who love him, since he tells the truth when he says, *When they rise from the dead, they neither marry nor are given in marriage, but are like the angels in heaven* [Mark 12:25]; and, *Come, you that are blessed by my Father, inherit the kingdom prepared for you from the foundation of the world* [Matt. 25:34]. And elsewhere it is said to another *who serves with gladness, Enter into the joy of your Lord* [Matt. 25:21, 23]. With him the divine Apostle says, *The trumpet shall sound and the dead in Christ shall* first *be raised incorruptible* [1 Cor. 15:52] and *then we the living who remain will be at once snatched up with them in the clouds, into the air, to meet the Lord, and so we shall always be with the Lord* [1 Thess. 4:17].

If such things as these are promised to those that love the Lord, how could anyone with his mind fixed solely on the word of Scripture say that heaven, and the *kingdom prepared from the foundation of the world* [Matt. 25:34], and the mystically hidden joy of the Lord, and the continuous and the completely uninterrupted rest and abode of the saints with the Lord – how could anyone moved by the Logos and longing to be a servant of the Logos say that these are the same as the earth? Rather, in this text I think that 'earth' means the steadfast disposition and strength, insusceptible to being deflected from goodness, possessed immutably by the gentle. They are always with the Lord, possess uninterrupted joy, have attained the kingdom prepared from the beginning, and been found worthy of rest and a place in heaven, and have inherited the *logos* of virtue, understood as if it were a kind of earth occupying the middle position in the universe. According to this principle, one who is gentle, living in the midst of honour and dishonour, remains tranquil, neither puffed up by praise nor downcast by insults. For the principle of virtue is naturally free of these; having renounced desire, it does not notice any provocations that crowd about it. Calmed from distress about these things, it has anchored the soul's whole strength in divine and priceless freedom. The Lord, desiring to grant this freedom to his disciples, said, *Take my yoke upon you and learn from me, for I am meek and humble in heart, and you will find rest for your souls* [Matt. 11:29]. He calls the rule of the divine kingdom *rest*, since he confers on those who are worthy lordship free from any servitude.

If he gives the indestructible power of the undefiled kingdom to the humble and meek, who would be so lacking in love and completely without desire for things good and divine as not to aim at the very summit of humility and meekness, so as to bear the imprint of the divine kingdom so far as is humanly possible, and take on in himself by grace the exact spiritual form of Christ, who is by nature and in being truly the great king? *In which*, says the divine Apostle, there is *not male and female* [Gal. 3:28] – that is, anger and desire. Of these, the first, like a tyrant, takes over our thinking and excludes our mind from the law of nature, while the second despises the one dispassionate cause and nature, itself alone desirable, making what is lower seem lovelier than it, and therefore giving the flesh preference over the Spirit, so that visible things appear more delightful than the glory and splendour of intelligible realities. It seduces the intellect by the sensual allure of pleasure from the divine apprehension of intelligible realities that are akin to it.

For the Spirit has conquered nature and persuades the intellect, stripped naked of its affection for the body, even though this disposition is quite natural, to lay aside moral philosophy, for this is necessary when it seeks affinity with the Word beyond being through simple and undivided contemplation, even though moral philosophy makes easier the severing from and passing beyond what belongs to the flow of time. For when the intellect has passed beyond attachment to the things of the senses, it is not reasonable that it should be burdened, as with a sheepskin, with moral preoccupations. The great Elias [or Elijah] shows this clearly, revealing this mystery in a figure through the things he did [4 Kgds 2:1–14]. On the one hand, at his ascension he gave to Elissaios [or Elisha] his sheepskin, by which I mean the mortification of the flesh, on which the magnificence of his moral decorum is established. For it represents the support by the Spirit against every opposing power, and a scourge of unstable and ever-flowing nature, of which the Jordan was a type. He did this so that his disciple, Elissaios, might not be held back from passage into the holy land, swamped in the muck and slippage of attachment to material things. Meanwhile, Elias himself departed to God in freedom, no longer hindered by attachment to any of the things which are. And so, simple in desire and unconfused in will, he made his dwelling with the One who is simple by nature, through the interconnected natural virtues, harnessed to one another in knowledge, like horses of fire.

For Elias knew that the disciples of Christ must be freed from unequal dispositions, whose difference is evidence of inner estrangement. For the passion caused by desire creates a diffusion of vital spirit around the heart, while irascible passion, when roused, clearly causes a boiling of blood. One who is already, as it were, *living, moving and being* in Christ [Acts 17:28], has put from himself the unwelcome production of unequal dispositions, no longer bearing in himself, like *male and female* – as I have said – the contrary dispositions of these passions, lest his reason become enslaved to them and subject to their restless vacillation. Naturally mastered by the brightness of the divine image, *logos* persuades the soul to be moulded of its own choice to the divine *likeness* [Gen. 1:26] and to belong to the great kingdom essentially brought into being by the God and Father of all. It becomes an all-radiant dwelling of the Holy Spirit, and receives – dare I say it – the whole authority of knowing the divine nature, so far as possible. In accordance with this, production of what is worse is naturally put aside and replaced by what is better, *even like God* [Phil. 2:6], while the soul, according to the grace of its calling, preserves unsullied in itself the substance of the good things given to it. In such a soul Christ ever desires to be born mystically, becoming flesh in those who are saved, and making the soul which gives birth to him a virgin mother; for, to put it briefly, such a soul does not have, in its condition, the marks (like *male and female*) of nature subject to generation and corruption.

Let no one be put off, hearing the corruption of generation brought forward. For having dispassionately and with right *logos* examined the nature of things which come to be and pass away, he will find that generation clearly begins from corruption and ends in corruption. Christ – that is to say, the life and *logos* of Christ and according to Christ – does not have the passions that are marks of this kind of generation. At least, if the Apostle Paul is speaking the truth when he says, *For in Christ Jesus there is not male and female* – by this signifying clearly the signs and passions of nature, subject to generation and corruption. Rather, in Christ there is only godlike *logos*, fashioned by divine knowledge, and the single movement of a will and intention that chooses virtue alone. He says, 'not *Greek and Jew*' [cf. Gal. 3:28], by this meaning different, or, rather, to speak more truly, contrary, opinions about God. The Greek foolishly introduces many original principles, dividing the single principle of the Godhead into opposed activities and powers, and thus creating a polytheistic piety, confused by the multitude of its objects of worship, and made ridiculous by its many forms of worship. The Jew, conversely, introduces a single original principle, which is narrow, incomplete and practically non-existent, since it is bereft of Word and Life. This account, though opposed to the other, falls into an equally evil atheism – that is, disbelief in the true God – since it limits to a single person the principle of divinity. It conceives this person either without Word and Spirit or as having been itself endowed with Word and Spirit as qualities. In doing so this account fails to realize what kind of a god he would be, lacking Word and Spirit, or how he could be God, if he shares in them as mere contingent attributes, by participation alongside rational creatures subject to generation.

As I have said, neither of these accounts finds any place at all in Christ. Rather, in him there is only the *logos* of true piety and firm ordinance of mystical theology, which dismisses the dilatation of the Greek account and does not admit the contraction of the second, lest it represent the divine as torn apart by discord by multiplying natures – the Greek way – or render it passible – the Jewish way – by admitting a single person, deprived of Word and Spirit, of only regarding Word and Spirit as qualities, without itself being Intellect and Word and Spirit. Instead, mystical theology teaches us, who, called by grace, have been adopted through faith and brought to recognize the truth, to know one nature and power of the godhead, that is, one God, contemplated in Father, and Son, and Holy Spirit, as it were, a single uncaused Intellect, subsisting essentially, the begetter according to being of a single *Logos* without beginning, and the source of a single eternal Life, subsisting essentially as the Holy Spirit: triad in monad and monad in triad; not one in another, for the triad is not in the monad, as accident in substance, nor vice versa, for God is without qualities; nor as one and another, for the monad does not differ from the triad by otherness of nature, for the nature is simple and single; nor as one beside another, for the triad is not distinguished from the monad, nor the monad from the triad, by diminution of power; nor is the monad distinguished from the triad as something common and general is perceived different in thought only from the particulars that make it up: it is properly self-existent being and absolutely mighty power; nor as one through another, for there is no mediating relationship such as cause and effect, for it is absolutely self-identical and without relationship;

nor as one out of another, for the triad is not from the monad either by derivation or by promotion, being ingenerate and self-revealed – but the same is said to be, and understood to be, truly monad and triad, both by the *logos* of its being and the mode of its existence, the same wholly monad, not divided into *hypostases*, nor confused by the monad, lest polytheism be introduced by division, or atheism by confusion.

As it avoids these misunderstandings, the account which is in Christ is radiant with truth – by which I mean the *logos* of Christ, the new proclamation of truth, in which there is *not male and female* – by which I mean the signs and passions of nature subject to corruption and generation – *not Greek* and *Jew* – that is, the opposed accounts of divinity. There is not *circumcision* and *uncircumcision* [Col. 3:11], which are plainly the modes of worship corresponding to these. Circumcision: because by its misuse of the symbols of the law, it makes out the visible creation to be evil and slanders the creator as the source of evils. Uncircumcision: because of the passions, divinizes creation and sets the creature against the creator. And together both lead to the same evil: insolence against God. Nor is there *barbarian* and *Scythian* [Col. 3:11] – that is, the fissure deliberately made in our single nature, which sets it at odds with itself, and to its own undoing introduces the unnatural law of killing one another into human society. Neither *slave* and *free* [Col. 3:11] – clearly the irrational division of this same nature, dishonouring what is naturally of equal honour, allied to a law that grants masters to tyrannize over those who possess the dignity of the image [of God]. *But Christ is all and in all* [Col. 3:11], fashioning by means beyond nature and law in the Spirit the architecture of the kingdom without beginning, which, as is manifest, is naturally characterized by humility and gentleness of heart, the confluence of these virtues revealing the *human* being made *perfect* according to *Christ* [Col. 1:28]. For everyone who thinks humbly is also always gentle, and every gentle person also thinks humbly, since he knows that his very being is on loan. He is gentle because he recognizes the use of the powers with which he is naturally endowed: by *logos* giving their service to the creation of virtue and withdrawing their activity completely from the senses. Therefore, his intellect is unceasingly moving towards God, but as regards sense-perception he is in no way moved, having no awareness of all that grieves the body; nor does he allow grief to leave its mark on his soul, and distort the joy-creating disposition in his soul. For he does not consider what is painful to the senses the deprivation of pleasure, for he considers companionship of his soul with the Word to be the only pleasure, the loss of which is unending torment that naturally encompasses all the ages. Therefore, he leaves behind the body and everything to do with it, and is carried eagerly to divine companionship, so that, were he to rule over the whole world, he would reckon as his only real loss failure to attain by grace that deification for which he longs.

Let us cleanse ourselves, therefore, *from every pollution of flesh and spirit* [2 Cor. 7:1], that we may hallow the divine name, as we quench the desire which makes pretence of being shocked by the passions. Let us also check by means of *logos* our anger which rages intemperately after pleasures, so that we may receive the kingdom of the God and Father which comes through gentleness.

Let us now join to what has gone before the next clause of the prayer, saying:

Your will be done, as in heaven, so also on earth.

One who mystically offers God worship in accordance with his rational power alone, purified of both desire and anger – this person has fulfilled the divine will on earth as the ranks of angels do in heaven. He has become through all this a fellow worshipper with the angels, and shares their dwelling, as the great Apostle says, *Our citizenship is in heaven* [Phil. 3:20]. For with them there is no desire to slacken intellectual tension through pleasure, nor anger to enrage them and make them bark indecently at their fellow creatures, but only *logos* alone, which naturally leads rational creatures to the primordial *Logos*. In this alone does God rejoice and this alone he seeks from us, his slaves, and this he shows us when he says to the great David, *For what is there for me in heaven, and what have I desired from you upon the earth?* [Ps. 72:25]. But nothing is offered to God in heaven from the holy angels save *rational worship* [Rom. 12:1], which he seeks also from us by teaching those who pray to say, *Your will be done, as in heaven, so also on earth.*

Therefore, let our *logos* be roused to seek after God, our desirous faculty to long for him, and our irascible faculty struggling to hold fast to him. Or, to speak more precisely, let our whole intellect stretch out towards God, straining by a certain tension in the irascible faculty, burning with longing to the utmost degree of desire. For imitating in this way the angels in heaven, we shall be found to be worshipping God through all things, manifesting on earth the same way of life as the angels, equally having our intellect in no way inclined towards anything that falls short of God. For following a way of life in accordance with prayers, we shall receive as our daily and life-sustaining bread, for the nourishment of our souls and for preserving the vigour of the good things bestowed on us by grace, the *Logos* who says, *I am the bread which came down from heaven, to give life to the world* [John 6:41, 33]. Nourished by virtue and wisdom, we shall each in our due degree receive him who has become all things and has been embodied in manifold ways – as he alone knows – in each of those being saved, while still living in this present age, in accordance with the meaning of the clause of the prayer, which says:

Give us today our daily bread.

I think that by *today* is meant this present age, as if someone, taking account of the broader context of the prayer, were to render this clause of the prayer: *Our bread* – which you originally prepared for our human nature to render it immortal – *give today to us* who for the present life belong to mortality, that the nourishment of *the bread of life* and of knowledge may conquer the death of sin. The transgression of the divine command did not allow the first man to become a partaker of this bread, for, if he had been filled with divine food, he would not have succumbed to the death of sin. The Saviour himself led me to this interpretation of the clause we are considering, when he expressly commanded his disciples to take no thought at all for earthly sustenance, saying, *Do not worry about your life, what you shall eat or drink*, nor *what* you will put on *your body*

[Matt. 6:25], *for it is the people of the world* that *seek after all these things* [Luke 12:30] – but, rather, *seek first the Kingdom of God and his righteousness, and all these things will be added unto you* [Matt. 6:33].

How, then, does he teach us to pray for things which he previously commanded us not to seek? Obviously, he did no such thing! We are to ask in prayer only for what we are commanded to seek. Whatever, therefore, a command does not allow to seek after is doubtless forbidden to ask for in prayer. If, then, the Saviour commanded us only *to seek the Kingdom of God and his righteousness*, then surely he urged those who long for divine gifts also to seek this kingdom through prayer, so that, having obtained through prayer the gracious gift of those things which we seek by nature, he might unite the will and intention of those who ask to the will of the one who bestows grace, making them one and the same in a union of relationship.

But if we are also ordered through prayer to request bread that passes away – bread, by which our present life is naturally sustained – let us not cross the boundaries of the prayer, voraciously entertaining many cycles of years, nor let us forget that we are mortal with a life that passes like a shadow [cf. Job 8:9]. Rather, let us, without anxiety, in prayer ask for bread one day at a time, showing that, as philosophers after Christ, we are making our life a rehearsal of death, anticipating nature in will and intention and, before death comes, severing our soul from its bodily cares. In this way our soul will not transfer its natural appetite to material things, nailing itself to what is perishing, nor learn greed, thus depriving itself of the abundance of divine benefits. Let us, then, flee with what strength we can muster from a fondness for matter, washing away our involvement in it, like dust from our spiritual eyes.

Let us be content only with what sustains our present life, not with what affords us pleasure. And let us pray to God, as we have been taught, to preserve our soul from slavery, not dominated, through the body, by anything visible. Let us show that we eat in order to live, rather than being guilty of living in order to eat – behaving as possessing a rational, rather than irrational, nature. And let us be careful guards of the prayer, showing through what we ask for that we hold fast to the one and only life in the Spirit, seeking to secure it through the use we make of this present life. It is for the sake of life in the Spirit that we manifest such affection for this present life as not to refuse to support it by bread alone, but to preserve its natural good health without decay – so far as we can – not that we may live, but that we may live to God [cf. Rom. 6:10], making our body, formed by the virtues, a messenger of the soul, and our soul, once convinced of the good, a herald of God. So, we limit our petition for bread to one day only, not daring to extend it to a second day, for the sake of the giver of the prayer.

Having thus disposed ourselves in deed in accordance with the meaning of the prayer, we can now proceed, in purity, to the next words of the prayer, which state:

And forgive us our debts as we forgive our debtors.

If we say, in accordance with the first interpretation of the previous clause, that *today* is a symbol of the present age, anyone who in this present age seeks through prayer the incorruptible bread of wisdom, from which the original transgression has divided us as by a wall, knows that his only pleasure lies in the attainment of divine things, bestowed, according to nature, by God and preserved, according to will, by the free choice of the one who receives them. He knows, too, that the only pain lies in failure to attain these things. It is the Devil who prompts this failure, and it is brought about by everyone who wearies of divine things through the slackness of his intent and does not preserve the precious object of his love by his settled intent. One who is not in the least inclined to anything in the visible world and therefore not overwhelmed by any bodily affliction: such a one truly and dispassionately forgives those who sin against him, for no one can absolutely seize the good he set his heart on, which is by nature unassailable.

He presents himself to God as an example of virtue (if we dare speak in this way), for by saying, *Forgive us our debts as we forgive our debtors,* he encourages the Inimitable to imitate himself, and to treat him as he has treated his neighbours. For if he wants to be forgiven by God, as he has forgiven the debts of those who sinned against him, then clearly just as God dispassionately forgives those who forgive, so too he, remaining dispassionate whatever happens to him, forgives those who offend him. He does not allow his intellect to be stamped by any memory of past woes, lest, by inwardly dividing his human nature, he set himself at odds with another human being, though he himself is human. For when the intention is united with the *logos* of nature, the reconciliation of God with nature naturally takes place, because otherwise, if nature remains self-divided in its intention, it cannot receive God's ineffable gift of himself. And surely this is why God wants us first to be reconciled with one another: not so that he may learn from us to be reconciled with sinners and to forgive the penalty for many terrible crimes – but that he may purify us from passions and show that the quality of grace granted those forgiven accords with their inward disposition.

For he has made it manifestly clear that when the intention has been united to the *logos* of nature, the free will of those who have achieved this cannot be at odds with God, since nothing contrary to *logos* is to be observed in the *logos* of nature. In fact, this principle is a law both natural and divine, whenever the movement of the will and intention arises in accordance with itself. But if there is nothing contrary to *logos* in the *logos* of nature, it is likely that the deliberative will, moved according to the principle of nature, will always be inclined towards God, forming a fruitful disposition, created by the grace of One who is by nature good, to bring virtue into being.

Such, then, will be the disposition when he prays of a person who petitions the bread of knowledge. After him, the other sort of person – the one who seeks out only material bread because of nature's requirement – will arrange his affairs in the same way. He will forgive his debtors, especially since he knows that he is, by nature, mortal. Thereafter, expecting what must naturally happen on a daily basis because of its uncertainty, he anticipates nature by his deliberate choice and becomes a free and independent corpse as far as the world is concerned. This is according to the saying, *For your sake we are killed all day long, we are reckoned as sheep for the slaughter* [Ps. 43:23,

Rom. 8:36]. For this reason, he is poured out to all [cf. Phil. 2:17], so that he may carry with himself no trace of this world's depravity, being, rather, transferred to ageless life, and that he may receive from the judge and Saviour of all an equal repayment of the things which he has lent out here. For a disposition, pure as regards those who have grieved him, necessary to both parties for the sake of their mutual profit, God established for the sake of all, but especially because of the power of the last clause, which runs thus:

And do not lead us into temptation, but deliver us from the evil one.

The *Logos* makes clear in these words that if anyone does not perfectly forgive those who stumble, and present his heart to God purified of grief and made resplendent with the light of reconciliation with his neighbour, he will miss out on the gracious gift of the good things he has prayed for. Furthermore, by a just judgement, he will be given over to temptation and the evil one, so that he may learn to be purified from his faults by setting aside his own reproaches against others. Here he calls temptation *the law of sin* [Rom. 7:23], which the first man did not have on coming into being, and the evil one, the devil who mixes this law of sin with human nature and by deceit persuades the soul to transfer its appetite from what is allowed to what is forbidden and thus turn to the transgression of the divine command. So the rejection of the incorruption granted by grace became a fact. Or, again, some say that temptation is the voluntary assent of the soul to the passions of the flesh, and what is evil the actual way of satisfying an impassioned disposition. From neither of these does the just judge set anyone free who does not forgive his debtors their debts if he prays for such deliverance merely in words. Rather, the judge allows such a one to be defiled by *the law of sin* and abandons one whose will is cruel and ruthless to the dominion of the evil one, that is to say, to *dishonourable passions* [Rom. 1:26], sown by the devil, which have been preferred to nature, whose creator is God. Moreover, God does not prevent one who is voluntarily disposed to the passions of the flesh, nor does he redeem him from actually satisfying his inclination to such passions, because he has less regard for nature than insubstantial passions. In his eagerness for these things, he has ignored the *logos* of nature. Had he followed that *logos*, he would have known the difference between submitting to a law of nature, and submitting to the tyranny of passions which comes about not naturally, but through a deliberate choice. He would have known to preserve the law of nature by the pursuit of what is natural, to drive far from his will acquiescence to the passions, guarding nature by *logos*, for nature is pure and blameless, free from hatred or discord, and to have re-established his will as nature's companion, free from assault by anything not bestowed by the *logos* of nature. Therefore, having put away from himself all hatred and all unnatural discord, when he prays this prayer, he will be heard, and receive a twofold, rather than a single, grace from God, receiving forgiveness of his own past failures, and protection and redemption for those that are to come, no longer allowed to enter into temptation nor be enslaved by the evil one, for this one reason: being ready to make this one petition for his neighbour – to forgive his debts.

Therefore, let me step back a little and briefly recount the meaning of what we have just been saying: if we want to be delivered from the evil one and not to enter into temptation, let us believe in God and forgive our debtors their debts – *For*, it says, *if you do not forgive others their* sins, *neither will your heavenly Father forgive you* [Matt. 6:14–15] – not only to receive forgiveness for all our offences, but also to conquer *the law of sin*, no longer left to undergo experience of it, and let us trample on the serpent, the wicked begetter of that law [cf. Gen. 3:19], from whom we plead to be delivered. For we have Christ as our general who *has overcome the world* [1 John 5:4–5, John 16:33], who has armed us *with the laws of the commandments* [Eph. 2:15], and who, by helping us to reject the passions, naturally restores nature to itself. Since he is the *bread of life* [John 6:35] – of wisdom, knowledge and righteousness – he makes our desire for him insatiable and as we fulfil the Father's will we make clear from the way we live our lives how like we are to the angels in our worship of him, as we imitate the way they are well-pleasing to God in heaven. Thence, again, he urges us on to ascend to the highest summit of things divine, to *the Father of lights* [James 1:17], and he brings us to perfection as *partakers of the divine nature* [2 Pet. 1:4] through participation in the Spirit by grace, so that we are called *children of God* [John 1:12], wholly, without limit and immaculately encircling him who himself worked this grace and is by nature the Son of the Father, from whom and through whom and in whom *we live and move and have* – and shall have – *our being* [cf. Acts 17:28].

Let us, then, make the aim of the prayer to look to the mystery of deification, so that we may know what we were like and what the self-emptying of the only-begotten in the flesh has made of us instead, and know, too, whence he has taken us up – from the lowest place in the universe, where we were weighed down by sin – and to where he has raised us up by the power of his kind and loving hand. Let us love all the more the one who thus wisely prepared for us this salvation, and show through our actions that the prayer has been fulfilled, so that we manifest and proclaim that God is truly our Father by grace, rather than making it all too clear that the father of our life is really the Evil One who is always seeking, through *dishonourable passions* [Rom. 1:26], to exercise tyranny over nature. Let us not, unawares, exchange death for life, for each of the 'fathers' we have mentioned naturally gives recompense to his supporters: the one awarding eternal life to those who love him; the other causing death, on the pretext of voluntary temptations, to those who come close to him. For, according to Scripture, there are two modes of temptation or trial: the pleasurable, and the painful; the former is voluntary, the latter unchosen. The former is generative of sin: into this we have been ordered to pray not to enter according to the teaching of the Lord, who says, *And do not lead us into temptation*, and *Watch and pray, lest you enter into temptation* [Matt. 26:41]. The latter, painful trial is a penalty for sin, which, by various unchosen pains, punishes the sin-loving disposition. If we endure these pains, especially if we are not attached to them by the nails of wickedness, we shall hear the words of the great James, saying clearly: *Consider it all joy, brethren, when you meet with various temptations, because the testing of your faith produces endurance, while endurance produces proven character, and let proven character have its complete work* [James 1:2–4, Rom. 5:3–4]. The evil one wickedly deals in both sorts of temptation, both the voluntary and the involuntary. In the first case, by sowing bodily pleasures in the soul and exciting it, he contrives to separate the soul from divine love. In the second case, wanting to corrupt nature through pain, he cunningly seeks to force the soul cast down by exhaustion from its pains, to slander the creator in its thoughts.

But recognizing the intentions of the evil one, let us pray to avert voluntary temptation, so that our desire may not be diverted from the love of God. Let us endure nobly involuntary temptations, which come upon us with God's permission, so that we may make clear that we have preferred nature's creator to nature. May *all* of us *who call on the name of our Lord Jesus* [Rom. 10:13] be delivered from the pleasures the evil one offers us now and set free from pains that are to come by our participation in the reality of the good things to come, stored up for us and already revealed in the same Christ our Lord, who, alone with the Father and the Holy Spirit, is glorified by all creation.

Amen.

Anonymous, *A Discourse on Abba Philemon*

ANONYMOUS, A DISCOURSE ON ABBA PHILEMON (10TH OR 11TH C.?)

This lovely tale tells of the deeds and teaching of a monk named Philemon. Its origin and setting are murkier than has previously been supposed. While set in Egypt and imagined on that basis to have been written there in the sixth or seventh century, the language is frequently marked by later Byzantine usage and the setting could as easily be Athos in the tenth century. It must have been written by the twelfth, since Peter of Damaskos refers to it in his *Treasury of Spiritual Knowledge* (*Philokalia* 3:74–281).

The *Discourse* is generally thought to be the earliest witness to the Jesus Prayer in its full form, although short prayers are witnessed from the earliest days of monasticism, and Diadochos is our first witness to devotion to the name of Jesus. Whether Philemon is really the first to commend the Jesus Prayer does not matter so much as do his striving after holiness, his willing instruction of interested brethren and the teaching within which the Jesus Prayer is contextualized. It is one of very few narrative pieces in the *Philokalia*, although much of the tale is given to homilies and instructions. Yet Philemon's daily life, with its liturgical rhythms and emphasis on practice, is a valuable reminder that the loftier theology of gnomic texts is intended to be lived, rather than merely read.

Sources

Text: *PHILOKALIA* (1782): 485–95; *Philokalia* (1893/1982): vol. 2, 241–54

A Very Beneficial Treatise Concerning Abba Philemon

It is said of Abba Philemon the hermit that he shut himself up in a certain cave not far from the Lavra of the Romans, as it was called.[1] While there he pursued ascetic contests, turning over in his mind what Arsenios the Great is said to have asked himself: 'Philemon, why did you come here?'[2] So Philemon laboured in that cave for a long time, making cord and stitching it into baskets. He gave these to the steward of the Lavra and received in turn small loaves for his sustenance. He ate nothing save bread and salt, once a day. He *made no provision* at all in this life *for his flesh* [Rom. 13:14], devoting himself to contemplation. Enveloped by divine illumination, he came to experience unspeakable mysteries and continued in joyfulness. When he went to the church on Saturdays and Sundays, he walked alone, always deep in thought. He allowed no one to approach him, lest his contemplation be cut short. In church he stood in a corner with his face turned to the ground, and poured out fountains of tears, ceaselessly clinging to mourning, the memory of death and the example of our Holy Fathers – especially Arsenios the Great, in whose footsteps he strove to walk.

When heresy arose in Alexandria and its environs, he withdrew and went to the Lavra next to Nikanor.[3] There a most God-loving man, Paulinos, received Philemon, allotted him a place of his own and established him in perfect stillness. For a year Paulinos allowed absolutely no one at all ever to meet with him. Indeed, even he did not trouble Philemon, save for the time it took to give him his required bread. On the Feast of the Holy Resurrection of Christ, Paulinos and Philemon were talking together, and the subject of the eremitic condition came up. Knowing that this was the preferred goal of his most pious brother he implanted in him ascetic thoughts, taken from the Scriptures, and the holy fathers, revealing through everything he said that it is impossible to please God without perfect stillness, as had been shown to that divine oracle, Moses. He showed, too, that stillness gives birth to discipline, discipline to weeping, weeping to fear, fear to humility, humility to foresight, and foresight to love. Love makes the soul healthy and dispassionate, and then one knows that one is not far from God.

Philemon said to him, 'You must totally purify your mind through stillness and engage it in endless spiritual activity. For just as our eye apprehends sensible objects and marvels at their sight, the pure intellect apprehends intelligible things and at once is astonished by spiritual contemplation and becomes hard to move from it. The more our intellect is stripped of passions and purified, the more is it found worthy of knowledge. But the intellect is perfect when it tramples down even knowledge of the essences of creatures and is united instead to God. For when it has royal dignity, it refuses to go begging any longer. Neither is it swollen with baser desires, even if you offered all the kingdoms of the world [Matt. 4:8]. If, therefore, you desire to acquire all these virtues, stop worrying about everyone, and, taking flight, flee the world, and walk eagerly in the way of the Saints. Own just a tattered *cloak*, *a dirty cassock*, humble clothes, *simple character, artless discourse*, an unpretentious gait, *unaffected speech. Live in penury and be derided by all.*[4] Above all, guard your intellect and be watchful, be patient when the going is hardest, and preserve intact and undisturbed every blessing you have been granted. Attend carefully to yourself, to accept no subtly introduced pleasures. For the soul's passions are lulled to sleep by stillness, but if provoked or irritated they generally become savage and compel those who have them to sin all the more, just as bodily wounds become hard to heal when scratched at and scraped. An idle word, therefore, can separate the intellect from the memory of God, as the demons shove their way in and the senses believe them. For it is a great and fearful contest, guarding the soul. You must, therefore, be separated from the whole world and *deliver your soul from its affection for the body, and so to become without city, homeless, without belongings,* income, *property, business, company, uninstructed in human* affairs; you must be humble, compassionate, good, meek, still, *prepared to receive in your heart the stamp of divine knowledge. For it is not possible to write in wax, unless one has* first *smoothed away the letters previously written there*. For the Great Basil teaches us these things.[5]

'Such is the chorus of Saints: a choir separated entirely from life in this world. Guarding their heavenly thinking untroubled, they have been made resplendent with divine laws. And through their pious acts and words they flash like lightning, having put to death *their members upon the earth* [Col. 3:5] through self-control with both fear and desire of God. By ceaseless prayer and meditation on the divine Scriptures, the soul's intellectual eyes are opened to see the King of angels. Then arises great joy and a fierce yearning kindled swiftly in the soul. The flesh, too, being exalted together with soul by the Spirit, the whole human being becomes wholly spiritual. The craftsmen of blessed stillness and a restrained life who have separated themselves from every human comfort – they alone converse in purity with the Master who is alone in the heavens.'

The same God-loving brother, having heard these things and his soul being wounded with divine yearning, took up dwelling with Philemon in Sketis, where the greatest of our holy fathers travelled the way of piety. And so they dwelt in the Lavra of St John Kolobos, entrusting their daily needs to the steward of the Lavra, because of their desire to live in stillness.

So they dwelt, by the grace of God, in all stillness, making their appearance unassumingly on Saturday and Sunday, but for the rest of the week each one doing his own prayers in accordance with their rule. This was the rule of the holy Elder: during the night he quietly chanted the whole Psalter and the Odes, and he recited one section of the Gospel. After that he would sit by himself saying, 'Lord, have mercy', so earnestly and so long that he could no longer speak out loud. Then he would sleep, and at first light again chant the First Hour, and then sit in his dwelling facing the east and chanting verses in succession.[6] Then he would again recite by heart from the Apostle and the Gospel.[7] So Philemon passed every day, ceaselessly chanting and praying [1 Thess. 5:17], being so nourished by contemplation of the heavens that his intellect would often be drawn up into contemplation and he would not know whether he was still on earth. Therefore, when the brother saw Philemon so unflinchingly dedicated to his rule and completely changed by divine thoughts, he said to Philemon, 'Father, why do you toil in old age, *mortifying and enslaving your body* [1 Cor. 9:27]?' Philemon said in response, 'Believe me, child, God has set such eagerness and yearning in my soul for the rule that I cannot match its intensity but yearning for God and the hope of good things to come conquer my bodily infirmity.'

And so he sent his intellect soaring with desire to heaven, not only at the times mentioned, but even during mealtimes. Another time, then, a brother who dwelt with Philemon asked him, 'What is the mystery of contemplation?' Since Philemon saw that this brother was desirous of learning and insistent besides, he said to him, 'I will tell you, though you are by nature a child, that should someone's intellect be purified to its utmost, God reveals to it the contemplations of ministering powers and orders.' So the same brother asked him, 'Why are you more delighted with the Psalter than all the rest of divine Scripture? And why, when you are chanting quietly, do you recite the words as though conversing with someone?' Philemon said to him, 'I say to you, child, God has conceived the power of psalmody in my humble soul even as he did in the prophet David. And I cannot be parted from the sweet delight of manifold contemplations contained in them. For they contain the whole of divine Scripture.' Philemon admitted this to that inquisitive brother with much humility, after he had been pushed to it, and only for the brother's benefit.

A certain brother, by the name of John, came from the coast and cast himself before our Holy and Great Father Philemon. John clasped his feet and said to him, '*What shall I do*, Father, *that I may be saved*? [Luke 18:18, Acts 16:30]. For I see that my intellect is distracted and pulled this way and that where it ought not to go.' Philemon paused a little, then said, 'This passion belongs to those outside, and it remains since you do not yet possess perfect desire for God. For the warmth of that yearning and of the knowledge of God has not yet entered you.'

The brother said, 'And so what shall I do, Father?'

Philemon said to him, 'Go, and for now keep in your heart a hidden meditation that can purify your mind from these problems.'

The brother, being unfamiliar with what Philemon described, said to the Elder, 'What is this hidden meditation, Father?'

So Philemon said to him, 'Go. Keep watch in your heart while in your mind you say, watchfully and *with fear and trembling* [Phil. 2:12]: "Lord Jesus Christ, have mercy on me." For the Blessed Diadochos has handed this down to beginners.'[8] So John departed, and, with God's cooperation and the Father's prayers, he kept stillness and was delighted with the meditation – for a little while. And then it left him, suddenly, and he could not cultivate it watchfully or pray. So he returned to the Elder and revealed to him what had happened.

Philemon said to him, 'Behold, for a little while you have seen the footprint of stillness, and you have experienced its activity and the sweet delight that comes from it. Have this, therefore, always in your heart. Whether you are eating or drinking, whether you are in a group or outside your cell, or even if you are on the road, let no opportunity pass you by to pray this very prayer, to chant psalms, or to meditate on prayers and psalms, with a watchful mind and unwandering intellect. Do not let your intellect be idle even in a moment of urgent necessity, as you pray and meditate silently. For thus you can understand the depths of divine Scripture and the power hidden therein, and you can offer your intellect ceaseless activity, that you may fulfil the apostolic saying: *Pray without ceasing* [1 Thess. 5:17]. Pay careful attention, therefore, and guard your heart against accepting any sort of wicked, empty, or useless thoughts. Instead, at every time, whether sleeping, waking, eating, drinking, or gathering, let your heart secretly in thought meditate on the Psalms or pray, "Lord Jesus Christ, Son of God, have mercy on me." When you are chanting out loud, take care not to speak with your mouth while your mind is distracted with other things.'

And again, the brother asked, 'I see many empty fantasies in dreams.' The Elder said to him, 'Do not be afraid or discouraged. But, before you go to sleep, say many prayers in your heart and resist those thoughts, so that rather than being dragged about by the Devil's desires, God may receive you instead. Do all you can to go to sleep after psalmody and attentive meditation, and do not be careless and allow your mind to take in alien thoughts. Lie down, meditating on what you were praying, that these things may set you right as you sleep and *converse with you when you rise* [Prov. 6:22]. Also, say the holy symbol of the orthodox faith before you sleep.[9] For believing rightly about God is the fount and protection of all good things.'

Again, the brother asked Philemon, saying, 'In your love, Father, tell me what sort of activity your intellect has? Teach me, please, that I may also be saved.' Philemon said, 'Why do you want to pry into these things?' But the brother had already risen and grasped the Saint's feet, kissing them and begging Philemon to answer him. Many hours later, Philemon said, 'You cannot bear it right now, for maintaining the work suitable for each sense belongs to a man who has acquired a disposition for the good things of righteousness. Nor can someone not yet totally purified from this world's vain thoughts be vouchsafed such a gift. Therefore, if you are really desirous of such things, lay hold of this hidden meditation with a pure heart. For if your prayer and meditation on the Scriptures remain constant, the intellectual eyes of the soul will be opened for you. Then great joy will come to your soul, with an indescribable piercing desire, while your flesh is set alight by the Spirit, so the whole person becomes spiritual. Whether God vouchsafes you to pray undistractedly with a pure intellect at night or during the day, do not cling, then, to your own rule. Rather, stretch out towards God with all your strength as you are joined to him and as he himself enlightens your heart as to what spiritual activity you ought to take up.'

Then Philemon added: 'Once a certain elder came to me and, having been asked by me about the condition of his intellect, said, "For two years I persisted in entreating God with my whole heart and supplicating him incessantly, that he might give me to have the prayer that he gave to his disciples stamped in my heart without end or distraction. And, seeing my labour and endurances, our generous Lord granted my petition."'

Philemon said also this: 'When thoughts of vanities arise in the mind, they are the diseases of an idle and indolent soul. It is therefore fitting that, as it is written, "*we preserve our own* intellect *with every guard*" [Prov. 4:23]; that we chant without distraction; and that we pray with a pure intellect. So then, brothers, God wants us to show our zeal for him in labours first and then in love and ceaseless prayer, and he will show us the way of salvation. It is obvious that there is no other way leading up to heaven except perfect stillness, flight from all wickedness, the procurement of good things, perfect love for God, and being united with him in holiness and righteousness. If someone achieves these, he will return swiftly to the heavenly country. Whoever wants to ascend to this height must always *mortify* their *members upon the earth* [Col. 3:5]. For whenever our soul enjoys the contemplation of real goodness, it turns to none of the passions roused by pleasure. Instead, having rejected every bodily luxury, it receives the manifestation of God with a pure and undefiled mind. We need, therefore, careful guard, bodily labours, and purification four our soul, that we may cause God to dwell in our hearts and thereafter unerringly fulfil his divine commandments. And then God, through the grace of the Spirit he has established in us, sends forth his own activities like the sun's rays and teaches us to guard his laws without fail. Through toils and trials must we purify the *image, according to* which we were made rational and receptive of all understanding and even *likeness to God* [Gen. 1:26], being refashioned for royal dignity and bearing our senses re-forged in the furnace of trials to undiluted purity. God made human nature to partake of every good thing and capable of intellectually contemplating the choirs of *angels*, the glories of *dominions, powers, rulers, authorities* [Eph. 1:18], the *unapproachable light* [1 Tim. 6:16], and his glory that outshines the sun.

'Now, when you have accomplished a virtue, do not let your thoughts be exalted against your brother, as though you have achieved something where he has been careless. For this is the beginning of pride. Moreover, take care with all your strength to do nothing for the sake of pleasing people. If you are struggling with passions do not make excuses, and do not get discouraged if the warfare persists. Instead, get up and cast yourself before God with your whole heart, and say with the Prophet: "*Execute justice, O Lord, on those who wrong me, for I am powerless against them*" [Ps. 34:1]. Seeing your humility, he will swiftly send you his assistance. When you are travelling with someone, allow no vain discussion, but instead give your intellect its appropriate spiritual activity, that it can develop a good habit and forgetfulness of the world's pleasures, and you will attain the shores of dispassion.'

When Philemon had finished catechizing the brother with these and many other words, he dismissed him. But after a little while, the brother came back to him and started a new line of interrogation, saying, 'What shall I do, Father, for sleep weighs me down during my nightly prayer rule and does not permit me to pray watchfully or to keep vigil very long? Also, what if I want to do some handiwork while I chant?' Philemon said to him, 'When you can pray watchfully, do not take up handiwork. If, however, you should be gripped by despondency, then move around a little, threaten your thought, and take up handiwork.' The brother said to him in turn, 'Master, are not you weighed down with sleep during your prayer rule?' Philemon said to him, 'Not really. But, if sleep does approach, I rouse myself and recite from the Prologue of John's Gospel [John 1:1–18], straining my mind's gaze towards God, and sleep vanishes immediately. I do the same with thoughts: when one comes upon me, I counter it with tears as though it were fire, and it vanishes. You, however, cannot be armed this way, at least not yet. Instead, you must always keep at your hidden meditation and the daily prayers ordained for us by the Holy Fathers – that is, the Third, Sixth and Ninth Hours, and Vespers. Strive also to pray during the night. Strive with all your strength to guard yourself from doing anything to please people or to harbour enmity with your brother, lest you separate yourself from your God. Strive to guard your mind from disturbance, being very careful with thoughts from outside.

'Whenever you are in church and are about to partake of the Divine Mysteries of Christ,[10] do not depart until you receive perfect peace. Stand in one place and do not budge until the dismissal. Understand that you are standing in Heaven, about to meet God with his Holy Angels, and to receive him in your heart. Prepare yourself with great *fear and trembling* [Phil. 2:12], lest you join unworthily with the holy powers.' Having armed the brother well with these words, and, having commended him to the Lord and the Spirit of his grace, Philemon dismissed him.

Besides all this, the brother who dwelt with Philemon related the following. Once, being seated next to him, I asked him whether he felt the demons' assaults when seated in desolate places. He said, 'Forgive me brother, but should God allow the trials and temptations sent to me by the devil to strike you, I do not think you could endure their bitterness. I have spent seventy years or more enduring trials and temptations, and I have dwelt in various desolate places in utmost solitude. I have experienced and suffered such things that it would do no good to relate their bitterness to those who have not experienced stillness. But in trials and temptations I have always done this: *I have placed* all *my hope in* God [Ps. 77:7], with whom I signed the contract of renunciation. And he has immediately delivered me from every necessity. Therefore, my brother, I no longer make my own plans. For I know him who takes care of me, and so bear more lightly the temptations that come upon me. This alone do I offer you from my experience: *Pray without ceasing* [1 Thess. 5:17]. For I know that however terrible the torments may be, so many are the crowns procured for the one who endures them: these are the commitments we receive from the just judge.

'Now that you know this, brother, do not slip into laziness, now that you realize you stand in the midst of battle and that those who fight God's enemy on our behalf are exceedingly numerous. For how could we dare a frontal assault on so fearful an enemy of our species unless the exceedingly mighty right hand of God's Word, which watches out and watches over us, also sustained us? How did human nature resist his attacks? *For who, it says, will uncover the front of his clothing? Who could pierce the plate of his chest? From his mouth there come burning torches and skittering sparks of fire. From his nostrils come a fume of burning smoke, of lit coals. His very soul is coals. Flame issues from his mouth; in his neck is power increased. Behind him follows destruction; his heart has grown hard as a stone, it stands like an unbreakable anvil. He makes the deep boil like a cauldron; he regards the sea as an ointment pot. He sees every exalted thing and rules over all that live in the waters* [Job 41:5, 11–14, 16, 23, 26]. Our fight, brother, is against this one. Scripture sketched such and so great a tyrant, but victory over him comes easily to those who have lawfully professed the solitary life, for two reasons. First, by renouncing the world and through bravery in virtues, they possess nothing of his. Secondly, we have one who fights on our behalf. For tell me who has come to the Lord and received in his intellect the fear of God, and has not had his nature refashioned? Or who, having adorned himself with divine laws and deeds, has not made his soul utterly resplendent? Or has not prepared himself to flash forth in divine ideas and thoughts? No, he does not let his soul be idle. For he has God raising up his intellect to launch it insatiably at the light. A soul so frequently roused to action is not permitted by the Spirit to luxuriate in passions. Rather, like a king breathing bitterness and terror against his enemies, cutting them down mercilessly and never retreating, he finds victory in battle through practical virtue, raising his hands to heaven, and through the intellect's prayer.'

This same brother related also that Philemon would never allow himself to hear an idle word. In fact, if someone carelessly related a matter that would not help the soul, Philemon would not respond at all. When I left on some duty, he never asked why I had left, and when I returned he did not ask where

I had been. Once, I had to sail to Alexandria because of a pressing need, and thence to the Queen of Cities[11] on a Church matter. Having bid farewell to the most pious brethren there I went up, having sent no message to God's servant, Philemon. After I spent a good while there, I finally returned to Philemon at Sketis. When he saw me he grew joyful and kissed me, but then, having offered a prayer, he sat down without asking me anything and instead remained engaged in contemplation. Later I desired to test him, and so I waited for days without giving him bread to eat. But he never demanded any or even asked about it. After all this I bowed before him and said, 'In your love, Father, tell me, were you not hurt that I did not bring you bread according to our custom?'

He said, 'Forgive me, brother, but even if you fail to give me bread for twenty days, I still will not ask it of you. For as long as I can endure in soul, I can endure in body.' That is how much he was devoted to contemplation of the true good. He used to say, 'From the time I came to Sketis I have not permitted my thoughts to leave my cell. Nor have I accepted any thought in mind save the fear of God and the judgement seats of the age to come. I have ruminated on the judgement threatening sinners, the eternal fire, the *outer darkness* [Matt. 25:30], how the souls of sinners and the righteous fare, and also *of the good things laid up for the righteous.*[12] I have thought about how *each* receives *his own wage, according to his own labour* [1 Cor. 3:8]: one for his increased toils, one for his almsgiving and unfeigned love, one for his willing poverty and renunciation of the whole world, another for humility and utmost stillness, another for his extreme submission and another for his life of exile. As I consider all these things, I permit no other thought to operate in me, and I can no longer be among people or busy my mind with them, lest I be separated from more divine thoughts.'

He added a story about a certain monk, saying, 'He had reached dispassion and used to receive the bread of delight from the hand of an angel, but he grew careless and was deprived of this honour. For when the soul grows slack and the intellect loses its keen attention, night seizes the soul. For wherever God does not shine, everything is confounded as in thick darkness, making it impossible to gaze at God alone and to *tremble at his words* [Isa. 66:2]. For *I am the God who is near, says the Lord, and not a distant God. If someone be hidden in secret, will I not still see them? Do I not fill heaven and earth? says the Lord* [Jer. 23:23–4].' Philemon also recalled many others who suffered similarly, to which he added Solomon's fall. He said, 'Solomon had received such wisdom and was glorified by all, for he was like *the Morning Star that rises at dawn* [Isa. 14:12], illuminating all with his shining universal wisdom – and for the sake of a little pleasure, he lost his glory [3 Kgds 11:1–13]. Carelessness is a frightening thing. We must *pray without ceasing* [1 Thess. 5:17] lest some thought steal in and separate us from God, distracting our intellect from him. For a pure heart, having become entirely a receptacle of the Holy Spirit, purely gazes on God himself as in a mirror.'

'Hearing this,' said the brother, 'and considering his actions, I realized that fleshly passions were totally inoperative in him. He was always desirous of better things, and you could see him being formed by the divine Spirit, groaning with *unutterable groans* [Rom. 8:26], being recollected to himself and testing himself, struggling lest some intrusive thought muddy his mental purity, and some disgrace hiddenly come to attach itself to him. As I saw these things,' said the brother who dwelt with him, 'and was roused to long for similar accomplishments, I entreated him constantly and repeatedly asked him: "How can I gain your intellectual purity?"'

He said, 'Go. Labour. For you require labour and toil in your heart. For things worthy of diligence and toil do not accrue to us who have fallen asleep. After all, one cannot gain the land without toil, either. Whoever desires to find spiritual advancement must first of all renounce their own desires and obtain instead perpetual mourning and voluntary poverty, attend not to the sins of others but to theirs and theirs alone, weep for them day and night, and hold no human friendship. A soul afflicted by its miseries and goaded by the memory of past sins becomes dead to the world, and the world dies to it: which is to say, fleshly passions become inoperative for them and they for the passions. For one who has renounced the world, submitted to Christ, and devoted themselves to stillness, loves God, guards the *image*, and is enriched with the likeness [Gen. 1:26]. For they receive again from God the abundance of the Spirit, and become the dwelling of God rather than demons, presenting righteous deeds to God. A soul, purified from worldly life and free from all pollutions of the flesh, having neither *spot nor wrinkle* [Eph. 5:27], will receive the crown of righteousness and shine bright with the beauty of virtue.

'If mourning is not present when someone begins their renunciation, there will be no spiritual tears, no memory of everlasting punishment, no true stillness, no persistent prayer, no psalmody, no meditation on the divine Scriptures. But if these have not become a habit that drives someone to the constancy of endurance to practise them with the intellect willingly or not, and if fear of God does not flourish in their mind, then such a person leans to the end on their friendship with the world and cannot find intellectual purity in prayer. For piety and the fear of God purify the soul from passions, prepare the intellect to become free. These lead it to natural contemplation and cause it to touch even theology, which it receives in the form of beatitude, which offers pledges here and now to those who seek it and preserves the soul unshakeable. Let us, therefore, attend with all our strength to practice in virtue, through which we are led upwards to piety, which is mental purity, the fruit of which is natural and theological contemplation. For a brilliant and supremely theological intellect says that *practice is the stairway to contemplation*.[13] If we are heedless about practical virtue, we will be bereft of all philosophy. For even if someone has climbed to the summit of virtue, they still need ascetic labour to bridle the body's disordered impulses and to guard the safe preservation of thoughts. Even thus someone may scarcely attain the indwelling of Christ. For spiritual courage is added to us only as much as righteousness abounds in us. When the intellect is perfected the whole of it is mingled with God, is illuminated with divine light, and has the unspeakable mysteries revealed to it. Then will our intellect truly learn *where there is prudence, where strength, where there is understanding*

to know everything, *where longevity and life, where the light of
the eyes and peace* [Baruch 3:14]. It will have the opportunity
to enjoy these things, though for now it is engaged in fighting
the passions. For both virtues and vices blind our mind: vices
prevent it from seeing virtues, virtues from seeing vices. But
when our intellect finds the other side of war and is granted
spiritual gifts, then the whole becomes radiant and frequently
roused to action by grace. Then it stands steadfastly in contemplation of spiritual things. Such an intellect is no longer bound
to things here but *has passed from death to life* [John 5:24].

Whoever has accepted our zealous way of life and who would
approach God must have an innocent heart and pure mouth,
and so hymn God worthily with the pure word proceeding
from a pure mouth. For the soul united to God converses with
him continually. Brothers, let us choose to climb the peak of
virtues, and not remain nailed to the passions on earth. Whoever struggles, whoever has advanced to draw near to God,
who has found participation in holy light, and is wounded with
yearning for God – he *takes delight in the Lord* [Ps. 36:4] with
a spiritual, even an incomprehensible, joy. So the divine Psalmist: *Take delight in the Lord and* may *he give you your heart's
wishes. He will display your righteousness like light and your
judgement like midday* [Ps. 36:4, 6]. What desire is so keen in
a soul, so unbearable, as that which comes from God to a soul
purified from every vice, which says from a sincere disposition,
I am wounded with love [Song 5:8]? 'The lightning flash of
divine beauty is forever indescribable and ineffable. Our language does not describe it, our hearing does not perceive it.
Even if you speak of the rays of the morning star, the radiance
of the moon, the light of the sun, they all pale in comparison
with that glory – less like it even than the middle of the night
or shadowy gloom compared to a clear noonday.' I quote that
oracle, Basil, who, having received and been taught by his experience, handed this on to us in his teachings.[14]

The brother who dwelt with Philemon related these things
and more. However, one should not marvel at another story
of his, which contains a great demonstration of Philemon's
humility. Having for a long while been elevated to the priesthood

and grasping heavenly things in knowledge and virtue, Philemon nevertheless so fled from the dignity of the divine Liturgies that for much of the time of his ascetic struggles he scarcely allowed himself to draw near to the holy altar.[15]

As to receiving the Divine Mysteries, he lived with such exactitude that whenever he happened to have a conversation with people, he would not partake, even though he had said nothing worldly and had only had the conversation for his interlocutors' benefit. When he was about to receive the Divine Mysteries, he importuned God with prayers, psalms and confessions. He trembled at the priest's voice, when, at the time of the Eucharist, the priest addressed the church, saying, 'Holy things for those who are holy'.[16] He explained that then the whole church is full of holy Angels, while the King of the heavenly powers himself mystically presides, and is transformed into body and blood in our hearts. For the same reason he would say, 'We must only dare to approach holy Communion in the ineffable mysteries of Christ innocently, purely, as though outside our very flesh, with neither doubt nor uncertainty, and so partake of the enlightenment of these mysteries. For many of our Holy Fathers beheld the Angels standing guard around them, and for that reason kept silence themselves, speaking to no one.'

Philemon also said that if he had to sell his own handiwork, then, to avoid any lie, oath, chatter or other form of sin that might follow, he would stand there and pretend to be a fool. Everyone who wished to buy could take what they wanted and pay what they wished. He made palm-baskets, as they are called, and gratefully accepted whatever money was offered without saying anything, this true philosopher.

St Symeon the New Theologian, *One Hundred and Fifty-Three Practical and Theological Chapters*

ST SYMEON THE NEW THEOLOGIAN
(949–1022/1027)

St Symeon was born into a wealthy provincial family and sent off to Constantinople to be educated with a view to a life at court. He never found that path fulfilling and, at around twenty, experienced a vision of light – of God as light. Such visions would be more common in his later years, but for now he remained in the world a little longer. It seems, then, that what Symeon experienced in his worldly youth was not the kind of vision that Athonite monks would later describe as the pinnacle of life spent in interior prayer and stillness, but it was decisive for the perspective he would develop on Christian aspirations. In 977 he joined the Stoudios Monastery under the tutelage of Symeon 'the Pious'. Under this elder our own Symeon would learn to refract all monastic community through an intimate and intense relationship with a 'spiritual father'. His attachment was such that he was forced to leave Stoudios not long after and move to the Monastery of St Mamas, where he would stay about twenty-five years. Symeon was soon ordained priest and made abbot. As a monastic leader, he had mixed results – on the one hand, his monks mutinied and expelled him for three years; on the other, he seems to have reconciled all parties. His commitment to the memory and glorification of Symeon the Pious, as well as teaching on confession and spiritual direction, to which his claims of divine visions added further complications, led Symeon to resign the abbacy and be condemned in an ecclesiastical court for heresy. By this period, Symeon was called 'the New Theologian', perhaps as an insult, synonymous with 'heretic'. Eventually, though, he was vindicated and, although he chose to remain in exile in a close-knit monastic community writing poetry, his fame would last and the name would stick – but now as a tribute to his status alongside Sts John the Evangelist and Gregory Nazianzen, as a teacher of orthodoxy in word and deed.

Symeon emphasized tears and compunction, the continuing gifts of the Holy Spirit, including ecstatic visions of light, and deification that amount to union with God achieved in intensely bodily and even erotic terms. The text translated here, *One Hundred and Fifty-Three Chapters*, is a pastiche of chapters, drawn from both Symeon's own works and elsewhere, in conscious imitation of *On Prayer* (by Evagrios, in this collection), which also had 153 short chapters. This set of 153 chapters, though, breaks down as follows:

1–118 come from Symeon's *Catecheses*, and include many themes from his teaching that appealed to later hesychast monks, including visions of light, experiences of the Holy Spirit, and the gift of tears. 119–52 are actually from St Symeon the Pious, and describe the ascetic life within a coenobitic context, with emphasis on traditional practices and values. 153 is a very loose version of ss. 30–31 of the *Life of Symeon the New Theologian* by his disciple St Niketas Stethatos.

Sources

Text: Chapters 1–118: J. Darrouzès and L. Neyrand (eds.), *Syméon le Nouveau Théologien: Chapitres théologiques, gnostiques et pratiques*, Sources Chrétiennes 51 (Paris: Éditions du Cerf, 1980).

Chapters 119–52: H. Alfeyev and L. Neyrand (eds.), *Syméon le Studite: Discours ascétique*, Sources Chrétiennes 460 (Paris: Éditions du Cerf, 2001).

Chapter 153: Niketas Stethatos, *The Life of Saint Symeon the New Theologian*, ed. Richard P. H. Greenfield, Dumbarton Oaks Medieval Library 20 (Cambridge, MA: Harvard University Press, 2013).

Alternative text: *PHILOKALIA* (1782): 755–82; *Philokalia* (1893/1982): vol. 3, 237–72.

One Hundred and Fifty-Three
Practical and Theological Chapters

1. Faith means dying for Christ's sake in fulfilment of his commandments and believing this very death to be the procurement of life. It means regarding poverty as wealth, meanness and disregard as true glory and grandeur. It means believing that in owning nothing one possesses everything – or, rather, that one gains *the unsearchable wealth of* the full knowledge of *Christ* [Eph. 3:8]. Finally, it means seeing everything visible as clay and smoke.

2. Faith in Christ means not merely scoffing at the delights of this life, but enduring and bearing every trial that comes upon you, whether in insults, tribulations or troubles, so long as God chooses and until he visits us. For it says, *Patiently I waited for the Lord and he attended to me* [Ps. 39:1].

3. Those who put their parents before God's command in anything do not possess faith in Christ. They are judged entirely by their own conscience, if indeed they have a living conscience about their own faithlessness! For it belongs to the faithful never in any way to transgress the commandment of *our great God and Saviour, Jesus Christ* [Tit. 2:13].

4. Faith in God gives birth to a desire for good things and a fear of punishment. In their turn, this desire for better things and fear of worse punishments make our keeping of the commandments exact. The exact keeping of the commandments convinces us of our frailty as humans, while comprehension of our true frailty begets the memory of death. Someone who procures the memory of death as a constant companion will seek to learn with all his effort what sort of things will happen to him after his departure and withdrawal from this life. Striving always to know about things to come, he ought first to rid himself of everything present. For so long as he is mastered by attachment – even a meagre one – to things present, he cannot gain knowledge of things to come. Even if he tastes this knowledge thanks to God's providence, then – unless he very swiftly renounces everything by which and in which he was mastered through attachment, and becomes wholly given to such knowledge and refuses to think willingly about anything else – then *even* the slight knowledge he seems *to have will be taken from him* [Matt. 25:29].

5. Renunciation of the world and total withdrawal, which entails exile from everything in life – materials, habits, opinions and faces – as well as denial of body and will, becomes the harbinger of tremendous benefit for him who has made his renunciation vigorously and in good time.

6. One who flees the world does not, at the outset, give his soul even an hour of consolation – even if all his relatives and friends compel him to do so. For the demons suggest this to them, so that they may quench his heart's fervour. For even if they cannot entirely trip you up in your purpose, they can make your heart slacker and totally weak.

7. When you are found to be courageous, refusing comfort in all the pleasures of this life, then, indeed, the demons will arouse sympathy in your relatives, making them weep and wail on your account – before your very eyes! You will know the truth of this when you remain inflexible in face of this provocation: you will see those same relatives suddenly kindled to rage and hatred against you. You will see them spurning you as an enemy and refusing even to see you.

8. When you see all the trouble your parents, siblings and friends complain of on your account, laugh at the demon who in one way or another brings about such opposition to you. With fear and great zeal, distance yourself and beg God fervently to bring you swiftly to the harbour of a good father, in which God himself will give rest to your wearied and burdened soul. For the sea of life offers many occasions of dangers and even of ultimate destruction.

9. Whoever desires to hate the world needs to have love for God in the very depths of his soul and have continual memory of him. Nothing else makes a person abandon all these things with joy and reject them as so much rubbish.

10. Do not desire to remain with the world at all even for good reasons, which, rather, are irrational pretexts, but, when you are called, obey straight away. Nothing pleases God so much as our readiness, since ready obedience with poverty is better than delay with much wealth.

11. While the world and everything in it pass away, God alone is eternal and immortal. So rejoice, all you who have abandoned corruptible things for his sake! For not only are wealth and possessions corruptible, but every pleasure and enjoyment of sin is corruption itself. Only God's commandments are light and life and called this by all.

12. Brother, if consumed by fiery zeal, you have hastened to a monastery or spiritual father, do not make use of baths, food or other bodily consolations for the sake of rest, even if you are exhorted by him or your ascetic brethren. On the contrary, be ever prepared for fasting, for suffering, for exacting self-control. However, should your father in the Lord urge you to partake of a little comfort, you are to be obedient, not seeking to follow your own free will in this matter. If he does not urge you, then you will bear with joy whatever you have chosen voluntarily to do for the good of your soul. Keeping to this rule, you will always be self-controlled and abstinent in all things, as well as renouncing your own will in everything. Moreover, you will preserve undying the unifying flame in your heart, which compels you to despise everything.

13. When the demons do everything they can think of and still cannot alter or impede our godly purpose, then they stealthily influence people who feign piety and attempt through them to impede those who genuinely struggle for it. First, as though moved sincerely by love and sympathy, these hypocrites exhort us to allow ourselves some bodily rest, lest – so they say – our body be weakened and we fall into despondency. Then they invite us to profitless conversations and make us waste our days in such drivel. If some zealous person, having obeyed

them, becomes like these hypocrites, they turn and laugh at his destruction. On the other hand, if he is not led on by their words but, rather, keeps himself a stranger to all, circumspect and sparing in his words – then these hypocrites are moved to envy and do everything they can until they have hounded him from the monastery! For dishonoured vainglory cannot bear to see humility praised right in front of it.

14. The vainglorious person chokes at seeing a humble person weeping tears that benefit him twice over: by God who is moved to mercy and by humans who offer him praise that he never sought.

15. From the moment you attach yourself entirely to your spiritual father, know that you are alienated from all worldly pursuits – I mean human affairs and possessions – that lead you astray. Without him you will not do or practise any of those things. Indeed, you will not ask him to allow you anything great or small, unless he on his own initiative either allows you to receive it or gives it to you with his own hand.

16. Without the permission of your father in God, do not give alms from the goods which you have brought to the monastery, nor allow someone else to distribute them on your behalf. For it is better to be poor and a stranger and regarded as such, than to distribute your goods and give them to the poor, while you are still a novice. If you have pure faith, you will entrust everything to the will of your spiritual father, as to the hand of God.

17. Do not ask to be given a cup of water, even if you have a fever, until your spiritual father, moved by himself, prescribes it. Constrain yourself and compel yourself in everything, persuading and telling your train of thoughts, 'If God wishes.' And, if you are worthy to drink, God will reveal it to your spiritual father, and he will say to you, 'Drink.' Then and only then – drink with a pure conscience, even if it is not at the right time for refreshment.

18. Someone who has experienced spiritual benefit and obtained genuine faith, calling on God as witness to the truth, said, 'I have resolved on my part never to ask my father if I might eat, nor drink, and never to partake of anything at all

without him, until God gives him assurance to command me. Holding to this,' he said, 'I have never failed in my aim.'

19. Someone who has palpable faith in his father in God, when he sees him, reckons that he sees Christ. He firmly believes that when he is with his father and following him, he is with Christ and following him. Such a one will never long to talk with another, nor will he prefer any worldly thing to the memory and love of his spiritual father. For what is greater or more beneficial than to be with Christ, both in the present and in the life to come? What is more beautiful or sweeter than the sight of him? If he is worthy of conversation with his father, he will without doubt draw eternal life from it.

20. Someone who is disposed to love and pray for those who insult or wrong him, who hate him or even rob him, makes great progress very quickly. For when this is felt in the heart, your thoughts are drawn down into an abyss of humility and the sources of tears, in which the soul, with its three powers, is engulfed. It also leads his mind up to the *heaven of dispassion*[1] and renders it contemplative; the taste of goodness from there leads him to count as dross everything in the present life and to accept food and drink neither often nor happily.

21. Not only must the ascetic refrain from wicked actions, but he must also endeavour to be free even of contrary thoughts and concepts. He must strive to spend his time in spiritual considerations that benefit his soul, so that he may live without concern for the things of this life.

22. If someone has stripped quite naked, but still has his blindfold on and will not take it off, he still cannot see the light, even if the rest of his body is naked. So it is if someone rejects all worldly affairs and possessions and even escapes the passions themselves: unless he frees the eye of his soul from the worries of this life and from wicked thoughts, he will never see the intelligible light – which is our Lord and God Jesus Christ

23. As a veil is laid over the eyes, so worldly thoughts and the worries of this life come upon the eye of the soul – that is, the mind. As long as such thoughts continue, we shall not see. But as soon as they are cast off by the memory of death,

then we shall clearly behold the *true light, which enlightens everyone who comes into the world* on high [John 1:9].

24. Someone blind from birth will neither understand nor believe the power of what has been written, while one deemed worthy to see will bear witness that what has been said is true.

25. Someone able to use their physical eyes knows when it is night, and when it is day, but a blind person knows neither. So also someone who looks up spiritually, and can see with the eye of the intellect, beholds the true and inaccessible light, but when, from negligence, he turns back to his former blindness, he is deprived of light, he feels keenly this loss quite clearly and is not ignorant why this has happened. Someone blind from birth knows nothing of all this either from experience or from personal activity, unless by hearsay he learns something about matters he can never behold. If he tells others what he has heard, neither he nor those who hear him will know what he is talking about.

26. It is impossible at once to stuff the flesh with food to satiety and spiritually to enjoy intellectual and divine delights. As much as one cares for his belly, so much will he deprive himself of that delight. To the extent that he mortifies his body, so will he be filled with spiritual nourishment and consolation.

27. Let us abandon everything on earth: not just wealth, gold and other material possessions of this life, but let us utterly cast off from our soul even the desire for such things. Let us hate not only the body's pleasures, but also its irrational movements, and let us strive to mortify it through toil. For it is because of our body that desires are roused and lead to action, and as long as it lives, our soul is of necessity quite dead and finds every one of God's commands very difficult, or even impossible.

28. Just as the flame of a fire rises ever higher, however you turn the wood from which it was kindled, so the heart of someone vainglorious cannot be humbled; and if you try to help him, it will be elevated more and more. Whether reprimanded or admonished, he reacts with exceeding violence; when praised or encouraged, his elation is beyond measure.

29. Someone practised in answering back has become for

himself a two-edged sword; unwittingly he destroys his own soul and makes it a stranger to eternal life.

30. Someone who answers back is like one who voluntarily makes himself a hostage to his king's enemies. For contradicting is a fish hook baited with self-justification: deceived by it we swallow the sharp hook of sin. Then the miserable soul finds itself caught by this means – as by the tongue and throat – by the spirits of wickedness. Sometimes it is raised up to the height of pride, sometimes cast down into the maelstrom of sin's abyss, and condemned together with the spirits that fell from Heaven.

31. Someone whose heart suffers bitterly when slighted or insulted should know from this that he still cherishes in his bosom the ancient serpent. If, then, he bears it with silence or responds with great humility, he weakens it and renders it inert. But if he replies with bitterness or speaks rashly, he has given the serpent strength to spread its venom in his heart and savagely to devour his innards. Thereafter the serpent is strengthened day by day to consume the wretched soul's strength and accomplishment of good things, so that it lives in sin and is completely dead to righteousness.

32. If you desire to renounce the world and be thoroughly taught the Gospel life, procure for yourself a teacher who is neither inexperienced nor prone to passions, lest you be taught the diabolic, rather than Gospel, life. For what is learned from good teachers is good, and what is learned from bad teachers is bad – wicked crops grow from wicked seeds.

33. Beseech God earnestly with prayers and tears [cf. Heb. 5:7] to send you a holy and dispassionate guide. Search the divine Scriptures yourself, and particularly the practical writings of our holy Fathers, so that, having compared the teachings of your teacher and your superior with them, you may behold them as in a mirror and learn them thoroughly: what is in accord with the divine Scriptures embrace and hold fast in your mind; what is false and alien discern and cast away, lest you be led astray. For many, as you well know, have gone astray and become false teachers in these days [cf. 2 Pet. 2:1].

34. Anyone who cannot see but still undertakes to guide others deceives them and brings those who follow him into a

pit of destruction in accordance with the Lord's saying: *If the blind leads the blind, both will fall into a pit* [Matt. 15:14].

35. One who is blind to the One is quite blind to everything, but one who beholds in the One contemplates all things. For abstaining from contemplation of all and yet, at once, seeking to enter into contemplation of all, he finds himself outside what he seeks to contemplate. Being in the One he sees all things and being in the region of the all he sees nothing at all. One who beholds in the One through the One sees distinctly himself, everybody and everything; hidden in it he sees nothing at all.

36. One who has not put on the image of our Lord Jesus Christ, *the heavenly man* and God, with full consciousness and awareness, in his rational and intellectual humanity, is still only *flesh and blood* [1 Cor. 15:49–50]. For he cannot receive a feeling of spiritual glory through his understanding, just as those blind from birth cannot know the light of the sun through understanding alone.

37. One who hears, sees and senses in this way knows the power of what has been said, since he already bears *the image of the heavenly man* [1 Cor. 15:49], having also *come to the perfect manhood of the fullness of Christ* [Eph. 4:13]. Such a one is well able to guide the flock of Christ on the path of God's commandments. Anyone who does not know what has been said and takes it otherwise evidently has not kept his soul's senses clear and healthy; it would be better for him to be led than to lead others at their peril.

38. If you look on your teacher and guide as God, you cannot answer back. If, however, someone supposes and says that you can, beware, for he is deceived. For he does not know what attitude those who are God's have towards God.

39. Someone who believes that his life and death are in the hand of his shepherd can never contradict him. It is ignorance of this that begets contradiction, which procures intelligible and eternal death.

40. Before the accused receives his sentence, he is given a chance to speak to the judge about what he has done. After his deeds have been laid bare and the sentence given by the judge, he has nothing to say to his jailers, whether small or great.

41. Before a monk enters this tribunal and before what is in his heart has been laid bare, perhaps he is allowed to answer back, whether through ignorance or, as he supposes, to keep his own thoughts hidden. But after the disclosure of his thoughts and a pure confession, he is no longer allowed to contradict the one who, after God, is his judge and master until death. For the monk, from the moment he has entered this tribunal and laid bare the secrets of his heart, is convinced from the beginning, if he has any understanding at all, that he is worthy of countless deaths. He believes, too, that through his obedience and humility he will be delivered from every torture and punishment, at least, if he truly understands the nature of the mystery.

42. One who guards these things indelibly in his own mind will never be moved in his heart, if he is disciplined, rebuked or reproached. However, one who falls into such evils – I mean answering back and not trusting his spiritual father – is carried piteously into the trap and the pit of Hades while still alive. That man becomes a house of Satan and all his impure power, as a *son of unbelief* and *destruction* [Eph. 2:2, John 17:12].

43. I exhort you to turn these principles of obedience over continually in your mind, and to strive with all zeal not to tumble down into the aforementioned evils of Hades. Rather, fervently beseech God like this, day by day, and say: 'God and Lord of all, possessing authority over every soul and breathing being, alone able to heal me, attend to the prayer of my wretched self; kill and destroy by the presence of your All-Holy Spirit the dragon lurking in me; make me worthy, in my poverty stripped of every virtue, to fall in tears at the feet of my holy father; fill his holy soul with sympathy that he may show mercy on me. Lord, give humility to my heart and thoughts befitting a sinner who has determined to repent in you. Do not in the end abandon a soul that has once confessed and submitted to you, chosen and esteemed you above the whole world. For you know, Lord, that I want to be saved, despite the obstacle of my ingrained wickedness. But for you, Master, *all things are possible that are impossible with humans* [Matt. 19:26].'

44. Those who *with fear and trembling* [Phil. 2:12] have laid a good foundation of faith and hope in the courtyard of piety; who have *set their feet firmly* [Prov. 3:26] on the rock of obedience to their spiritual fathers; who listen to what their fathers command as though it came from the mouth of God; and who on this foundation of obedience have built a stable edifice in humility of soul: these have immediate success. This first and great accomplishment is accomplished for them: to deny themselves. For the fulfilment of another's will, rather than one's own, leads not only to denial of one's own soul, but also to dying to the whole world.

45. The demons rejoice with a monk who answers back to his father, while the angels marvel at someone who is humbled even unto death. For such a one *works the work of God* [John 6:28], becoming like the Son of God, who fulfilled obedience to his own Father *even unto death, death on a cross* [Phil. 2:8].

46. Great and untimely heartbreak darkens and obscures the mind and drives away both pure prayer and humility from the soul. It creates toil for the heart, and then makes it forever hard and calloused. Through all this, the demons work despair among the spiritual.

47. As you are a monk, you will encounter such things and find a great zeal and yearning for perfection in your soul, desiring to fulfil every commandment of God and not to fall into sin even in an *idle word* [Matt. 12:36]. You will yearn not to fall behind any of the Saints of old in active virtue, knowledge, and contemplation. You will also see yourself prevented by the one who *secretly sows tares* of discouragement from climbing to such a height of holiness, insinuating within your mind thoughts and saying, 'It is impossible for you to be saved in the midst of the world, and to keep God's commandments without exception.' Then you must sit down in a corner of your cell, withdraw into yourself and gather your thoughts together, and speak good counsel to your soul, saying, '*Why are you deeply grieved, my soul, and why do you trouble me? Hope in God, for I will make confession to him.* It is not my works that will be *the salvation of my face*, but *my God* [Ps. 41:6]. For who *will be justified by works of the law* [Gal. 2:16]? *No one living will be justified before your face* [Ps. 142:2]. I hope to be saved from my faith in God himself, freely through his ineffable compassion. *Get behind me, Satan*, and I *reverence the Lord my God* [Matt. 4:10], from my youth I worship him who is able to save me by his mercy alone. Go away, therefore, from me! God who made me *according to his image and likeness* [Gen. 1:26] will destroy you utterly.'

48. God asks nothing from us save this and only this: not to sin. This is not achieved by keeping the law, but by scrupulously guarding the divine image in us and our heavenly dignity, so that, standing in our natural state and clothed with the radiant garment of the Spirit, *we dwell in God and he in us* [1 John 4.13], being called gods by adoption and *sons of God* [Matt. 5:9], and *signed with the light* of the knowledge of God [cf. Ps. 4:7].

49. Bodily despondency and torpor, which come upon the soul through laziness and carelessness, not only estrange us from our habitual rule of prayer, but darken the mind and fill it with discouragement. Thence thoughts of cowardice and blasphemy bubble up in the heart and, tempted by the demon of despondency, we cannot even enter our accustomed place of prayer, but, hesitating, entertain absurd thoughts about the Maker of all. So then, knowing the cause of these things and where they all come from, earnestly go into your accustomed place of prayer and, falling down before the God who loves humankind, beseech him with groaning and tears with a grieving heart for deliverance from the burden of despondency and from wicked trains of thoughts. Then you will be swiftly granted freedom from all these things, if you knock hard and persistently.

50. One who possesses purity of heart has conquered cowardice. One who is still being purified sometimes overcomes it and sometimes is overcome by it. One who does not struggle at all, however, is either completely unaware that he has become a friend of passions and demons alike, and, sick with vainglory and self-conceit, *imagines himself to be something when he is nothing* [Gal. 6:3], or has become enslaved to cowardice, mentally trembling like a child, and full of fear *where*, for those who fear the Lord, *there is no fear* [Ps. 13:5], nor any occasion for cowardice.

51. One who fears God is not afraid of the attacks of demons, nor their feeble assaults, nor even the threats of the wicked. Rather, like a flame or burning fire, he goes about night and day in hidden and gloomy places. He puts the demons to flight; rather than fleeing from them himself, they take to their heels lest they be scorched by the fiery ray of divine fire that radiates from him.

52. One who walks in the fear of God will not be afraid of going about among wicked men, for he has within himself the fear of God, carrying the invincible weapon of faith, which empowers him to do anything, even those things that seem difficult and even impossible to most people. Rather, like a giant among monkeys, or a roaring lion among dogs and foxes, through his trust in the Lord he terrifies them by his firmness of purpose, and puts them out of their wits, wielding the word in wisdom like an *iron rod* [Ps. 2:9].

53. Not only the solitary or one under obedience, but also the abbot and superior of many who himself serves them, ought to be free of anxiety, that is, unambiguously free from all the concerns of this life. For if we are anxious, we will be found transgressors of God's commandment that says, *Do not be anxious in your soul about what to eat or what to drink or what to wear; for all these things the Gentiles seek after* [Matt. 6:25]. And again, *See that your hearts be not weighed down with indulgence, drunkenness, and the cares of this life* [Luke 21:34].

54. No one worried in his thoughts about the affairs of this life is really free. For he is possessed by worry about these things and enslaved, whether they concern himself or others. Whoever is free from these concerns does not worry about this life, whether on his own account or for others, even if he happens to be a bishop, an abbot or a deacon. However, he will not be idle, nor neglect what is slight or of little value. He will do and carry out everything for the glory of God, accomplishing all without anxiety throughout the whole of his life.

55. Do not destroy your own dwelling in your desire to build your neighbour's. Come, brother, consider what they call perfect withdrawal from the world: the complete mortification of one's

own will, followed by detachment from family, neighbours and friends; and the denial of all these. See how troublesome and difficult the enterprise is, lest having decided to do this, and pulled down your own house, you find yourself quite incapable of building your neighbour's.

56. Unless you possess total detachment from the affairs and goods of this life, do not assume responsibility for the management of such matters, lest you get lost in them and, instead of receiving the reward for your service, you suffer condemnation for robbery and sacrilege. If this is required as an obedience by your abbot, act as though you were handling blazing fire: steer clear of the provocation of thoughts by confession and repentance and you will be preserved unharmed by the prayer of your abbot.

57. One who has not become dispassionate neither knows what dispassion is nor believes that anyone could attain it here on earth. For unless you have *first denied yourself* [Matt. 16:24] and eagerly poured out your own blood for the sake of this truly blessed life, how could you imagine that anyone else could choose to do these things for the sake of attaining dispassion? Likewise, someone who thinks he possesses the Holy Spirit without actually possessing it can never believe, if he hears of the Spirit at work in those who indeed have the Holy Spirit, that anyone in our generation could be roused and moved by the divine Spirit, or come to know him with full consciousness in a vision, just like the apostles of Christ and the saints of old. For everyone judges his neighbour's affairs, whether virtuous or wicked, in accordance with his own state.

58. Dispassion of soul is one thing and dispassion of body another. For while the soul's dispassion thoroughly sanctifies the body by its own radiance and the Spirit's effusion of light, the body's dispassion by itself cannot benefit in any way the one who possesses it.

59. Imagine someone raised by a king from utter poverty to wealth and resplendent dignity, clothed by him in rich clothes, and called to stand in his presence. Such a one will look upon the king with longing and love him all the more as his benefactor. He will be fully aware of the robes in which he has been

clothed, and the dignity granted him, and the wealth he has been given. Likewise also the monk who has truly withdrawn from the world and its affairs, who has drawn near to Christ, who has felt himself called and been raised up to the heights of spiritual contemplation through fulfilment of the commandments. He gazes unerringly on God himself and clearly understands the change that has been wrought in him. For he sees the grace of the Spirit ever shining around him, which is called a garment and the royal purple – or, rather, which is Christ himself, since those who believe in Christ have been clothed by Christ [Gal. 3:27].

60. Many read the divine Scriptures or hear the passages read, but few are able to know rightly the power and meaning of what is read. Sometimes they declare things said in the divine Scriptures to be impossible; sometimes they reckon them completely incredible. Sometimes they engage in poor sorts of figurative reading[2] and judge things said about the present time as referring to the future, or they take what is said about the future as having already happened or as happening on a daily basis. So, they have neither right judgement in these matters nor true discernment in things divine and human.

61. We believers ought to consider all believers as one, and reckon that Christ is in each one of us, and in this way be inclined by our love for him to be ready to lay down our *own lives* for him [John 15:13]. We have absolutely no right to say or think that someone is wicked, but, rather, should look on all as good, as we have said. For even if you see someone troubled by the passions, do not hate your brother, but the passions that war on him. If you see him tyrannized by desires and predispositions towards sin, be all the more compassionate, lest *you* yourself *be tempted* [Gal. 6:1], as you are subject to the changes of unstable matter.

62. Someone who is false because of hypocrisy, blameworthy from his actions, easily wounded by some passion, or lapses even a little because of carelessness – such a one is not numbered among the healthy but is instead cast out as useless and discreditable. Otherwise he will make the links of the chain break at a moment of tension, and wreak separation between

the inseparable, causing grief both to those at the head of the chain on account of the last, and to the last, distressed at their separation from those in front.

63. In the same way as someone quenches a burning furnace by throwing sand on the flame, so the *cares of this life* [Luke 21.34] and every attachment to cheap and paltry things annihilate the fervour kindled in our heart at our beginning.

64. One who conceives the fear of death loathes all food, drink and adornment in clothing. He does not eat bread with pleasure, nor drink water. He will allow his body only as much as it needs to keep it alive. He will deny his own will and at the discretion of those to whom he is subject become a slave of all.

65. One who enslaves himself to his spiritual fathers through fear of punishment would not choose – even if commanded – tasks that assuage his heart's toil or those that dissolve the bond of fear. Nor will he obey those who would lead him to such things, whether they do so affectionately, sycophantically or from a position of authority. Instead he will prefer whatever amplifies his heart's toil, and will choose tasks that tighten the bond of fear. He will cherish whatever strengthens his torturer, and cleave to them, not as expecting ever to receive freedom from them. For hope of deliverance makes hard labour lighter, which is of no use for someone engaged in fervent repentance.

66. For everyone embarking on a godly life, fear of punishment and the toil that is born of it is helpful. Anyone who imagines he can make a beginning without such toil, bonds and someone to inflict them does not merely lay the foundation of his activity on sand [cf. Matt. 7:26], but seems to think that he can establish his dwelling in the air without foundations: something wholly impossible. For this toil itself gives birth to almost all our joys, and this hard bond itself will break the bonds of all our sins and passions, and this torture will itself procure not death but eternal life.

67. A person who does not choose to escape and flee the toil born of fear of eternal punishment, but, rather, follows it with his heart's purpose and binds its bonds more tightly about himself, is like someone who takes the shorter path and presents himself before the *king of kings* [1 Tim. 6:15]. When this

happens, at once he beholds his royal glory, however faintly, and immediately his bonds fall away, his fear of torture flees far from him, and the miserable toil of his heart is turned to joy, as it becomes a spring, flowing forever with fervent tears like a river, inwardly at peace, full of gentleness and unutterable sweetness, still freely, unflinchingly and brooking no hindrance running the way of God's commandments in complete obedience: something impossible for beginners, but reserved for those who have advanced to the middle state of progress, and for those who are being perfected this very spring becomes light for hearts suddenly changed and transformed.

68. One who has the light of the All-Holy Spirit within cannot bear to see it but falls headlong to the ground. He cries and shouts in astonishment and great fear, as though seeing and enduring something beyond nature, beyond word, beyond concept. He becomes like someone whose innards have been set on fire [cf. Jer. 20:9]: consumed by the flame, he cannot bear the burning, and is as if outside himself and wholly unable to contain himself. Bathed in an endless flow of tears, he is refreshed by them, and the fire of his desire is enkindled even more vehemently. From within, tears flow in abundance and being washed by their flow he shines more brilliantly than lightning. When entirely consumed by fire, he becomes like light itself, then will the saying be fulfilled: *God is united with gods and known by them*[3] insofar, perhaps, as God is already united with those attached to him, and revealed to those who know him.

69. Before attaining to mourning and tears, *let no one deceive* us *with vain words* [Eph. 5:6], nor let us mislead ourselves: there is no repentance in us, no true diligence, no fear of God in our hearts; nor do we accuse ourselves; our soul has not become conscious of the judgement to come and eternal punishment. For if we had accused ourselves and become conscious of our impending fate, we would have immediately shed tears. For without tears, neither can our hard hearts be softened nor our souls come to possess spiritual humility, nor can we be humble. Nor can such a one be united to the Holy Spirit. Without being united to the Spirit through purification, one can neither come to contemplation and knowledge of God nor be worthy to be instructed in the hidden virtues of humility.

70. Those who dissemble virtue appear in one way in the sheepskin of the monastic habit [cf. Matt. 7:15], but inwardly [cf. Rom. 7:22] in quite another way, perhaps *filled with all manner of wickedness* [Rom. 1:29], full of *envy, selfishness* [Gal. 5:20], and the stench of pleasure; they are honoured as dispassionate and holy by most people, who do not have their soul's eye cleansed, and cannot *recognize them by their fruit* [Matt. 7:20]. But those who live in piety, virtue, and *simplicity of heart* [Acts 2:46] and are truly holy are judged by most people to be like anyone else, and treated with disdain, as they pass them by.

71. Such people, rather, count someone loquacious and showy to be a teacher and spiritual; they judge someone quiet, with few words, to be a dumb peasant.

72. Anyone who speaks under the inspiration of the Holy Spirit is dismissed by the arrogant who are sick with diabolical pride as arrogant and proud, for they are wounded by his words rather than pierced by compunction. Instead, they heap praises on one who spins words from his own gut or bits and pieces of learning, and deceives them about their salvation, and approve him. So it is that there is no one among them who can see things rightly as they are and exercise discernment.

73. *Blessed are the pure in heart*, says God, *for they shall see God* [Matt. 5:8]. Purity of heart is not realized by one virtue or two, or even ten, but all the virtues together, as it were, united into one and brought to perfection. And even so it is not the virtues alone that can make a heart pure without the presence and activity of the Spirit. The blacksmith plies his art with his tools, but he cannot make anything without the activity of fire. So too one does everything one can, making use of the virtues as tools, but without the presence of spiritual fire his deeds remain powerless and unproductive, and they cannot cleanse the filth and putrefaction of the soul.

74. From divine baptism we receive remission of sins, are freed from the ancient curse and are sanctified by the presence of the Holy Spirit. But perfect grace – according to the saying,

I will dwell in them and walk among them [2 Cor. 6:16] – is not yet given. Perfect grace belongs to those who are firm in faith and manifest it in their deeds. For if, after we are baptized, we incline towards wicked and shameful actions, and so cast off entirely our sanctification, by repentance, confession and tears, we receive forgiveness analogous to that first remission of sins, and so receive sanctification together with grace from on high.

75. Thanks to repentance the pollution caused by shameful deeds is thoroughly washed away, and after that there comes about participation in the Holy Spirit. Not simply, but in accordance with the faith, disposition, and humility of those who repent with all their soul. Not only that, but afterwards it is necessary to receive perfect remission of sins from our spiritual father. For this reason it is good to repent daily in accordance with the express commandment. For *Repent, for the Kingdom of Heaven is at hand* [Matt. 3:2] shows that the practice of repentance is without end.

76. The grace of the All-Holy Spirit is given to those souls betrothed to Christ as a pledge. Just as, without a pledge, a woman has no certainty that the union with her husband will ever certainly take place, so also a soul receives no firm assurance that it will ever be united with her master and God forever, or that she will be united with him mystically and ineffably, or that she will enjoy his unapproachable beauty, unless she receives the pledge of grace, and in full conscience possesses him in herself.

77. Unless the marriage contract bears the signatures of trustworthy witnesses, the pledge is not sure. Nor is the illumination of grace certain before the keeping of commandments and the possession of virtues. For what the witnesses are to the contracts, so are the virtues and the keeping of commandments to the spiritual pledge. It is through these that each of those who are going to be saved receives complete possession of the pledge.

78. First the agreements are written, as it were, by the keeping of commandments and then are signed and sealed by the virtues. Then Christ the bridegroom gives his ring to the betrothed soul, which is the pledge of the Spirit.

79. Just as before their wedding the bride receives only the pledge from her bridegroom, and must wait eagerly until after the wedding to receive the agreed dowry and the gifts specified in the contract, so too the bride, which is the Church of the faithful, and the soul of each of us, receives from our bridegroom, Christ, at first only the pledge of the Spirit, and waits until after our departure hence[4] to receive the eternal good things and the Kingdom of Heaven. But the Church and our souls are assured through the pledge that those good things contracted with Christ will not prove false.

80. Suppose the bridegroom were delayed on a journey [cf. Matt. 25:5], or detained in some other business, and meanwhile the wedding had to be put off – if in anger the bride disdained her love for her betrothed, and cancelled or tore up the wedding contract, then immediately she would forfeit her hopes in her bridegroom: so naturally it is the case with the soul. If one of those engaged in spiritual combat were to say, 'How long have I to go on suffering?', and then went on to neglect completely his ascetic labours, become careless in keeping the commandments, abandon constant repentance, he would, as it were, have cancelled and torn up the wedding agreement. Straight away he would forfeit the pledge and lose entirely his hope in God.

81. Just as if a bride were to transfer her affection for her own lawful bridegroom to another, and slept with him openly or secretly, not only could she hope to receive none of those things promised her by her bridegroom but could rightly expect blame and punishment under the law – so naturally it is the case among us monastics. If someone were to change his love for our bridegroom, Christ, to a desire for something else – whether openly or secretly – and if he sets his heart on it, then he will be hateful and loathsome to the bridegroom, and unworthy of union with him. For Christ says, *I love those who love me* [Prov. 8:17].

82. It is necessary that each one learn from such signs whether he has received the pledge of the Spirit from Christ, our bridegroom and master. If he has received it, let him endeavour to hold it fast. If he has not yet been counted worthy

to receive it, let him endeavour through good works and deeds and fervent repentance to receive it and to guard it by keeping the commandments and further acquisition of the virtues.

83. Just as the roof of any house is supported by the foundations and the rest of the building, so the foundations are fashioned to be necessary and useful for holding up the roof; and neither can the roof fulfil its natural function without foundations, nor can the foundations serve any useful purpose without a roof. So too is God's grace preserved through the keeping of the commandments, while the keeping of the commandments through God's free gift is laid down as foundations. Neither is the grace of the Spirit accustomed to abide in us without our keeping the commandments, nor is the keeping of the commandments of any use or benefit for us without God's grace.

84. Just as a house left roofless owing to carelessness of the builder is not merely uninhabitable, but also brings ridicule on the builder, so it is with one who lays the foundations of keeping God's commandments, and who sets up walls of lofty virtues: unless he receives the grace of the Spirit by his soul's contemplation and knowledge, he remains imperfect, and is pitied by the perfect. He is deprived entirely of the grace of the Spirit for two reasons: either he has been careless in repenting, or else, having recoiled before the dense ranks of the virtues as before some boundless wood, he has left undone one of them that seems to us of little worth, but is really indispensable for finishing the house of the virtues, so that without it the house cannot receive a roof through the grace of the Spirit.

85. If, for this reason, the Son of God, God himself, came down on the earth, to reconcile us, *though we were enemies* [Rom. 5:10], to his own Father, and to unite us in full consciousness to himself through the Holy Spirit, consubstantial with him, what other kind of grace will he find who falls away from this? He will certainly have neither reconciliation with God nor union with him through participation in the Spirit.

86. One who partakes of the Holy Spirit is delivered from impassioned desires and pleasures, but is not separated from the bodily necessities of nature. Since he has been freed from the

bonds of impassioned yearning, and has been joined to immortal glory and sweetness, he is compelled to be unceasingly on high and to pass his time with God, and never, even for an instant, to withdraw from the inexhaustible delight of contemplating him. But, since he is also fastened to the body and to corruption, he is pulled down by them, dragged along and brought back to earthly things. His distress at this must be as great, I should think, as that of a sinner when his soul is separated from the body.

87. Just as for one who loves the body, life, pleasure and the world, separation from such things is death, so too for one who loves purity, God, the immaterial and virtue, the slightest distance of his mind from such things is in truth death. For if someone who sees this perceptible light shuts his eyes for a moment or has them covered by another, he is vexed, grieved, and cannot bear it at all, especially if he were gazing at some wonder or something he just had to see. And so with someone who is illumined by the Holy Spirit, and who sees those *good things* – really and intellectually, waking and sleeping – *which eye has not seen and ear has not heard, and which have not entered into the human heart* [1 Cor. 2:9], things *into which angels long to peer* [1 Pet. 1:12]: how much more will he not be grieved and afflicted, should someone drag him away from beholding such things? This will seem to him to be death, and, in truth, alienation from eternal life.

88. Many have blessed the eremitic, and many the mixed or coenobitic, life. Still others have praised the leadership of the laity, their admonition, teaching and administration of the churches, by which different people are accustomed to be nourished in body and soul. For myself I would rather not prefer one to another, nor count one praiseworthy and another blameworthy, but everywhere and in everything to count all-blessed a life lived through God and for his sake.

89. Just as human life is supported through various arts and sciences, with each person exercising his own art and making his own contribution, in turn giving and receiving, everyone living and satisfying naturally their bodily needs, so we see the same thing when it comes to spiritual matters, with one pursuing one

virtue and another pursuing another, one pursuing one way of life and another pursuing another, but all running together towards the same goal.

90. The goal of all those who struggle to live in accordance with God is to be pleasing to Christ our God, to receive reconciliation with the Father through participation in the Spirit, and so, through this, to find their own salvation. For this is the salvation of every human soul: if this goal is not attained, our labour is empty and our effort futile. Every way of life is unprofitable that does not lead to this goal.

91. Suppose someone has abandoned the world in everything, and withdrawn to the mountain in search of stillness, but then writes ostentatiously to those in the world, blessing them, flattering them and praising them: is he is not like someone who has divorced his wife, a shameless and utterly vile adulteress, and who has *journeyed to a far country* [cf. Luke 15:13] to be free even from memory of her, but then he forgets the reason why he came to the mountain and longs to write to that adulteress's lovers – her fellow debauchees, if I may put it so – even blessing their happiness? In his intention, he shares the same passions as those debauchees: certainly in his heart and mind, if not in his body. It is as if he approves their sexual congress with her.

92. Just as those who purify their senses and hearts from every wicked desire while living in the world are praiseworthy and blessed, so are those who dwell in *mountains and caves* [Heb. 11:38] worthy to be blamed and rejected, if they desire human praise, blessing and glory. For they will be as adulterers to God *who searches* our *hearts* [Rom. 8:27]. For one who wants his story, his name and his way of life to be reported in the world makes himself a prostitute, far from God, as of old the Jewish people, as David said [Ps. 105:39].

93. One who has, by unflinching faith in God, bid farewell to the world and all that is in it believes that *the Lord is merciful and compassionate* [Ps. 102:8], and receives those who approach him in repentance. He knows that God honours his servants with dishonour, enriches them through extreme poverty, glorifies them through insults and belittlement, and

restores them through death to partake of and inherit eternal life. Through these trials he longs, like the *deer thirsting for* the immortal *fount* [Ps. 41:2], and ascends the heights as on the steps of a ladder, on which angels ascend and descend [cf. Gen. 28:12], coming to the aid of those who climb. God sits on high, attentive to the strength of our purpose and zeal, not because he is glad to watch us toiling away, but because, in his loving kindness, he wants to reward us as if we were owed it.

94. The Lord does not permit those who approach him without hesitation to fail completely but, seeing them unequal to the task, he works with them and aids them, stretching out his mighty hand to them, and lifting them up to himself. He works with them visibly and invisibly, in ways known and unknown, until at last, having ascended the entire ladder, they draw near to him, and are wholly united with him in everything, forgetting everything earthly. Yes, they are with him there, *whether in the body or out of the body I do not know* [2 Cor. 12:2], and as his fellow citizens they enjoy ineffable good things.

95. It is right that we first bend our necks to the yoke of Christ's commandments, neither provoking him nor drawing back, but walking rightly and eagerly in them until death, and making ourselves again truly the new paradise of God, until the time when the Son with his Father through the Holy Spirit enters and dwells in us. Then, as God dwells in us entirely and has become our sole teacher, whatever he requires of us or whatever service he entrusts to us, God will undertake and perform eagerly as seems best to him. It is not allowed to seek this out before the right time, nor can it be taken or received from mortals. Rather, we must stick to the commandments of our God and Master and wait on his command.

96. After undertaking some ministry in divine matters with distinction, if we are required by the Spirit to be transferred to another ministry, activity or service, let us not resist. For God does not want us to be idle or to remain in one and the same activity on which we have embarked until our death, but to make progress, being ever-moving towards the attainment of better things, grounded in the divine will and not our own.

97. One who strives to put to death his own will should

follow God's will and in himself should substitute God's will for his own, implanting and grafting God's will in his own heart. He should look assiduously at his seedlings and grafts, to see whether the former have taken root in the heart's depths and are growing, and whether the latter have been completely cicatrized and become one with the tree. He should see whether they are growing, and blossoming, or even bearing sweet, ripe fruit, so that he can no longer tell the soil that first received seed, nor the trunk on which the graft was made, so incomprehensible and ineffable is the life-bearing plant.

98. To one who cuts off his own will out of fear of God, God gives his own will – imperceptibly, and so unknown to him – and preserves it like an indelible seal in his heart, and opens the eyes of his mind to recognize it, and gives him strength to fulfil it. The grace of the Holy Spirit is active in these things and without it nothing happens [cf. John 1:3].

99. If you have received remission of all your sins, either through confession or through being clothed with the holy and angelic habit, this will be a cause of such love, thanksgiving and humility! For, being worthy of many thousands of punishments, not only were you delivered from them, but you have been counted worthy of adoption, glory and the Kingdom of Heaven! Turning all this over in your mind and always meditating on them, be ready and well prepared not to dishonour the One who has honoured you and pardoned your many thousands of faults, but, in everything you do, glorify and honour him, that he may in return all the more glorify you, whom he has honoured more than the whole visible creation, and may call you his true friend.

100. As much as the soul is more honourable than the body, so much greater is the rational human being than the entire cosmos. As you contemplate the greatness of the creatures in the world, do not imagine for this reason that other creatures are more precious than you, O mortal, but look to the grace that has been given to you and, learning the value of your intelligent and rational soul, sing a hymn to the God who has honoured you beyond everything visible.

101. Let us consider how we glorify God. For he is glorified

by us in no other way than he has been glorified by his Son. For in the same way that the Son glorified his Father, so also was the Son glorified by the Father [cf. John 17:4]. Let us, therefore, pursue this way with zeal, that we may glorify him who has accepted to be called *our Father in Heaven* [Matt. 6:9] and also be glorified by him with Jesus' glory, *which he had with him before the world was* [John 17:5]. This way involves the cross – that is, our putting the whole world to death – trials, temptations, and the rest of Christ's sufferings. Bearing these with much endurance, we imitate Christ's sufferings and through them glorify our God and Father as his children by grace and as *fellow heirs with Christ* [Rom. 8:17].

102. A soul that does not feel completely free from ties and attachments to visible things cannot bear grievous circumstances or the insults of mortals and demons without distress, but, as if bound by attachment to human concerns, is injured at the loss of money, vexed at being deprived of goods, and greatly stricken by the wounds inflicted on its body.

103. If someone has torn his soul away from affection and desire for perceptible things and has bound it to God, not only will he think nothing of the wealth and property he sees about him, and keep himself unmoved when he is deprived of them, as though they belonged to aliens and strangers, but he will bear with joy and fitting thanksgiving any bodily discomfort, observing always, with the divine Apostle, that our outer nature is wasting away while our inner nature is being renewed from day to day [cf. 2 Cor. 4:16]. Otherwise, it is not possible to endure with joy the afflictions permitted by God, for in such cases there is needed perfect knowledge and spiritual wisdom. Someone bereft of such knowledge and wisdom is always walking in the darkness of ignorance and hopelessness, unable to behold at all the light of long suffering and consolation.

104. No one pretending to be learned in mathematical science will ever be counted worthy to catch a glimpse of or to behold the mysteries of God, unless he first chooses to be humbled and become a fool, casting off the knowledge to which he presumed. One who does this and follows with unwavering faith those wise in divine matters – allowing

himself to be led by the hand – will enter with them into the city of the living God, and guided and enlightened by the divine Spirit, he will see and be taught that which no other mortal knows or can ever see or learn; then he will come to be *taught by God* [John 6:45].

105. The disciples of those wise in this world consider those *taught by God* to be fools, though in truth they are fools themselves, having been muzzled by the foolish outer wisdom which, according to the divine Apostle, *God has made foolish* [1 Cor. 1:20]; and which the inspired voice calls *earthly, natural, demonic*, full of *faction* and envy [James 3:15–16]. Such, being outside the divine light, cannot see the marvels within, and so they reckon that people wrapped in divine light, who see and teach what lies within, have been led astray, while, in truth, they themselves are lost, having never tasted God's ineffable delights.

106. There are even now holy and dispassionate people, filled with divine light, living in our midst, who have so *put to death whatever in them is earthly* [Col. 3:5], ridding themselves of every impurity and impassioned desire, that they never consider anything evil nor seek to provoke it and, even when drawn towards evil by another, experience no change in their customary dispassion. Those who ascribe stupidity to such saints and who disbelieve those who teach divine things in the wisdom of the Spirit would have known that there are such people if they were actually attentive to what is read and chanted from Scripture daily. For if they had come to perfect knowledge of the divine Scripture, they would trust the good things made mention of by God and given to us. But since, because of their self-conceit and carelessness, they have not partaken of such beautiful things, out of disbelief they calumniate those who have partaken and teach them.

107. For this reason those who are filled with grace and made perfect in knowledge and wisdom from above want to visit and see people who live in the world, only that they might procure for them some profit through reminding them of God's commandments and through good works, that they may perhaps hear, and perhaps understand, and be persuaded, since those

who are not *led by the Spirit of God* [Rom. 8:14] *walk about in darkness* and *neither know where they are going* [John 12:35] nor what they are stumbling against. For perhaps one day they will recover from their besetting self-conceit and receive the true teaching of the Holy Spirit and, hearing the will of God genuinely and sincerely, they will repent, and come to partake of some spiritual grace. But if the holy cannot procure such benefits for the worldly, then, mourning the hardness of their hearts, they will return to their cells, praying night and day for their salvation. Indeed, those who unceasingly converse with God and are abundantly filled with every good thing will never be grieved over anything else but this.

108. What is the purpose of the incarnate dispensation of God the Word, proclaimed throughout the divine Scriptures, and read among us, but not understood? Surely it is that he who participated in what is ours makes us participate in what is his. For it was for this reason that the Son of God became the Son of man, that he might make us humans the sons of God, by grace leading our human race to what he is by nature. He made us to be born from above in the Holy Spirit [cf. John 3:3], directly leading us into the Kingdom of Heaven. Or, rather, he granted us grace to have the Kingdom *within* us [Luke 17:21], so that we are not merely in hope of entering in, but as really possessing it we may cry out: *Our life is hidden with Christ in God* [Col. 3:3].

109. Our self-determination and freedom of choice are not taken away by baptism; rather, baptism grants us freedom no longer to be under the tyranny of the Devil against our will. It is up to us after baptism whether of our own will we abide by the commandments of our master, Christ, into whom we were baptized, and journey on the road he has appointed for us, or whether we turn aside from this straight road and through wicked deeds turn again to our adversary and enemy, the Devil.

110. Those who after baptism yield to the wiles of the Evil One and practise what he counsels *alienate* themselves *from the* sacred *womb* of baptism, as David says [Ps. 57:4]. For the nature after which we have been created none of us can change or alter; rather, having been created good by God – for

God made nothing evil – we are immutable in the nature and essence in which we were created. So, whatever we choose and wish after our voluntary intention, the same we do, whether for better or worse. Just as a sword, whether used for good or ill, is not changed in its own nature, but continues to be iron, so also we human beings act and perform what we have chosen, as we have said, and do not depart from our own nature.

111. To have mercy on one person will not save us, but to scorn one person will dispatch us to the flames. The words, *I was hungry, I was thirsty*, were not spoken of a single occasion, nor of just one day, but, rather, the whole extent of our life. So also with *feeding* Christ, *giving him to drink*, and *clothing him*, and all the other deeds [Matt. 25:35]: doing them not once, but throughout our whole life and on every occasion, it is this that our Lord and God confessed he had received from his servants.

112. One who gives food and drink to a hundred people, and was able to give to others, but sent them away, although they all besought him and cried out – such a one will be judged by Christ as having refused him nourishment, since Christ is in all of these and looks for us to nourish him in *each of the least of these* [Matt. 25:40].

113. One who grants to all everything needed for the day, and then the next day, although he could do it again, neglects some of the brothers and allows them to perish from hunger, thirst or cold; it is as if he had let Christ himself die, and scorned the one who said, *Inasmuch as you did to one of the least of these, you did for me* [Matt. 25:40].

114. In this Christ has accepted to be seen in the face of each poor wretch, and he made himself like every poor person, so that none of those who believe in him might disparage his brother, but each, regarding his brother and neighbour as his God, might reckon himself as the least, as much with his brother as with the one who made him, and receive and honour his brother as God, and empty himself of all he owns for his brother's service, as Christ our God emptied himself of his own blood for our salvation.

115. One who has been commanded to consider his neighbour as himself [cf. Luke 10:27] ought to keep to this commandment

not just for a day but for his whole life; one who has been enjoined *to give to whoever asks* [Matt. 5:42] should do this for the whole of his life; and one who wants others to do for him the good things he wants for himself will be required to do these things for others [cf. Matt. 7:12].

116. Just as one who regards his neighbour as himself cannot bear to have anything more than his neighbour, so, should he have something and not share it ungrudgingly, even if it makes him poor and so renders him equal to his neighbours, he will not be found to have fulfilled his master's commandment. It is the same, too, if one wants to give to all who ask, but, when he is down to his last obol or a crust of bread, turns away someone who asks him. So too with someone who does not do for his neighbour what he wants, so that another may do it for him. Furthermore, one who has given drink, food and clothing to every last beggar and has done everything else for them too, but scorns one person and passes him over, will be reckoned as one who passed over Christ God when he was hungry and thirsty.

117. These commands will perhaps appear burdensome to all, so they will think it reasonable to say to themselves, 'Who, then, can do all this so as to minister to all, to feed everyone, and in no case to pass over anyone?' Well, let them listen to Paul, proclaiming quite explicitly that *The love of Christ constrains us, for we are convinced that if one died for all, then all died* [2 Cor. 5:14].

118. Just as the comprehensive commandments contain in themselves all the more particular commandments, so also the comprehensive virtues embrace within themselves the more particular ones. So one who sells his goods and distributes them to the poor, and at once becomes a beggar, has fulfilled all the particular commandments in one fell stroke; and so he no longer needs to give to any who asks, or to turn away those who want to borrow from him [cf. Matt. 5:42]. So too the one who prays unceasingly has in this action included everything, and is no longer under obligation to *praise the Lord seven times a day* [Ps. 118:164] or *evening, morning and midday* [Ps. 54:17]. For he has already fulfilled everything that we pray and chant according to rule at set times and hours. So also he who has acquired consciously within himself the God who gives *knowledge to humankind* [Ps. 93:10] has traversed the whole of holy Scripture and reaped the whole harvest from his reading, and will no longer need to read books. For why? He has come to speak together with the God who inspired the authors of all divine books and has been initiated by that God into the ineffable heart of hidden mysteries. Yes, he himself will be for others a God-inspired book [cf. 2 Tim. 3:16] bearing in himself the *old and new* mysteries [Matt. 13:52] written *by the finger of God* [Exod. 31:18], and finally he will have accomplished all and come to rest *from all his works* [Gen. 2:2] in God the sovereign perfection.

119–52: from Symeon the Pious

119. Nocturnal emissions during sleep take place for a variety of reasons: gluttony, vainglory and the demons' envy. It happens from long vigils, when the body is finally relaxed in sleep, and from fear of suffering this very thing. When someone is a priest, it may happen because of the divine Liturgy or because of Communion that while lying in bed he dallies with thoughts of fear lest he suffer a nocturnal emission and, when he has fallen asleep, he suffers precisely that – this happens by the demons' envy. There are other reasons too: if someone has seen a beautiful face during the day and then contemplates it mentally, he goes to sleep with lustful thoughts. Because of his slackness he does not drive them off and so falls during sleep – and perhaps even while awake on his bed. Or there are some fellows, indolent in my view, who sit around discussing passion-filled things, whether they themselves are full of passion or not. Then when they come to bed and turn these things over in their mind, they fall asleep in dalliance with such thoughts and so experience a nocturnal emission during sleep. Perhaps someone has been harmed by another simply during a conversation. For this reason, we must always be attentive to ourselves and meditate on the Prophet's words, *I saw myself always before the Lord, for he is my right hand, that I may* *not be shaken* [Ps. 15:8], and stop ourselves from hearing such conversations. Often people who are taking a rest from prayer are driven into carnal movement, just as we have shown in the chapter on prayer.

120. Brother, strive from the beginning of your renunciation to plant good virtues in yourself, so as to be useful to the whole human race and in the last times to be magnified by the Lord. Do not be familiar with your abbot, as we have said elsewhere, nor seek any honour from him. Do not seek to be friendly with pre-eminent monks, nor hang about their cells, knowing that in this not only will the passion of vainglory start to take root in you, but you will also be hateful to your abbot! How that happens, let him understand who can. Sit in your cell, whatever it is, in peace and do not, on pretext of piety, turn away someone who wants to meet you, but, rather, greeting him with fatherly good will, you will not be harmed, even if he has been sent to try you. If you do not see any good coming of this, you must pursue a path more beneficial to you.

121. Then, always have the fear of God and each day assess yourself as to what you have done – good and bad. Then forget about the good things, lest you fall into the passion of vainglory. As for the bad ones, procure tears for those, through confession and intense prayer. Let your self-interrogation run thus: when the day is over and the night has come, start a dialogue within yourself, 'How, then, have I passed the day with God's help? Have I condemned anyone, abused them, scandalized them, killed them? Have I looked on anyone's face with passion? Have I disobeyed or been careless in the service set me by the abbot? Have I been angered at anyone? When I stood at the *synaxis*,[5] did I let my mind linger on inconsequential matters? Or, being weighed down by indolence in church, did I abandon my rule?'[6] When you can find yourself innocent of all these – which is impossible, of course, for *no one* is *pure from defilement* for a *single day of his life* [Job 14.4], and no one *will boast that his heart is pure* [Prov. 20:9] – then cry out to God with many tears: 'Lord, *forgive me everything in which I have sinned, in word and deed, in knowledge and ignorance.*'[7] *For we fail in many things* [James 3:2] and do not even know it.

122. Every day you must confess every thought to your spiritual father and receive with all assurance whatever is said to you by him as though it comes from God's mouth. Present these things to no one else, saying that 'Having asked my father this and that, he told me this other thing, and did he speak well or no? Should I do it for my healing?' Such words are full of unbelief towards your father, and harm for your soul such as mostly befalls mere novices.

123. Next, look on everyone in the *coenobium* as saints, and see yourself alone as a sinner and the least, considering that as all of them are going to be saved, you alone will be punished on that day. As you stand at the *synaxis* and consider these things, do not stop weeping shamelessly in compunction, saying not a word to any who look askance at this or are scandalized by it. If you see yourself slipping from this activity into vainglory, then, exit the church and do it *in secret* [Matt. 6:4]. Afterwards return swiftly to your own proper place. This activity is exceptionally good for novices, and especially during the Six Psalms, the chanting of the Kathismata Psalms, the reading of Scripture, and the divine Liturgy.[8] Take care to condemn none, but set it in your mind that 'Whoever sees me lamenting this way is aware that I am a terrible sinner, and they pray for my salvation.' If you consider things in this way and always do what I have advised, you will be greatly benefited, you will draw God's grace, and you will become a partaker of God's promised beatitude.

124. Do not visit another's cell, save the abbot's, and that rarely. Instead, if you wish to consult him about some thought you have, do so in the church. After the *synaxis*, return straightway to your cell, or to your work. After Compline,[9] having bowed before your abbot's cell and asked his prayer, prostrate yourself once more and return to your cell with silence. For one attentive Trisagion[10] before sleep is better than four hours' vigil spent in fruitless conversation. In like manner, wherever compunction and mourning are, there too is divine illumination, and in its presence despondency and illness are driven out.

125. Have no particular affection for anyone whomsoever – but especially not for a novice – even if you think him to live an excellent life, and certainly not if he is suspicious. For such affection drives you from spiritual love to passionate love most of the time, and you will fall into unhelpful temptations. This happens especially to those engaged in spiritual struggle. Likewise, humility and continuous prayer will teach this, though time does not permit a detailed discussion of it here. Let him understand who can [cf. Matt. 11:15 and 24:15].

126. Consider yourself a stranger to every monk in the *coenobium*, and even more so to those known to you in the world. Love all equally and see all the pious and struggling as saints. Pray fervently for those who are indifferent towards you. In like manner, as we have made clear already, consider all people saints and so hasten to be cleansed of your own passions through tears. That way, having been illumined by grace to consider all equal, you may attain to the beatitude of the *pure in heart* [Matt. 5:8].

127. Brother, think about what is called 'perfect renunciation of the world': it is the total mortification of one's own will and the detachment from and denial of one's parents, relations and friends.

128. Then, in the same way, comes the stripping off of one's belongings and distributing to the needy, according to the saying, *Sell your goods and give to the poor* [Matt. 19:21]. Make yourself forget anyone for whom you had a special attachment, whether bodily or spiritually.

129. Then make confession of all the hidden things of your heart – that is, everything done by you from your infancy to the present hour – to your spiritual father or abbot, as though to God himself who *tests our heart and minds* [Ps. 7:10]. For you see how John *baptized with a baptism of repentance* and *all came to him confessing their sins* [Mark 1:4–5]. For, from this baptism great joy comes to the soul and relief to the conscience, according to the prophetic word: *First declare your sins that you may be justified* [Isa. 43:26].

130. Hold to this thought with assurance: on your entrance to the *coenobium*, all your relatives and friends are dead, and you must consider as father and mother none but God and your abbot. No longer should you ask anything from your

parents by way of bodily necessity. And if something is sent to you out of their concern for you, receive it and pray for their well-being – and then give their gift to the hostel or clinic. Do this in humility, for it does not belong to the perfect but to the least of monks.

131. Do every good deed with humility, thinking of him who said, *When you have done everything, say that 'we are worthless servants, who have done no more than what we ought to do'* [Luke 17:10].

132. Watch out never to take Communion while you have something against someone – even just a provocative thought – until you can effect a reconciliation through repentance. Nevertheless you will learn this by prayer.

133. Be ready each day to receive every affliction, thinking all of them to be supremely beneficial, and give thanks to the holy God. For from these comes confidence that cannot be put to shame, according to the great Apostle: For *affliction produces endurance, endurance character, character hope, and hope does not put us to shame* [Rom. 5:3–5]. Also, those *things which eye has not seen and ear has not heard, which have not entered into the human hearts* [1 Cor. 2:9] – according to the promise that does not deceive – will be for those who, with the cooperation of grace, show endurance in afflictions. Without grace, of course, it is impossible to accomplish anything.

134. Keep nothing material in your cell, save for a rush basket, a sheepskin, a cloak and the clothes you wear – not even a needle! If possible, not even a stool. For there is a saying about this. Again, let him understand who can.

135. Again, do not bother the monk set over you even about necessities, save what is required by your rule, and these things only when he calls you to give them to you himself. Receive them with thanksgiving as from God, and cope with them. Never ever allow yourself to be swayed by a subversive thought to exchange them for something else, and never buy anything else. Wash your tunic twice a year, when it is dirty, and like an unknown beggar, with all humility, ask to borrow something to wear from another brother, until your own has been dried by the sun, and then return it with thanksgiving. Do the same with your cloak and anything else.

136. Toil with all your might in your work of service. Persevere in your cell in prayer with compunction, attentiveness and constant tears. Never think that 'Today I have laboured so much that I may subtract a bit from my prayer on account of bodily exhaustion.' For I tell you that however much someone forces himself to exertion in service, if he loses his prayer, he will find that he has lost a great possession. That is how things are.

137. Be the first to arrive for *synaxes* in the Church, and be the last to depart, except for some pressing need. Especially do this for Matins and the Liturgy.

138. Be completely subject to the one set over you, by whom you were tonsured, and fulfil without discussion every task he assigns you even unto death – even if it seems to you impossible. In this way imitate him *who was obedient unto death, death on a cross* [Phil. 2:8]. It is not only your abbot whom you are to obey in everything, but your whole brotherhood and the monk who has been entrusted with assigning the various tasks to be done. But if what is commanded proves beyond your strength, then make a prostration and ask forgiveness. And if this is refused, then, reckoning that *the Kingdom of Heaven belongs to the violent, and the violent take it by force* [Matt. 11:12], force yourself.

139. Prostrate yourself with *a broken heart* [Ps. 50:19] at the feet of your whole brotherhood, as someone unnoticed and of no account, indeed barely existing. Indeed, one who behaves thus in life, I dare to say, becomes clairvoyant and with the help of grace foretells many things. Such a one mourns the faults of others while remaining undistracted by attachments to material things, since the intensity of his spiritual and divine longing prevents him from falling among them. There is nothing marvellous about foretelling, for it often happens owing to demonic agency. Again, let him understand who can. Although, should someone begin hearing confessions, perhaps he will lose this gift, since he is wholly engaged in examining the thoughts of others. If, again, with great humility he ceases from confessions – that is, from speaking and listening – then he may well be restored to his former condition. God alone understands the knowledge of such things. I, being seized with fear, dare not declare anything about them.

140. Have your mind always with God – asleep and waking, at table and in conversation, in your manual work and in every other activity – in accordance with the prophetic word: *I beheld the Lord always before me* [Ps. 15:8]. Likewise, consider yourself more sinful than everyone. When this memory is prolonged, illumination, like a ray of light, naturally enters the intellect. The more you seek this with great attention, with undistracted understanding, with great effort and tears, the more radiant it seems. Manifest, illumination is loved, loved it purifies, purifying it assimilates to God, as it illumines and teaches how to discern the good from the bad. Still, my brother, much effort is needed, with God, to make illumination dwell within your soul and make it radiant, just as the moon brightens the gloom of night.

It is necessary to guard against the assault of evil thoughts – of vainglory and self-conceit – lest you condemn someone whom you see doing something wrong. For the demons, when they see your soul freed from passions and temptations through the indwelling of grace and its own peaceful condition, attack with precisely such thoughts as these. Still, your *help is from God* [Ps. 7:11].

Let your mourning be continuous and your tears unquenchable. Take care not to be harmed by your abundant joy and compunction, lest you reckon that these gifts come from your own effort and not from God. For then they will be taken away from you, and you will seek greatly in prayer and not find and will know only what a gift you have lost. But no, Lord! Lord, may we not be deprived of your grace!

Still, brother, should this happen, *cast your* infirmity *on God* [Ps. 54:23]. Rise up, stretch out your hands, and pray like this: 'Lord, have mercy on me, the sinner, the infirm and worthless, and send down upon me your grace, and do not *permit me to be tempted beyond my ability* [1 Cor. 10:13]. Behold, Lord, my many sins, that have led me into such despair and evil thoughts. Lord, even if I wish it, I cannot reckon the loss of your consolation because of the demons and my own self-conceit. For I know that they stand arrayed against those who fervently accomplish your will. But I accomplish their will daily, so how will I be tempted by them? I am ever tried by my own sins. And now, Lord, my Lord, if it be your will and beneficial for me, let your grace enter again into your servant, so that, seeing this, I may rejoice in compunction and weeping, being enlightened by this ever-shining illumination, being guarded from defiled thoughts, from every wicked deed, and from the words and deeds in which I fail daily. May I receive assurance of addressing you freely, Lord, from the afflictions which daily befall your servant at the hands of demons and humans. And cutting off of my own will, may I be mindful of the good things that remain *for those who love* you [Rom. 8:28]. For you have said, Lord, that *Whoever asks receives, whoever seeks will find, and to the one who knocks it will be opened* [Matt. 7:8].'

In addition to these, brother, persevere, beseeching whatever other things God will put into your mind. Do not be weakened by despondency; and the good God will not abandon you.

141. Persevere until the end in the cell allotted you at the beginning by your abbot. If, because of its age or ruinous condition you are troubled in your thoughts, then make a prostration yourself before the abbot, and humbly bring it to his attention. If he listens to you, be glad; if not, give thanks anyway, remembering your Master who *had nowhere to lay his head* [Matt. 8:20]. For if you trouble him about this twice, thrice, even four times, it will bring about familiarity, then faithlessness and, finally, contempt.

So if you desire to live a peaceful and tranquil life, seek out no bodily comfort at all from your teacher. For at the beginning you did not vow this only, but also to be despised by all and counted as nothing, according to the Lord's commandment [cf. Matt. 16:24, 5:11, etc.], and to bear it all. If, then, you wish to save your faith and love for your director and to regard him as a saint, keep to these three things: do not ask for things for your comfort, do not take liberties with him, and do not go on visiting him – as some are allowed to do, on the grounds that they are helped by him. This is not sound, but merely human. I am not condemning you, however, for not hiding from him every thought that comes to you. For if you keep to these things, you will pass through the sea of this life without storms, and you will regard your father – whatever he is like – as a saint.

If you approach your father in church to ask him about a thought, you will probably find another brother ahead of you, who has come for the same reason – or perhaps for other reasons – and you may see yourself neglected. Do not be annoyed or take it badly. Instead, stand by yourself with your arms folded until he is finished, and it is your turn. This often happens with the fathers – perhaps deliberately – to test us and grant us pardon for past sins.

142. Fast during the three forty-day periods.[11] Fast two days out of three during the Great Lenten Fast, except for a great feast and Saturdays and Sundays. During the other two, fast every other day. On the remaining days of the year, eat once only, except on Saturdays, Sundays and feasts. Never eat to satiety.

143. Endeavour to become a good example to the entire brotherhood, in respect of every virtue: humility, meekness, almsgiving, obedience even in the most meagre matters, in lack of anger and detachment, voluntary poverty and compunction, innocence and artlessness, simplicity in habits, and being a stranger to everyone, in care for the sick and consolation of the afflicted. Do not turn away anyone who needs your help lest they disturb your converse with God. *For love is greater than prayer.*[12] Be sympathetic also with all; reject vainglory, familiarity and reproof. Do not demand things of your abbot or his attendants. Maintain your respect for all the priests. Be attentive in prayer and artless in your disposition. Show love for all. Do not, for your own glory, investigate and *search the Scriptures* [John 5:39] out of curiosity. For prayer with tears and the illumination that comes from grace will teach these things.

When questioned about some appropriate matter, with great humility you should teach the truths of divinely inspired deeds from your own life (but made to seem like another's), with grace leading the way. Teach with your thinking free of vainglory, and whoever seeks it out may find benefit. Do not turn away someone seeking a beneficial word about his thought. But take on yourself his failures, whatever they may be, and weep and pray for him. For this is a sign of love and perfect sympathy. Do not drive away someone who comes to you, because you wish to avoid being harmed by the mere hearing of such failings – for when grace cooperates with you, nothing will harm you even if, perhaps, you suffer the attack of a thought since you are human. (Only, because harm might come to others, hold this consultation in a private place.) For if you have been filled with grace, you will not succumb to the thought's attack. Remember – we are taught *not to seek our own good but the good of others*, that they may be saved [1 Cor. 10:24].

As we have already said, you must guard for yourself a life free of business and possessions. Then, being roused by grace, you will consider yourself a greater sinner than all. How this happens, I cannot say. God knows.

144. Spend the hours of your nightly vigil in this way: two hours in spiritual reading, duly praying with compunction and tears. Then chant whichever *kanon* you wish,[13] and psalms – the Twelve Psalms, if you like[14] – and the *Blessed are those who are blameless in the way* [Ps. 118]. Say the prayer of St Eustratios.[15] Do all this when nights are long. When they are short, perform a shortened service, according to the power given you by God. For without him you can do no good thing, as the Prophet says: *A man's steps are directed by the Lord* [Ps. 36:23]. And our Saviour himself says, *Without me you can do nothing* [John 15:5].

Never receive communion without tears.

145. Eat what you are given, whatever it may be, and likewise take wine without grumbling (but in moderation!). If you are stuck in your cell because of some infirmity, have raw vegetables with oil. Should one of the brothers send some morsel to you, accept it with thanksgiving and humility, like a guest. Receive it from him, whatever it is and whatever

sort of day it is – unless it is cheese or eggs. Send the left-overs to another brother, who is poor and pious. If you are invited to a meal, accept a little of everything set before you, according to the command, but preserve self-control. When you rise from table, prostrate yourself like a stranger and beggar, returning him thanks and saying 'May God reward you, holy father.' Refrain from conversation, even if it could be profitable.

146. If a brother comes to you because he has been afflicted by the abbot, the steward or someone else, console him thus: 'Believe, my brother, that this has happened to test your character. For this has happened to me in various ways, and I have been grieved because of my own pettiness. But then I was assured that these things are to test me, and I bear them grate-fully. You should do the same now, and, indeed, rejoice in such afflictions' [cf. Rom. 5:3–5]. Even if he resorts to insults, do not turn him away, but, rather, comfort him as grace directs you. For there are various ways of discernment, and as you know his condition and his words, keep him company, and do not let him depart unhealed.

147. If it happens that a brother falls ill and you cannot visit him for some time, you must send ahead to him, explaining and saying: 'Believe, holy father, that I learned of your illness today and I beg your forgiveness.' Then, having gone, made a prostration and said a prayer, speak to him thus: 'How has God strengthened you, holy father?' Then, having sat down with arms folded, be silent. If others are there who have come to visit him, take care not to talk with them, whether about Scripture or natural philosophy – especially if you have not been asked! – lest you come to grief later. For this is what often happens to brothers who are too simple.

148. If you happen to be sharing a meal with pious brothers, you must partake of what is set before you without scruple, whatever the food may be. If you have been ordered by some-one not to partake of fish or something else like that, and these are set before you – then, if the person who ordered you is close at hand, go and persuade him to permit your partaking. If he is not present, or you know that he will not permit it, but you still do not wish to scandalize your brothers, then explain everything to him after the meal, and beg his forgiveness. If you do not wish to do either of these, then it is better you not go to the meal. For you will profit in two ways: you will flee the demon of vainglory and you will spare your brothers scandal and trial. If, however, they set out for you more carnal foods,[16] keep to your rule, though even so it is better to partake a little of all you are given. Likewise, when invited to any meal, follow the principle of the Apostle: '*Eat everything set before you, and do not scruple over it for the sake of conscience*' [1 Cor. 10:25].

149. If someone knocks on your door while you are at prayer in your cell, open it for him. Sit down then, and humbly converse with him if he suggests something profitable. Even if he is weighed down by affliction, strive to minister to him by word or deed. Then, when he departs, close the door, take up your prayer again and finish it. For likewise helping those who visit you amounts to reconciliation. Do not, however, do this with worldlings. With them, you should first finish your prayer and then converse.

150. If, when you are praying, you feel frightened, are disturbed by some noise, or if something shines like light, or anything else happens – do not be disturbed. Rather, persist all the more intensely in your prayer. For demonic trouble, terror and derangement happen to make you weak in prayer and, when you have got into that habit, they will take you captive. Now if, when you have finished your prayer, another kind of light shines on you, which you cannot describe, and your prayer is filled with joy, and your desire is for better things, while tears flow with compunction – know that this is divine visitation and succour. If this goes on for a long time, lest something more happen to you because of the continual flow of tears, make your intellect captive to something bodily, and in this to humble yourself. Take care not to abandon your prayer out of terror at your enemies. Rather, be like a child who, when frightened by some bogeyman, dispels his fear by taking refuge in the arms of his mother or father. So you, too, having recourse to God in prayer, will put fear to flight.

151. If, as you are sitting in your cell, a brother comes and asks you about fleshly combat, do not turn him away. Rather, converse with him with compunction from whatever things God's grace suggests to you or which you have found through practice, and only then send him away. When he is leaving, make a prostration before him and say: 'Believe me, brother, I have hope in God's love for humankind that this kind of warfare will flee from you. Only do not succumb to it or give up.' When he has left, rise, call to mind his struggle, stretch out your arms to God with tears and pray with groans for your brother, saying, 'Lord God, *who desires not the death of a sinner*,[17] since you know what is good for my brother, please accomplish it in your providence.' And God who knows your brother's faith in you and your sympathy for him in love, as well as your pure prayer on his behalf, will lighten his warfare.

152. All these activities, my brother, are needful for compunction. And you must accomplish them with a broken heart, with endurance and with thanksgiving. For they are the cause of tears, purify the passions, and obtain the Kingdom of Heaven. *The Kingdom of Heaven belongs to the violent, and the violent take it by force* [Matt. 11:12]. For if you accomplish these activities, you will entirely break your old habits and perhaps even the mental suggestions of them. For darkness naturally gives way to light, and shadow to sun. For if someone is puffed up in his thinking and is, therefore, careless in these activities at the outset, then he becomes a mere busybody, he is robbed of grace, and then falls into a multitude of evils. Yet he knows his own infirmity for he is filled with cowardice. Whoever accomplishes these good activities, however, must not reckon them the fruit of his own effort, but, rather, the result of God's grace.

You must purify yourself first in accordance with the saying: *First be purified and then converse with the pure one*.[18] A mind that has been purified through numerous tears and has received the illumination of divine light – which the whole world would not be large enough to hold [cf. John 21:25] – loves to dwell intellectually among the good things to come. It closely observes these things as God has revealed them and rejoices in them spiritually as the Apostle says: *The fruit of the Spirit is love, joy, peace, meekness and patience* [Gal. 5:22].

153: from Niketas Stethatos

153. The holy and blessed Symeon was asked what sort of person a priest ought to be. He responded, saying, 'I am not worthy to be a priest. Yet I have learned with certainty what sort of person one who is going to minister to God should be. First, he should be pure not only in body, but even more so in his soul. Moreover, he should also be free from participation in any sin. Secondly, he should be outwardly humble in disposition and inwardly contrite in character. When he stands at the holy and sacred table,[19] he should see the divinity with his intellect at the same time that he sees with his senses the holy gifts laid out visibly. Not only this but a priest should have a conscious awareness that the one who is invisibly present in these gifts dwells within his own heart, so that he can offer supplications with confidence, speaking with the God and Father as a friend with a friend [cf. Exod. 33:11], saying irreproachably, *Our Father in heaven, may your name be hallowed* [Matt. 6:9]. This prayer clearly shows that he has the one who is by nature Son of God dwelling in himself, together with the Father and the Holy Spirit. I have known such priests. Forgive me, fathers and brothers.'

He [Symeon] said something else as though about someone else, so as to obscure himself and flee *human glory* [John 5:41, 12:43]. But, being compelled by his affection for others, he revealed himself. 'I heard,' he said, 'from a hieromonk[20] who confided in me as his intimate friend the following: "I have never served the Liturgy without seeing the Holy Spirit, just as I saw it descending upon me when the Metropolitan ordained me: as he spoke the prayer of making a priest and placed the *Euchologion*[21] on my miserable head." When I asked this old monk if he saw the Holy Spirit then and in what form He appeared, he said, "Simple – formless – but like light." So I marvelled at first, seeing what I had never beheld. As I considered what this might be, the Holy Spirit said to me silently – but I had the knowledge of a voice: "So I visit all the prophets, the apostles, and those who are even now God's elect and holy ones. For I am the Holy Spirit of God."'

To Him be glory and power unto the ages. Amen.

Ps-Symeon, *Methods of Holy Prayer and Attentiveness*

PS-SYMEON (13TH C.?)

We know nothing of the author of this piece, save that they (or later copyists) believed that the name of Symeon the New Theologian would best legitimize their spiritual practices. There is little of St Symeon here, and the text probably comes from the thirteenth century. However, its value is not measured by its purported authorship. Rather, this short piece contains some of the *Philokalia*'s most intimate teaching on physical techniques of prayer, including patterns of breathing designed to align the rhythm of the Jesus Prayer with one's heartbeat. The *Methods of Holy Prayer and Attentiveness* is a full-fledged hesychast treatise in which every element of that spirituality – interiority, continual prayer, use of the Jesus Prayer – is aligned and powerfully embodied.

Sources

Text: Irénée Hausherr, 'La méthode d'oraison hésychaste', *Orientalia Christiana* 9 (1927): 54–76

Alternative text: (as Symeon the New Theologian, in demotic) *PHILOKALIA* (1782): 1178–85; *Philokalia* (1893/1982): vol. 5, 81–9

Methods of Holy Prayer and Attentiveness

There are three ways of prayer and attentiveness, through which the soul is either led up or dragged down. It is led upwards when it makes proper use of these ways, each in its own time; it is dragged downwards, when it seizes them in an untimely and unspiritual fashion. Watchfulness and prayer are bound together as the soul is with the body – neither of them subsists without the other. Watchfulness and prayer are mixed in two ways. First, watchfulness opposes sin, as a sort of scout or advance guard, and then prayer follows immediately to remove and annihilate the shameful thoughts that have been captured by the mental guard, since attentiveness by itself cannot accomplish this feat. This is the gate of life and death: attentiveness and prayer. If we keep our prayer pure through watchfulness, we improve, but if we carelessly pollute it, we shall ourselves get worse.

Since, then, we said that attentiveness and prayer are divided three ways, we must clarify the characteristics of each in turn. Thus, whoever desires to find life and wishes to practise virtue can with assurance choose the better of these various states, once they are clearly distinguished. Otherwise, he may inadvertently lay hold of the worse and overlook the better.

Concerning the First Way of Prayer

These are the characteristics of the first way of prayer. Someone stands in prayer, with hands and eyes uplifted, looking heavenward with his intellect. His intellect is filled with divine images and imagines heavenly beauties, the ranks of angels, *dwellings of the righteous* [Ps. 117:15], and, in short, during prayer he gathers together in his intellect what he has drawn from the Scriptures, and arouses his soul to divine yearning, gazing intently to heaven, even letting his eyes shed tears. So, little by little, his heart is puffed up and exalted, and takes this experience as divine consolation: so he prays that this feeling may go on forever. Now, these signs are all signs of delusion – for even something good ceases to be good when it does not take place in a good way. If someone lives a solitary life and keeps entirely to himself, he cannot avoid derangement. Even if he does not fall into this passion, he can hardly advance to the achievement of virtues – let alone dispassion.

This sort of attentiveness leads people to the delusion of thinking that they see lights with their waking eyes, or smell sweetness, or hear voices, and other such things. Some people are so completely possessed by demons that they wander from place to place and land to land in their madness. Others failing to recognize the one *who transforms himself into an angel of light* [2 Cor. 11:14] take the devil as he presents himself, and thereafter remain intransigent until death, unable to accept correction from others. Others fall into self-harm and suicide, brought to this by their deceiver. Others still hurl themselves off cliffs. But who could list all the varieties of the devil's deceit?

It is possible, though, for a person of understanding to learn from the foregoing what the profit born of this first method of prayer really amounts to. Even if someone avoids falling into these traps because he lives with others – for these things mostly happen to hermits – nonetheless they will spend their entire life without making any progress.

Concerning the Second Way of Prayer

This is the second way. The intellect withdraws from everything perceptible, keeping guard over external sense-perception. It gathers together all its thoughts, and advances, forgetting all the vanity of the world. Sometimes he subjects his thoughts to scrutiny; sometimes he is careful about the words of petitions he makes to God; sometimes he draws back to himself thoughts that have been taken captive; and sometimes when he has been seized by passion he begins again with violence to recover himself. It is impossible for one who fights in this way ever to make peace or be crowned victor. No, such a one is like someone fighting at night, who hears his enemies' voices and feels the wounds, but cannot see clearly who they are, whence they come, how they attack, let alone why – for it is the darkness in his mind that is the problem. A person who fights thus will not escape the spiritual invaders, but endures the struggle only to miss his reward. The attentiveness he imagines his has been stolen by vainglory. Subject to vainglory, he is mocked by it. Sometimes he blames and criticizes others for lacking the attentiveness he supposes himself to have. He sets himself up as shepherd of the sheep, but is like *someone blind* professing to *lead the blind* [Matt. 15:14].

These are the modes of the second method of prayer, from which one who really struggles can learn the harm it does. Of course, the second mode of prayer is much better than the first, just as a moonlit night is better than a night without light and starless.

Concerning the Third Method of Prayer

Look! Now we come to speak about the third sort of prayer. It is a matter strange and hard to explain. To the ignorant it is not merely hard to understand but almost impossible to believe. It is to be found only among very few. I think that a good of this kind has vanished together with obedience. For it is obedience that causes its lovers to detach themselves from this present wicked age, freeing them from cares and attachment to passions. They are thus enabled to pursue their chosen path, constant and resolute, at least if they can find an unerring guide. If you have through obedience become dead to any worldly or bodily attachment, what passing concerns could drag your intellect aside? What worry could distract one who placed the whole care of soul and body upon God and his own spiritual father, and who *no longer lives for* himself [2 Cor. 5:15], nor *desires man's day* [Jer. 17:16 LXX]? Thereafter, the intellectual distractions of the rebel powers, which, like ropes, drag the mind into myriad trappings of wicked thoughts, are shattered. The mind is revealed to be free, making war with authority, while it easily searches out and pursues the enemies' thoughts and offers prayers with a pure heart. This is the beginning of a monastic way of life. Without beginning in this way all ascetic struggle will be in vain.

This, the beginning of the third way of prayer, does not begin from gazing upwards, stretching out hands, gathering thoughts, and calling for aid from heaven. For those actions are, as we have said, properties of the delusion obtained through the first method of prayer. Nor, to reiterate, does it begin from the second mode, in which the mind fixates on exterior senses while failing to recognize interior enemies. For, as we have said, such a mind is attacked and does not counter-attack; it is wounded and does not know it; it is taken captive and is not strong enough to fend off its captors. Forever do *sinners plough upon its back* [Ps. 128:3] and even confront it face to face, making it vainglorious and arrogant.

Now, if you wish to embark on such light-giving and delightful activity, be ready now to make a start. Following exact obedience (whose portrait this treatise has already painted), you must do everything with a good conscience – for apart from obedience there is no pure conscience. You must first protect your conscience with respect to God, then to your spiritual father, and, finally, to other people and material things. As regards God, you must avoid doing anything that you know does not serve God; as regards your spiritual father, you must do, without addition or subtraction, whatever he commands you, in accordance with his own intention; as regards other people, you must not do to another whatever you hate yourself. You must guard against abuse of material things in every matter – food, drink and clothing. To put it simply, do everything as though in the presence of God, so as not to be convicted by your conscience in anything.

Since we have cleared the way and made a start on the notion of true attentiveness, it seems good to discuss further its properties clearly and briefly. True and unerring attention as well as prayer consist in this: that the intellect guard the heart while praying, always keeping watch over the heart inwardly; and offering petitions to the Lord from the depths of the heart. The intellect that *tastes* here and now *that the Lord is good* [Ps. 33:8] is no longer to be evicted from the dwelling place of the heart. For the Lord himself says by his Apostle [Peter], *It is good for us to be here* [Matt. 17:4], and, ever inspecting those inward places, he seeks and destroys those thoughts sown therein by our enemy. Nevertheless to the ignorant this way of life seems exceedingly hard and arduous, and not only to the uninitiated, but even to those who have had sure experience but have not yet tasted its delight in the depths of their hearts. But for those who enjoy its delights, who drink down its sweetness in their heart's throat, it is possible to cry out with Paul, *Who will separate us from the love of Christ?* and so on [Rom. 8:35]. For our holy Fathers heard the Lord saying that *from your heart proceed wicked thoughts, murders, adulteries, thefts, false-witness*, and that *these things defile a person* [Matt. 15:19–20]. They heard his exhortation to *clean the inside of the cup, that its outside also be clean* [Matt. 23:26]. So they gave up every other activity of virtue and strove instead after the thought of guarding the heart. For they clearly perceived that with this one activity – guarding the heart – they could master every other virtue with ease, and that without it virtue could not persist. Some of our Fathers termed this 'stillness of heart', others 'attentiveness', 'guarding of the heart', 'watchfulness and refutation', 'examination of thoughts', and some called it 'guarding of the mind'. But all of them in similar fashion tilled the earth of their heart and through this labour have attained to eating divine manna. Concerning this activity the Teacher says, *Rejoice, young man, in your youth, and walk blameless in the ways of your heart. Cast anger out of your heart. If a ruler's spirit rises against you, do not leave your place* [Eccles. 11:9–10, 10:4]. By *place* he means the heart, just as our Lord says, *From the heart proceed wicked thoughts* [Matt. 15:19]. And, again, *Do not be worried* [Luke 12:29], and *How narrow is the gate, and how confined the road that leads to life* [Matt. 7:14]. *Blessed are the poor in spirit* [Matt. 5:3] – that is, those who have no thought at all of this present age in them. The Apostle Peter says, *Be watchful, be wakeful, for your opponent the Devil walks about like a roaring lion, seeking whom he may devour* and so on [1 Pet. 5:8]. Paul writes to the Ephesians with utter clarity about guarding the heart, when he says, *Our battle is not against flesh and blood* and so on [Eph. 6:12]. Everything which our divine Fathers have declared in their writings about guarding the heart will be clear to those who seek these things zealously.

First of all you need to secure for yourself three things, and make a start on your quest. First, freedom from anxieties, whether reasonable or not – that is, you need to die to everything. Secondly, a pure conscience – that is, keeping yourself from being condemned in your own conscience. Thirdly, detachment – that is, having no inclination towards anything in this world or even your own body.

Then, having sat down in a quiet cell, in your own little corner, pay attention and do exactly as I tell you. Shut the door and remove your intellect from everything vain and transient. Bend your beard to your chest, directing your physical eye and your whole intellect on the middle of your abdomen – I mean, your omphalos, or belly button. Restrain the inhalation of breath through your nose so as not to inhale easily. Search intellectually within your inner parts to find the place of your heart, where all your soul's faculties love to make their dwelling. At first you will find darkness and inward heaviness. But, as you persist in this work night and day, you will find – what a marvel! – unspeakable delight. For as soon as your intellect discovers the place of your heart, it sees straight away things it never knew. For it sees both the air between the heart and itself made wholly luminous and full of discernment. Thereafter, should a thought arise, before it is completed or shaped into an image, the intellect uses the invocation of Jesus Christ to chase and destroy it. Then, the intellect harbours malice for the demons and with its natural rage aroused it engages in intellectual warfare. You will learn other things too, with God's help, as you lay hold of Jesus in your heart by the guarding of your mind. For it says, '*Sit in your cell and it will teach you all.*'[1]

Question. Why cannot the first and second modes of prayer perfect a monk?
Answer. Because they do not proceed in order. St John Klimakos confirms this when he says, 'Some diminish their passions, some chant psalms and spend most of their time in this, others persevere in prayer, while others spend their life gazing in contemplation in their depths. Let this riddle be solved in the manner of a ladder,' says he.[2] So then, if you want to ascend the ladder do not proceed from top to bottom, but from bottom to top. You must step on the first rung first, and then climb the rest in order. In this way it is possible to rise from earth to heaven. If, then, we wish to *attain to the perfect manhood of Christ's fullness* [Eph. 4:21 modified], let us set foot on the ladder in a childlike manner, and go up as children do through the stages of growth, so that we may, after progressing a bit, attain the measure of manhood and eldership.

The first stage of monastic life consists in diminishing our passions. This pertains to beginners.

The second rung and stage of growth – which brings a boy into spiritual adolescence – is assiduity in psalmody. For after the lulling and lessening of passions, psalmody is sweetened by the tongue and is valued by God, since it is impossible *to sing* to *the Lord in a foreign land* [Ps. 136:4]. This activity is the mark of those making progress.

The third rung and stage of growth – which ushers the adolescent into spiritual adulthood – is perseverance in prayer. This belongs to those who have already made progress. Prayer surpasses psalmody as the *perfect man* surpasses adolescent and child, according to whatever rung to which we come.

In addition to these, the fourth rung and spiritual stage of life is that of the grey-haired elder. This consists in the unmoving gaze of contemplation and belongs to the perfect. Behold! The way is complete, and the ladder finds its summit.

Considering that these activities have been ordained and divinely communicated by the Spirit, it is not otherwise possible for a child to grow to adulthood and ascend to the condition of a grey-haired elder, save through beginning (as we have said) with the first rung and advancing properly through all four so as to come to perfection.

For one who desires to be born anew spiritually the beginning of advancement towards light is the diminution of passions – that is to say, guarding of the heart. For otherwise it is impossible that the passions be diminished. Next comes intense practice in psalmody. For when the passions have been laid to rest and thoroughly reduced through opposition to them in the heart, the desire for reconciliation with God kindles the mind. Thereafter the intellect, being strengthened against the thoughts that blow across the surface of the heart, searches out and destroys them. And so the intellect applies itself assiduously to the second mode of attentiveness and prayer. This provokes the evil spirits to attack and the spirits of the passions are accustomed violently to disturb the abyss of the heart. But through the invocation of the Lord Jesus Christ they are destroyed and melt like wax in the fire. Once cast out of the heart these spirits stir up the surface of the intellect through the senses, but as this is superficial, swiftly a sense of calmness is regained, though one can never fully escape the attacks of the demons nor avoid fighting them. For such calm belongs only to one who has already *come to perfect manhood* [Eph. 4:21], manifest in total renunciation and enduring forever in the attention of the heart. The attentive person is raised little by little from these activities to the wisdom of old age, that is, the ascent to contemplation, which belongs to the perfect. One, therefore, who undertakes these activities in their own time and at a good pace can also – following the expulsion of passions from the heart and perseverance in psalmody – properly ward off the thoughts that are roused through the senses and the troubling of the surface of the intellect. He can lift up his physical as well as his intellectual eyes to heaven when he has need of it, and he can pray purely in truth – but occasionally or rarely, because of those who lie in ambush in the air. For this alone is demanded of us, that our heart be purified by our guarding of it. *If*, according to the Apostle, *the root is holy, then clearly so are the leaves* and fruit [Rom. 11:16]. But, apart from the way we have discussed, anyone who raises eye and mind to heaven, desiring to visualize something intelligible, will behold some idol rather than truth. Because the heart is impure, the second and first modes do not offer progress. We do not first put the roof on a house and then lay its foundation (since this is impossible), but the other way round: first foundation, then the building, and then the roof atop these together. Well, it is the same with these intelligible concepts. First, we guard our heart and diminish the passions within it and thus lay the foundation of our spiritual house. Then we drive back the breeze of evil spirits that rises against us through our external senses and quickly escape their war. In this way we fix the walls of our spiritual house atop the foundation. Then, finally, through perfect inclination towards God or withdrawal from the world, we extend the roof of the house, and thus we complete our spiritual house,

In Christ Jesus our Lord, to whom be glory unto the ages. Amen.

St Elias Ekdikos,
Gnomic Anthology

ELIAS EKDIKOS, THE PRIEST
AND LAWYER (11TH–12TH C.)

Nothing is known of Elias save what can be gleaned with difficulty from the highly elliptical and impersonal *Anthology*. He
seems to have been influenced by St Symeon the New Theologian and some manuscripts mention a rumour that he was a
'disciple' of Symeon, though whether personally or literarily we
cannot tell. The Gnomic *Anthology* is quoted in a saint's *Life*
written no later than the 1130s. On the basis of these details we
can say that Elias wrote probably in the later eleventh century.
There was another Elias, the Metropolitan Bishop of Crete,
around the same time, who wrote voluminous commentaries
on St Gregory Nazianzen and St John Klimakos, but this is
almost certainly a different person.

Manuscripts call our Elias a 'low-level priest and *ekdikos*'.
An *ekdikos* was a lawyer, effectively, but Elias was probably
an ecclesiastical *ekdikos*, which may have seen him receiving,
confessing and disciplining people seeking sanctuary in the
Church. The position was frequently filled by priests, which
makes sense of Elias's double titles. This position is best known
from Constantinople, and so it is quite possible that is where
Elias lived and worked. This is all we can say of him, really,
though it is possible that he was part of a monastic community,
given the affinities of his work with the style and themes of
gnomic literature popular among monastic writers.

The *Gnomic Anthology* describes the two phases of Christian life, marked not by a sharp change but a change in emphasis: the life of practical virtue and the life of contemplation. Contemplation is founded, for Elias, in practical virtue, freedom from passions and growing humility. Contemplation, though, requires an ascent even beyond discursive reason to a kind of direct and intuitive knowing. Prayer suffuses this whole process and growth, though its character changes with that of the one praying. The *Gnomic Anthology* is a particularly challenging read, full of elliptical expression and technical vocabulary which Elias develops through recurrence, motif and allusion.

NB: We have enumerated the four sections of the *Gnomic Anthology* separately; the original *Philokalia* has continuous enumeration in sections I and II (109 = 79 + 30) and sections III and IV (139 = 32 + 107).

Sources

Text: *PHILOKALIA* (1782): 529–48; *Philokalia* (1893/1982): vol. 2, 289–314

Gnomic Anthology

I. Brief Sentences for Serious Philosophers

If you approach carefully, you will find this treatise
A fount flowing with waters of virtue.

1. Every Christian who believes rightly in God cannot be free from anxiety, but must forever expect and accept temptation, so that when it comes he is neither perplexed nor troubled. He will gratefully endure the trouble of affliction and consider why, as he chants with the Prophet, *Try me, Lord, and test me* [Ps. 25:2], David did not say that *Your discipline* has destroyed me, but that it *set me upright in the end* [Ps. 17:36].

2. The beginning of good things is fear of God; their end is desire for God.

3. The beginning of every good thing is practical reason and rational practice. For neither practice without reason nor a word spoken without action is good.

4. Practical virtue is: for the body, fasting and vigil; for the tongue, psalmody, prayer and silence more valuable than speech. For the hands, practice means their working without complaint; and for the feet, their hastening at the first call.

5. All these are guided by mercy and truth, whose offspring is humility and the discernment that, according to our Fathers, accrues from it. Without discernment, humility cannot see its own extent. For practice that dishonours the yoke of reason is found wandering like some calf here and there among worthless things; while reason that discards the precious robes

of practical virtue is not becoming, even if it makes a show of seeming such.

6. The manly soul, burning with practical and contemplative virtue – like a woman who her whole life clutches two lamps – does beneficial things. Again, the opposite holds true for a soul persisting in pleasures.

7. Voluntary suffering does not suffice for a soul's complete deliverance from vice unless it remains undestroyed when burned by involuntary suffering. For the soul is a kind of sword: unless it *has passed through fire and water* [Ps. 65:12] – that is, voluntary and involuntary troubles – it is not preserved unbroken against the blows of circumstance.

8. There are three general causes of voluntary temptations: health, wealth and fame. So there are three causes of involuntary ones: loss, abuse and sickness. For some these are edifying, for others destructive.

9. There subsist together in our soul desire and sadness; in our body, pleasure and pain. The cause of pain is pleasure, for, desiring to flee the toilsome sensation of pain we take refuge in pleasure. Likewise, the cause of sadness is desire.

10. A virtuous person has goodness as a disposition; a vainglorious person has it as mere cunning. A zealous person has evil superficially; a lover of pleasure has it deep down.

11. For our soul, practical virtue means self-control in simplicity and simplicity animated by self-control.

12. For our mind, practical virtue means prayer in contemplation and contemplation in prayer.

13. One who hates evil is seldom found in it and then without much interest. But one who enjoys its causes is found in it attentively and all too often.

14. To those whose repentance is not purposive falls come continuously, while to those whose sin contradicts their purpose, repentance finds its fulfilment, and its cause is not great.

15. Let perception and understanding accompany your spoken words, so that the peaceful and divine Word be not ashamed to be found among these because of their temerity or immoderacy.

16. One who does not wrong his soul in actions does not necessarily keep it undefiled in words. Nor has the man who guards his soul in words not already defiled it with pollutions. For sinning is threefold.

17. You will not be able to gaze on the face of virtue so long as you think gladly of the face of vice. The latter will appear utterly hateful to you when you repudiate the taste of delicious food and even the sight of it.

18. The demons war on our soul principally through thoughts rather than external things, for things make war on us by themselves. The cause of this external war is hearing and seeing; of mental war, habit and the demons.

19. We find that the soul's propensity to sin is threefold: deeds, words and thoughts. The goodness of sinlessness is six-fold: for it guards the five senses from failure and the spoken word too. In these matters, if someone does not fall, he is perfect and able to bridle the other parts of the soul.

20. The soul's irrational part is divided six ways: the five senses and the spoken word. This last, if impassible, assists indivisibly in preserving the sufferer; but if it is found to be passible it receives his vice.

21. Neither can the body be purified without fasting and vigil, nor the soul without mercy and truth, nor the mind without converse with God and contemplation of Him. For in each these are the most significant pairs [of activities].

22. The soul walled about with the aforementioned virtues establishes endurance as its citadel undisturbed by the clamour of temptations. For *by your endurance you gain your souls* [Luke 21:19], says the Word. But if the soul's possessions be otherwise, then, like some unwalled city terrified of distant noises, it gets used to the bolts that protect it trembling with cowardice.

23. Not all who are prudent in matters of speech are prudent in matters of thought; nor will all those be found prudent in matters of external sense-perception. For even though sense-perception has all humans as its tributaries, they do not all render tribute alike. For in their simplicity, many do not know

how sense-perception requires them to honour it in matters pertaining to it.

24. Though moral wisdom is by nature undivided, it is cut into various portions: to one is given more, to another less, at least, until practical virtue, having increased and having the principal virtues in its retinue, fulfils for each all possible goodness. For many have received thinking in accordance with their lack of practical life.

25. Few will be found wise in things that accord with nature, but many in things contrary to nature. For by fear of natural things they have emptied out their whole natural thinking, they have very little understanding – mostly in superfluous matters and not ones by nature praiseworthy.

26. Time and good measure are table companions of blessed silence and truth its banquet. So when the father of lies [cf. John 8:44] comes and the soul is away at that banquet, he finds nothing of what he seeks.

27. The truly compassionate [or, generous] person does not merely give voluntarily of his abundance, but surrenders even what he needs to those who take it.

28. Some procure immaterial wealth by means of material wealth, in keeping with the laws of almsgiving; others, who have come to a perception of what cannot be stolen, give up material wealth by means of the immaterial.

29. Being wealthy in good things is dear to all; but it is grievous to one who divinely enriches others not to be allowed to rejoice in this for long.

30. To the soul, health seems to be external, but its sickness is internal, naturally accustomed to hide at the base of sense-perception. If that sickness must be bled out by the cutting of reproaches, and health be introduced by *the renewing of the mind* [Rom. 12:1], then he is a fool who shakes off reproaches and is not ashamed always to recline on the sickbed of insensitivity.

31. Do not be angry with one who involuntarily operates on you like a surgeon. Rather, seeing the horrid thing that he has cut away, blame yourself and bless him for having become the cause of your benefit, by God's dispensation.

32. Do not despair at the horror of your sickness. Rather, drive it away through the more powerful drugs of laborious practice, you who diligently seek health for your soul.

33. Do not recoil from one who gives you a timely sting. Assent to this and it will show you just how much good has rubbed off on your senses. And so you will eat the sweet food of health after having removed the filth of bitterness.

34. The more you feel pain, the more you should welcome the one whose reproach makes you perceive it. For he is the cause, as far as you are concerned, of perfect purification, without which your mind cannot come to the pure realm of prayer.

35. When you are reproached, you must either keep silent or gently defend yourself against your accuser – not in order to endear yourself to him, but to raise him up who has perhaps stumbled by accusing you in ignorance.

36. He who repents before it is demanded of him by the one whom he has justly grieved has lost nothing; if he repents only afterwards, he forfeits half his abundance. But he who is never found to have estranged another through grief gains for himself all that he has sown; and he who in everything puts the blame on himself gains more than he deserved.

37. One who has a high opinion of himself does not recognize his own defects, nor does the humble-minded recognize goodness as his own. For an evil ignorance hides them from the former, while an ignorance pleasing to God hides them from the latter.

38. A proud man does not like to be compared to his equals in his good qualities. In his failings, however, he is content to be compared with those who surpass him, reckoning as tolerable his own defect.

39. Censure makes the soul firm, while praise makes it relaxed, and more sleepy towards what is good.

40. The substance of wealth is gold, as humility is of virtue. So, just as someone who lacks gold is poor, even if he does not appear so to outsiders, so also one who engages in the spiritual struggle without humility will never be virtuous.

41. Without gold a merchant is not inherently a merchant, even if he is very experienced in trade. Neither will

one embarking on the ascetic life be found in possession of the delights of virtue without humility, even though he be very confident in his own good sense.

42. One who ascends in humility will be lower than his own estimate of himself, while one who climbs without it will seem higher than his own estimation. The humble cannot willingly accept to be compared even with the lowest and because of this is distressed when given the first place at table [cf. Matt. 23:6].

43. It is good for the spiritual contestant to consider himself not up to what is required of him, but in his actions to disregard his timidity. For in this way he will gain people's respect and be found an *unashamed worker* for God [2 Tim. 2:15].

44. One who is afraid lest he seem a stranger to those reclining in the bridal chamber [cf. Matt. 22:1-14] must either accomplish all of God's commands or in their stead accomplish just one: humility.

45. Mix self-control with simplicity and yoke truth to humility and you will be seen to be a guest of righteousness, at whose table every other virtue loves to gather.

46. Truth without humility is blind. For this reason it often uses dispute as a guide which, though it labours to rest upon something, finds nothing but the confirmation of resentment.

47. Kind habit testifies to the beauty of virtue, and tranquillity of our [bodily] members shows a peaceful soul.

48. Your primary good is not slipping up at all in anything. Second to that: neither hiding a fault in shame nor sinking further in it but, instead, being humbled, joining the one who accuses you in his accusation, and gladly receiving your punishment. Unless this happens, every offering to God is ineffective [cf. Matt. 5:24].

49. In addition to the voluntary, we must accept involuntary suffering – I mean that which comes from accusers, losses and illnesses. For one who does not accept these, but instead gives up in despair, is like someone who will only eat bread with honey and never with salt. That person does not have pleasure as his companion forever, but he will always get surfeit as his neighbour.

50. He who washes his neighbour's tattered cloak with

inspired words or stitches it up with meeting his needs may appear to be clothed in the garb of a slave [cf. Phil. 2:7], but is really the master. Let him take care to do this truly as a slave, lest, through vainglory, he lose his reward together with the dignity attaching to his authority.

51. Just as *faith is* naturally *the substance of things hoped for* [Heb. 11:1], so is sagacity the substance of the soul, and humility of virtue. And it is a marvel how things complete in themselves become defective without their substance.

52. *The Lord will guard your coming in and your going out* [Ps. 120:8]: that is, the intake of food and the output of words, guarded by self-control. For he who keeps both with self-control at once escapes the *desire of the eyes* [1 John 2:16] and assuages the anger that comes from frustration – in both these feats the spiritual contestant must above all be diligent and in every way zealous. For by these is practical virtue strengthened and contemplation made firm.

53. Some take great care over their intake of food, but remain careless about their output of words. Such people do not understand how to divert *anger from* their *heart* and desire *from* their *flesh*, as Ecclesiastes puts it [Eccles. 11:10]. It is through these that a pure heart is accustomed to be made by the renewing Spirit [cf. Ps. 50:12].

54. Frugality in food can be attained through a poorer quality of nourishment; blamelessness in words by a greater quality of silence.

55. Cauterize your loins with abstinence from food and unmask your heart with self-control in words. Then your desiring and incensive [or, irascible] faculties will come to be in service of what is good.

56. Sexual pleasure abates in ascetics as their bodies get older, but their pleasure in talking remains if they do not learn to curb it properly. You must, therefore, be zealous to scrape off the shame of the effect by dealing with its cause, lest, being found a stranger to the virtue of self-control, you be clothed in shame.

57. An ascetic needs to know when to nourish his body as an enemy to food, when as a friend, and when he must comfort

it in infirmity. He must not forget and give an enemy's foods to a friend, or a friend's to an enemy, or either of these to infirmity – because then he will find all three states fighting against him in time of temptation.

58. When someone at table considers nourishment preferable to luxury, then the grace of tears comes to dwell in him and begins to exhort him also to forget every other delight, as they are already swallowed up by the incomparable sweetness of tears.

59. In one who is puffed up tears dry up; they pour forth in one who loves *the narrow way* [cf. Matt. 7:13].

60. There is none who escapes grief – neither sinner nor righteous: the sinner, because he has not at all abandoned wickedness; the righteous, because he has not yet attained perfection.

61. Among the things that are up to us are the virtues that are within our power: prayer and silence. What is not up to us but, instead, mostly concerns our bodily constitution, includes fasting and vigil. Therefore, the spiritual contestant must go in quest of what is more accessible to him.

62. Patience is the house of the soul, for in it the soul is protected; humility is its wealth, for the soul is nourished through it.

63. Unless you endure troubles you will not be honoured with praises. If you pay attention to pain before indulging in pleasure, you will escape the grief it causes.

64. If you are not bound in a small matter, you will not be enslaved in a greater one. For greater evils are not generally formed before lesser ones.

65. If you pay attention to greater evils, you will be fearful of lesser evils. If you are seen to be scornful of these, you will give in to those.

66. You cannot reach the greater virtues without having grasped to the utmost what is within your own power.

67. In those where mercy and grace reign, everything will be pleasing to God, for truth judges nothing without mercy and mercy offers no kindness without truth.

68. Once you have blended self-control with simplicity, you will thereafter be in beatitude's embrace.

69. You will not see at all the passions that war against you, unless first letting the soil that nourishes them lie fallow.

70. Some strive only to purify their body's matter; others strive to purify their soul's too. For some have received strength enough only to fight sin in action; others, to fight passion – but only to very few is it given to fight desire itself.

71. The body's wicked matter is passion; the soul's, indulgence in pleasure; the mind's, attachment. Touch brings the accusation against the first, the other senses against the second, a contrary disposition against the last.

72. One who indulges in pleasure is neighbour to an impassioned man, and one passionately attached neighbour to the indulgent: the dispassionate one dwells far from them all.

73. A man subject to passion is one who is violently drawn to a thought's sinfulness, even if meanwhile he refrains from sinning in externals. One who indulges in pleasure actually commits the sin that comes from a thought, even if he suffers internally. But one passionately attached is given over to various ways of sinning through freedom, or, rather, through slavery. But he is dispassionate who does not know the difference between these various conditions.

74. Being subject to passion is eradicated from the soul through fasting and prayer; love of pleasure, through vigil and silence; attachment, through stillness and attentiveness. Dispassion is constituted by the memory of God.

75. From *the lips* of dispassion *drip* the *words of eternal life* [John 6:68], like *combs* of honey [cf. Song 4:11]. Who, therefore, would be deemed worthy to touch the lips of dispassion with his own? Or to *encamp between* her *breasts* [Song 1:13]? Or to imbibe the delightful *fragrance of* her *garments* – that is, to be clothed in laws of virtues which, it says, *are preferable to all scents* of sensible distinction [Song 4:10]?

76. Many have perhaps stripped off the robe of self-affection, few have disrobed their love of the world, and you will find only the dispassionate – and him who is called *least* [Mark 9:34, cf. Matt. 11:11] – stripped of vainglory.

77. Every soul will be stripped of its visible body, and the soul that has shared little in the pleasures of this life will be stripped of the *body of sin* [Rom. 6:6].

78. All of those who live will be corpses, but only those who have hated sin with their whole disposition will be made corpses to sin.

79. Who will see himself rid of sin before our common bodily death? Who knows himself and his own nature, what quality it is, before the impending shedding of the body?

II. Untitled

A soul wounded with bridal love,
Prayer knows how to unite with its bridegroom.

1. The rational soul is set on the frontier between perceptible and intelligible light. Through the former the soul is enabled to accomplish things of the body; through the latter, things of the Spirit. But, since the intelligible light has become dim in the soul while the perceptible has become clear through habit built up from the beginning, the soul cannot gaze fixedly on divine things unless it has come entirely into the intelligible light in prayer. The soul must dwell in the no man's land between darkness and light, being turned back and forth, according to its participation in light or its imagining in darkness.

2. An intellect subject to passions cannot enter through the *narrow gate* of prayer until it renounce the anxiety born of its attachment. It will always suffer as it busies itself about the camp of prayer.

3. Let prayer persist in your intellect, like a ray of light in the sun, for without prayer sensory concerns block the intellect of its natural radiance, like waterless clouds scudding overhead.

4. The power of prayer lies in voluntary abstinence from food; the power of such abstinence lies in neither hearing nor seeing anything worldly, except when absolutely necessary. One who is negligent of these at once deprives the house of fasting of its foundation and brings the house of prayer in his soul to ruin [cf. Matt. 7:24–7].

5. Unless the intellect becomes frugal in all sensory matters it cannot ascend nor realize its own dignity.

6. Fasting is a symbol of day, because it is apparent, while prayer is a symbol of night because it is hidden. He who travels through both as is appropriate to each will find the city he seeks, from which are *fled away pain, sorrow, and sighing* [Isa. 35:10].

7. Spiritual activity naturally subsists even without bodily labour. Blessed is he who has reckoned immaterial activity better than material labour. For through this activity he fills up what is lacking in material labour, having lived the life of prayer – hidden, but manifest to God.

8. The divine Apostle exhorts us to endure in faith, to *rejoice in hope*, to *persist in prayer* [Rom. 12:12] so that the goodness of joy may remain with us. If this is the case, then he who does not endure is not faithful, and he who does not rejoice is not hopeful, for he has rejected prayer, the cause of joy, by not persisting in it.

9. If an intellect that has from its inception dwelt among worldly thoughts has such affection for them, how much proper companionship will it not have in continual prayer? 'For', it says, 'the intellect is accustomed to spread out in the things among which it spends time.'[1]

10. Just as the intellect that has long been removed from its own dwelling place has forgotten the radiance it enjoyed there, so must it in turn become forgetful of things here to return back there through prayer.

11. As an infant at its mother's dry breasts so is our intellect found to be in prayer, unable to be consoled by it. But when on the contrary it finds consolation, then it is like a child lulled to sleep by pleasure in its mother's arms.

12. *There*, according to the woman in the Song – clearly meaning in the mournful bed of the virtuous life – the bride, that is, prayer, says to her lover, *I will give you my breasts* [Song 7:13], if you will dedicate yourself wholly to me.

13. Fondness for prayer is impossible unless you renounce everything material.

14. Save for life and breath, set yourself apart from everything else in prayer, if you wish to be with your intellect alone.

15. Evidence of an intellect devoted to God is single-phrased prayer [e.g., the Jesus Prayer], of sane reason a timely word, and of sense-perception that is free, simple taste: therefore, when there is evidence in all three cases, the faculties of the soul can be said to be in good health.

16. It is necessary for the nature of one who prays to be supple and malleable as with children, so that, like them, he may receive easily the openness that goes with prayer. Let him who loves to find intimacy in prayer not be careless.

17. Not all obtain the same goal in prayer: one finds this, another that. One prays that, if possible, his heart will always be gathered up in prayer; another, to transcend it; yet another, not to be cut off by thoughts during prayer. But all pray either to be maintained in what is good or not to be led astray by evil.

18. If because of prayer everyone is humbled (for he who prays spends his life in humility), then someone boastful outwardly is not praying in humility.

19. If one who prays keeps in mind the widow who moved the cruel judge to justice [Luke 18:2–8], then he will never despair because the good things promised us are slow in coming.

20. Prayer will not remain with you if you argue about things internally and dwell on outward matters. It will be seen to be returning to one who, for the sake of prayer, guards against both.

21. Unless the words of your prayer enter the very deepest part of your soul, no tears will be allowed to wash the cheeks of the face.

22. Wheat grows for the farmer, who has hidden out of sight the seeds he sowed in the earth. Tears well up for the monk who has attended diligently to the words of the prayer.

23. Prayer is the key to the Kingdom of Heaven: he who uses it as he should sees the good things laid up for those who love it. But he who has not found confidence in prayer sees passing things only.

24. In the time of prayer the mind cannot say confidently to God, *You have broken my bonds; I will offer you a sacrifice of praise* [Ps. 115:7–8], unless by desire for better things it has been delivered from cowardice, carelessness, sleepiness, gourmandizing, all of which cause us to fall.

25. He who is distracted in prayer stands outside the first veil [of the Temple]. He who is accomplished in the single-phrased [Jesus Prayer] stands within it. But he alone enters the *Holy of Holies* [Exod. 26:33, Heb. 9:4, etc.] who, at peace from natural thoughts, considers those things *that pass all understanding* [Phil. 4:7] and has thus been counted worthy to receive from thence some divine manifestation.

26. Whenever a soul, free from attention to external matters, has found union in prayer, then prayer, having enveloped the soul like a flame – just as fire engulfs iron [in the forge] – sets the whole aflame. And in that moment the soul remains the same, but cannot be touched, as neither can red-hot iron be touched by those who handle it.

27. Blessed is the man who in this life has been deemed worthy of such contemplation, and who beholds his own naturally clayish figure made fiery by grace.

28. To beginners the law of prayer weighs heavy, like some taskmaster. To those making progress it is as burning desire, driving a starving man to an elaborate feast.

29. To those who are pursuing practical virtue well, sometimes prayer overshadows them like a cloud and cools their burning thoughts. Sometimes it rains thoughts like tear drops and reveals spiritual sights.

30. The sound of the lyre when struck will be found sweet by an outsider, while a soul does not naturally feel compunction unless in prayer the secret calling echoes within it in spirit. For *we do not know how to pray as we ought*, and the rest [Rom. 8:26]: into this it urges the one who is praying.

III. Gnostic Matters

A mind is enlightened when drawn
To the height of gnostic contemplation,
Encountering the principles of things –
It is darkened again when enveloped in passion.

1. The gnostic needs to know when his intellect is in the place of intellection, when in the place of discursive thinking, and

when in the place of sense-perception. And again, in each case, he needs to know if his intellect is found to be there at the right time or the wrong time.

2. When the intellect is not in the realm of intellection, it is no doubt among discursive thoughts; when it is among discursive thoughts, it is not in the realm of intellection. But if it is in sensory perception, it is with everything.

3. The intellect arrives at intellectual reality through intellection; reason arrives at what is rational through discursive thought. Sense-perception arrives at what is to be done in the material world through imagination.

4. The intellect gathered to itself contemplates nothing either sensory or discursive. Instead, it beholds bare intellects and divine rays flowing with peace and joy.

5. The intellectual meaning of any reality is one thing, its *logos* another, and what falls to sense-perception is yet another. The first is essence, the second accident, the third the distinctive character of underlying matter.

6. An intellect that blazes numerous trails is clearly insatiate. An intellect that confines itself to the single path of prayer appears cramped before it reaches perfection and begs its partner to be set free from everything from which it has withdrawn.

7. An intellect drawn down from above will not return there again unless it achieves complete contempt for things below through diligent study of divine things.

8. If you cannot cause your soul to be alone with the thoughts that pertain to it, at least compel your body to keep to itself, contemplating continually its wretchedness. For thus, with time and by God's mercy, you will be able to return to the original dignity of nobility.

9. One engaged in ascetic struggle can easily submit his intellect to prayer; the contemplative, however, submits prayer to his intellect. The former limits his senses to manifest forms; the latter leads his soul to the principles [*logoi*] hidden in forms. The former persuades his mind to be ignorant of bodily principles [*logoi*]; the latter persuades it to contemplate bodiless ones. Now, the principles [*logoi*] of bodies, their properties and substances, are themselves bodiless.

10. When you free your intellect from the pleasant enjoyment of bodies, goods and foods, then what you have done will be reckoned a pure gift to God. Then will be given to you in return the opening of the eyes of your heart and ready meditation on the words of God written therein – which words will be considered *sweeter than honey and the honeycomb* in your spiritual *throat* because of their fragrant sweetness [Ps. 118:103].

11. You cannot make your mind victorious over bodies, goods and the desire for unnecessary foods, unless you lead it into the pure land of the righteous, wherein the memory of death and God wells up and then every shoot of desire will be cleared from the soil of your heart.

12. Nothing is more frightening than the idea of death or more marvellous than the memory of God. The former causes salvific sadness [cf. 2 Cor. 7:10], the latter gives delight. For *I remembered God*, says the Prophet, *and I rejoiced* [Ps. 75:4]. And a wise man says, *Remember your end and you will not sin* [Sirach 7:36]. For one cannot come into possession of God without first having experience of the harshness of death.

13. Until a mind beholds *the glory of God with face unveiled* [2 Cor. 3:18] the soul cannot say in its own perception, I *will rejoice in the Lord* and *delight in his salvation* [Ps. 34:9]. For the *veil* of self-affection *lies upon* its *heart* [2 Cor. 3:15] so that *the foundations of the inhabited world* are not revealed to it [Ps. 17:16] – that is, the principles [*logoi*] of created beings. And this veil is not lifted without voluntary and involuntary toils.

14. It was not after the flight from Egypt (which land symbolizes sin in action), nor after crossing the sea (which is slavery through attachment), but only after sojourning in the desert that lies between the arousal and activity of wickedness that the leader of the people of Israel was able to reconnoitre *the land of promise* [Heb. 11:9], which is dispassion, by dispatching his powers of seeing and observing.

15. Those who have sojourned in the desert – that is, in the non-activity of the passions – possess *the good things of the land* [Isa. 1:19] in hearing alone. Those who have reconnoitred

what lies in that land clearly have come to a mere apprehension of the contemplation of things seen there. But those who have been found worthy to enter into it have had their whole sensory array filled with the indescribable things of that land, like *milk and honey* [Exod. 3:8] – I mean, both first and second natural contemplation.[2]

16. He has not yet *been crucified with Christ* [Gal. 2:20] who still possesses the natural movements of his flesh; nor has he *been buried with Christ* [Rom. 6:4] who is drawn about by the soul's ideas. How, then, will such a person *rise with Christ to walk in newness of life* [Rom. 6:4]?

17. There are three comprehensive virtues for the soul – fasting, prayer and silence. Therefore, it is necessary that someone about to emerge from prayer alight on some natural contemplation, and one about to emerge from silence rest in virtuous discourse. Someone about to break his fast must turn to permitted refreshment.

18. When the mind lives among divine things, it saves what is *in the likeness* [of God] [Gen. 1:26], and is found to be good and compassionate. Now, having come among sensory things, provided it has done so in a timely and appropriate fashion, the mind gives and receives experience and, growing healthy again, it returns to itself. But if it has done so untimely and unnecessarily, it will be discovered to be an unwary general who is cut off from most of his army in the fighting.

19. The paradise of dispassion hidden within us is an image of what the just will obtain. Yet not all who are unable to come into dispassion's enclosure will be found outside the realm of the just.

20. The perceptible sun finds its rays excluded from shuttered houses. The intelligible sun will not bring its sweetness into a soul that expects it unless it keeps its senses closed off to visible things.

21. A gnostic is one who has disposed his soul's descents magnificently and its ascents humbly [cf. Ps. 83:6].

22. A bee that visits a meadow brings from it the ingredients for honey. A soul that goes about the ages infuses sweetness in its mind.

23. When a stag eats a poisonous serpent it seeks out springs of water to quench the venom.[3] A soul wounded by divine darts unceasingly longs for the love that is wounding it [cf. Song 2:5].

24. Simple thoughts grow in the monadic life, discursive thoughts in the dyadic. When thoughts have been banished from the fragmented soul, only intellects free from bodies introduce the soul to the principles [*logoi*] of providence and judgement, thus manifesting to it *the foundations of the earth* [cf. Ps. 81:5].

25. In the dyadic life it is not natural for *male and female* to be seen in a single gaze, but this will be found in the monadic life, since *in Christ Jesus* [Gal. 3:28], where the *likeness* [Gen. 1:26] is attained, the distinction of *male* and *female* will not be known.

26. Thoughts belong neither to the soul's irrational part (for thoughts cannot be in thoughtless beings) nor to its intellectual part (since there are no thoughts like these among the angels). Being offspring of the rational soul thoughts use the imagination like a ladder, ascending from sense-perception to the intellect, announcing to it things derived from the senses, and descending from mind to senses, introducing intellectual intuitions.

27. As people swimming up from deep water attempt to cling to one another for help, so will wicked thoughts be found, when the ship of vice is in danger of foundering on the flood of tears.

28. Thoughts gather about a soul according to its underlying quality, either to board it like pirates or like rowers to save it when in danger: pirate thoughts dragging the soul towards a sea of improper thoughts; rowers, seeking to find stability, steering the ship towards calm shores.

29. The soul, which longs to cast off vainglory at last – for vainglory is the seventh thought – unless it strips off the six thoughts that come before it will not be able to put on the eighth thought, which the divine Apostle knows as 'the heavenly dwelling', which can only be put on through groanings by

those who for its sake have stripped themselves of material things [cf. 2 Cor. 5:1–4].

30. Angelic thoughts naturally accompany perfect prayer; spiritual thoughts intermediate prayer; and thoughts about nature the prayer of beginners.

31. As the quality of the seed is usually seen in the ear of wheat, so is the purity of contemplation seen through prayer. The seed uses its enveloping spear-like sheath to repel scavenging birds. Contemplation has wise and rational thoughts in temptations to remove them.

32. In ascetic struggle, the soul's manifest qualities are like *the silvery wings of the dove*. In contemplation its soft and intelligible qualities are arrayed *in the sheen of gold* [Ps. 67:14]. For a soul that has not yet attained such beauty cannot *take wing and be at rest* [Ps. 54:7] there in *the dwelling of all who rejoice* [Ps. 86:7].

IV. Practical and Contemplative Matters, by the same author

Here is a meadow full of fruit:
Spiritual practice and contemplation.

1. Of old the ancients were commanded to offer the first fruits of their threshing floors and wine presses in the temple [cf. Exod. 22:29]. Now, though, we need to offer self-control and truth to God as first fruits of practical virtue. Of contemplative virtue, we must offer love and prayer. Through the former we burn up the impulses of irrational desire and anger, and through the latter vain thoughts and our neighbour's plots.

2. Self-control and truth are the beginning of practical virtue; its middle is moderation and humility; and its end is peace and the body's sanctification.

3. Practical virtue is not simply being able to do good things, but doing them as one ought. One who acts must be concerned with time and measure in his actions.

4. Contemplation is not merely beholding bodies as they are, but in seeing their inner principles to which they refer.

5. There is no unerring practice apart from contemplation, nor true contemplation without practice. For practice must be rational and contemplation practical so that by the first, vice be rendered powerless, while by the second, the virtue of kindness is powerful in well-pleasing acts.

6. The goal of practical matters is the mortification of the passions, the purpose of matters gnostic contemplation of the virtues.

7. As matter is to form, so is practice to contemplation, and as an eye is to the face, so is contemplation to practice.

8. Many *run in the arena* of ascetic practice but *only one receives the prize* [1 Cor. 9:24]: he who desires to come by means of contemplation to practice's limit.

9. In prayer the practising ascetic drinks the draught of compunction, but the contemplative gets drunk on the most potent cup [cf. Ps. 22:5]. The former philosophizes in matters according to nature, the latter forgets even himself in praying.

10. One engaged in ascetic struggle cannot endure spiritual contemplation for long; it is as if he has briefly sneaked out of his home to be entertained by someone.

11. As people of practical virtue *enter the gates* of God's commands *in* prayer, so contemplatives *enter* the *courts* of virtues *in hymns* [Ps. 99:4]. The former give thanks that they have been freed from their chains; the latter, that they have taken their enemies captive.

12. It is necessary to observe both the power of ascetic struggle and that of contemplation, lest you be borne about like a ship with the wrong rigging: either you risk danger from the violence of the winds, or you suffer loss of wind because of the sails' being too small for the hull.

13. Think of pious thoughts as rowers in the ship of the intellect, whose oars are the soul's vital faculties: irascibility, desire, will and free choice. The practical person stands always in need of these, but not always the contemplative. For at the time of prayer the contemplative says goodbye to everything, and seating himself at the tiller of discernment, he watches throughout

the whole night of contemplation, directing his praises to the One who holds the universe together. And maybe he takes up some kind of love song to chant to his soul as he beholds the swell of the salty sea and roar of the waves, and is full of awe at the divine judgements and ordinances.

14. Someone who has made some progress in ascetic struggle and contemplation does not propel his ship always with the oars, as sailors do, or solely with his spiritual sails. Rather, he uses both to accomplish what he needs for a fair journey, bearing gladly the toils of practice in accordance with the measure of his contemplation, and the principles [*logoi*] of endless contemplation because he is strengthened by practice.

15. The contemplative that possesses a nature running together with his deliberative will makes his journey a breeze, as it were. One engaged in ascetic practice, finding his state constraining his free choice, is submerged beneath a great wave of thoughts and risks coming near to despair under their weight.

16. Land that has not been well worked is not likely to provide the sower with abundant, pure seed; neither will anyone engaged in ascetic practice see the plenteous pure fruit of prayer unless he works carefully and without ostentation.

17. An intellect engaged in the ceaseless paths of prayer is like well-trodden earth: for as such ground will be smooth to gentle feet, so the intellect will be open and receptive to pure prayer.

18. In material matters, the mind has thought as its partner; in immaterial matters, unless the mind rejects thought, it will have it as *a thorn troubling* it [2 Cor. 12:7].

19. In prayer the practising ascetic finds that his knowledge of perceptible things forms *a veil upon his heart* [2 Cor. 3:15], which cannot be removed because of his entanglement in such things. The contemplative alone, because he is unattached, can *with unveiled face* behold in part *the glory of God* [2 Cor. 3:18].

20. Prayer joined to spiritual contemplation born of the Spirit is the *land of promise* [Heb. 11:9], in which knowledge of God's principles [*logoi*] of providence and judgement *flow* like *milk and honey* [Exod. 3:8]. Prayer joined to some natural

contemplation is Egypt, wherein a memory of denser, more earthy, desire is born in those who pray. Prayer which is simple is manna in the desert [cf. Num. 11:7]: because it is one and simple, it seals off from those who lack endurance the good things promised for which they long; for those who persist with such restricted nourishment, it grants them a taste for things greater and lasting.

21. Ascetic struggle with contemplation will be reckoned like a body with *a guiding spirit* [Ps. 50:14]; without contemplation, like flesh with a *wandering spirit* [Eccles. 1:14, etc.].

22. In the rational soul, sense-perception is a forecourt, reasoning a temple, the intellect a high priest. In the forecourt it stands, set about by untimely thoughts; in the temple, set about by timely thoughts; but, free from both of these, the intellect is found worthy to enter into the divine sanctuary.

23. *Lament and mourning and woe* [Ezek. 2:10] will be heard in the house of a soul engaged in ascetic struggle, because of its toil. But a *voice of rejoicing and praise* will echo from the house of the contemplative soul, because of its knowledge.

24. One engaged in ascetic struggle *longs to die* because of toils *and* come to *be with Christ* [Phil. 1:23]. But the contemplative is pleased, *rather, to remain in the flesh because of* his joy [Phil. 1:24], which he gets from prayer, and because of the benefit that this brings to his neighbour.

25. Among those who are more intelligent [λογικώτεροι] contemplation goes before ascetic practice; in those more rustic, ascetic practice precedes contemplation. Both come to the same good end, but it is seen to be quicker in those where contemplation precedes ascetic practice.

26. Contemplation of things intelligible [νοητά] is Paradise. The gnostic enters this in prayer as though it were his own house. One engaged in ascetic practice is like a passer-by who wants to peep in, but cannot because the garden wall has been set higher than his spiritual stature.

27. Bodily passions are like beasts, while passions of the soul are like birds. One engaged in ascetic practice walls off the former from his rational [*logikos*] vineyard, but cannot keep out the birds unless he comes to spiritual contemplation born

of the Spirit, with however much zeal he strives to guard himself inwardly.

28. One engaged in ascetic struggle cannot go beyond that moral decency, unless, following the example of the patriarch Abraham, he also goes outside the natural law, as Abraham left his native land, and beyond the stage appropriate to his time of life, as Abraham left his kinsfolk. Thus, he will receive as a seal the abandonment of pleasure in general, which has wrapped us about like a veil since birth and prevents us from receiving complete freedom.

29. A foal in spring cannot bear to remain in its manger and eat what lies there. Neither can a newly initiated intellect stand the strict food of prayer for very long. Rather, like that foal, it would much rather run around in the meadows of natural contemplation, which it finds through psalmody and spiritual reading.

30. Practical virtue has its *loins* – the soul's vital faculties – *girt* [Eph. 6:14] with fasting and vigil. Contemplative virtue keeps its intellectual powers – prayer and silence – burning like lamps. The former has reason [λογισμός] as a tutor; the latter has the indwelling Word [*Logos*] as a bridal escort.

31. An uninitiated mind is not permitted to enter the fruitful vineyard of prayer. It can only – and barely – hear the faint echoes of the psalms, like a poor man gleaning unwanted grapes.

32. Not all who come into a king's company can breakfast with him; nor will all who find success in prayer be seen in prayerful contemplation.

33. Timely silence becomes a bridle for anger, as does moderation in food for irrational desire, and the single-phrased [Jesus] Prayer for unruly thoughts.

34. The one who dives into the depths below for a material pearl will fail in his endeavour, unless he strips naked; so the one who dives into gnostic depths for the pearl of wisdom will fail, unless he divests himself of attachment to the world of the senses.

35. An intellect that encloses itself within the mind in prayer will find himself like a groom conversing with his bride in the bridal chamber. An intellect, not permitted to enter in, stands outside and cries out with groans, '*Who will lead me to a*

fortified city? Who will guide me until I no longer gaze upon vanity and raving falsehood in prayer [Ps. 59:11]?'

36. As unsalted food is tasteless to the throat, so is prayer entering without compunction to the intellect.

37. A soul still in pursuit of prayer is somewhat like a woman in travail. A soul that has attained it is like a woman who has given birth and is now full of joy at the birth of her child [cf. John 16:21].

38. Of old the Amorite dwelling on the mountain slew any he came upon who were trying to force their way through [cf. Deut. 1:44]. Nowadays a wicked forgetfulness pursues those who strive to ascend to the more lofty prayer of simplicity before attaining purity.

39. The demons are naturally very hostile to pure prayer, and the multitude of psalms does not astound them (as armies in the world frighten their enemies), but the harmony of three does: of the intellect with reason [*logos*], and reason with sense-perception.

40. Prayer on its own will seem sustaining like bread to those who pray. Prayer with some contemplation will seem nourishing like oil. Prayer without forms will seem like sweetly fragrant wine; those who drink their fill of this will enter into ecstasy.

41. A *wild ass* is said *to jeer at the city crowd* and the *unicorn* to be bound by none [Job 39:5, 7, 9]. An intellect that has surmounted thoughts of nature and of those contrary to nature alike jeers at the vanity of thoughts, and in prayer cannot be mastered by anything sensory.

42. Shaking a stick at dogs provokes them against oneself; forcing oneself to pray purely provokes the demons.

43. It is necessary for the spiritual contestant to constrain his sense-perception by frugal nourishment, and his intellect to the single-phrased [Jesus] Prayer. Having thus become detached from the passions, he will find himself caught up to the Lord while praying.

44. Those who pray while taking pleasure in the passions, because they are materially minded, are distracted in prayer by their thoughts as by the croaking of frogs. Those with moderated passion are delighted in prayer by manifold

contemplations, like nightingales hopping from branch to branch. But silence becomes the dispassionate, silence and a profound quietude from thoughts and intellectual images during prayer.

45. Of old, Maria, [the sister] of Moses, seeing the downfall of the enemies, took up the tambourine and led out the women to sing songs of victory [Exod. 15:20–21]. Now at this time, in praise of the soul that has conquered the passions, love, the greatest among the virtues, is roused to take up the cithara and embark on a song, like some contemplation, hard won long ago as an adornment to its beauty, and does not cease to praise God, rejoicing with those who surround it.

46. When in continuous prayer the words of the psalms are brought into the possession of the praying heart, then this heart, like good soil, as it were, begins on its own to bring forth various flowers: such as roses, the contemplation of the bodiless beings; lilies, the radiance of bodily realities; and violets, the manifold divine judgements, hard to understand.

47. A flame bears light, so long as it is bound to matter. A soul is God-bearing, so long as it is freed from matter. The flame rises up naturally so long as it has fuel; the soul will rise up until its consummation in divine love.

48. A soul that has perfectly denied itself and been wholly exalted to prayer does not come down when it wishes, now that it is found above creation, but only when it seems to be right to the One who orders all our affairs by weight and measure.

49. When listlessness has been driven from the soul and wickedness has been shaken out of the mind, then the intellect becomes naked in simplicity and an artless life. Then, free of every veil of shame, it sings to God *a new song* [Ps. 95:1]. Striking up a melody, it gives thanks in its delight by celebrating the dedication feast of its life that is to come.

50. When the soul in prayer begins to be roused to more divine activities, then, like the bride in the Song, it calls to its spiritual companions such things as these: *My beloved thrust his hand from the opening, and my stomach fluttered for him* [Song 5:4].

51. A soldier returned from war puts off the weight of his armour, and one engaged in ascetic struggle divests himself of thoughts when he comes to contemplation. For a soldier has no need of weapons unless he is in combat, and the contemplative has no need of thoughts, unless he turns back to sensory things.

52. Those engaged in ascetic practice see bodies in terms of convention, while contemplatives see them in terms of nature – but only gnostics behold the inner principles [*logoi*] of both.

53. Bodiless beings are known in the inner principles [*logoi*] of bodies, while in bodiless beings the Word [*Logos*] beyond being is known, to which every earnest soul hastens to return.

54. The inner principles [*logoi*] of bodiless beings are like bones hidden within perceptible things, which no one sees who has not got beyond attachment to perceptible things.

55. A soldier who has left war behind gets rid of his weaponry and a contemplative gets rid of thoughts as he returns to the Lord.

56. The general who fails to win spoils in war will find himself disheartened; so too one engaged in ascetic practice who fails to attain spiritual contemplation in prayer.

57. A deer bitten by a beast runs to springs of corporeal water; a soul wounded by the supremely sweet dart of prayer to rays of incorporeal light.

58. Our bodily eye cannot perceive the grain in wheat unless it is stripped of its husk, while an intellect engaged in ascetic practice cannot see its own nature unless it is stripped of the entanglements that wrap around it.

59. The stars are hidden at sunrise, and thoughts cease when the intellect turns back to its own kingdom.

60. When ascetic struggle has achieved its goal, the spiritual contemplations which pour over the intellect seem to come from outside, somewhat like the rays of the sun appearing over the horizon, even though they are really its own and embrace it because of its purity.

61. If, on coming down from Heaven above and giving its attention to those things constrained by nature, the contemplative intellect could speak out, it would say such things as: What is more astounding than divine beauty? What could be more graceful than the idea of God's grandeur? What kind of yearning

is so sharp and unbearable as that born from God in a soul purified of every vice, and able to say from its own experience: *I am
wounded with love* [Song 2:5]?

62. *My heart grew warm within me and a fire was kindled
during my meditation* [Ps. 38:4]: thus may one speak who has
not *grown weary of striving after* God in prayer and who has
not desired to see *another's comeuppance* [Jer. 17:16].

63. Let a soul engaged in ascetic struggle, which, after its
rejection of evils, is violently forced by thoughts inspired by
wicked demons to look upon vanity and raving falsehood, say
like the woman in the Song: *I threw off my cloak, how shall I
put it on again? I washed my feet, how shall I soil them?* [Song
5:3].

64. It belongs to a soul that loves God and is confident before
him to say, *Tell me, Good Shepherd* [John 10:11], *where you
pasture* your sheep, *where you rest* your lambs *at midday*, so
that, having followed them, *I may not be encompassed about
among the flocks of your companions* [Song 1:7].

65. The soul engaged in ascetic practice, seeking to master
the principle of prayer, but unable, cries out, like the woman in
the Song, such things as these: *Upon my bed at night I sought
him whom I love. I sought and found him not. I called him
and he heard me not. I will rise* through more intense prayer
*and walking around the city, I will seek my beloved in the
lanes and markets* [Song 3:1–2] – perhaps he, who pervades
everything and is outside all, will disclose himself to me and *I
will be satisfied in seeing his glory* [Ps. 17:16].

66. When the soul begins to be full of tears, because of the
joy that surrounds it in prayer, then it finds the confidence to
cry out, as a bride to her groom: '*Let my beloved come down
to his garden and let him eat* the hard-won consolation of *my*
weeping, like *ripe fruit*' [Song 4:16].

67. When a soul engaged in ascetic practice begins to marvel
at the Creator from the grandeur and beauty of his creatures
and to delight in the pleasure that comes from these, then it
cries out in amazement: 'How beautiful have you become,
my bridegroom, Paradise of your Father? You are a *flower of
the field* and his cedar *like the cedars of Lebanon* [Ps. 103:16

LXX, etc.]. *I have desired to sit down in his shade* [Song 2:1, 3], and *his fruit tasted sweet in my mouth*' [Song 5:3].

68. If someone who entertains kings in his home is resplendent, admired on all sides and full of all joy – how much more so will the soul be that receives the *King of kings* [Rev. 19:16, etc.] in a state of purity, according to the promise of him who does not lie. Still, such a soul ought to confirm itself in utmost piety, casting out everything opposed to God's presence, and welcoming in everything that is pleasing to him.

69. Will someone who expects to be called before a king the next day be found concerned with anything else than meditating on words to please the king? A soul that preserves this concern will not be found unprepared before yonder judgement seat.

70. Blessed is the soul that, daily expecting its Lord's return, makes nothing of all its labours by day or by night, because suddenly he will appear at dawn.

71. God sees all, but only those who see nothing else in prayer will see God. As many as see God are heard by him, and as many as are not heard by God do not see him. Blessed is the one who believes that he is seen by God: *his foot* will not *stumble* unless it pleases God [cf. Ps. 72:2].

72. The good things of the *Kingdom* that are *within us* [Luke 17:21] – which things an *eye* fond of outward appearance *has not seen* and hearing fond of honour *has not heard*, nor *has it entered into a heart* empty of the Holy Spirit [cf. 1 Cor. 2:9] – are pledges of the good things to be given by God to the righteous in his Kingdom that is to come. And one who may not eat of them, because they are the *fruits of the Spirit* [Gal. 5:22], cannot come to enjoy them.

73. The thoughts of people engaged in ascetic practice are like deer. For deer are sometimes found high on mountains for fear of hunters, and sometimes beneath in the valleys because they long for the [waters] in them. It is like this with thoughts: they cannot always be in spiritual contemplation, because they are not ready for it; nor can they be in natural contemplation, because they are not always in pursuit of rest. Thoughts of contemplatives, on the other hand, are disdainful of lower forms of contemplation.

74. Droplets of dew moisten furrows in soil. Tearful groans welling up from the heart soften the soul's dispositions in prayer.

75. No one will be found contemplating divinity understood in the Triad who has not transcended the material dyad and its neighbour, the [material] monad. Nor will anyone become loftier than this [the monad], unless he makes his intellect monadic with its intellections.

76. It will be found less hard to drive back a river's course from flowing downstream than for one praying to restrain his intellect's flow from being scattered among visible things and instead to be gathered to things on high, with which it has kinship, when he wishes – even though the intellect naturally belongs on high, whereas to check the flow of a river is unnatural.

77. Those who purify the intellect, casting off visible things within, are filled with such amazement and joy that they cannot give way to any other earthly thing, not even if all things we prize most highly were to flow together to them.

78. Merely mentioning the laws of nature suffices to cause us exceeding wonder. When understood well, they are found to be meadows in bloom, bursting into pure flowers with unfailing spiritual sweetness, like nectar from heaven.

79. Bees swarm around the queen bee of the hive among the dewy meadow flowers. The soul that is unceasingly in a state of compunction is surrounded by the intellectual [noerai] powers that assist it, for they are kindred with it.

80. In the visible world, the human appears as another world; in the intelligible world, the same is true of thought [logismos]. For the human is the herald of heaven, earth and all that lies between them, while thought is the interpreter of the intellect, sense-perception and all that concerns them. Without these – the human and thought – both worlds would be rendered deaf and dumb.

81. A captive freed after long servitude does not walk with such joy as a mind freed from entanglement journeys with delighted step towards the heavenly realm as to its own home.

82. To one who prays inattentively – scattered in thought – the psalm will be reckoned outlandish, and to the psalm he

himself will seem likewise outlandish. And to the demons, both seem raving mad.

83. Those to whom *the world has been crucified* are not the same as those *crucified to the world* [cf. Gal. 6:14]. For the former, the nails are fasting and vigil; for the latter, poverty and counting oneself as naught. Of course, without the latter, the labours of the former are of no value.

84. No one can pray purely who is ruled by passionate fondness of outward appearance and fondness for honour. For entanglements and thoughts of vanity are at home with these passions, and so they become like plaited cords binding the one who seeks to pray. They drag the intellect down, like a sparrow caught in a net, as it tries to rise in the time of prayer.

85. It is impossible for an intellect to become peaceful during prayer that does not possess, as a firm friend, self-control and love. For, with God's help, self-control struggles to remove the body's hostility towards the soul, as love does with hostility towards one's neighbour. Thereafter, the *peace that passes all understanding* [Phil. 4:7] descends and promises to make its dwelling in the one who has established himself in peace through these means.

86. It is necessary for one who strives *to enter the Kingdom of God* [Matt. 19:24] to abound in good things, which is his work of righteousness: in almsgiving, by supplying from his own lack; and in toils in behalf of peace, by meeting trials with long suffering in the Lord.

87. Neither the person lacking in virtue because of his carelessness, nor the one who thinks to abound in it because of self-conceit, will be found to enter the harbour of dispassion. For none has come into enjoyment of good things, save through justice, which is a mean between lack and excess in these things.

88. Land, if it yields only what is sown or even a little more, cannot make a farmer rich, only if it multiplies the seed many times over. Neither can his achievements make one engaged in ascetic struggle righteous, unless his zeal for God is found to be greater than what lies within his power.

89. Not all those who do not love their neighbour can bring

themselves to hate him, nor those who do not hate him love him. And it is one thing to begrudge your neighbour his progress, but quite another to refrain from getting in the way of his progress. But the lowest depth of wickedness is not just to snarl at your neighbour's success, but, rather, to dispute his good deeds, and claim that such things never happened.

90. Passions of the body are one thing, passions of the soul another. Those of the body are natural, those of the soul contrary to nature. One who has driven away the former, but taken no care for the latter, is like someone who sets up a high, thick fence against wild animals, but he still takes delight in the birds eating the truly splendid grapes of his rational vineyard.

91. First the soul imagines something evil, then desires it, then feels either pleasure or pain, and so comes to experience it, and finally unites with it, either visibly or invisibly. At every stage there are accompanying thoughts, save for the first movement – if it is not accepted, all the evil that accompanies it will be neutralized.

92. Those who are near to dispassion stumble in imaginings alone. Those who have moderated their passions stumble in desires. Those who abuse their necessary functions but feel grief come to perceive evil; those who do so without grief unite themselves to evil.

93. Pleasure resides in all the bodily members, but does not appear to trouble them all in the same way. With some people it troubles the desiring part of the soul through gluttony; with others the irascible part through a quick temper; and others again the rational part through wickedness, the cause of all the unholy passions.

94. It is necessary for the senses to open like the gates of a city. However, in opening up for essential matters, it is necessary not to allow foreigners desirous of war to enter and become established as a cause of strife.

95. Pleasure is the mother of desire; quick temper the mother of anger; wickedness, mother of bearing grudges. One who does not struggle against the rulers will find no peace with their followers. Neither can anyone enter the harbour of moderation in passion who needs to force himself to follow the commandments.

96. Those who ward off provocations do not allow thoughts [*logismoi*] to enter their rational [*logikos*] *vineyard* like wild beasts and wreak havoc among its *vines* [cf. Ps. 79:9–16]. Those who couple with them, but do not take pleasure in it, allow thoughts merely to enter and not to touch anything. Those who happily commune with the passions through thoughts, but do not consent, are like those who permit the solitary wild boar to enter the fenced field, but do not let it eat its fill of the clusters of grapes in the vineyard. Then, however, they find it stronger than they are, and so find themselves consenting often enough to passions.

97. Someone who still needs to guard carefully his self-control has not yet attained simplicity. For it is said, 'The one who is perfect no longer practises self-control', but only the one still engaged in ascetic struggle.[4] For such a one is like someone who has a vineyard or a field, not amid many others, but off in some corner. For that reason it needs a lot of guarding and watching. But for one who has achieved simplicity, no one dares to touch his vineyard, for it is as if it belonged to a king or an influential courtier, even the mention of whom inspires fear, making thieves and passers-by alike tremble at the thought of trespassing.

98. Many ascend the cross of painful suffering, but few accept its nails. For many subject themselves to voluntary trials and tribulations, but only those who have perfectly died to the world and the rest it offers subject themselves to what comes to them against their will.

99. Many will put off all the *garments of skin* [Gen. 3:21], save the last – that of vainglory – which is only cast off by those who have come to loathe its mother, that is, self-indulgence.

100. One who refuses *praise from people* [Rom. 2:29] and accepts no bodily relaxation: such a one has been stripped naked of the last *garment* of vainglory and thereupon becomes worthy *to be clothed* with the radiance of the *dwelling place from heaven*, sought after with so many *groans* [2 Cor. 5:2].

101. Activity is one thing, the act achieved another. The act of sin accomplished is demonstrable, but the activity of indulgence in pleasure is only roused internally, not outwardly. The

self-indulgent are like people who have not left their own land, but must nevertheless pay tribute in goods that will satisfy their foreign masters.

102. When our sense of taste rules in pleasures, the other senses cannot help but follow, even if in colder bodies the genitals seem to be at peace, as with the elderly, which seem insensitive to the burning of lust, because so withered. Yet the barren adulteress will not be vindicated as temperate because she has not given birth. We might say that perfect chastity really consists in being neither passionately roused within, nor charmed by what is seen.

103. The desiring aspect of the soul is revealed for what it is by foods, bodily shapes, and voices, whether enchanting or otherwise; by knowledge, sight and hearing – whether it is found using these, abusing them or something in between.

104. In those matters where fear does not guide, our thoughts will be found in confusion, like *sheep without a shepherd* [Mark 6:34]. Thoughts will be disciplined and in good order within the sheepfold, when fear accompanies them or takes a lead.

105. Fear is the son of faith and the herdsman of God's commandments. But one who does not possess its mother – faith – will not be found worthy to be a sheep in the Lord's pasture.

106. With good things, some possess only the rudiments, others possess them in part, and yet others in their entirety. Of those who lack them in their entirety, the first will be found to be like a simple soldier, the second like one of higher rank but without any money: the soldier can guard only his own dwelling from those who seek to seize it, while the other is not given the honour due to his rank by those he meets.

107. Those who encourage us to indulge in the pleasures of the palate, when we are imperfect, are like those who encourage us to reopen a wound already healed, to scratch itches because of the pleasure it gives, to eat foods that cause fever, or to fence off our [spiritual] vineyard and then allow the *mind of the flesh* [Rom. 8:6] to enter, like some *wild boar* [Ps. 79:14], and to devour our good thoughts like so many grapes. It is imperative not to trust them, nor heed the untimely flattery of humans or

passions. Rather, fortify its fence through self-control until the fleshly passions, like beasts, cease their howling; and until vain thoughts no longer descend to damage the vineyard of your soul, flourishing with contemplations in Christ Jesus our Lord, to whom be glory unto the ages. Amen.

Nikiphoros the Monk,
On Watchfulness and the Guarding of the Heart

NIKIPHOROS THE MONK (13TH C.)

St Gregory Palamas describes Nikiphoros in his *Triads* as a convert of sorts. Originally from Italy, Gregory says, he renounced both homeland and the Roman Church, and joined the Byzantine, settling on Mt Athos. St Gregory affirms that, even there, Nikiphoros sought out secluded places and stillness where he could pray and be attentive. However, ecclesiastical politics found him even there. Nikiphoros himself writes that the emperor Michael VIII Palaiologos sent delegates to Athos to demand the monks' agreement to union with the Roman Church following the Council of Lyons in 1274. Michael had reconquered Constantinople from the Franks in 1261, and union of the Roman and Byzantine Churches was intended to cement the restoration of the Byzantine Empire. The Athonite monks did not agree. Nikiphoros recounts a debate, held in the context of imperial remonstrations on Athos, between a 'Christian' and a 'Latin', in which the latter's positions are systematically reduced and the Orthodox (Byzantine) dogma vindicated. He says that, after this, he and other recalcitrant monks were exiled to Cyprus, in December 1276. We do not know when he died, but probably before 1300.

On Watchfulness and the Guarding of the Heart sees Nikiphoros developing another imagined debate, between a hesychast monk and 'a new Nikodemos' who does not understand the method of interior prayer. Nikiphoros develops his argument through a *florilegium*, an anthology of extracts from authoritative figures, some of whom would also be included in the *Philokalia*. He concludes with an original discussion of interior prayer, techniques of breathing, and the need for spiritual direction. Nikiphoros aims at two goals simultaneously: explaining the method or 'science' of interior prayer, and proving its validity in the context of ascetic and theological tradition.

The result may be thought of as a microcosmic *Philokalia*. Readers will have to excuse the more numerous notes in this text, which serve primarily to reference and contextualize the various works that Nikiphoros quotes, some of which are included whole cloth in the *Philokalia*.

Sources

Text: *PHILOKALIA* (1782): 869–76; *Philokalia* (1893/1982): vol. 4, 18–30

On Watchfulness and the Guarding of the Heart

As many of you as are smitten with desire for the majestic and divine illumination of our Saviour Jesus Christ – As many of you as wish to receive and feel the fire from beyond the heavens in your heart – As many of you as are striving for reconciliation with God in feeling and experience – As many of you as have abandoned everything in this world to find and obtain the *treasure hidden in the field* of your hearts [Matt. 13:44] – As many of you as wish to have your soul's lamp lit with bright flame from now on, and so have given up everything here – As many of you as wish to know and receive, by spiritual experience, the Kingdom of Heaven within you [Luke 17:21] – Come! And I will expound for you knowledge of this eternal, or, rather, heavenly life, or, rather, a method which leads you without pain or sweat *to the harbour of dispassion,*[1] without the fear of any being deceived or terrified by the demons. Such terror when we stray in disobedience somewhere far outside the life I will show you, just like Adam, who disregarded God's commandment and attended instead to the serpent and trusting him. Filled to repletion with the fruit of deceit, Adam pitiably cast himself and all who came after down to the nadir of death, darkness and decay. Therefore, return to yourselves! It would be truer to say, let us be restored to ourselves, brethren, abhorring the serpent's counsel together with every distraction that would have us crawling in the dirt. For we can hardly attain reconciliation and fellowship with God unless, so far as is up to us, we are first reconciled with ourselves, or, rather, enter into ourselves. It is a wonder that cutting ourselves off from the world's distraction and vain cares actually allows us to grasp the *Kingdom of Heaven* that *is within us* [Luke 17:21]. This is why the monastic way of life is called *art of arts and science of sciences*,[2] since this holy life does not procure for us corruptible things that divert our intellect from what is better and choke it. Instead, strange and unutterable good things are announced to us, *Which neither eye has seen nor ear heard, neither have entered into human hearts* [1 Cor. 2:9], for here below *our struggle is not with flesh and blood, but with the powers, the authorities, the world-rulers of the darkness of this age* [Eph. 6:12]. If, then, the present age is darkness, let us flee from it! Let us flee in our thoughts that there may be nothing in common between us and God's enemy. For to be a friend of this present age is to *become God's enemy* [James 4:4], and who could possibly help someone who has become God's enemy?

Therefore, we are to imitate our fathers and seek the treasure in our hearts as they did, and having found it let us hold it with all our might, at once cultivating it and guarding it. For we have been commanded from the beginning to do this. Perhaps some other Nikodemos has been spotted arguing about these matters and saying, 'How can someone enter into his own heart work or reside there?' In the same way Nikodemos once contradicted the Saviour, saying, '*How can someone enter a second time into his mother's womb and be born, when he is old?*' [John 3:4]. Our new Nikodemos will get the same answer: that *The Spirit blows where it will* [John 3:8]. And if we are so faithless and doubtful about the tasks of ascetic struggle, how will those of contemplation ever come to us? For practical virtue is the entrance to contemplation. Now, since doubters need written demonstrations to be fully convinced – come, bring us the lives and writings of the saints! Let us include them in this treatise for the benefit of many, so that our doubter may be convinced by them and have his doubt dispelled.

Beginning from our own great father, let us set out these words and deeds, which we have excerpted and gathered from the works of our fathers, presenting them as much as possible in their proper order, to confirm what I have been saying.

From the *Life of our Holy Father Antony*:[3]

Once two brothers came to Abba Antony. Their water had failed while they travelled. One died and the other was dying. Having no more strength to journey on, he lay down on the ground, expecting to die. Antony, being seated on his mountain, called two monks who happened to be there and dispatched them, saying, 'Take a jar of water and run along the road to Egypt. For two brothers were coming. One has just died, and the other soon will unless you hurry! This was revealed to me while I prayed.' The monks went straightway, found the dead brother and buried him. They revived the other with water and took him to the old man. The distance was a day's journey. If someone asks why Antony did not speak before the first man died, he is asking the wrong question. For the judgement of death did not belong to Antony, but to God, who passed judgement concerning the one and revealed the situation of the other. The miracle that belonged to Antony and no other was that he kept his heart watchful on the mountain, as the Lord revealed to him things happening far off. Do you see that Antony became a seer of both God and the future because he was watchful in his heart? For God is revealed to our intellect in our heart, at first, as says John of the Ladder, purifying his lover, and then as light illumining the mind and making it radiant.[4] Now let our discussion go through the rest in order.

From the *Life of St Theodosios, Head of the Coenobium*:[5]

The divine Theodosios *had been so struck with the sweet dart of love and so bound with its chains that in his actions was fulfilled the exalted and divine precept, 'You shall love the Lord your God with your whole heart, your whole soul and your whole mind'* [Matt. 22:37, Deut. 6:5]. *But this could only happen if his soul's natural capacities focused the very activities of his soul, not for anything in this world, only in desire for their Maker, so much that when offering comfort he terrified many and when rebuking he was lovable and sweet in everything. Who is so exceedingly profitable in talking with the crowds, so incredibly capable of gathering his senses and turning them inward that he could persist in total calm, whether*

*with people in the bustling world or those in the desert? How
did he remain the same whether among the crowds or by himself?* Behold, this great Theodosios who, because he gathered
his senses and led them inward, was *wounded with love* [Song
2:5] of his Creator.

From the *Life of St Arsenios*:[6]

*This was the rule kept by the marvellous Arsenios: neither
to propose scriptural inquiries nor even to give written orders.
Not because he was incapable, for how could that be? For
who finds speaking well as easy as speaking simply to others?
Rather, the reason was that he was habituated to silence and
averse to demonstration. This is why, even though he was very
diligent in attending liturgy, he neither saw others nor was seen
by them, but instead would stand behind a pillar or other ob-
struction and conceal himself entirely from the company of
others. He did this because he desired to attend to himself and
to gather his intellect within himself, and so be more easily
raised to God.* So here again – *this divine man, this earthly
angel*,[7] gathers his mind within so that here and now he may be
easily drawn to God.

From the *Life of St Paul in Latros*:[8]

The divine Paul passed his whole life among mountains and
deserts [Heb. 11:38], *having wild beasts as his neighbours and
table companions. Once, however, when he came down to the
Lavra, he sat in charge of the brothers there. He encouraged
and taught them to be neither faint-hearted nor careless in the
toilsome work of virtue, but to cling attentively and discern-
ingly to the Gospel life, and bravely to resist the wicked spirits.
Furthermore, he introduced them to a method by which they
could unlearn their impassioned predispositions and so avoid
even the seeds of passion.*

My goodness! How does this divine Father teach his innocent pupils a method of averting the onslaughts of passion? It
is none other than the guarding of our mind. For to this and
only this does a successful outcome belong. Now, let the argument proceed.

From the Life of St Sabbas[9]

When the divine Sabbas saw that someone had *renounced all*, had *closely learned the rule of* monastic conduct, and could already *guard his intellect* to *fight off hostile thoughts* – and, moreover, banished entirely *the memory of worldly things* from his mind – then Sabbas *would grant* him a cell *in the Lavra*, should he have a weak and sick body. *Should* he *instead be* healthy and *capable, Sabbas turned him to* building a cell.

Do you see how Sabbas, that oracle of God, enjoined the guarding of the mind on his disciples, and only then grants them a cell and allows them to sit in it? What will we do who sit idly in cells and do not even know whether there be such a thing as guarding of the mind?

From the *Life of Abba Agathon*:[10]

A brother asked *Abba Agathon*, saying, 'Tell me, Abba, *what is greater, bodily toil or interior guard?*' And Agathon said, '*A human being is like a tree. Bodily labour comprises the leaves, but inward guards the fruit. As it is written, "Every tree not bearing good fruit is uprooted and cast into the fire"* [Matt. 7:19]. *This shows that all our diligence is for the sake of fruit, that is, the guarding of our intellect. But the leaves are needed for shelter and adornment, which things bodily labour offers.*'

It is marvellous how this holy man denounced those who lack the guarding of the intellect, telling those who boast in practical virtue alone that *every tree not bearing fruit* – clearly the guarding of the mind – but possessing leaves only – that is, practical virtue – *is uprooted and cast into fire*! Your verdict, Father, is terrifying.

From Abba Mark's *Letter to Nicholas*:[11]

So, you wish, my child, to procure your very own lamp, to shine the intelligible light of spiritual knowledge within you, so that you can walk without stumbling in the deepest night of this age [cf. John 11:9]? *You wish for your steps to be prospered by the Lord and you greatly desire the way of his Gospel* [cf. Ps. 36:23], *in accordance with the prophetic saying – that is, you desire to be compassed about with fiery faith in the more*

*perfect evangelical commandments, and to become a commu-
nicant of the Lord's sufferings through desire and prayer? If
you desire all this, well then, I will show you a marvellous
method and design, which requires a spiritual way of life – not
requiring bodily toil or struggle, but discovering instead labour
of soul and mind, and attentive thoughts. It works together
with fear and love of God. Through this plan you can easily
turn aside the whole enemy phalanx. If you wish to claim victory against the passions then, having retreated into yourself
through prayer and working together with God, and having
plunged into the depths of your heart, hunt down these three
strong giants: I mean forgetfulness, indifference and ignorance,
the mainstays of the intelligible foreigners, through which the
rest of the passions sneak in, operate, live and grow strong in
the souls of lovers of pleasure. Then, through much attentiveness and mental control, together with a helping push from
above, you will have discovered evils unknown to many and
you can finally be delivered from the three mighty giants. The
tracks of forgetfulness, ignorance and indifference fade entirely
in the soul, and are wiped out of existence by the concord of
true knowledge, memory of God's word and good desire, operating through grace in the soul, which works diligently to unite
them, and zealously guards them.*

Do you see the harmony of these spiritual words? Do you see
how clearly they reveal the knowledge of attentiveness? Look,
then, at our next selection and how it reasons with us.

From St John Klimakos:[12]

*A solitary is one who struggles to enclose the bodiless in its
bodily dwelling – a paradox. A hesychast is that man who said,
'I sleep, but my heart keeps vigil' [Songs 5:2]. Shut the door
of your cell to the body, the door of your tongue to speech,
and your inward gate to spirits. Being seated on the heights,
keep guard over your vineyard if you know how, and you will
see how, when, whence, how many, and what sort of thieves
have come to enter and steal your grapes. When the watcher
grows weary, he rises and prays. When he sits back down he
clings to his activity more courageously. Guarding of thoughts*

is one thing, protection of the intellect another, and the latter is as far from the former as east is from west [Ps. 102:12], *and as much more wearisome. Just as thieves, seeing royal weapons lying somewhere, do not ordinarily approach that place, so also the monk who has united prayer to his heart is not generally robbed by spiritual thieves.*

Do you see the clarity of this great father's marvellous practice? But we, as though *wandering in darkness* [Ps. 81:5] and trampling on life-saving sayings of the Spirit as in some night battle, shut our ears to it and pass it by. Well, look instead to what lies before us, which our Fathers have written to lead us to watchfulness.

From Abba Isaiah:[13]

When someone separates himself from the [thief on the] *left-hand side* [Luke 23:39–42] *he will know precisely all the sins which he has committed against God – since one cannot see one's sins unless one has first been removed from them by a bitter separation. Those who have gained this measure have discovered weeping, supplication and a feeling of shame before God as they remember their wicked affection for the passions. Let us strive, therefore, brethren, as much as we can, and God will work with us according to the multitude of his mercy* [Ps. 105:45]. *If we have not guarded our heart as our fathers did, yet have been as diligent as we could be to keep our bodies sinless, as God requires, we believe that in the time of famine which has overtaken us, he will offer us mercy as he does with his Saints.*

This great man here offers consolation to the particularly infirm, when he says, *If we have not guarded our heart as our fathers did,* yet have been as diligent *as we could be to keep our bodies sinless, as God requires, he will offer us mercy.* Great indeed is the compassion and concession of such a father!

From Makarios the Great:[14]

The most important attribute of a spiritual athlete is that, having entered into his heart, he makes war on Satan and hates him utterly. Having wrestled with Satan's thoughts, let him do battle with him. If someone guards his visible body against corruption and fornication, but inwardly cheats on God and fornicates in thought, his virginal body offers no benefit. For it is written, *Everyone who looks on a woman to desire her has already committed adultery in his heart* [Matt. 5:28]. *For there is fornication accomplished through the body and a fornication of a soul that cavorts with Satan.*

This great father seems to contradict the afore-quoted father, Abba Isaiah. Not so! For Makarios surely recommends *'for us to preserve our bodies as God requires'*, but, since God seeks purity not just in body but also in spirit, Makarios also urges exactly what is found in the Gospel commandments.

From Diadochos:[15]

Whoever dwells always in his own heart lives far from the pleasures of life, for, walking by the Spirit, he cannot see the desires of the flesh [cf. Gal. 5:24-5]. *Such a one walks within the citadel of the virtues and himself possesses the virtues as gatekeepers. Therefore, indeed, the machinations of the demons are, in the end, impotent against him.*

The Saint says rightly that *the machinations of the* enemies remain *impotent against him* when, clearly, we pass our time somehow in the depth of our heart, and all the more as we linger there. But I know that *time will fail me* [Heb. 11:32] as I wish to include the writings of all our fathers in this exposition. Therefore, I will recall one or two more and then bring my argument to a close.

From Isaak the Syrian:[16]

Be sure to enter into your inner chamber [Matt. 6:6] *and you will see the heavenly chamber. For they are one and the same, and in a single entrance you will contemplate both. The ladder to that heavenly kingdom is hidden in you, in your soul, that is. Wash yourself, therefore, from sin, and you will find ascents by which you can ascend.*

From the Karpathian:[17]

We need much struggle and toil in prayer until we find an

undisturbed state, a kind of other heaven in our heart wherein
Christ dwells. As the Apostle says, 'Do you not know that
Christ dwells within you? Unless, of course, you are discred-
ited' [2 Cor. 13:5].

From Symeon the Theologian:[18]

The Devil with his demons, because of whom humanity was
expelled from Paradise and from God through transgression,
found himself the temerity to shake up every human being's
intelligence intellectually, night and day – in some more, some
less, some quite a lot indeed. Our intelligence cannot be fortified except by the ceaseless memory of God. Then, if divine
memory, having been inscribed on our heart by the power
of his cross, it will strengthen and confirm our intelligence.
Everything in our spiritual contest, in which each Christian
strips down in the stadium of faith in Christ to compete, is
directed towards this end. If not, competition is in vain. All
our various ascetic disciplines of suffering for God's sake are
for the sake of such a contest, that through it we may move
the Good One to pity to give us again our ancient dignity, and
that Christ be sealed in our intelligence. So says the Apostle:
My children, with whom I am in travail until Christ be formed
in you [Gal. 4:19].

Learn well, brothers, how swiftly this spiritual art – that is,
method – leads its practitioner to dispassion and the vision of
God. Are you convinced yet that all practical virtue is reckoned
by God as leaves on a tree still without fruit? Are you not yet
assured also that for every soul that lacks watchfulness of mind
practical virtues will turn out merely to be vanity? Let us be
diligent, then, not to devote ourselves to pointless matters and
end our lives as fruitless trees.

Question. We know from the present discourse what the
practice of those most pleasing to the Lord is. Likewise, we do
not doubt that there is a certain activity which swiftly frees the
soul from passions and binds it to the love of God, and that this
activity is necessary for everyone enlisted to Christ's service.
Far from doubting, we are thoroughly convinced! We would
really like to learn what attentiveness is and how someone can

be enabled to find it, for we are entirely uninitiated in such a thing.

Answer. In the name of our Lord Jesus, who said, '*Without me you can do nothing*' [John 15:5], whom we invoke as our aid and fellow worker, I will attempt, so far as I can, to elucidate what attentiveness is and how – God willing – it is achieved.

From Nikiphoros Himself:

Some Saints called attentiveness 'watching the intellect', others a 'guard of the heart', 'sobriety', 'intellectual stillness' or other names besides. They all mean the same thing. Think how someone might say 'bread', another 'slice' and another 'biscuit'. Learn carefully what attentiveness is and what its properties are. Attentiveness is the expression of undiluted repentance. It is restoration of soul, hatred of the world and return to God. Attentiveness is rejection of sin and reception of virtue. It is an indubitable assurance of the forgiveness of sins. Attentiveness is the beginning of contemplation, or, rather, the prerequisite of contemplation since through it God, having taken notice of it, shows himself to the intellect. Attentiveness is tranquillity of the intellect, or, rather, stability of the soul, granted to it through God's mercy. Attentiveness is purification of thoughts while memory of God is both shrine and steward of the endurance of what befalls us. Attentiveness is a cause of *faith, hope and love* [1 Cor. 13:13]. For unless someone has faith, how could he accept the external injuries which befall him? And unless he gladly welcomes injuries, he cannot not say to the Lord, *You are my protector and refuge* [2 Kgds 22:3]. And unless he *makes the Most High* his *refuge* [Ps. 90:9], he cannot enter the embrace of God's love. Most, therefore, and probably all, gain this attentiveness, this greatest of all great accomplishments, from instruction. For they are rare indeed who have gained it untaught, by sheer force of activity and fervour of faith – and *an exception is not the rule*.[19]

So you see, we must seek out an unerring guide so that we may learn from their example of attentiveness and imitate them, having been taught the defects of both right and left, which is to say not only defects but also excesses introduced from the evil one. As they make clear from examples of the *things they suffered when tempted* [Heb. 2:18], they unambiguously present this spiritual path, so we can walk it more easily. If there is no guide, we must seek one diligently. If one is not discovered, then, having first invoked God with *a contrite spirit* and tears [Isa. 65:14], entreat him with your poverty. And then, do what I will tell you.

You know that the breath we draw in is air and we exhale it for the heart's sake, for the heart is the source of the body's life and warmth. Therefore, the heart attracts the breath [or, spirit], to expel its own heat out through exhalation and maintain its own good temperament. Another cause, or, rather, servant, of this arrangement is the lungs, which, since they were fashioned by the Creator to expand and contract like a bellows, drawing in air painlessly and expelling the air contained. So too the heart, drawing in coolness through the breath [or, spirit] and dispersing its heat, preserves unfailingly the function for which it was created, namely the maintaining of life.

You, therefore, having sat down and collected your intellect, lead it through the path of your nostrils, whence your breath [or, spirit] enters into your heart. Drive your intellect down and force it to descend with your indrawn breath [or, spirit] into your heart. Once it has entered into your heart, it will no longer be unhappy and things thereafter will not be joyless. Rather, when someone who has journeyed far off returns home, there is nothing that can remove him from his joy, because he has been allowed to see his wife and children again. Just so, when the intellect has been united with the soul it enjoys unutterable pleasure and delight. Therefore, brother, instruct your intellect not to depart quickly from your heart. At first, the intellect is frequently neglectful because of the confinement and narrowness of being within your heart, but when it becomes accustomed to this, it ceases to be infatuated with outside distractions. For *the Kingdom of Heaven is within you* [Luke 17:21] – observing carefully and seeking it out through pure prayer, the intellect comes to regard everything external as abhorrent and hateful. Now, if you enter through your intellect into the place of the heart, as I have described – then, thanks be to God! Glorify him! Leap with joy! Cling always to this activity, and it will teach you things you do not know.

But you must learn this, too: while your mind remains there in your heart, do not keep silent and idle thereafter. Have, rather, as your task and meditation the ceaseless repetition of 'Lord Jesus Christ, Son of God, have mercy on me.' And never ever cease from this prayer. For this prayer, which preserves your intellect without distraction, proves it impregnable and invulnerable to the enemy's attacks, and daily leads it to love and divine yearning.

If, however, you are very sick, my brother, and so cannot enter into the place of your heart as I have commanded you, then do what I now tell you and you will, with God's help, find what you seek. You know that the intelligence lies in the breast. For while our lips keep silence, within our breast we speak, we deliberate, and we offer prayers, psalms and the rest, in good order. As regards the intelligence, then, remove every thought from it (for you can if you want to), and instead replace it with the prayer 'Lord Jesus Christ, Son of God, have mercy on me.' Compel your intellect to utter this inwardly, always, instead of entertaining any notion. Once you have mastered this practice, the entrance to your heart will therefore be opened to you without doubt, just as we have written to you and as we have learned by experience. Then, along with much sought-after and delightful attentiveness, will come to you the whole chorus of virtues – *love, joy, peace* and the rest [Gal. 5:22], through which you will obtain all your requests in Christ Jesus our Lord, to whom with the Father and the Holy Spirit be all glory, power, honour and worship, now and forever and unto the ages of ages.

Amen.

St Gregory of Sinai,
One Hundred and Thirty-Seven
Very Beneficial Chapters

ST GREGORY OF SINAI (*c.*1275–*c.*1346)

St Gregory of Sinai lived in tumultuous times, as the Byzantine Empire was finding its footing after the Frankish occupation of Constantinople (1204–61), but the rapidly eroding frontiers were plagued by incursions of Seljuk Turks, Catalan pirates and others. St Gregory was born near Smyrna on the Anatolian coast (modern-day Turkey) and was captured by Turkish raiders when he was fifteen. He was eventually ransomed and released on Cyprus, from where he made his way to St Catherine's Monastery in Sinai. After training there as a monk and absorbing traditions of prayer and reflection developed there, he made his way to Athos, where he stayed almost two decades before pirate attacks there forced him to flee. He would eventually wind up in Paroria (now south-eastern Bulgaria), dying on 27 November 1346, or maybe 1347.

St Gregory is a hinge in the rise of hesychast spirituality. He absorbed traditions associated with Sinai, from writers like St Hesychios and St Philotheos, both of whom drew deeply on St John Klimakos. But when he came to Athos he would have encountered a flourishing garden of monasteries and monks deeply committed to continuous prayer, the inner life and the panoply of spiritual practices that enable these. In Gregory we can see the aspirations of Athos and the tradition of Sinai together. It is significant, too, that he taught and guided a young St Gregory Palamas, who would become the greatest defender of hesychasm and articulator of its theological underpinnings.

In the *One Hundred and Thirty-Seven Very Beneficial Chapters*,

Gregory writes in the gnomic tradition of Evagrios, St Diado-chos and St Maximos. He covers a range of topics – thoughts, virtues, vices, demonic attack, fasting, etc. – from a variety of angles, but it is worth noting especially how he conceives of stillness (*hesychia*, hence, 'hesychast') as an integral dimension of prayer, and how he sets both within the rhythms of liturgical offices and daily monastic life. Stillness becomes the linchpin of development in interconnected virtues in the human being that Gregory describes as a microcosm of the created world, destined for reunion with God in prayer.

Two notes on language: first, we have included the Greek word *logos* in brackets where Gregory plays with its numerous shades of meaning. Second, we have referred to certain kinds of monastic as 'hesychast' since, by Gregory's day, the term *hêsu-chastês* had come to mean not just a 'hermit' or 'solitary', but someone who engaged in the kinds of prayer and meditation that Gregory discusses at length. See the Glossary for more on both *logos* and *hêsuchia*.

Sources

Text: *PHILOKALIA* (1782): 879–905; *Philokalia* (1893/1982): vol. 4, 31–62

Very Beneficial Chapters Arranged
in an Acrostic

*Of which the acrostic is: Various Chapters about Command-
ments, Teachings, Admonitions and Promises; then concerning
Thoughts, Passions and Virtues; and finally Stillness and Prayer.*

1. No reasonable being can possess or attain its natural state
of mindfulness without purity and incorruption. For a habit of
irrationality introduced by the senses has overlaid purity, while
incorruption is subject to the state of fleshly corruption.

2. It is only those reasonable beings who have become holy
through purity that manifest their natural state of mindfulness. For none of those adept at speaking wisely can attain
pure mindfulness, for they have corrupted the higher exercise
of reason through evil thoughts. Meanwhile, the material and
loquacious spirit of worldly wisdom, while leading towards
ever greater realms of knowledge, lends crudeness to our thinking. The combination of the two – wide-ranging knowledge
with crude conceptuality – falls short of real wisdom and contemplation, as well as of undivided and unified knowledge.

3. Regard the knowledge of truth as properly a feeling of
awareness owing to grace. Everything else should really be
called impressions of thinking and proofs of worldly things.

4. Those who fall from grace suffer this because of their
unbelief and carelessness, while those who find it again do so
through faith and zeal. One advances, because of faith and
zeal, to what lies ahead, while one reverts to what lies behind
because of unbelief and carelessness.

5. Being dead and being insensible are equivalent, like being
blind intellectually and physically blind. For the dead have lost

their capability of life and activity. The one who does not see has been robbed of the divine light that makes them see and be seen.

6. Few receive both strength and wisdom from God. For one partakes of divine goods, while the other reveals them. But to partake and pass on both? That is a truly divine and super-human feat.

7. The heart, free from thoughts and roused to activity by the Spirit, is a true sanctuary even before the life to come. For there, everything will be said and done spiritually. One who has not obtained this state here and now is a stone, fitted by his other virtues for placement in the divine temple, but he is not himself a *temple* and priest *of the Spirit* [1 Cor. 6:19].

8. Humans were fashioned incorruptible – without the bodily humours – and so they will rise. They were neither made immutable nor again mutable, since they have the cap-acity of changing, or not, by a habit of willing. For the faculty of will does not bestow perfect immutability on nature, for that remains a prize of the immutable deification to come.

9. Flesh is generated from corruption. Eating, defecating, proud bearing and sleeping, too, are natural properties of wild and domestic animals. Because of Adam's transgression, we have been made like beasts, and have fallen away from our proper and God-given goods: we have become animal instead of rational, and beasts instead of gods.

10. Paradise is twofold: sensible and intelligible. The sens-ible in Eden [Gen. 2:8], the intelligible from grace. The place of Eden is so lofty as to be in the third heaven, as those who have inquired scientifically affirm, having been planted by God with all kinds of most fragrant plants. It was neither perfectly in-corruptible nor entirely corruptible. It was fashioned between decay and incorruption, so as to exist forever, luxuriant with fruit and sprouting new shoots, always having some fruit ripe and new fruit ripening. For as leaves rot and ripe fruit falls to the earth they become fragrant soil, and they do not stink of decay as plants in the world do. This arises from the great abundance and sanctification of the grace that always prevails there. Thus, the river Okeanos, which was established to water Paradise, flows through it and, as it leaves Paradise, is divided

into four beginnings and carries soil and fallen leaves thence as it flows to Indian[1] and Ethiopian lands and deposits them there. There, the Phison and Gehon merge and forever flow round those regions, until they are divided again, one watering Libya and the other the land of Egypt.

11. Flowing or corruptible creation, they say, was not fashioned so at first, but was later corrupted unwillingly and, as Scripture says, *subjected to vanity* [Rom. 8:20] – that is, to humanity. Not willingly, perhaps, but, rather, for the sake of him who subjected it in hope of renewing corrupted Adam. Christ, having renewed Adam and sanctified him, and, although bearing a mortal body for the sake of our transient life, still he renewed creation, though he has not yet delivered it from corruption. Some say that creation's delivery from corruption means a change of sensible things for the better,[2] others that it is their complete transference.[3] For Scripture habitually affirms present difficulties simply and artlessly.

12. Those who receive grace, as in conception, and are pregnant by the Spirit, either expel the divine seed through sin, or are deprived of God by intimacy with the enemy who lurks within them. Expulsion of grace occurs through the activity of the passions, but complete deprivation because of the practice of sin. For a soul addicted to passions and sin, being deprived and bereaved of the grace it has expelled, will be an abode of passion – not to say, demons – both now and in the age to come.

13. Nothing so turns anger into joy and gentleness as courage and mercy: courage shattering those outside and mercy those inside, like two siege engines.

14. Many who perform the commandments seem to be travellers who, not yet having reached the city, remain outside. For they make their way mindlessly, having inadvertently deviated from the straight and royal roads – that is to say, the vices that are so close to the path of virtue. For the commandments, which seek only the divine will, demand that we do neither too little nor too much, but pursue a purpose pleasing to God. Without that, our labour is in vain, not *making straight the ways of God* [Isa. 40:3], as Scripture puts it. For in every action we must seek out the goal of the matter.

15. Seek the Lord on the way, which is to say, in your heart, through his commandments. For when you hear John crying out and commanding everyone *to prepare the roads* and *make ways straight* [Matt. 3:3], understand this to mean 'commandments', 'hearts' and 'practices'. For nothing but rectitude in heart can construct the straight road of the commandments or an unerring practice.

16. When you hear Scripture speaking of *rod* and *staff* [Ps. 22:4], understand these as: on a prophetic reading, 'judgement' and 'providence'; on a moral one, 'psalmody' and 'prayer.' For being judged by the Lord with the *rod* of discipline, we are educated towards return. Disciplining our enemies with the rod of courageous psalmody, we are confirmed in prayer. Having, then, the *rod and staff* of our intellect's practice in hand, let us not cease disciplining and being disciplined until we have fled judgement both now and in future, and become wholly subject to providence.

17. It belongs to the commandments always to prefer the commandment that embraces them all: the memory of God, which says, *Always remember the Lord your God* [Deut. 8:18]. Through memory the commandments are lost, and through it they can be kept, since at the outset forgetfulness destroyed the memory of God and so revealed the man to be denuded of every good.

18. Those engaged in spiritual struggle make progress towards our original dignity by two commandments – obedience and fasting – for it is through what is contrary to these that every vice has entered the race of mortals. Now, those who keep the commandments through obedience return to God more swiftly; those who keep them through fasting and prayer, more slowly. Obedience is well-suited to beginners, fasting to those in the middle way, who have attained spiritual knowledge and self-mastery. For keeping obedience to God pure through the commandments belongs to very few and it demands effort even from those who have attained self-mastery.

19. *The Law of the Spirit of Life* [Rom. 8:2], according to the Apostle, operates and speaks in the heart, just as the law of the letter [cf. 2 Cor. 3:6] operates in the flesh [cf. Rom. 7:5]. For

the Law of the Spirit frees the intellect *from the law of sin and death* [Rom. 8:2], while that of the letter makes it an unwitting Pharisee who understands and performs the law bodily, and only keeps the commandments to be seen by people.

20. The complex of all the commandments joined and knitted together in the Spirit [Eph. 4:16] has an analogy in the human person, whether he is called perfect or imperfect in accordance with his progress. The commandments are like the body; the virtues, like the bones, since they are inner qualities become habitual. Grace, as a living soul, is moved, and breathes life into the practice of the commandments, just as the soul gives life to the body. Carelessness or zeal reveal whether one is an infant or mature, measured against Christ's maturity [cf. Eph. 4:13], both now and in the age to come.

21. If you want that body of commandments to grow, you must zealously yearn for the genuine spiritual milk of motherly grace. For everyone who seeks to grow in Christ is nurtured with this milk of grace. Wisdom offers fervour from her own breasts as milk for growth, while to the perfect she gives her gladness as honeyed food for purification. As it says, *Honey and milk are under your tongue* [Song 4:11]. Solomon called the Spirit's nutritive and nourishing power 'milk', and its purifying power 'honey'. The great Apostle praises the difference of activities, saying, *I have given you milk to drink, like children, and not solid food* [1 Cor. 3:2].

22. He who seeks the meaning of the commandments without practising them, wanting to learn them only through study and reading, is like someone who imagines a shadow instead of truth. For the meaning of the truth is only found by those who partake of truth. But when the uninitiated and inexperienced in truth seek its meaning, they find only *wisdom made foolish* [1 Cor. 1:20]. The Apostle called them *natural*, since they lack the Spirit [1 Cor. 2:14], even if they pride themselves on the truth.

23. Just as the eye looks at letters and receives sensible ideas from them, so too the intellect, when it has been purified and returned to its primordial dignity, looks to God and receives divine representations from him. Instead of a book, it has the Spirit; instead of a pen, the intellect and tongue. *My tongue,*

it says, *is a pen* [Ps. 44:1]. Instead of ink, it has light. So then, dipping the intellect in light and producing light, it writes the spiritual meaning of things on the pure hearts of those who listen. Then the intellect understands the saying about how *The faithful will be taught by God* [John 6:45, Isa. 54:13] and how, as the prophecy puts it, *God teaches* a person *knowledge* in spirit [Prov. 30:3].

24. Understand that faith roused to action in the heart is the unmediated law of commandments. For through faith every commandment gushes up and effects the enlightenment of souls, in which the fruits of true and active faith are self-control, love and, finally, God-given humility, which is the beginning and strength of love.

25. True knowledge of things visible and invisible is the truthful glory of beings. The glory of visible things is knowledge of what is perceptible to sense; of invisible ones, knowledge of what is perceptible by intellect and of things rational, intelligible and divine.

26. The definition of Orthodoxy is to see with purity the two dogmas of the faith, and from them to know the Triad and the Dyad. In the case of the Triad to contemplate and know it in the unity without confusion or division; in the case of the Dyad, of Christ's natures in one person: that is, to confess and know one Son in two natures both before and after his Incarnation, glorified without confusion in two wills, both divine and human.

27. It is necessary to confess piously the three unmoving and unchanging properties of the All-Holy Trinity: begottenness, unbegottenness and procession. That is: the Father is unbegotten and unoriginated; the Son is begotten and likewise unoriginated; the Holy Spirit proceeds from the Father and through the Son (as the Damascene says[4]) and is coeternal.

28. Faith in grace, roused by the Spirit through the commandments, suffices for salvation, provided that we have guarded it and have not preferred a dead faith unable to give life to one *living and active* [Heb. 4:12] in Christ. For the form and life of faith active in Christ suffice for the believer. Nowadays, however, ignorance has been teaching pious Christians a dead and unfeeling faith in words alone instead of faith in grace.

29. The Trinity [or Triad] is simple unity [or monad] since it is without quality or composition. A Trinity in unity: for one God is three persons who possess between them complete but unconfused mutual interpenetration.

30. God is always known and spoken of in a threefold way, for God is uncircumscribed and yet through the Son and in the Holy Spirit is the preserver and provider of all things. Whenever one of these is named, it cannot be considered or even mentioned without or apart from the others.

31. Humans have intellect, word [*logos*] and breath [or, spirit]. Neither is there intellect without word, nor word without breath, each being itself yet inhering in the others. For intellect speaks through word, and word is manifest through breath. According to this analogy, each human being bears an obscure image of the archetypal and nameless Trinity and by this shows now what it means to be *in accordance with the image* [Gen. 1:26–7].

32. For our God-bearing fathers taught by analogy that the Father is intellect, the Son is word [*Logos*], and the Holy Spirit is truly breath [or, spirit]. Thus they taught the holy, supernatural Trinity that transcends essence, the one God in three persons, having bequeathed us true faith and an *anchor* of *hope* [Heb. 6:18–19]. For, according to Scripture, knowing one God is *the root of immortality* and *understanding the power* of the unity in three persons is *complete righteousness* [Wisd. 15:3]. So, again, this is how we understand the Gospel saying that '*This is eternal life, that they may know you the only true God* in three persons, *and Jesus Christ whom you have sent* in two natures and wills' [John 17:3].

33. As punishments differ, so do rewards. Punishments are in Hades, according to the Scripture that says, *In a dark and shadowy land, in a land of eternal darkness* [Job 10:21–2]. There sinners dwell until the Judgement and they return to it through God's verdict. For what else could passages like *Let sinners be turned back to Hades* [Ps. 9:18] and *Death shepherds them* [Ps. 48:15] refer to, except the final verdict and eternal condemnation?

34. 'Fire', 'darkness', 'worm' and 'Tartaros' [Mark 9:43–8] refer to: the comprehensive passion of pleasure, the universal ignorance of darkness, the titillation and trembling of wantonness in everything, and the rotten stench of sin. Like the pledges and first fruits of punishment, each of these latter is shown already operative in the souls of sinners through their disposition.

35. Dispositions of passions are pledges of punishments, just as activities of virtue are pledges of the Kingdom. It is necessary to understand and say that the commandments are activities, the virtues dispositions, just as they say vices are dispositions built through habit.

36. We get what we deserve, even if the crowd thinks otherwise. For divine justice metes out eternal life to some, eternal punishment to others. Each group, having lived in the present age either well or badly, is recompensed appropriately to their deeds, while the quantity and quality of their appropriate recompense are proportional to their disposition and activity in passion or virtue alike.

37. Souls that luxuriate in pleasure are *lakes of fire* [Rev. 19:20, etc.] in whom the stench of passions reeks like mire and breeds the sleepless worm of incontinence – that comprehensive unhealthiness of the flesh – as well as snakes, frogs and leeches of wicked desires, which are cursed and poisonous thoughts and demons. Such a condition has already received the pledge of future punishment.

38. Just as the first fruits of punishments are hidden in the souls of sinners, so the pledges of good things operate and are partaken of through the Spirit in the hearts of the righteous. For virtuous conversion is the Kingdom of Heaven, just as the disposition of passions is punishment.

39. '*Night is coming*', according to our Lord's saying [John 9:4], and refers to the total inertia of the impending darkness. Interpreted differently, 'night' is Antichrist, who is and is called 'darkness'. Or, on a moral reading, 'night' refers to regular indolence, which like a dark night numbs the soul in the sleep of insensitivity. For, just as night-time makes everyone sleep, and is an image of death in its lifelessness, so with the drink of troubles the night of future darkness renders sinners dead and senseless, drunk with pain.

40. *The judgement*, according to the Gospel passage, *of this world* [John 12:31] is the unbelief of the impious, in agreement with the statement that *He who does not believe has already been judged* [John 3:18]. The judgements of providence are visitations aimed at restraining us or turning us back from sin, while judgements of our purposes test whether our dispositions turn in action towards good or evil, according to the verse in the Psalms, *Sinners were alienated from the womb* [Ps. 57:4]. For God's just judgement then is manifest in unbelief, discipline or ascetic struggle: rebuking some, having mercy on others, bestowing crowns or punishments. For those sunk in unbelief are completely impious, while those in need of discipline are believers, but careless, and are therefore educated philanthropically. Those who have become perfect in virtues or in vicious sins will have their recompense.

41. Unless it is kept undefiled, or restored to its original purity through the Spirit, our nature cannot become one body and spirit in Christ, either now or in the future harmony. For the embracing and unifying power of the Spirit does not generally complete the new garment of grace by sewing an old and ragged cloth of passions onto it [cf. Matt. 9:16].

42. He who has received and maintained the gift of newness in the Spirit [Rom. 7:6] will have equality with Christ's *appearance* when he ineffably undergoes miraculous deification. But no one will be *one in Christ* [Gal. 3:28] or a *member of Christ* [1 Cor. 6:15] unless he becomes a partaker of grace here and now and possesses in himself the *appearance of truth and knowledge* [Rom. 2:20].

43. The Kingdom of Heaven is like a tabernacle made by God according to the pattern he revealed to Moses [Exod. 25–31, 35–40], even having in the age to come two sanctuaries divided by curtains [Exod. 25:40]. Into the first sanctuary all will enter who are priests of grace. But into the second, as it is intelligible, only those will enter who in the darkness of theology now perfectly celebrate as hierarchs the triadic liturgy. Having Jesus as founder of their mysteries and their first hierarch before the Trinity, they will enter in the tabernacle which he himself established, illumined ever more richly with his splendid radiance.

44. Our Saviour called the various ways of ascent and advancement towards our future state *many mansions* [John 14:2]. For, although there is one Kingdom, there are many differences within: heavenly, earthly, and differences in accordance with virtue, knowledge and the degree of deification. For, although all will shine in the same heavenly firmament, yet *the glory of the sun is one thing, that of the moon another, that of the stars different still, and even star differs from star in glory*, as the Apostle says [1 Cor. 15:41].

45. You become an intimate companion of the angels, and nearly as incorruptible as the bodiless ones, when you have purified your intellect with tears, already raised up your soul by the Spirit, and made your flesh radiant by the Word and fashioned your *naturally clayish figure* into a *fiery* temple of divine effulgence.[5] Since, indeed, bodies become incorrupt when they lose the humours and denser parts.

46. The body of incorruption will be earthy, but lacking humours and density, being so reformed unspeakably from a *natural* to a *spiritual body* [1 Cor. 15:44] as to belong at once to soil and heaven, thanks to the subtlety of its likeness to God. For as it was originally fashioned, so it will be raised, to be *conformed to the image of the Son* of Man [Rom. 8:29], according to its perfect participation in deification.

47. The *earth* belonging to *the meek* [Matt. 5:5] is either the Kingdom of Heaven or the Son's divine–human state, towards which we come who have received the birth of adoption by grace and renewal through resurrection. Or again, *holy ground* [Exod. 3:5] is a deified nature; or perhaps this land is purified for such earthly people as are deserving. In another sense, the *land* taken *as inheritance* [Num. 33:54] is the divine and waveless calm of the *peace that surpasses understanding* [Phil. 4:7] reserved for true saints, in which the *generation of the upright will be* settled [Ps. 111:2], where nothing will buzz about demanding their attention.

48. Dispassion is the *land of promise* [Heb. 11:9], where *milk and honey* well up [Exod. 3:8], which are delight in the Spirit.

49. In the age to come the saints will share silently one with another their inner thoughts, given voice in the Holy Spirit.

50. If we do not know what God made us to be, we will not recognize what sin has made of us.

51. All who have received the *fullness of Christ's* maturity are thereafter of the same *stature* in spirit [Eph. 4:13].

52. Those who do the work get the recompense, but their rank and condition in the future life will reveal their work's quantity and quality, i.e. their measure.

53. It says that the *sons of* Christ's *resurrection*, the saints, will be intellects – that is, *equal to the angels* [Luke 20:36] – by virtue of incorruption and deification.

54. In the age to come, they say, angels and saints will never cease or desist from advancing in the increase of spiritual gifts, because they are desirous of good things. For that age knows neither slackening nor diminution of virtue into vice.

55. Understand that for now *mature manhood* [Eph. 4:13] means having received the likeness of the stages of Christ's life, like a pledge. In the age to come, however, the power of deification will reveal its completion.

56. One who is now perfect in virtue corresponding to their spirit's stage of life will possess in the age to come dignity and deification equal with others of the same stage.

57. They say that true belief is knowledge, which is to say, contemplation of the Spirit; and that an accurate interpretation of dogmas is knowledge of true faith.

58. Astonishment means total elation of the soul's faculties towards the majesty of God's glory, disclosed as an undivided unity. Or astonishment is a pure and perfect straining towards God's boundless power in light. Ecstasy is not merely the heavenward rapture of the soul's faculties, but also the complete transcendence of the senses. *Eros*, or yearning – and it is twofold – is the spiritual inebriation that inflames desire.

59. Properly speaking, there are two kinds of ecstatic spiritual *eros* – one in the heart, one conducive to ecstasy. The first belongs to those still being illumined, the second to those perfected in love. Both put the intellect out of its senses as it

is roused to ecstasy. If *eros* is really divine, it is spiritual inebriation drawing those who think in accordance with nature
to what is better. Through this drunkenness the perception of
worldly attachments is destroyed.

60. The origin and cause of thoughts are memory, properly single and simple, but divided by Adam's transgression,
through which it lost the divine memory and perished, having
by its own capacities become composite instead of simple, and
variegated instead of singular.

61. Return to its primal simplicity cures our original memory
from being a wicked, destructive memory of thoughts. For
Adam's transgression not only fashioned our soul's simple
memory of goodness into an instrument of vice, but it also
corrupted all the soul's faculties, having diminished its natural
appetites for virtue. Properly speaking, divine memory, made
firm through prayer, can be said to cure our natural memory by
raising it above nature and uniting it to the Spirit.

62. Sinful acts provoke passions; passions arouse thoughts;
thoughts give rise to fantasies, as memory begets a multitude
of notions. The cause of memory's consequent fragmentation is
forgetfulness, the offspring of ignorance. Ignorance comes from
laziness,[6] laziness from lustful appetites. The mother of lustful
appetites is uncontrollable emotions, caused by committing evil
deeds. Evil deeds are provoked by a mindless desire for wickedness and a disposition towards the senses and what they perceive.

63. In the rational soul, thoughts operate and arise; in the
irascible, bestial passions; and in the desiring part, the memory
of animal lust. In the intellectual [soul], it is imaginary appearances; and in the discursive, it is concepts.

64. The approach of wicked thoughts is like the flow of a
river. We are provoked to sin by these thoughts, and in assent-
ing to them our heart is overwhelmed as by a flood tide.

65. Understand *deep mire* [Ps. 68:3] to mean slippery pleasure, the muck of lust, or the weight of material things. Weighed
down with these, the impassioned intellect drowns itself with
thoughts in an abyss of despair.

66. Scripture has often called the principles [*logoi*] of
actions 'thoughts' [*logismoi*], just as it calls principles concepts

[*noêmata*], and vice versa. This happens because the action of such things is immaterial but is shaped into a form through material things and woven together with them, so that the non-material provocation is known and called by its material manifestation.

67. Trains of thoughts are the demons' words [*logoi*] and forerunners of the passions, just as reasons [*logoi*] and concepts [*noêmata*] are forerunners of actions. For it is impossible for anything to be good or bad in action unless it has first suggested its thought, since, really, an attacking thought is the as yet formless motion of an action of some sort.

68. Matter begets simple thoughts of things, while demonic provocation *contrives wicked* ones [Sirach 27:22]. Thus, natural reasons [*logoi*] and thoughts [*logismoi*] differ in comparison with both those that are against nature and those that transcend nature.

69. Thoughts lead to corresponding alterations in individuals of different classes, though generally natural thoughts can turn easily into unnatural ones, and thoughts in accord with nature into supernatural ones. However, the thoughts responsible for change and generation into others are: for demonic individuals, thoughts from matter; for material people, thoughts from provocation; and for divine people, natural thoughts. Natural thoughts can, after all, beget supernatural ones. Each has a cause and genesis that effects alteration towards its cognate outcome in one of these four directions – either material, demonic, natural or supernatural.

70. Note that causes have been placed before thoughts, thoughts before fantasies, fantasies before passions, passions before demons. Like some chain and order among disorderly spirits have they been cunningly linked, one to the next. Except that none operates on its own. They are only roused to action by the demons: neither does the imagination fashion images, nor passion operate, without carefully hidden demonic power. Even if Satan has fallen in ruin, he is yet strengthened by our laziness, as he vaunts arrogantly over us.

71. The demons shape our intellect, or, rather, conform themselves to us and provoke us according to whichever passion's

disposition prevails and operates in our soul. For the demons take a passion's disposition as an opportunity for fashioning its image in our imagination. Thus, whether waking or sleeping, they show us variegated and multiform fantasies. For the demons of desire are transformed sometimes into pigs, sometimes asses, sometimes lusting and fiery horses. Demons of licentiousness, in particular, are depicted sometimes as Hebrews, while demons of anger are sometimes transformed into foreign peoples, sometimes into lions. Those of cowardice are transformed into Ishmaelites, those of licentiousness into Idumeans, those of drunkenness and intemperance into Hagarenes. While demons of arrogant greed are transformed sometimes into wolves, sometimes into leopards. The demons of malice are transformed sometimes into snakes and sometimes vipers, sometimes into foxes. The demons of shamelessness are transformed into dogs, those of despondency into cats. Sometimes the demons of lust are transformed into serpents, sometimes into crows and jackdaws. Soul-like demons, especially the aerial ones, are transformed into birds. This range of fantasies has a threefold cause: the forms of spirits are shaped according to the tripartite nature of the soul, so that the resultant image is also threefold. Images of birds, beasts and domestic animals correspond to the rational, irascible and desiring powers of the soul, respectively. For the three ruling passions take arms against the three powers of the soul and the demons transform themselves, according to congenital likeness, into whichever passion our soul has gained as its disposition, and so attack us.

72. The demons of pleasure frequently attack like fire and coals. For pleasure-loving spirits inflame the desiring part and, having confounded our mind, darken the whole soul. For the cause of fever, turmoil and darkness alike lie, properly speaking, in the pleasure of the passions.

73. The *darkness* of ignorance is the *night* of the passions [Ps. 103:20]. Or, again, *night* is the realm that generates the passions, where the viceroy of darkness reigns. Here we meet the *beasts of the field and birds of the sky* [Gen. 2:19], and the *serpents of the earth* [Gen. 1:25] – which are figures of the *howling* spirits *seeking to snatch* us for *their food* [Ps. 103:21].

74. At the time when the passions are active, some thoughts precede them and some follow. Thoughts precede fantasies, while passions follow them. Likewise, passions precede the demons, and the demons follow them.

75. The source and cause of the passions are the abuse of things, while such abuse is due to inclination, the result of a willing disposition. The will is tested by provocation, caused by the demons: they are permitted, through God's providence, to reveal the quality of our self-determination.

76. The soul's impassioned disposition is *the fatal* venom *in the sting* of *sin* [1 Cor. 15:56]. For one who has been voluntarily habituated to the passions is unmoving and fixed in them.

77. Passions are described in various ways, and are divided first into those of the body and those of the soul. Passions of the body are subdivided into painful and sinful ones. The painful passions are either diseases or educative. Passions of the soul are divided by faculty of the soul: those of desire, those of anger and those of reason. Passions of reason are either imaginative or conceptual. Of these some are willed in accordance with its abuse; others are involuntary, in accord with necessity. These lattermost passions are called 'blameless', and the Fathers sometimes call them either 'consequent properties' or 'natural properties'.[7]

78. Some passions are bodily and some are of the soul. Those of the soul's desiring part differ from those of its irascible part, and both differ from those of its rational part. In this last, some passions belong to the intellect, some to the mind. However, all share some characteristics with each other, and each cooperates with the others: bodily passions with those of desire, passions of the soul with those of its irascible part. Again, rational passions cooperate with intellectual ones, and these with passions of the mind and memory.

79. Passions of anger are: wrath, bitterness, yelling, quick temper, rashness, affectation, boasting, et cetera. Those of desire are: grasping, licentiousness, incontinence, greed, love of pleasure, love of money, love of self (the worst of all). Passions of the flesh are: fornication, adultery, impurity, insatiability, injustice, gluttony, despondency, boastfulness, love of adornment,

irrational love of this life, et cetera. Passions of the soul's rational part are: unbelief, blasphemy, malice, cunning, idle curiosity, dissemblance, abusive speech, slander, condemnation, belittling others, jocularity, hypocrisy, lying, indecent speech, empty speech, treachery, sarcasm, ostentation, people-pleasing, fluctuation, perjury, pointless chatter and the rest. Passions of the intellect are: self-conceit, pompousness, self-satisfaction, strife, contention, self-pleasing, contradiction, disobedience, vain imagining, day-dreaming, love of show, love of glory and pride (the first and last of all evils). Passions of the mind are: distractions, fluctuations, captivities, darkening, blindness, abductions into error, provocations, assents, turns, inclinations, flickers, movements like these. To put it simply: all bad movements contrary to nature have been mixed in the three powers of the soul, just as good movements subsist in those powers in accord with nature.

80. Oh, what sublimity did David show in his wonder at God, when he said, '*Your knowledge was made wonderful beyond me, for I cannot attain it – it is too strong* [Ps. 138:6]; it is unattainable for my weak knowledge and capacity.' How incomprehensible is our very flesh in its composite formation, which is triadic in each part yet a single harmony of its own members and parts. The flesh is honoured also with the seventh and second numbers, which manifest time and nature respectively. Thus, our flesh itself is an instrument of God's glory, which, when considered physiologically according to the laws of nature at work in it, reveals the Trinitarian grandeur.

81. The laws of nature are various compositions of active members – which the word called 'differences' because of the complexities of members' individual characteristics. Or again, the natural law is the potential activity of each part and member. For just as God activates and moves all creation, so the soul rouses and moves each member of the body to its own proper activity. We must discover by what principle God-bearing men have called anger and desire sometimes capacities of the flesh, and sometimes capacities of the soul. And we affirm that, for those who know them precisely, the words of the saints have no incongruence. Rather, both accounts are true and the saints very wisely use the terms interchangeably, as is fitting, because

both body and soul come into being unutterably in accord with the mode of coexistence, such that the soul is already complete, but the body incomplete because it will grow through nourishment. The soul, since it was made rational and intellectual, has from its formation a capacity for directing appetite and an irascible capacity that moves it to steadfastness in *eros*. For irrational anger and mindless desire were not created together with the soul, just as these did not formerly exist in the flesh, which was, rather, fashioned incorruptible and without humours, on which desire and bestial anger follow. After the transgression, emotion and desire necessarily penetrated the human, who had fallen under decay and the grossness belonging to irrational beings. When, therefore, the body rules, it opposes the will of the soul in matters of emotion and desire both. But when the mortal is subject to the rational, it follows the soul to good activities. For when the imported properties of the flesh were mixed indiscriminately with those of the soul, then the human being was made like *cattle* [Ps. 48:13], being subjected to the law of sin out of natural necessity – turning from rational to bovine, from human to bestial.

82. God did not create emotion and bestial desire together with the soul that was fashioned rational through his inspiration and intellectual through his vivifying in-breathing [Gen. 2:7]. Rather, with the soul God made a capacity for directed appetite and, additionally, a capacity for persuasion at once courageous and erotic. Neither did God introduce anger and irrational desire to the body when he fashioned it. Rather, through the transgression, it later received these things in addition to mortality, corruptibility and bestiality, in which it came to subsist. For the body, say theologians, was created incorruptible (just as it will rise) but receptive of mortality, in the same sense as the soul is called dispassionate. Both body and soul were together corrupted and mixed by primary natural law of their mutual interpenetration and communication of properties. The soul was reshaped by passions, or, rather, by demons, while the body was assimilated to irrational animals by its dispositional activity and the dominion of corruption. The powers of both having become one, body and soul came

to be a single beast, having become irrational with emotion and mindless with desire. Thus was the human being *likened to cattle*, according to Scripture, *and assimilated to them* [Ps. 48:13], in every way.

83. The source and formation of the virtues are a good purpose, or, therefore, aiming at the Good, just as God is cause and fount of every good thing. The source of the Good is faith or, rather, Christ the rock of faith, whom we have as the source and foundation of all the virtues on which we stand and build everything good. For he is *the chief cornerstone* [Eph. 2:20] and unites us to himself, the *pearl of great price* [Matt. 13:46]. Seeking this *pearl* the monk enters the depth of stillness and *sells all his own* desires through obedience to the commandments, that he may thereafter obtain Christ [Matt. 13:46].

84. The virtues are equal one with another, and are all gathered into one and together make up a single definition and form of virtue. However, some virtues are greater than others because they are more comprehensive and essential than most or, indeed, all. These include divine love, humility and divine endurance. Of the last our Lord said that *By your endurance you will gain your souls* [Luke 21:19]. He did not say, 'by your fasting' or 'by your vigils'. I speak of endurance bestowed by God, which is the queen of virtues, the foundation of virtuous deeds. Endurance is itself peace amid war, calm in the gale, an unshakeable foundation in those who cultivate it. Neither arms nor spears, nor enemy camps loosed against it, nor even the demons' disorder and the shadowy enemy battleline can harm the person who has found endurance in Christ Jesus.

85. Although they produce each other as well, virtues (except divine ones) take their genesis from the three faculties of the soul. For the source and principle of the four general ([or, cardinal] virtues in natural matters – moral wisdom, courage, moderation and justice, from which and in which the rest subsist – and of the divine virtues too, are the divine wisdom of theologians, inspired by the Spirit. Wisdom acts in four ways in the intellect, not bringing into operation all the virtues together at once, but each individually, at the right time and as it determines: moral wisdom as light; courage as a nimble

capacity and ever-moving inspiration; moderation as a sancti-
fying and purifying power; and righteousness [or, justice] as a
soothing dew of purity that cools the fever of passions. In these
ways, wisdom brings into activity all the virtues, as has been
said, to each one who has attained perfection, in the appropriate way.

86. Pursuit of the virtues by one's own zeal does not grant
the soul full strength, unless by grace the virtues have first come
to exist substantially in the soul's disposition. For each virtue
carries its own charism in accord with its activity, so that, by
disposition and nature of goodness, it can draw partakers to
itself without their any longer needing to choose. And when
this has been given to us, it is thereafter preserved unalterable
and unchanging. For the virtues have the Spirit's grace living in
them like a soul in its members, rousing them to action. Thus,
without grace, the whole throng of virtues is a corpse, while to
those who imagine they possess or accomplish them, so long as
they lack grace, virtues are only types and shadows of goodness, and not images of truth [Heb. 10:1].

87. There are four general virtues – courage, moral wisdom,
moderation and justice – and eight that, through either excess
or defect, trail behind them. These eight are vices as far as we
are concerned, though they are called and considered virtues
by worldly types. The two doubles of courage are: by excess,
audacity; by defect, cowardice. Of moral wisdom they are: by
excess, crafty dealing; by defect, ignorance. Of moderation they
are: by excess, folly; by defect, licentiousness. Of justice they
are: by excess, foolish disadvantage; by defect, arrogant greed.
For not only the general and natural virtues, but the practical
ones as well, are means, or mid-points, superior to every defect
or excess. Thus, the general virtues have free choice in partner-
ship with the rectitude of the will; the other eight have change
and self-conceit as their partner. That virtues are the mid-
points of rectitude, take as witness the Proverb that says, *You
will straighten all good mid-points* [Prov. 2:9]. Thus, all virtues
subsist in the soul's three faculties, in which they are born and
built, having the four general virtues – or, rather, Christ – as
foundation of their dwelling. Thus, the natural virtues are

purified through practical ones, while divine and supernatural virtues are given in the goodness of the Spirit.

88. Of the virtues, some are practical, some natural and some divine (because they come from the Spirit). The practical ones belong to free choice, the natural to our constitution and the divine to grace.

89. As our soul is generative of the virtues, so also it is of the passions. But, while it is accustomed to give birth to virtues in accordance with nature, it generates passions contrary to nature. The inclination of the soul's will suffices for the generation of either good or evil, like the fixed foot of a compass or the fulcrum of a scale: to whichever the soul inclines, this it takes as partner, and this it activates. Intention is the underlying material for both kinds of activity, since it bears both within itself: with virtues, by its own generation; with vices, by free inclination of the will.

90. Scripture calls the virtues *young women* [Song 1:3 or Ps. 67:26], because of their conjugal intercourse with the soul, and because they are contemplated with it in one spirit and body. For the form of a young woman is a symbol of love, and the shape of these sacred virginal virtues is a sure sign of purity and holiness. For grace habitually transmutes divine things into qualities that express them and unerringly endues divine things with an appropriate form in those who can receive them.

91. Although there are eight passions in the front rank, three of these loom particularly large: gluttony, greed and vainglory. The other five follow: fornication, anger, sadness, despondency and pride. Likewise, three comprehensive virtues oppose these: abandonment of property, continence and humility. Alongside these the others follow: innocence, meekness, joy, courage and counting oneself as nothing, and the whole entourage of virtues. Not everyone who wants can learn and know the strength, activity and scent of each individual virtue or vice. That belongs only to those who do and suffer in word and deed, and who have received from the Spirit *gifts* of *knowledge* and *discernment* [1 Cor. 12:8–10].

92. Some virtues are active and some are activated. The latter, dwelling in us, activate when necessary, whenever,

however and however much they choose, while we ourselves activate these in accordance with our free choice and the moral disposition gained by habit. On the other hand, the active virtues are formed substantially, while we are conformed to their habit, like an impression in wax, since, indeed, the mode of all our practices is but an impression of the heavenly archetypes. For intelligible things are communicated to very few people before their future enjoyment of incorruption. For now we activate and receive, not the virtues themselves, but merely their impressions and the ascetic struggle they demand.

93. According to Paul, one who partakes of and is able to transmit Christ's enlightenment to others by his own activity *administers the Gospel* [Rom. 15:16]. He sows the word like a divine seed in the fertile souls of those who hear him: Let *your word* be *seasoned with the grace* of divine goodness, that I may give grace *to those who listen with faith* [Col. 4:6, Heb. 4:2]. Again, calling those who teach and those who are taught 'farmers' and *a field* [1 Cor. 3:7–9], he wisely shows teachers to be husbandmen and sowers of the divine word, and their students to be rich soil for the virtues, fertile and fruitful. For true *ministry*, properly speaking, is not only the activity of divine things, but also one's reception and communication of good things.

94. Different is the word spoken for the purpose of teaching, and is gathered in many different ways from four sources: from study, from reading, from ascetic practice and from grace. Just as water is by nature one thing, but is altered and varied into particular characteristics according to the different soils over which it flows, so that water tastes bitter or sweet, briny or brackish, likewise the word emerges and is altered in accordance with the moral disposition of each and so is known by its activity and the benefit it confers.

95. This spoken word is to be enjoyed by each rational nature, so, just as there are many different foods, the soul receiving the word of teaching experiences pleasure in different ways. Instruction forms the soul's moral character; reading nourishes it like *still waters* [Ps. 22:2]; ascetic practice is like *green pasture* [Ps. 22:2] that strengthens it; and teaching imparted through grace is like *an intoxicating cup* [Ps. 22:5] that fills it

with ineffable joy, or like *oil gladdens the face* [Ps. 103:15], and makes it radiant.

96. Really, though, not only does the soul possess these things in itself as its life, but when it hears them from others, it perceives them as instruction, whenever love and faith together lead the way. One hears by faith and the other teaches with love, fashioning teachings [*logoi*] on the virtues without pomp or ostentation. For the soul learns from disciplined study, finding in reading nourishment, taught by ascetic practice to make it one's own inwardly, as a most delightful wedding gift; and finding enlightenment from the Spirit, as a bridegroom who enters into union with her and fills her with delight. For *every word that proceeds from God's mouth* [Deut. 8:3, Matt. 4:4] means words that come forth through the Spirit from the mouths of saints. This is the Spirit's supremely sweet inspiration in action, on which only the worthy feed. Although the Word is nourishment for all intelligent beings, here below very few thoroughly enjoy the Spirit's words. Most only know and partake through memory of echoes of spiritual words and do not yet share with full awareness in *the true bread* [John 6:32] of the coming age, which is the *Word of God* [John 1:1, Heb. 4:12]. For in that age, this bread is the sole food for the saints, offered in such abundance as to be never exhausted, never depleted, never again sacrificed.

97. Without intellectual feeling, it is impossible to taste the pleasure of divine things with full awareness. Someone who has blunted his senses and made them useless as regards perceptible things neither sees nor hears nor smells, being paralysed, or, rather, half dead. In the same way someone who has mortified his soul's natural faculties through passions has numbed them to the activity of and participation in the Spirit's mysteries. For someone who neither sees nor hears nor perceives spiritually is a corpse, because Christ does not live in him, nor is he moving and active in Christ.

98. The senses have an activity equal to and the same as the soul's powers – dare I say, one and the same? – especially when they are healthy. For the soul's powers live and operate through the senses, and the vivifying Spirit is mingled with both. For,

properly speaking, someone is sick when they suffer from the general illness of the passions, forever lounging in the clinic of laziness. For when there is no satanic strife setting them against the law of the intellect and the Spirit, the senses behold sensible things and the powers of the soul contemplate with clarity intelligible entities. When the senses have been gathered into one and become a unity through the Spirit, then they know directly and essentially the natures of things human and divine. They behold their *logoi* or principles, and, so far as possible, contemplate purely the one source of all, the Trinity.

99. One who practises stillness should first have these five virtues as a foundation on which to build: silence, self-control, vigilance, humility and endurance. Then come the three practices pleasing to God: psalmody, prayer and reading; or, if they are infirm, a little handiwork. These virtues we have listed not only embrace all other virtues, but they also sustain one another. From dawn the hesychast is to devote himself to the memory of God through prayer and stillness of heart: praying diligently at the first hour; then at the second hour reading; at the third, singing psalms; at the fourth, praying; at the fifth, reading; at the sixth, singing psalms; at the seventh, praying; at the eighth, reading; at the ninth, singing psalms; at the tenth hour, eating; at the eleventh, let them rest a bit if they need to; at the twelfth hour, let them sing Vespers. Passing the course of the day in this fashion, they will be well-pleasing to God.

100. Like bees making honey, we must collect the most useful bits from all the virtues and, receiving thus a little from all, to mix a great concoction of virtuous practices, from which the honey of wisdom flows to gladden souls.

101. If you wish to pass the time of night more easily, listen. Night vigil has three programmes: for beginners, those on the way and mature monks. The programme for beginners is this: to sleep half the night, from Vespers to midnight, and then to keep vigil from midnight until dawn. The programme for those on the way is to keep vigil for an hour or two after Vespers, then to sleep for four hours, then rise again for Orthros, chanting and praying the six hours until dawn. Thereafter, chant the First Hour and sit and keep silence as described above, either

keeping to the sequence of the hours or else continuing in unceasing prayer, thus establishing a firm habit of prayer. The third programme, for the mature, is simply to stand and stay awake the whole night.

102. Listen to what we say about food: a pound of bread suffices for anyone contending for stillness, while they should drink two small cups of unmixed wine and three of water. They should eat from provisions on hand, not as much as nature seeks in its desire, but only as much as forethought with self-control dictates. The best and briefest plan for those who wish to conduct themselves carefully is to maintain their practice of the three comprehensive virtues – we mean fasting, vigil and prayer, which have together been established as the surest support of all virtues.

103. Stillness requires *faith* above all, endurance *with one's whole heart* and *strength* and power [Mark 12:30], *love* and *hope* [1 Cor. 13:13]. For if you have faith, even though you fail to achieve what you seek here below out of carelessness or for some other reason, it is not quite impossible that at their death they will not be assured of the fruit of their faith and spiritual struggle and to behold their freedom – which is Jesus Christ, the redemption and salvation of souls, the Word at once God and human. But if you lack faith, however, you will be utterly condemned at death, although, really, they *have already been judged*, as the Lord says [John 3:18]. For one enslaved to pleasures, who seeks *glory from humans* and not from *God* [John 12:43], is faithless, it says [cf. John 5:44], even if they appear to be faithful in word. Such a one has unwittingly deceived himself and will hear that *Because* you did not receive me in your heart, but cast me away behind you, *I too will cast you away* [Ezek. 5:11]. For the faithful person must be of good hope and trust in God's truth, to which all the Scriptures testify, and must confess their own infirmity, lest they receive this twofold and inexorable condemnation.

104. Nothing brings about a *contrite heart* and *humbled* soul [Ps. 50:19] so much as solitude, embraced in self-awareness and silence in everything. Likewise, nothing else so ruins the state of stillness and strips it of its divine power as these six

comprehensive passions: bold speech, gluttony, talkativeness, distraction, self-inflation and self-conceit, that mistress of the passions. Someone who has readily accustomed themselves to these is gradually darkened the further they go until they finally become totally insensate. But if they turn back and make a new beginning with eagerness and faith, they will find again what they seek, especially if they do so in humility. But if through their carelessness even one of these passions still reigns within, then the complete roster of passions will march forth in company with ruinous unbelief and make their soul a barren wasteland like another Babylon, subject to the tumults and terrors of the demons. Thus, *their end will be worse than their beginning* [Matt. 12:45], having become an irascible enemy and accuser of those who keep stillness, sharpening their *tongue* against them like a *sharp*, two-edged *sword* [Ps. 56:5].

105. The waters of the passions – from which is fed the dirty and turbid sea that floods the soul of stillness – are not to be crossed save in the light and nimble ship of all-embracing renunciation and self-control. For the torrents of passions, fed from intemperance and love of worldly things, drench the earth of our heart and deposit all sorts of rot and material for thoughts. These floods make for confusion in the intellect, troubling the mind, and weighing down the body. They render our soul and heart careless, dark and numb, and cast both alike far from their proper disposition and natural perception.

106. Nothing makes zealous souls so relaxed, careless and mindless as real self-love, that nurse of the passions. For whenever someone prefers bodily rest over toils for virtue, and imagines that productive knowledge consists in refusing to work hard – especially the easy little workouts of the commandments – then self-love naturally makes the soul ill at ease for the arena of stillness, while it renders inertial laziness powerful and insuperable.

107. The first and finest doctor for those infirm in God's commands but who have decided to vomit up the troubling darkness within is nothing but unquestioning obedience with faith in everything. This drug is a life-giving compound of virtues for those who drink it, and a blade that cleans scabbed

wounds at a stroke. One who has chosen in faith and simplicity to cultivate obedience above all has cut off all the passions at once. They have not only attained stillness, but have accomplished it already through obedience. They have found Christ, becoming and being called Christ's imitators and servants.

108. Unless your way of life and working is tinged with grief it is impossible to endure the burning heat of stillness. For if with a sense of grief you meditate on the terrors that await us before and after death before they come to pass, you will possess endurance and humility, the two foundations of stillness. Without these, efforts to achieve stillness will forever be accompanied by apathy, leading to self-conceit, from which distractions that take the mind prisoner will multiply and induce lethargy. Then dissipation, the daughter of laziness, makes the body flabby and slack, and renders the mind darkened and hardened. Jesus is then hidden away, being crowded out by the host of ideas and thoughts that occupy the mind.

109. To experience with full awareness the torments of conscience either now or in the age to come is impossible for everyone, but only for those who, in this world or the next, are deprived of glory and love. Such torment is like a tormentor punishing the guilty in a multitude of ways, or ever appears like a tyrant's sharp sword, unsheathed to strike with indignation or reproach. Once the conscience has been awakened, what is called indignation, or, by others, natural *anger* (which they command us to *sharpen* as a *relentless sword* against our enemies [Wisd. 5:20]), is roused in three ways: against enemies, against nature and against the soul. If, having been victorious, the conscience should subjugate the two (sin and flesh) to the one (the soul), it is transmuted into a mountain of courage ascending to God. But if the soul submits to sin and flesh, then conscience becomes in the end a merciless torment for the soul, as it has become enslaved to its enemies of its own free will. Thereafter the soul engages in the most shameful practices, because it has lost its state of the virtues and fallen, alienated from God.

110. Of all the passions two, really, are the hardest and heaviest: fornication and despondency, which encompass

and exhaust the wretched soul. These two go in tandem and mutually support each other, being hard to fight and harder to defeat – in fact, they cannot be completely conquered by our own efforts. Fornication may abound in the soul's desiring part, but it embraces indiscriminately the matter naturally belonging to both soul and body, having all its pleasure mixed into every member. Then despondency grips the soul's leading faculty afresh, strangling the whole soul, and the flesh too, like bindweed, and makes their nature sluggish, careless and even paralysed. These passions are removed (though not completely bested before one attains blessed dispassion) whenever the soul, having received in prayer from the Holy Spirit a strength that offers the soul rest, power and a deep peace, rejoices because of stillness. Fornication is the beginning, the queen, the mistress, the all-embracing pleasure of pleasures. Its sibling, laziness, is the insuperable chariot bearing Pharaoh's viziers [Exod. 15:4]. Through fornication and laziness the origins of the other passions have entered into our wretched life.

111. The beginning of intellectual prayer is the activity, or purifying power, of the Spirit, and the mystical ministry of the intellect. In like fashion, the beginning of stillness is attention, its middle is enlightening power and contemplation, and its end is the intellect's ecstasy and rapture to God.

112. Prior to the enjoyment to come that transcends the intellect, the intellect's intellectual activity is a spiritual sanctuary that mystically as a pledge offers and partakes of the *Lamb of God* [John 1:29] on the altar of the soul. Eating the *Lamb of God* on the soul's intelligible altar is not merely knowing or partaking of it, but even becoming like the Lamb as an image in the age to come. For here below it is the inner meaning [the *logoi*] of the mysteries that we receive, as we hope there to receive them in reality.

113. For beginners, prayer is like a fire of joyfulness kindled in the heart: for the perfect, it is like a vigorous, fragrant light. Or again, prayer is the preaching of apostles, the activity of faith, or, rather, immediate faith, the *substance of things hoped for* [Heb. 11:1], love in action, angelic movement, power of the bodiless beings, at once their task and delight. It is God's

Gospel, heartfelt assurance, hope of salvation, sign of innocence and symbol of holiness. It is the recognition of God,
the manifestation of baptism, purification of the font. It is the
pledge of the Holy Spirit [2 Cor. 1:22], Jesus' great joy. It is the
soul's delight, God's mercy, sign of deliverance, seal of Christ,
ray of intelligible sunlight, *morning star* of *hearts* [2 Pet. 1:19].
It is the confirmation of Christianity, the demonstration of
reconciliation with God, grace of God, wisdom of God (rather,
the beginning of wisdom itself), manifestation of God, task of
monastics, way of life of those who practise stillness, origin
of stillness, a sure sign of an angelic way of life. What else
could be said? Prayer is God, who *works all in all* [1 Cor. 12:6],
because the activity of Father, Son and Holy Spirit – which
Spirit *works all things* in Christ Jesus [1 Cor. 12:11] – is one.

114. If Moses had not received the rod of power from God,
he would not have become *a god to Pharaoh* [Exod. 7:1] to
plague Pharaoh and Egypt both. The intellect, too, unless it
grasps the power of prayer, cannot shatter sin and the opposing powers.

115. One who speaks and acts without humility is like someone building a house in winter, without clay. But to find and
know this with experience and knowledge belongs to very few.
Those who try to talk about humility in words are like people
trying to measure the abyss. We, being but blind men who have
impetuously imagined some little thing about this great light,
say this: humility, properly speaking, possesses neither humble
speech nor humble appearance. It is neither compelled to think
humble thoughts, nor does it blame itself when humiliated.
Such activities are, perhaps, its occasions and forms, or even its
various modes, but humility itself is grace and *a gift from above*
[James 1:17]. As our Fathers say, there are two kinds of humility: first, *holding oneself below all*, *and* secondly, *ascribing
one's achievements to God.*[8] The first is humility's beginning,
the second its end. Those who seek humility should bear in
mind and consider these three things: that they are the worst
of sinners; that they are the most despicable of creatures, since
their state is unnatural; and that they are so much more pitiable
than the demons, since they are the slaves of the demons. You

ought to say to yourself: How could I know with any accuracy how many or what sort of sins others have committed? Because of our ignorance, my soul, we are beneath everyone, like *earth and ashes* [Gen. 19:27] to be trodden underfoot. How can you not account yourself more shameful than all creatures that live according to nature as they were made, when I through boundless offences have sunk down to an unnatural state? Truly, wild beasts and cattle are purer than me, sinner that I am! Therefore, I am lower than all, dragged down to Hades and lying there even before my death. Who is not fully aware that the one who sins is worse than the demons because he is their slave in thrall to them, and even in this present life shares with them in the darkness of imprisonment? Truly, the one ruled by demons is worse than them, and, therefore, wretch that I am, I will inherit with them the abyss! If before death you are dwelling in the ground, in Hades and the abyss, how can you deceive yourself, by calling yourself righteous? Have you not made yourself a sinner, profane, even a demon by your wicked works? Alas, for your self-deception and delusion, you superstitious, you impure dog, who for these reasons are consigned to fire and darkness!

116. Wisdom moved by the Spirit is, according to theologians, the power of intelligible, pure and angelic prayer, the sign of which is that, while praying, the mind appears completely formless and does not see itself or anything else in gross materiality, while that light frequently causes the senses to withdraw inward. For the mind then becomes immaterial and radiant with light, as it is indescribably united with God into a single spirit.

117. We are drawn and guided to God-given humility by seven different qualities that give rise to and complement the others: silence, humble-mindedness, humble speech, humble bearing, self-blame, contrition and setting oneself last. Silence in knowledge gives birth to humble-mindedness, and from this are born the three ways of humiliation: speaking humble words, bearing oneself humbly and unassumingly, and always blaming oneself. These three in turn give birth to the contrition that comes from God's permitting temptation, which some call

providential discipline and *humiliation thanks to the demons*.[9]
Contrition, in its turn, quite naturally and in fact sets the soul
below all and the last of all since it is subservient to all. These
last two modes lead to perfect and God-given humility, which
is called a '*a certain capacity, perfection* in *all* virtues'[10] – and
this humility ascribes all accomplishments to God. So then,
first of all is silence, from which humble-mindedness is born.
This gives birth to the three modes of humiliation. They give
birth to the single mode of contrition. From contrition is born
the seventh mode, the primal form of humility – regarding
oneself as lower than all – which is also called 'providential
humility'. Providential humility bears in turn the God-given,
perfect, unaffected and true humility. The first form of humility comes about thus: unless a person has been abandoned,
vanquished, enslaved, and subject to every passion, thought
and spirit; and, having been so conquered, discovers no help
from his own works, from God or anything else at all, even the
slightest thing; and so he becomes desperate and is humiliated
in everything – unless all of that happens he cannot be contrite
and hold himself lower than all. He simply cannot regard himself as the last, the servant of all, worse than the demons since
he is tyrannized and conquered by them. This is the 'providential humility' of divine Providence, through which is granted
the second humility, lofty and divine. The second humility is
divine power activating and making all things. Through this a
person sees himself always as a tool of humility for the accomplishment of God's *wonders* [Ps. 95:3].

118. In our generation when the passions' tyranny rules in us
thanks to the multitude of temptations, it is impossible to find:
substantial spiritual contemplation of light, an intellect free of
imagination and fluctuation, true activity of prayer that ever
flows from the centre of our heart, resurrection and elevation
of soul, divine astonishment and departure from everything
here, complete ecstasy of a mind out of its sense in the Spirit,
an intellect's rapture from its own faculties, or a soul's angelic
motion inspired by God, driving it to the steep and infinite
ascent. For the intellect – especially among the light-minded –
generally fantasizes about these things before their time, and

ends up losing what little bit of that divinely given disposition that it had and becoming completely necrotized. We must, therefore, with all discernment, neither seek things before their time, nor, when we have them, cast them off and fantasize about others. The intellect naturally and quite easily imagines the aforementioned activities and conjures up what it has not attained. There is no small fear that someone who has become a cultivator of fantasies rather than stillness will be deprived of all they have been given and maybe even be so deceived as to lose their wits.

119. Not only is faith a gift of grace, but so is prayer made active. For prayer made active by the Spirit through love reveals true faith, which contains visibly the life of Jesus. Conversely, whoever has not seen prayer made active in themselves possesses only a dead, inanimate faith. Of course, someone would not really be called faithful who believes in mere word alone and not with a faith made active in God's commandments or the Spirit. We must, therefore, either reveal faith visibly by our progress in deeds, or possess a faith made active with deeds and shining with light. As the Apostle says, '*Show me your faith from your deeds and I will show you my deeds* from my faith' [James 2:18]. Here the Apostle shows that the faith that comes from grace is revealed by doing the commandments, just as the commandments are accomplished and shine *by grace through faith* [Eph. 2:8]. For faith is the root of the commandments, or, rather, the spring that waters and nurtures them. Though faith is by nature undivided, it is divided into two aspects: confession and grace.

120. The short ladder for those living in obedience – which is at once both small and great – has five rungs leading towards perfection. First there is renunciation; secondly, submission; thirdly, obedience; fourthly, humility; and fifthly, love – which is God [1 John 4:8]. Renunciation leads one fallen out of Hades and cuts the bonds of slavery to matter. Submission discovers Christ and serves him, as he himself said, *My servant follows me, and where I am, there my servant will be* [John 12:26]. Where is Christ? Sitting *at the right hand of the Father* [Rom. 8:34]. Therefore, the servant must be wherever his master is, his foot set ready to

climb upwards; indeed, even before making a start on ascending in his own way, he has already been raised up and is ascending with Christ. Obedience, put into action by keeping God's commandments, puts the ladder together from the different virtues, and puts them in the soul as rungs by which to ascend [Ps. 83:6]. Thence humility, which lifts up, receives the soul and bears him up to Heaven, delivering him to love, the queen of the virtues. It sets him before Christ as an offering. Thus, by this brief ladder one who is truly obedient ascends easily to Heaven.

121. There is no shorter way to the Kingdom on high than this little ladder of virtues which effaces the five passions opposed to obedience: namely, disobedience, contradiction, self-gratification, self-justification and deadly self-conceit. These are the parts and members of the rebellious demon that gulps down those who fake obedience and hurls them to *the Dragon* of *the Abyss* [Rev. 20:2–3]. Disobedience is the mouth of Hades, contradiction its tongue, *like a sharp sword* [Ps. 56:5]. Self-pleasing sharpens its fangs; self-justification is its breastplate; self-conceit that casts down to Hades, the vent of its all-consuming stomach. Whoever conquers the first of these through obedience has cut off the rest at a stroke and by this single rung leaps swiftly to Heaven. It is truly a marvel, more than ineffable, that our Lord who loves us humans has made it so we can ascend instantly to Heaven through a single virtue – or, rather, command – just as through a single transgression we have tumbled down into Hades and remain there.

122. The human being is another, second, world, called 'new'. As the divine Apostle says, *If someone is in Christ they are a new creation* [2 Cor. 5:17]. For through virtue a human becomes and is described as heaven, earth and everything that makes up the world. *Every principle* [logos] *and every mystery exists for* this new human being, to quote the Theologian.[11] For, as the Apostle says, *Our battle is not against flesh and blood, but against the rulers and authorities of the darkness of this present age, against the spiritual powers of wickedness in heavenly places of the ruler of the air* [Eph. 6:12, 2:2]. It is, therefore, fitting that those who war against us in secret do so in another great world of nature, that of the powers of

our souls. Three such *rulers* stand arrayed against the three powers of our soul, and march out against each of them, and it is precisely where we have made progress and accomplished something that they launch their attack.

First, the dragon, the *ruler of the abyss* [Rev. 20:2], whose strength lies in the loins and belly, where desire resides, challenges and threatens those who are attentive in heart. Through the pleasure-loving giant of forgetfulness, he hurls against them a burning array of *flaming darts* [Eph. 6:16]. For him, desire is like another sea and abyss, into which he plunges, coiling his way through it, stirring it up and making it foam and *boil* [Job 41:23]. Thus, he inflames it with sexual longing, so that it overflows with torrents of pleasure which cannot be slaked for it is insatiable.

Second, *the ruler of this world* [John 12:31] takes a stand against those engaged in practical virtue, as he makes war against the soul's irascible part. With the help of his giant of indolence, he fashions all manner of tricks and devices for his spiritual warfare from the passions, as though entering, as it were, into another world, a theatre, and arena. There he wrestles with those who bravely resist him; he is sometimes victorious and sometimes worsted, and so shames us or gains for us crowns in the sight of the angels. He forever arrays his battle line against us and fights us continually.

Third, the *ruler of the air* [Eph. 2:2] assaults those who exercise their mind in contemplation. Together with the aerial spirits of cunning wickedness, he presents illusions as he approaches the rational and intellectual part of the soul. With his giant of ignorance he troubles and clouds the elevated mind, as if it were an intellectual heaven, filling it with the fantastic and misty apparitions of spirits and deceptive transmutations of lightning and thunder, squalls and thick clouds. With such fantasies he induces the intellect to cowardice.

Each ruler opposes one of our soul's three parts and attacks it with its giant. Wherever that ruler makes war, there is our contest.

123. Though they were once intellects, these rulers fell from their immateriality and subtlety and took on a certain material thickness. Each becomes corporeal in accordance with the order or activity with which it is endowed when active. Since, like humans, these lost angelic pleasure and were deprived of divine luxury, they have had to revel in dust, just like us, and they have become in some sense material by their disposition towards material passions. Do not be surprised, at least, that our soul, which had been created rational and intellectual *according to the image of God* [Gen. 1:26], has become bestial, insensate, almost mindless from its indulgence in material things, all because it ignored God. For habit generally refashions nature and alters a being's natural activity in accordance with its free choice. Some spirits, then, are turgid, weighty, unruly, irascible and vengeful. They are like carnivorous beasts gaping at material pleasure and luxury. Like bloodthirsty dogs they show their affection in gobbling rot with those they possess. They have fat, material flesh as both home and meal. Others are intemperate and watery, waiting in the stagnant pool of desire like leeches, frogs and serpents, sometimes changed into fish, as they slither through the briny pleasure of intemperance, which they have for enjoyment. Like fish with a kind of oily and tender nature, they swim in the sea of drunkenness. Delighting in the fluidity of irrational pleasures, they forever rouse waves, swells, and squalls of thoughts and pollutions in the soul. Other spirits are light and subtle. Being aerial spirits, they shake the soul's contemplative faculty, presenting it with violent winds and fantasies. Sometimes these spirits are *transformed* into birds and sometimes *into angels* [2 Cor. 11:14], and so deceive the soul. They conjure up memories of familiar things, altering and deforming every spiritual contemplation in those labouring but who have not reached purification and the *discernment of spirits* [1 Cor. 12:10]. For there is no spiritual thing into which they do not change their appearance in our imagination. For they arm themselves against our condition and the measure of our progress, and they establish themselves, bringing delusion instead of truth and fantasy instead of contemplation. Scripture testifies about these spirits, when it speaks of *beasts of the field, birds of heaven, and creeping things of the earth* [Hos. 2:14], revealing the distinctions between the spirits of wickedness.

124. The uprising of the passions and the war of the flesh against the soul come upon us in five ways: first, when the flesh abuses beings; secondly, when it tries to do unnatural things as though they were natural; thirdly, when it is armed against the soul by the demons because it has become such good friends with them; fourthly, when it is unruly on its own because it has been shaped by passions. Finally, warfare can come from the envy of demons permitted to oppose us for the sake of humility when they have failed in the first four ways.

125. There are, in fact, three causes of warfare, but they can operate in us from or through anything at all: they are habit, abuse of beings and, with God's providential permission, the demons' envious attack. However, the flesh's uprising or *desiring contrary to the* soul *and the* soul *contrary to the flesh* [Gal. 5:17], which is to say, the flesh's passions contrary to the soul and the soul's valorous acts contrary to the flesh, share the same mode of disposition and activity. Sometimes, though, our enemy himself is emboldened to fight us without cause or reason, since he is shameless. Do not allow this blood-sucking leech, my friend, to drain your veins dry! Do not give ground to the snake and dragon, and *you will* easily *trample* the insolence of *the lion and dragon* [Ps. 90:13]. *Groan* until you *take off* the flesh and *put on your heavenly dwelling* [2 Cor. 5:2, 4] and the likeness *according to the image* of Jesus Christ who made you [Gen. 1:26].

126. Those who are really just flesh, who welcome self-love, are ever enslaved to pleasure and vainglory. Envy takes root in them. Wasting away with malignity and regarding their neighbour's success with resentment, they falsely accuse good things of being the wicked offspring of delusion. They neither accept nor believe in the things of the Spirit, while by their feeble faith they are unable to behold or to recognize God. Probably such people as these will, in keeping with their own blindness and faithlessness, hear *I do not know you* [Matt. 25:12]. The one who asks must have faith, when hearing an answer they must believe what they have not seen, must learn to understand what they believe, must teach what they have understood, and thus generously multiply the talent in those who receive it with faith

[Matt. 25:14–30]. If they disbelieve what they have not seen, disregard what they have not known, and teach what they have not learned to understand, they will regard with malice those who teach things from practical experience. Such a one will be rebuked and his whole portion will be with those who possess only *the gall of bitterness* [Acts 8:23].

127. According to people truly wise in speech a teacher is someone who comprehends things through his general knowledge, dividing and joining them like parts of a single body, and demonstrating their shared significance in accordance with their difference and identity. Alternatively, a teacher is someone said to be capable of demonstrating the truth of things. Or, again, a teacher is in fact a spiritual man who, in a comprehensive speech, distinguishes and unites the five universal and primary properties divided among all beings, but which the incarnate Word united. Such a teacher is able to enlighten others, not thanks merely to the demonstrative account itself, but thanks to the contemplations of beings shown him by the Spirit.

A true philosopher is someone who through beings perceives their cause or knows beings from their cause. He comes to unity beyond comprehension and faith beyond mediation, and so not only learns about but experiences divine things. Or again, a philosopher is, properly speaking, an intellect well versed through experience in practical and theoretical virtue. The perfect philosophical intellect has perfected moral, natural and theological philosophy, the love of wisdom, or, rather, love of God. This intellect has been taught by God: in moral philosophy, what to do; in natural philosophy, to behold the principles [or *logoi*] of things; in theological philosophy, contemplation and exactness in dogmas.

Or again, a divine teacher of divine matters is one who distinguishes what truly is from what partakes of being and non-being, distinguishing the principles [or *logoi*] of the former from those of the latter, seeing them with inspired eyes. He distinguishes the intelligible and invisible from the perceptible and visible, and the sensible and visible world from the invisible world that cannot be perceived, for the visible is an image of the invisible, and the invisible the archetype of the visible. It says that *impressions are emitted from things unimpressible, and shapes from things shapeless,*[12] so that the shapeless and unimpressible is revealed spiritually through an impression or shape, and vice versa. This divine teacher easily sees each in the other and makes this clear by *the word of truth* [2 Tim. 2:15]. He does not weave the knowledge that illuminates like the sunshine of truth with analogies and allegories, but, rather, articulates and demonstrates with utmost clarity the words of the truth of both type and archetype, by his knowledge and spiritual power.

A divine philosopher, on the other hand, is one who has been directly united with God through ascetic struggle and contemplation, and has become and is called a friend of God, since he has befriended and loved the first, creative and true wisdom more than any other affection, wisdom or knowledge.

He is only a philologist [one who loves words] and not properly a philosopher – even though, as the great Gregory points out, vainglory has unwittingly usurped the name of philosophy[13] – that is, someone who loves and studies the wisdom of God, reflected in creation down to its final echo, not studying this philosophy ostentatiously for the sake of praise or human glory, lest he be a lover of matter and not a philosopher of God's natural wisdom.

A s*cribe who has been educated in the Kingdom* of God is one who studies contemplation of God through practice and persists in stillness, who *brings forth from his heart's treasure new things and old* [Matt. 13:52]. *New and old* refer to Gospel and prophecy, or the New and Old Testaments, respectively, or to doctrinal and practical matters, or even legal and apostolic ones. For these are mysteries *new and old*, which the scribe, being someone of practical virtue, *brings forth*, having been educated in a way of life pleasing to God. The scribe is everyone engaged in spiritual struggle who still occupies himself bodily in virtuous practices. A divine teacher is one who through natural contemplation stands amid the knowledge and principles of beings, and demonstrates everything in spirit by the discriminating power of the mind. A true philosopher is one who with full awareness and immediately possesses within himself supernatural union with God.

128. Those who without the Spirit write and speak out of a desire to edify the Church are *natural humans who do not possess the Spirit*, as the divine Apostle says somewhere [Jude 19]. Such people are condemned by the curse saying, '*Woe to them that believe themselves wise and are learned in their own sight!* [Isa. 5:21]. For they speak on their own, and it is not *the Spirit of God that speaks in* them' [Matt. 10:20], as the Lord says. People who speak their own thoughts before being purified have been deceived by the spirit of self-conceit. Proverbs says of this, *I saw a man who considered himself wise. But a fool has more hope than he* [Prov. 26:12]. And Wisdom admonishes us, *Do not be wise in your own opinion* [Rom. 12:16]. The divine Apostle himself, full of the Spirit, agrees, saying, *We are not sufficient in ourselves; our sufficiency is from God* [2 Cor. 3:5]. And . . . *rather, we speak in Christ as being from God and before God* [2 Cor. 2:17]. The words of such men are shapeless and shadowy, for they speak without drawing from the living fount of the Spirit. Rather, they speak from the stagnant puddle of their own heart, where leeches, serpents and frogs of desire, delusion and intemperance are nurtured. The water of their knowledge is stinking, muddy and tepid. Those who drink of it are made thoroughly sick, and moved to nausea and vomiting,

129. *We are the body of Christ*, says the divine Apostle, *and individually members of it* [1 Cor. 12:27]. Again, *You are one body, one spirit, just as you have been called* [Eph. 4:4]. For just as *a body without spirit is dead* [James 2:26] and senseless, so too one who has been mortified in passions through negligence of the commandments after his baptism becomes inert and unenlightened by the Holy Spirit and Christ's grace. Though possessing the Spirit through faith and rebirth, they are inactive and unmoving through the deadness of the soul. Though the soul is one and the members of the body many, the soul rules them all, and vivifies and moves those receptive of life. If some bodily members have been so cooled by some illness as to be dead and immobilized, the soul still sustains them in itself, even though they are lifeless and insensate. So also the whole Spirit of Christ is present without mixture in all the members of Christ, activating and vivifying all those capable of receiving life, but also embracing as his own those too weak to partake in his love for humankind. Therefore, every believer partakes through faith in the Spirit's adoption, but through carelessness and faithlessness becomes inert and unilluminated, deprived of the light and life of Jesus. Every believer, then, is a member of Christ who possesses Christ's Spirit, but can become inactive, immobile and unreceptive to participation in grace.

130. We speak of eight general forms of contemplation. The first is contemplation of the uncreated God, without form or beginning, the cause of all, the one triadic Godhead that transcends being. The second, contemplation of the order and reality of the intelligible powers. The third, contemplation of the constitution of beings; fourth, contemplation of the economy of the descent of the Word to be with us; fifth, contemplation of the universal resurrection; sixth, contemplation of the second, dread coming of Christ; seventh, contemplation of eternal punishment; and eighth, contemplation of the Kingdom of Heaven. Four concern things that have already happened, and four concern things future and as yet invisible. The latter are beheld from a distance, discovered by people who have, through grace, obtained great intellectual purity. Let anyone who aims without light at any of these know that he is envisaging mere fantasy and not contemplation, for he fantasizes and is deluded by the spirit of fantasy.

131. See now, we must say what we can about delusion too, since for many it is hard to recognize and almost uncatchable, thanks to its endlessly inventive ambushes. Though it has its beginning and cause in pride alone, it is said that delusion appears in two modes – or, rather, it attacks and latches on in two ways: in imagination and in action. The first is generally the cause of the second and the second of a third, which deranges the mind. Self-conceit is the origin of fantastic contemplation, i.e. causing the Deity to be pictured in some shape, from which follows the delusion of deceptive fantasies, through which blasphemy is begotten. Alongside these offspring, delusion in fantasy gives birth to cowardice at strange apparitions, both waking and sleeping. This is called trembling and agitation of soul. Delusion follows pride, blasphemy follows delusion,

cowardice blasphemy, and trembling cowardice. Finally, the derangement of one's natural wits follows trembling. Such is the first mode – delusion in imagination.

The second mode, delusion in action, has its beginning in the attachment to pleasure that is born from apparently natural desire. For from pleasure is born an unspeakably impure intemperance, which thoroughly heats one's whole nature, muddies the soul's guiding element by intercourse with mental images, and drives the intellect to derangement. By inebriating the soul with its feverish activity, this delusion renders it utterly deranged, and causes it to utter false prophecies, raving of visions and words of supposedly holy people, as though revealed through it, but really just drunk in the torpor of passion. Finally, it perverts his character into something demonic. People in the world, living in delusive deceit, call such people 'butterflies' or 'poor little souls', when they are seen sitting or flitting about saints' shrines, apparently inspired, roused and afflicted by them, and speaking for the saints. We should really call these 'butterflies' demoniacs, dupes of deceit and slaves of delusion, and absolutely not prophets and foretellers of things present and things to come. The demon of intemperance, having darkened their intellect with the smoke of pleasure, drags them out of their wits, showing them fantasies of saints and revealing to them discourses and spectacles. Sometimes the demons themselves even appear to reduce these dupes to terror. For, having bound them with the *yoke* of *Beliar* [2 Cor. 6:14–15], the demon of intemperance weighs them down and impels them to practise their delusions, to keep them as prisoners and slaves until death, when he will escort them to punishment.

132. It is important to know that delusion has three general causes, through which it attacks people: it comes from pride, from the demons' envy, and from God's withdrawing from us in order to test and train us.[14] In turn, the cause of pride is superficiality; of envy, progress; and of withdrawal, a sinful lifestyle. Delusion coming solely from demonic envy or self-conceit is quickly healed, especially when we humble ourselves. However, in order to correct our sinful way of life God often allows us to be handed over to Satan on account of sin to persist until death in order to grant us forgiveness. Sometimes God allows even the innocent to be tormented for the sake of their salvation. It is important to know that the demon of self-conceit prefers to dwell in those who do not take care to be watchful in their heart.

133. All the faithful are truly anointed at their renewal [i.e., baptism] as priests and kings, as the ancients were anointed figuratively. For they were types and figures of what we experience in truth. This is the case with all of us, not only with some of us. For our kingdom and priesthood are not of the same mode and form as theirs, for theirs were symbolic. Nor do nature or grace and our calling admit a difference among us as regards this anointing so as to make a distinction among those anointed; but we have one and the same calling and faith and ritual form. It reveals and manifests, according to the word of truth, that the one anointed is pure, dispassionate and wholly consecrated to God, now and in the age to come.

134. One who speaks wisdom with his mouth and meditates on understanding in his heart [Ps. 48:4] clearly discerns in created beings God the Word, the personal wisdom of the God and Father. Since he possesses the inner principles of their archetypes stamped on created beings, through the living and active Word he *speaks with his mouth wisdom* from wisdom. Being illuminated in his *heart* by the power of a transformative *understanding* on which he *meditates* in the Spirit, he can by that understanding bring illumination to those who listen with faith.

135. The great opponent of truth is delusion that today draws humans to destruction. (Through it the ignorance of darkness reigns in the souls of the lazy, alienating them from God. They hardly realize that the God who renews and enlightens us even exists, or else believe and accept this only in thought, and not in their deeds; or else they imagine that God revealed himself only in former times, and not to us. Or else they think that the Scriptural testimonies about God apply only to those who wrote them, and not to themselves. Thus, denying true religion that comes through knowledge, *they blaspheme* against *right belief* about God [Jude 8]; they read the Scriptures in a bodily way, dare I say Judaically, and deny an awakening now through the soul's resurrection, and choose to dwell in the tombs of ignorance.) Today's destructive delusion consists in these three passions: faithlessness, wickedness and laziness, which mutually support and generate each other. For faithlessness is a teacher of wickedness, and wickedness is a sibling of laziness, the symbol of which is sluggishness. Conversely, laziness is the birth-giver of wickedness, as our Lord says: *You wicked and sluggish servant!* [Matt. 25:26]. And wickedness is the mother of faithlessness. For every wicked man is also faithless, since one who does not believe does not fear God either. From faithlessness, then, laziness is born, the mother of contemptuousness, through which everything good is left undone and everything evil practised.

136. Perfect orthodoxy in matters of doctrine consists of true belief about God and unerring knowledge of all that is. Therefore, one ought to glorify God thus: Glory to you, Christ our God, glory to you, because you, God the Word beyond being, have become incarnate for us. Through this great mystery of your economy, Our Saviour, glory to you!

137. According to the great Maximos, there are three ways of composing written words that are beyond reproach and unobjectionable: to remind oneself, to help others or as an act of obedience.[15] Most writings have been composed out of obedience, for those who humbly requested the account. But one who writes about virtues simply to please an audience, or for glory and fame, has *already received* his *reward*, as it says [Matt. 6:5]. He will receive no benefit now nor any reward in the age to come. Rather, he will be condemned for courting popularity and deceitfully *peddling the word of God for profit* [2 Cor. 2:17].

St Gregory Palamas, *To Xenia*

ST GREGORY PALAMAS
(*c*.1296–1357/9)

St Gregory was born to an aristocratic family, and educated appropriately to his status; at his first chance he ran off to join a monastery on Mt Athos. Despite Turkish incursions and summonses to councils, he would live there on and off from 1314 until 1350, when he could finally enter nearby Thessaloniki to take up the position of Metropolitan Archbishop, to which he had been appointed in 1347. His early years on Athos were formative in the practices of continuous and interior prayer in silence: in short, hesychasm as it had come to be understood among Athonite monks. In 1334, however, discussions of reunification between the Roman and the Byzantine Churches led a Greek monk in Italy, Barlaam the Calabrian (*c*.1290–1348), to question what kind of knowledge humans could have of God. The premiss shared by Christians on both sides was that the Deity is unknowable in its essence – God is unbounded by any category of thought and, therefore, impossible to know *as God is*. This led Barlaam, who had read some of the works of what would become the *Philokalia* (Nikiphoros the Monk, Ps-Symeon and Gregory of Sinai), to decry hesychast practice of prayer and to deny monks' claims that through this prayer they 'see' God in a vision of light. Gregory began to write in defence of Athonite practices and to develop the theological distinctions that could explain and underpin both interior prayer and the vision of light, which he would argue is at once available to the senses and uncreated, an eternal activity (*energeia*) of the Deity. This would lead Gregory ultimately to the distinction for which he is most famous: that God is unknowable in essence (*ousia*) but knowable in activity (*energeia*). The complexity comes in making sense of the relationship between *ousia* and *energeia*, whether the latter really amounts to an experience of God as such, or whether it is some subordinate category, and Palamas devoted thousands of pages to proving that experience of God's *energeia* is experience of God, full stop.

Over the next decade Gregory refined this position through polemics, first with Barlaam and later with Gregory Akindynos and Nikephoras Gregoras. Councils were held in 1341, 1344, 1347 and 1351 to determine the orthodoxy of the hesychast position as encapsulated by Palamas. He was vindicated in 1341 against Barlaam, in 1347 against Akindynos and in 1351 against Gregoras and Akindynos both. The 1344 council had sided with Akindynos and condemned Palamas. This same period of theological foment was subject to civil war between rival claimants to the imperial throne, and the bishops present at the synods had to take political as well as theological sides. One reason Palamas was condemned and then vindicated was that fortunes had changed in the civil war. But, from 1351, despite Gregoras's continued opposition, and the lasting war of words between the men, Palamas's position was secured as Orthodox dogma, and hesychast prayer quickly became the dominant form of Byzantine spirituality, being taken up with gusto in Slavic lands as well as other monasteries in what remained of the Empire. Gregory himself was Metropolitan Bishop of Thessaloniki from 1351 to his death on 14 November 1357 (or possibly 1359), with a brief period of imprisonment at the hands of the Ottoman Turks in 1354–5.

Gregory is the summit of the *Philokalia*, in whose writings the practice of continuous interior prayer is both presented and given a robust theological underpinning. He writes in the tradition of others collected here and is the lens through which Nikodemos and Makarios read them. The text presented here, *To Xenia* (1345/6), concerns the pitfalls and practices of monastic life as one moves through practical virtue towards interior prayer and the more perfect exercise of the intellect. It is very much in line with texts included here from Gregory of Sinai, Diadochos, Evagrios and others. We do not know anything about the nun Xenia save what is written here – older and in charge of daughters of 'the great king', perhaps including Maria Palaiologina, daughter of Andronikos III Palaiologos (r. 1328–41).

Sources

Text: *Ascetic Oration* 3, in P. K. Chrestou (ed.), 'Ἀσκητικὰ συγγράμματα', in Γρηγορίου τοῦ Παλαμᾶ συγγράμματα, vol. 5 (Thessaloniki: Ekdoseis Oikos Kyromanos, 1992), 193–230.

Alternative text: *PHILOKALIA* (1782): 929–49; *Philokalia* (1893/1982): vol. 4, 91–115

To *the most pious among nuns,*
Xenia: Concerning passions, virtue
and what is born of intellectual study

1. Conversation, not only with the people in general, but even with those who share their chosen life, is truly disagreeable to those zealous in the monastic life. For it interrupts the continuity of their most well-pleasing conversation with God and splits the unified concentration of their intellect, which constitutes true and inward monasticism, into duality and sometimes fragments it totally. Therefore, one of the fathers, when he was asked why he fled human company, responded, 'I cannot be with God when among people.'[1] Another, describing such things from his own experience, refused not only conversation, but even the sight of other people, because it can weaken the stable quietude of those hesychasts who practise intellectual stillness.

2. On a careful examination you will find that the memory of someone visiting or the expectation of a sojourn and its likely meetings do not allow the soul's rational intellect to remain undisturbed. Oh, but someone who commits words to paper wraps his intellect in sharper anxiety. Should he be one of those who have progressed and attained the love of God in the strength of his soul, then though this love continues active while he writes, it is less focused and undiluted. But if, like me, he is one of those who still falls into numerous psychic illnesses and affections, who need to cry out to God continuously, 'Heal me, for I have sinned against you!' – well, it makes no sense to abandon his supplication before being healed and turn willingly to anything else. You see, he converses both with his correspondents and with people not present, and he hands over his private conversation to an unknown audience – including

such company as he would rather avoid – for written words generally endure long after the death of their author.

3. For this reason, many of the hesychastic fathers have refused to write a single thing, though they could have offered wonderfully beneficial words. I, having totally abandoned their exactitude, have developed a habit of writing – but only when need compels me. Some readers, who have at some point looked upon our writings with envious eyes to discern occasions for their malice, have made me even more hesitant. These people are, as the great Dionysios says, *passionately attached to meaningless letters and words, to unfamiliar syllables and phrases, which their soul can make no sense of.*[2] Really, it is an irrational, perverse custom, no use at all to those who want to understand divine matters, to focus on isolated passages rather than the purpose of what is said.

4. I know well the reproaches I have endured at their hands: not that I have failed to write in accordance with the fathers, for this accord has, by Christ's grace, been preserved in my writings. No, they allege that I have written about matters I am unworthy of, like some Uzzah I imagine, attempting with my own staggering reason to right the slipping cart of truth [1 Paral. 13:11]. The only difference is that we were visited not by God's anger, but, rather, his moderate discipline, and so our attackers were not permitted to prevail over us. Yet this was probably owing to my unworthiness, for I was neither worthy nor capable, it seems, of suffering for the sake of truth and so sharing with joy in the suffering of the saints.

5. What, then? Was not our father Chrysostom, who even while clothed in the body was joined to *the Church of the first-born in heaven* [Heb. 12:23], who wrote about piety so surely, wisely and beautifully – was not such a great man cut off from the Church and banished on charges of writing and believing Origenist heresies?[3] And Peter, too, the leader of the supreme chorus of our Lord's disciples, says that there are things *hard to understand*, in the letters of the great Paul, *which ignorant and unstable people perverted to their own destruction* [2 Pet. 3:16].

6. I, too, because of a little abuse from those who have raised

their hands against me – although they have been condemned by a synod – was considering giving up writing altogether. Except that now you, sacred elder, have persisted with imploring letters and instructions until you persuaded me to attempt once more some words of encouragement, though you hardly need it. For by the grace of Christ you have grown reverend in both age and understanding, and through years of practice, having divided your life appropriately between obedience and stillness, you have studied the law of sacred promises. Through both you have scraped smooth the parchment of your soul and prepared it to receive and retain the divine characters. Ah, but this is the way with a soul utterly captivated by yearning for spiritual teaching: it never gets its fill.

7. Therefore, Wisdom says of herself, *Those who feed on me will hunger still* [Sirach 24:21]. The Lord who implants this divine yearning in the soul says of Mary, who chose this good portion, that *it will not be taken from her* [Luke 10:42]. Maybe, though, you really want those encouraging words for the daughters of the emperor living under your tutelage, and especially for the nun Synesis. Since she is from your family, you yearn to marry her to the bestower of immortality, whom indeed you imitate. Just as for our sake he truly assumed our form, you have now assumed the persona of a novice who needs instruction. Well then, I am not rich in words generally, and especially in such as you ask, but, out of obedience to the commandment to *give to the one who asks* [Matt. 5:42], I will show my good purpose and pay the debt of Christlike love with what little I have.

8. Know, then, sacred elder – or, rather, let the young women who have chosen to live a godly life learn through you – that there is such a thing as death for our naturally deathless soul. When the beloved theologian says, 'There is *sin unto death* and *sin not unto death*' [1 John 5:16], he is referring to a 'death' of the soul. The great Paul, too, says, *Worldly grief brings about death* [2 Cor. 7:10], which absolutely means a death of soul. Again, he says, *Arise, O sleeper, and Christ, who has risen from the dead, will shine upon you!* [Eph. 5:14]. From what group of 'the dead' is he called to rise? Obviously, from those

who have been killed by fleshly desires that war against the soul. Thus, the Lord called those who live in this empty world 'dead'. For he did not allow his disciple who asked to bury his own father, commanding him instead *to follow*, having *left the dead to bury their own dead* [Matt. 8:22]. In this passage the Lord calls the living 'dead', since they are utterly dead in soul.

9. Just as its separation from the soul is death for the body, so separation from God is the death of the soul, and this is properly death, the death of the soul. God made this clear through his commandment in Paradise, when he said to Adam, *On the day in which you eat* of the forbidden tree, *you will die by death* [Gen. 2:17]. For at that moment, even though his bodily existence would persist for another nine hundred and thirty years, Adam's soul was killed because it was separated from God by his transgression.

10. Thanks to Adam's transgression, death latched on to the soul, and thus not only debased it and cursed the human being, but also made the body itself liable to all kinds of suffering and disease, and then, having made the body a corruptible thing, in the end handed it over to death too. For then, after the dying of his inner self because of his transgression, earthy Adam heard that *The land is cursed in your works! It will grow thorns and thistles for you, and you will eat your bread by the sweat of your brow until you return to the earth from which you were taken. For you are earth and you will return to the earth* [Gen. 3:17–19].

11. Even if the bodies of transgressors and sinners will rise as part of the future rebirth in the resurrection of the righteous, it is only to condemn them to *the second death* [Rev. 20:14]: that is, to eternal punishment, the sleepless worm, *the gnashing of teeth* [Matt. 8:12, etc.]; *outer, palpable darkness* [Matt. 8:12]; the shadowy and unquenchable *Gehenna of fire* [Matt. 5:22, etc.], in accordance with the prophet who said, *Transgressors and sinners will burn together and there will be none to quench them* [Isa. 1:31]. All of this constitutes the *second death*, as John teaches us in his Apocalypse [Rev. 20:14]. Hear, then, the great Paul, who says, *If you live according to the flesh, you will die. But if by the spirit you kill the body's habits,*

you will live [Rom. 8:13]. Here he refers 'life' and 'death' to
the age to come: 'life' means enjoyment of the eternal kingdom,
while 'death' means eternal punishment.

12. Thus, the transgression of God's commandment became
the harbinger of all death, both of body in the present age and
of soul in that unending punishment. Properly, death means
the soul being unyoked from divine grace and hitched instead
to sin. Those who understand things know that this is the death
to be feared and fled. For those who think carefully, this death
is more frightening than punishment in Gehenna. Let us flee
this death with all our might! Let us cast off everything, let go
of everything, renounce every attachment, action and purpose
that diverts and distances us from God, which together constitute such a death! She who has feared this and mistrusted her
flesh will not fear the approach of bodily death, since she has
dwelling within her the true life that gains its inviolability by
that death. For, as the soul's death is properly death, the soul's
life is properly life.

13. The soul's life is union with God, just as the body's union
with the soul is its life. For, as the soul, torn from God by the
transgression of his command, was killed, so it is vivified again
when united to God through obedience to his commandment.
For this reason, our Lord says in the Gospels that *The words
that I speak are spirit and life* [John 6:63]. Peter, who learned
this by experience, said to Jesus that *You have the words of
eternal life* [John 6:68]. However, the *words of eternal life* pertain to those who obey, while for the disobedient that same
commandment of life becomes death. Thus, the apostles, being
the *fragrance of Christ*, were *a stink of death to death* to some,
but to others *the fragrance of life to life* [2 Cor. 2:15–16].

14. Again, though, this life does not belong to the soul alone,
but to the body as well. For it will render the body immortal
through the resurrection, delivering it not only from mortality
but also from the never-ending death of that future punishment, and the body, too, will receive eternal life in Christ:
without toil, sickness, sorrow [Isa. 35:10] and, truly, without
death. The soul's death (that is, transgression and sin) is followed by bodily death and with it our dissolution into earth

and our end in the clay; this is in turn followed by the soul's imprisonment in Hades. So too the soul's resurrection (which is its return to God through obedience to his commandments) is followed by the body's resurrection as it is reunited to the soul. Upon this resurrection follows true incorruption for those who will spend eternity with God, having become *spiritual* instead of *fleshly* [2 Cor. 2:14] and living *as the angels* of God *in heaven* [Matt. 22:30].

15. *We will be caught up*, it says, *in the clouds to meet the Lord in the air and so we will always be with the Lord* [1 Thess. 4:17]. The Son of God, having become human in his love for humankind, died in the flesh, and his soul was separated from his body but not from his divinity. Therefore, when his body was resurrected, he took it up into heaven in glory. So it is with those who live godly lives now: when separated from their body they are not separated from God, while in the resurrection they will take their body to God as they enter together *into indescribable joy* [1 Pet. 1:8] *where Jesus has entered as our forerunner* [Heb. 6:20] and enjoy together *the glory that will be revealed* in Christ [1 Pet 5:1]. For they will partake not only of resurrection, but of the Lord's ascension and all divine life. Not so those who have lived fleshly lives now and have been found to lack any communion with God at the hour of their death. For although all will be raised, each, it says, *will be raised in their own order* [1 Cor. 15:23]. So, those who here *kill the body's habits by the spirit will live* there with Christ in divine and truly eternal life [Rom. 8:13]. On the other hand – I hate even to say it! – those who, by following the flesh's desires and passions, have killed the spirit here will there be condemned with the creator and begetter of evil and handed over to inescapable, endless punishment. This is the second and final death.

16. Where did true death, which fashions and presages temporal and eternal death for both soul and body, have its beginning? Where else than in the land of life? For this reason – alas! – Adam was immediately condemned to exile from the paradise of God since he had taken on an existence which carries death and is, therefore, incompatible with the divine

paradise. Similarly, the true life that grants true and deathless life for both soul and body will have its beginning in this place of death. Let no one who refuses to seek eternal life in the soul here and now be deceived with vain hopes of somehow getting it there! Let them not hope to receive God's love for humankind then, because that is the time for retribution and vengeance, not compassion and philanthropy. That will be a time *that reveals* anger, *wrath* and *God's just judgement* [Rom. 2:5]; a time that manifests his mighty and outstretched hand casting the faithless into punishment [Ps. 135:12]. Woe to those who fall *into the hands of the living God* [Heb. 10:31]! Woe to those who, instead of learning now the power of God's wrath through fear and through their deeds having a foretaste of God's compassion, learn there the Lord's anger by direct experience. For this is the use of the present time: God has permitted us this life and even offered it to us precisely as a place of repentance. If it weren't like this, then someone would die as soon as they sinned, and what would be the point of that?

17. Despair, therefore, has no place among humans, even though the evil one insinuates it in various ways both in those who live indifferently and even in those engaged in ascetic struggle. For since our present life is a time of repentance, then the very fact of our continuing existence offers the promise of God's warm welcome to the sinner who wants to return. Autonomy always accompanies our present life, and it presupposes, as its material, the ways of life and death alike: anyone wishing to embrace one and flee the other will travel, so far as possible, whichever of the two ways chosen. Where, then, will despair find a place when everyone can always grasp eternal life whenever they choose?

18. Can you see the magnitude of God's love for humankind? To begin with, he does not render a just judgement against us faithless ones. Rather, being patient, he offers us time to return. During this time of forbearance, he *gives* us *authority*, should we choose it, to become his children [John 1:12]. Why speak of becoming his children, though? He actually gives us authority to be united with him and to be with him in spirit. Yet, during this same time of forbearance, if we do the opposite and love

death instead of true life, he does not rescind that authority – not just that, but he keeps recalling us and, as in the parable of the vineyard [Matt. 20:1–16], goes about from dawn until the very sunset of our existence seeking and turning us to the works of life. Following the parable, who is the one calling and hiring? It is *the Father of our Lord Jesus Christ, the God of all consolation* [2 Cor. 1:3]. What is the vine which God calls us to work? It is the Son of God, who says, *I am the vine* [John 15:5], and no one *can come to* Christ, as he says in the Gospels, *unless the Father draws them* [John 6:44]. Who are the vine branches? Us! Again, we hear him saying, *You are the branches; my Father is the vine-dresser* [John 15:5, 15:1].

19. The Father who *reconciles us to himself through* his Son, *not considering our failures*, calls us, not because we busy ourselves in inappropriate activities, but because we are *idle* [Matt. 20:3], even though idleness is sin and we *will give account for every idle word* [Matt. 12:36]. As I've said, though, God who overlooks each person's pre-existing sins [cf. Rom. 3:25], exhorts them again and again. What does he call those who respond? He calls them *workers* in his vineyard [Matt. 20:8]. The work means toiling away on vine branches – clearly referring to ourselves. Then – oh, the unfathomable greatness of God's love for humankind! – he rewards and pays those who labour over themselves! 'Come,' he says, 'receive the eternal life I have abundantly provided and, as though I owed it, I myself will pay the wage of your labour in travelling the way of life, and even just desiring it from me.'

20. Who does not owe her ransom to the one who ransoms us from death? Who will not confess her gratitude to the giver of life? Besides all this, God promises us a wage on deposit, an unutterable wage: *For I have come*, Christ says, *that they may have life and have it in abundance* [John 10:10]. What is the *abundance*? It is not just that of our being with him and living together, but that he will make us into his brothers and sisters and fellow heirs. This *abundance*, it seems, is the *wage* given to those who hasten to the life-giving vine and become its branches, who labour on their own behalf and cultivate it for their own sake. What have they to do? First, they prune off

everything superfluous that stops them producing fruit worthy of the divine storehouse. What is to be pruned? Wealth, luxury, vainglory, everything transient and temporal, every wicked and loathsome passion of soul and body, all the refuse of a wandering intellect, every sound, sight and harmful word that can be recalled in one's soul. For unless a great effort is made to root these things out and prune the offshoots of the heart, they will never produce *fruit for eternal life* [Rom. 6:22]. Those who live in marriage strive for this purity, but only with enormous difficulty.

21. For this reason, all who through renewal attain to our merciful God have looked to that life with a keener mental glance, and have become lovers of its good things avoid marriage, since *in the resurrection*, according to our Lord, *they neither marry nor are given in marriage, but are as the angels of God* [Matt. 22:30]. So, whoever wishes even now to be like the angels of God and the children of the resurrection is right to avoid sexual intercourse. Besides, the motivation to sin found its first foothold in us thanks to a wife. Marriage, then, must be rejected by those who wish never to offer any foothold to their opponent.

22. If our body is so obstinate and unresponsive to virtue, and we have to bear it about like an inborn enemy, why, then, do we trust it? How much do we exacerbate the difficulties of virtue by being bound to a wide variety of bodies? How will the woman who is bound by nature's chains to husband, children and all those blood relations find the freedom to which she is called? How will she who has allowed herself to be anxious over such people devote herself tranquilly to the Lord? How will she find peace who is bound to such crowds by marriage?

23. Therefore, the true virgin – who imitates the virgin born of a Virgin, the bridegroom of souls that have lived as they ought in virginity – flees not only sexual intercourse but also worldly company. She has renounced all family that she may, with Peter, confidently affirm to Christ that 'we have left everything and followed you' [Matt. 19:27]. According to Scripture, an earthly bride leaves her father and mother for the sake of her mortal bridegroom and is joined with him [Matt. 19:5]. Why,

then, should it be a novelty that a virgin do the same thing, and
leave her relations for the sake of the bridal chamber and bridegroom greater than this whole world? How, indeed, should she
whose *citizenship is in Heaven* [Phil. 3:20] have family on the
earth? How, then, should she, a child not of flesh but of spirit,
have father, mother or other blood relatives? How should she
who, because she has renounced fleshly life, forever flees her
own body as much as possible have any attachment whatsoever
to alien bodies? But, if 'likeness is affection', as they say,[4] and
like embraces like, then the virgin will become like what she
cherishes, and again fall sick with love of the world. But, says
Paul, who escorts us to the spiritual bridal chamber, *Affection*
towards the world is enmity towards God.[5] So then, she runs
the risk not only of being cut off from the bridegroom greater
than this world, but of falling into enmity with him. Now, do
not be surprised or confused if Scripture does not blame those
who, through marriage, concern themselves with the things
of the world rather than of the Lord, while forbidding those
who have professed their virginity to God even to touch people
in the world and barring them from enjoying any comfort –
although, of course, Paul does say clearly to those in marriage,
The time is short, and henceforth those who have wives ought
to be as those who do not, and those who use this world ought
to be as those who do not [1 Cor. 7:29, 31]. Anyway, for my
part, I consider marriage more irksome than the trials of virginity. For experience shows that simply fasting is easier than
restraint in the presence of food and drink. Indeed, one could
say quite rightly that if someone has not deliberately chosen
to be saved, we have nothing to say to her. But, if someone is
concerned with her own salvation, let her know that the life of
virginity is more efficacious and easier than marriage.

24. Now, let us leave all this behind. Instead, think back,
virgin bride of Christ, to that branch of the vine of life which I
discussed above. For the Lord says, *I am the vine, you are the*
branches, and my Father is the vine-dresser. He prunes every
branch bearing fruit in me, that it may bear much fruit [John
15:1-2, 5]. Consider this work of pruning as an example of
both the fruit of your virginity and the bridegroom's affection

for you, and let it spur you to rejoice and increase your ambition in obedience to him. Put differently, gold that has some bronze mixed in it is said to be adulterated, while melted bronze that has gold shavings mixed in it shines and glitters brighter than it would have by itself. So also, O virgin, it is glorious for non-virgins to long for your way of life, but dishonourable for you to desire theirs. That yearning returns you to the world for two reasons. First, because you, who should have died to the world, would be attached to those living in it and so would live with them. Second, you would come to value the same things they would wish for themselves and their families: wealth, splendour, glory and contentment in those things. Thus, you would eventually abandon your bridegroom's intention for you. For he clearly denounces all these pursuits in the Gospels, when he says, Woe to the wealthy! *Woe to those who laugh! Woe to those who are sated! Woe to you when all people say you do well!* [Luke 6:24–6].

25. Why does he denounce such people? Is it not because they are dead in soul? What kinship does the bride of life have with the dead? What companionship does she have with those travelling on a completely different path? For *broad and spacious* is the way along which those in the world are carried, and unless they restrain themselves and mix in some of your ways, they will fall utterly into *destruction* [Matt. 7:13]. You enter, however, through *the cramped and narrow gate and road to life* [Matt. 7:14]. No one who has taken on herself the swelling mass of earthly glory, the spreading dissolution of pleasure, or the weight of goods and property, can enter through the narrow gate and way.

26. However, when you hear that the worldly way of life is *broad*, do not regard it as being free of pain. No, it is most unhappy and fraught with calamity. For Christ calls it *broad and spacious* because there are many traversing it, each of them spattered with the detritus of ever-flowing matter. But your way is especially *narrow*, O virgin, since it cannot allow even two to walk abreast. Therefore, many of those who had previously been held by the world have, after being widowed, denied the world in their zeal for your heavenly way of life and chosen to

walk your path that they might share your crowns. Paul commands that such women be honoured, as they have persisted *in prayers and supplications* with hope in God [Rom. 15:30, 1 Tim. 5:5]. For even though some grief is characteristic of your way of life, it is conducive to consolation, formative of the Kingdom of Heaven, and effective for salvation, while both the delights and griefs of a worldly life are fatal. For *worldly grief*, it says, *causes death, but godly grief effects* steadfast *repentance unto salvation* [2 Cor. 7:10].

27. For this reason, it is the very opposite of worldly goods that our Lord blesses, saying, *Blessed are the poor in spirit, for theirs is the Kingdom of Heaven* [Matt. 5:3]. Why, when he says, *Blessed are the poor*, does he add, *in spirit*? So that, as he blesses and welcomes the poor, he may demonstrate the soul's humble modesty. Why, then, did he not say, 'Blessed are those who are poor with respect to spirit' (since in this way he could demonstrate the mind's measure), but, instead, *Blessed are the poor in spirit*? So that he might teach us that poverty in body is blessed and formative of the Kingdom of Heaven, certainly, but only when it is achieved for the sake of the soul's humility, is united with that humility and takes its beginning from it. For, having blessed the *poor in spirit* he marvellously showed the character, the root and beginning, as it were, of the poverty we see among the saints: clearly, their *spirit*. For this spirit, which is wrapped in the grace of the Gospel proclamation, causes *a spring* of poverty to well up from itself, which *waters the whole face of* our *earth* [Gen. 2:6], which is to say, our *outward self* [2 Cor. 4:16], and makes a paradise of virtues grow. Such poverty is blessed by God.

28. According to the prophet, *the Lord has* given *a brief account* upon the earth [Isa. 10:23] of the cause of the variety of voluntary poverty. When he had shown and blessed its cause, he included also concise teaching on its many effects. For someone can be poor, thrifty and self-controlled, by choice no less, just to get human glory. Such a person is not *poor in spirit* [Matt. 5:3]. For hypocrisy is born of such self-conceit, which is the very opposite of poverty in spirit. For someone, however, who possesses an afflicted, measured and humbled

spirit, it is impossible not to rejoice also in visible thrift and humility. For that person considers herself unworthy of glory, happiness, prosperity and all such things. And she who believes herself unworthy of these is the pauper blessed by God – she is truly poor and does not go after it with half-measures. Thus, the divine Luke said, *Blessed are the poor*, without needing to add 'in spirit' [Luke 6:20]. These are the ones who hear and follow, who are made like the Son of God, who says, *Learn from me, for I am meek and humble in heart, and you will find rest for your souls* [Matt. 11:29]. By the same token, *theirs is the Kingdom of Heaven* [Matt. 5:3], for *they are Christ's fellow heirs* [Rom. 8:17].

29. The soul has three parts and is distributed into three powers: the rational, the irascible and the desiring. It is sick in all three, and Christ heals in ascending order, reasonably beginning his therapy with desire. For desire becomes the material of emotion, and when these are disposed badly, both become material for our wandering mind. Contrariwise, our soul's irascible capacity could hardly be healthy unless our desire is first cured; nor the rational, unless both irascible and desiring are already healed.

30. Close inspection would reveal that the first evil born of the desiring part is love of wealth. For desires that help humans continue living are not blameworthy, and so these are naturally with us from earliest infancy, while avarice sprouts a little later in childhood. Its late arrival demonstrates that avarice is not natural, but instead begins in our free choice. The divine Paul rightly called it the *root of all evils* [1 Tim. 6:10], since it generally gives birth to miserliness, fraudulence, conniving, thievery and just about every form of grasping for advantage – which he termed a second *idolatry* [Col. 3:5]. Avarice even provides material subsistence to nearly every form of evil not directly born of it.

31. As many of these evils as are born of material desire are the passions of a soul lacking fervour in doing good. While passions arising from free choice are more easily expunged than those arising from nature, underlying disbelief in God's providence renders those which emerge from avarice very difficult

to expel. For those who disbelieve providence put their trust in possessions instead. On hearing the Lord say that *It is easier for a camel to pass through the eye of a needle than for a rich man to enter the Kingdom of Heaven* [Matt. 19:24], she waves away the heavenly and eternal Kingdom and yearns instead after earthly and transient wealth. Even when wealth is unattainable, its very desire causes catastrophic losses to those who long for it. As Paul says, *Those who yearn to be rich fall into temptations and the Devil's traps* [1 Tim. 6:9]. But even when it is available, and has been shown to be nothing, those who have not learned from experience will still thirst for it as though it were still out of reach. For this hateful love is not born of need – it is quite the other way round. Really, love of wealth comes from the same stupidity as that man showed who *pulled down* his *barns and built bigger ones* and was most justly called *fool* by Christ our common master [Luke 12:13–21].

32. How is she not a fool who, for the sake of what cannot help, casts off everything that is most beneficial? For no one's *life consists in the abundance of her possessions* [Luke 12:15]. She does not become a wise merchant who reduces her necessities so far as possible and adds them to the principal of truly fruitful and profitable trade or planting. And what a planting! Even before harvest-time arrives, the seed is multiplied a hundredfold, which demonstrates in advance, we might say, that the future profit and timely harvest are unutterable and unimaginable, inasmuch, paradoxically, as the seeds come from narrow little storehouses. We are left, then, with no good pretext for desiring wealth. They fear need who do not totally believe in Him who promises to *add all things to* those who *seek the Kingdom of God* [Matt. 6:33]. Indeed, while surrounded with every luxury, they harp on the excuse of need and so never reconsider their sick and destructive desire. Instead, always hoarding more, they lay up for themselves a useless burden. Worse, while yet living they close themselves up in a strange and novel tomb.

33. Corpses are simply buried in the earth, but a greedy person's intellect is buried alive in gold dust. This tomb stinks more than earthly ones to those whose senses are healthy, and all the

more as the dust is piled up. For the festering sore of those miserable buried men is overpowering, and stinks to heaven, to the
angels of God, and even to God himself. By this they become
loathsome and truly repugnant, *stinking because of their fool-
ishness*, as David put it [Ps. 37:6]. Voluntary poverty – that is
to say, poverty in spirit, which the Lord blessed – delivers us
humans from the reeking, deadly passion of greed.

34. It is impossible for the monastic suffering from this passion to be obedient. But if he persists in cherishing his greed,
he runs the risk of falling also into incurable bodily ills. Gehazi
and Judas, from the Old and New Testaments respectively,
are sufficient examples of this. For on Gehazi's body leprous
sores broke out, which indicated his unhealed soul [4 Kgds
5:27]. Judas, after hanging himself in the field *of blood* (Matt.
27:8], fell *headlong, burst open in the middle and spilled his
guts* (Acts 1:18]. If renunciation precedes obedience, how can
it be the other way round? And if renunciation stands as a
kind of elementary education in the monastic way of life, how
could someone who has not renounced worldly goods possibly
endure its more advanced curriculum? What, will one who is
untested in obedience simply keep herself in stillness in a cell,
meditating and devoting herself to prayer on her own? *But
where your treasure is*, says the Lord, *there is your* intellect
[Matt. 6:21]. How, then, will one whose mind is stretched out
towards the one *seated at the right hand of majesty in Heaven*
[Heb. 1:3] *lay up treasure on earth* [Matt. 6:20]? How will one
inherit the Kingdom, who is prevented by passion from accom-
modating anything pure in the intellect? Therefore, *blessed are
the poor in spirit, for theirs is the Kingdom of Heaven* [Matt.
5:3]. Do you see now how many passions our Lord cut off with
this one Beatitude?

35. Yet this is not all, since we have said that the first offspring of evil desire is love of matter. But there is a second
even more to be shunned, and a third no less evil. What is the
second? Love of glory. As we grow older, this passion joins
the love of flesh, though even for adolescents that passion is
like a vile prelude to the love of glory. I can tell you now that
the first form of love of glory consists in well-adorned bodies

and expensive clothes, which our fathers call 'worldly vanity' to distinguish it from other kinds of vanity, which affects those known for virtue, who are affected by self-conceit and hypocrisy, through which our enemy contrives to pillage and destroy their spiritual wealth.

36. All these things are completely healed in two ways. First, in regard to perception and desire of heavenly honour when those who desire that honour consider themselves unworthy of it; second, in regard to enduring lowliness among people, when they consider themselves deserving it. Furthermore, it is preferable to desire God's glory rather than one's own, as it says: *Not to us, Lord, not to us, but to your own name give glory!* [Ps. 113:9]. Even if someone is aware of having accomplished something praiseworthy, the cause of its accomplishment must be referred to God, and to him the praise for it, instead of praising themselves. Thus, they will rejoice, having received virtue as a gift, rather than exalting themselves as though they possessed it in their own right. Thus, they will be humbled, fixing the eyes of their minds on God day and night, *as the eyes of a handmaid on the hands of her mistress*, as the Psalmist puts it [Ps. 122:2]. They are afraid, lest, having been separated from God, who alone bestows and preserves them in goodness, they be dragged down into the pit of wickedness, which is what someone suffers who is enslaved to self-conceit and vainglory. Withdrawal from the world, dwelling in a monastery and remaining in one's cell assist marvellously in healing this passion. It is especially helpful to recognize the weakness of one's freewill and to consider oneself unable to socialize. What else are these habits but the very poverty in spirit that our Lord blessed?

37. If you recognize the shame that accompanies the passion itself, you will flee vainglory as fast as you can. For when you desire praise from humans you court dishonour from the very deeds done to attain it. You can see that, when you study hard and imagine great things, glorying in famous ancestors or beautiful clothing or other such things, you really show that you still cling to infantile thinking. For all these things are dust. And what is less worthy of honour than dust? A nun who uses her clothes not simply for protection and warmth,

but because it is soft and glittering, does not merely proclaim to all the fruitlessness of her soul, but decks herself in the shamefulness of courtesans. Let her hear, rather, the one who said that *Those who wear soft clothes are in the palaces of kings* [Matt. 11:8] and Paul's statement that *our citizenship is in Heaven* [Phil. 3:20]. Let us not be cast out of Heaven into the dwellings of the *world-ruler of the darkness* of this present age [Eph. 6:12, cf. 2 Cor. 4:4] for the sake of foolish ostentation in our clothing.

38. Those, too, who pursue virtue for human glory suffer the same thing. For they have forgotten that they *have their citizenship in Heaven* [Phil. 3:20] and so – alas! – drawing the Davidic curse on themselves, they *cause* their *glory to dwell in the dust* [Ps. 7:6]. Their prayer cannot be on high in Heaven, and all their zeal crashes down, because it does not bear the wings which divine love fashions out of our heavenly deeds on earth. Thus, they endure the toil but reap no fruitful rewards. Why do I speak of fruitlessness of rewards? To be sure, they bear fruit: shame, inconstancy in thoughts, captivity of intellect and inner turmoil. It says, *The Lord has scattered the bones of people-pleasers. Let them be ashamed, for God has brought them to naught* [Ps. 52:6]. This passion of vainglory is subtler than all others. Therefore, she who battles against it needs not just to flee from coupling with it or consenting to it, but to consider and guard against its initial attack as though that were already consent. Even then she can scarcely outrun a speedy defeat. If she practises watchfulness thus, the initial attack actually leads to compunction; if not, it prepares a place for pride. One who gives way to pride can scarcely be recalled – really, she comes to be incurable. For pride is the Devil's fall. However, even before that, the passion of 'people-pleasing' causes such harm to those who suffer it that they *are shipwrecked in their faith* [1 Tim. 1:19]. As our Lord says, *How can you believe in me who receive glory from people but do not seek glory from God alone* [John 5:44]?

39. What have you to do with human glory, my friend? Or, rather, with the empty name of glory – a name not only barren but which negates it? And not only that, but it gives birth to

envy of others? Malice, what is it but potential murder, patron first of that primal bloodletting and later of the killing of God? What does this passion do for nature? Preserve it? Guard it? Refresh it to strengthen and heal it? No one could seriously claim any such thing. No, I think the following proves that it is an abuse of language to make excuses for envy. Should someone examine the matter closely, she will find that the same desire for glory is patron and denouncer of most of our most shameful acts, at those times shamelessly casting off its mask and shaming its lovers, even if those teachers of Greek doctrines imagine that there are no achievements in this life without it. Alas! What delusion! For they are not ashamed to proclaim such nonsense.

40. We, however, who are named for him who through his own love for humankind christened all that is ours have not been taught thus. We have him as overseer of all we do. Looking to him they do through him and for his sake all that is best, doing it all to God's glory and certainly not striving to please humans. This accords with Paul, that supreme initiate of our lawgiver: *For if I still pleased people I would not be Christ's servant* [Gal. 1:10].

41. But let us see if the third brat born of evil desire is also destroyed by blessed poverty. The third spawn of a soul sick with desire is gluttony, from which comes every fleshly impurity. How do we claim this is third and last, when it is naturally planted in us from our conception? In fact, the natural processes pertaining to childbearing are detected in infants at their mother's breast. So, why should we call gluttony the last disease of fleshly desire? Since those drives are proper to our nature – and whatever is natural is blameless since it was made by God – so that through them we might *walk in good works* [Eph. 2:10]. Therefore, while these drives are not of themselves proof of a sick soul, they become so for those who abuse them. So, whenever *we take thought for our flesh to accomplish its desire* [Rom. 13:10], then the passion becomes evil and the beginning of fleshly passions, and love of pleasure our soul's sickness. And so, the intellect is the first to suffer such passions, wherefore, since the wicked passions originate first in the mind,

the Lord said that *wicked thoughts emerge from the heart* and *those are common to all people* [Matt. 15:19–20]. In fact, before the Gospel the Law says, *Watch yourself, lest a hidden and transgressive word arise in your heart* [Deut. 15:9]. However, although the ill-disposed intellect is first to suffer, it is stamped by the representation of perceptible bodies from below through the senses and so delights in them. It is roused to abuse first and especially through the eyes, which can draw in pollution from a distance. Our foremother Eve offers a clear testimony of this: first *she saw that the fruit was beautiful to look at and pleasant to* contemplate [Gen. 3:9], and then, having consented in her heart, took and ate from the forbidden tree.

42. We rightly said that yielding to the beauty of bodies precedes and preludes the other shameful passions. It is, therefore, a patristic precept neither to observe others' beauty too closely nor to delight in our own. Although the passions are observable in children, they help in natural self-preservation and do not conduce to sin until the mind becomes subject to passion. At a young age, therefore, these passions are not wicked. It is from an intellect subject to passion that the fleshly passions arise, so it is necessary for the healing to begin with the intellect. If you want to quench a conflagration, cutting at the flames from above achieves nothing, while removing its fuel immediately brings the fire to an end. So it is with lustful passions: unless you dry up the inward fountain of thoughts by prayer and humility, you labour in vain, even if you are armed against those thoughts with fasting and bodily suffering. If you sanctify the inward root through humility and prayer, you will gain sanctification outside too. This seems to me to explain that apostolic injunction to *gird your loins in truth* [Eph. 6:14], as it has been perfectly interpreted by one of our fathers: that *contemplation restricts our desiring faculty* and restrains the passions lying below our loins and stomach.[6] That being said, we still need bodily suffering and moderation in our diet, lest the unruliness of thought grow more violent. Therefore, nothing heals all the passions of the flesh save bodily suffering and prayer offered from *a humbled heart* [Ps. 50:19] – which is the poverty in spirit that our Lord blessed.

43. If, then, you want to be rich in *holiness, without which no one will see the Lord* [Heb. 12:14], remain in your own cell, enduring suffering and praying in humility. Dwelling properly in your cell is the haven of self-restraint, but everything outside it – especially what goes on in the marketplace and at festivals – is full of lustful turmoil arising from unseemly sights and sounds, which drowns the wretched soul of that monastic who falls into it. You could also call the world a raging fire of wickedness that takes conversations for its fuel and burns to cinders every form of virtue. No such raging fire is found in the desert. As for you, your desert is your cell. Stay in it and be hidden for a while, at least until the storm of your passions has passed. When passion has blown over, the public will not harm your regimen. For then you will truly be a pauper in spirit and will gain the Kingdom instead of passions. You will be glowingly blessed by him who said, *Blessed are the poor in spirit for theirs is the Kingdom of Heaven* [Matt. 5:3].

44. How could they not be rightly blessed who trust not in possessions but in Christ, who yearn to please none other than him, who live in his presence in humility and the rest of the virtues? Let us be poor in that way: humbled in spirit, suffering in the flesh and without property in our lives. Let us be so poor that the Kingdom of God may be ours and that, having inherited it, we may attain our blessed hopes. When the Lord set out the comprehensive headwords of the Gospel of our salvation, he did not simply include as many virtues as he banned vices in a single Beatitude, while blessing those who through repentance prune down their own souls' passible part. No, he also blessed many other things whose analogy lies not in pruning, but in the violence that comes from ice and frost, snow, sleet and bitter winds – simply put: the hardships of winter and summer, which plants must endure, exposed as they are to cold and heat, yet without which nothing planted in the ground can ever come to fruition.

45. What, then, are these things? Why, the variegated attacks of temptations, which she who will bear fruit for the farmer of spirits must bear gratefully. Imagine if someone pitied the hardships of plants, and set a wall around their shoots and put a roof over them, permitting nothing terrible to happen to them. Even if she prunes and cleans all round them, and does everything else assiduously, still she will get no fruit. Instead, she must permit them to endure everything, so that when the hour of spring puts an end to winter's misery her plants will bud, bloom, burst with leaves and give new fruit under the shade of their blooming shoots. Having spent a bit of time in the harsher sun, the fruit will mature, ripen, and be ready for harvest and enjoyment. So too, if someone will not nobly bear the crushing distress of temptations, even if she lack no other virtue, she will never bear fruit worthy of the divine wine press or grain ready for the everlasting barn. Every serious Christian is perfected through endurance of voluntary and involuntary toils, whether they come from outside or are borne within. For whatever a cultivator's consideration and the natural turning of seasons add to plants accrue also to us, Christ's rational vine branches, as we obey the Farmer of our souls voluntarily and willingly. Without our enduring things that befall us unchosen, whatever we have done by choice will not attain a divine blessing. For our love for God obtains approval especially through the affliction of temptations.

46. Nevertheless we must first correct whatever is voluntary in the soul, and then, when we have thus grown accustomed to brush aside both pleasure and glory, we will also withstand unsought attacks. She who, because of her poverty in spirit, despises pleasure and glory, and instead believes that she requires the harsher medicines of repentance, both anticipates every affliction and accepts every trial as though she deserved it. She rejoices when she meets them because she greets them as the purification of her soul. She makes that moment matter for heartfelt and effectual supplication to God. She considers that it produces and guards her soul's good health and so, not only does she bear no grudge against her tempters, she actually thanks them and prays for them as her benefactors. Therefore, she not only receives the promised forgiveness for sins [Matt. 6:14], but also attains to the Kingdom of Heaven and the divine blessing, having been blessed by the Lord on account of her lifelong patience in a spirit of humility.

47. Having set out a brief summary of spiritual pruning, let us now set out something of the fecundity it leads to. After having blessed those who, thanks to their spiritual poverty, have obtained wealth that cannot be taken away, Christ (the only blessed one) makes mourners to share in his own blessedness, saying, *Blessed are those who mourn, for they shall be comforted* [Matt. 5:4].

48. Why did Christ link mourning to poverty? Because mourning always accompanies poverty. But, says the Apostle, the *sorrow* that accompanies *worldly* poverty *works death* for the soul. But the *sorrow* that accompanies *godly* poverty achieves *salvation not to be repented of* [2 Cor. 7:10]. Of necessity, an involuntary grief follows the involuntary poverty of the world, while godly, voluntary poverty is followed by voluntary grief. Since blessed mourning necessarily emerges from and is joined to godly poverty in this world, mourning hangs on poverty as its whole cause, and they are both classed as spiritual and voluntary. But let us see how supremely blessed poverty gives birth to blessed mourning.

49. A little earlier in this treatise we distinguished four forms of spiritual poverty: in thinking, in body, in regard to abundance in this life and in regard to trials coming from external matters.

As an aside, let no one who has heard us describing these separately suppose that they are separated in practice, since in reality they are accomplished together. Therefore, they have been enclosed within a single Beatitude, which wondrously shows the shared root, as it were, and harbinger of the others: our spirit. For when our spirit is wrapped in the grace of the Gospel proclamation, it gives from itself a fount of poverty that *waters all the face of* our *earth* [Gen 2:6] – that is, our *outer self* [2 Cor. 4:16] – and renders it a paradise of virtues.

Now then, as there are four forms of spiritual poverty, each gives birth to a corresponding form of mourning and its accompanying comfort.

50. First, consider again voluntary bodily poverty and humility, which consist of hunger, thirst, sleepless nights and just about every sort of patient bodily suffering, and, in addition,

the reasonable limitation of our senses. Now, through this poverty and from these activities, not only is mourning born, but
tears as well. Just as insensitivity, callousness and hardness
of heart are naturally born of relaxation, luxury and ease, so
from a controlled and restricted diet are born affliction of heart
and compunction, which preserves us from all bitterness and
embraces every sweet gladness. For *without a trembling heart
it is impossible*, it says, *to be delivered from evil.*[7] Tripartite
abstention, from food, sleep and relaxation, afflicts the heart,
and when, by this affliction, the soul is delivered from evil
and bitterness, it receives instead an entirely spiritual delight.
And this delight is the comfort for the sake of which our Lord
blesses mourners. John, too, who built a spiritual *Ladder* out
of words for us, says that *'Thirst and vigil afflict the heart; the
heart, being afflicted, wells up with* tears.'[8] And one who has
been tested, it says, *will laugh* in her tears with blessed laughter,
when, as the Lord announced, she has been comforted [Luke
6:21]. The mourning that blessedly comforts those who have
it takes its origin from a godly bodily poverty. So, secondly,
how can mourning come from frightened thinking and inspired
humility in one's soul?

51. To begin with, self-accusation always accompanies
humility of soul. It begins with the fear of punishment, vividly
bringing before our very eyes a terrifying image of conflicting
ideas of hell combined in a single place of punishment. Then it
adds to the fear of what is due by the realization that the punishment is unimaginable, and therefore worse even than what
has been said, and – to add further to our dismay – that it is
endless. For heat, cold, darkness, fire, movement and immobil-
ity, bonds, horrors and the tearing jaws of undying beasts are
gathered there in a single condemnation – and not even this
suffices to describe that terrible place which, according to the
Scripture, *has not entered into the human* mind [1 Cor. 2:9].

52. Why this useless, inconsolable and endless grief? It is
grief stirred up in those who have sinned against God from a
recognition of their offences. There, convicted of their sins and
robbed of any hope of improvement, despairing of salvation,
they feel the pain of grief multiplied by the unwelcome prick of

conscience. The realization that this grief will not end leads to further grief, to another terrible darkness, a burning that knows no relief, and a helpless abyss of despondency. Here and now grief is supremely profitable, for God responds with mercy, for, having considered our situation, he has descended to be with us and promised comfort to those who mourn. The comfort he has promised is himself, for God is and is called Comforter [John 14:16]. Thirdly, do you know the grief that comes from a humbled soul or the comfort that follows?

53. By itself self-accusation is like an intellectual weight laid on the soul's rational faculties. After a while it compresses, crushes, and squeezes out salvific *wine that gladdens human hearts* [Ps. 103:15] – that is, our *inner self* [2 Cor. 4:16]. Compunction is just such a wine. Together with mourning, it squeezes out the passions and, having delivered the soul from their terrible weight, fills it with blessed joy. This is why *those who mourn* are *blessed, because they will be comforted* [Matt. 5:4]. Mourning comes also from voluntary poverty, that is, poverty in belongings and comforts joined to poverty in spirit, which, when accomplished in conjunction with each other, are perfect and pleasing to God. If, therefore, you listen carefully you will understand just how the mourning that comes from such poverty arises in us and what comfort it holds. For, when someone bids farewell to all her worldly goods and so renounces possessions, either distributing them or scattering them in accordance with the commandment, then her soul leaves behind all its anxiety over worldly goods, and is allowed to turn towards self-examination free of all external and material distractions.

54. Should one's intellect escape everything perceptible and rise above the turbulence it causes and observe the *inner self* [2 Cor. 4:16], it immediately perceives the ugly mask it has acquired from wandering about in the lower world and so hastens to wash this off through mourning. Then, when this hideous veil has been lifted and the soul is not shamefully distracted with various attachments, it goes tranquilly into its true *inner rooms* and *in secret prays to its Father* [Matt. 6:6]. The Father grants it first peaceful thoughts, which make it receptive of other charisms, and with this humility, which is generative

of all virtue and embraces it. This humility does not consist in readily available words and expressions, but is, rather, that humility to which the good and divine Spirit testifies, that the same Spirit creates as he renews our inward parts.

55. In peace and humility, as in the safety of a walled paradise for the intellect, the whole orchard of true virtue flourishes. In their midst arise the sacred palaces of love, in the forecourts of which blooms unutterable joy, a sure possession and prelude of the age to come. For voluntary poverty is mother of freedom from anxiety, which is mother of attentiveness and prayer, which are the mothers of grief and tears. These wipe out our predispositions to passion. When those have been removed like stones from the road, the way of virtue is travelled more easily, and the conscience becomes blameless. Grief and tears also cause joy to well up and the blessed laughter of the soul.

56. Then, indeed, is the misery of weeping made sweet and *God's sayings* become *like sweetness in the throat, sweeter than honey on the tongue* [Ps. 118:103]. Then is supplication in prayer transformed to thanksgiving, while meditation on the divine testimonies is *the heart's delight* [Ps. 118:111], together with *hope unashamed* [Rom. 5:5], which is the preliminary experience of that sweet taste. Mingling with joy and thanksgiving, hope learns in part the *surpassing wealth* of God's goodness [Eph. 2:7] – as in the saying, *Taste and see that the Lord is good* [Ps. 33:9] – that is, the delight of the righteous, the joy of the upright, the gladness of the humble, the comfort of those who mourn for God's sake.

57. What, then? Is this the extent of consolation and these alone the gifts of sacred betrothal? Does the Bridegroom really not reveal himself in every way purer than these to such souls as have been bathed in blessed mourning, purified and set apart as brides through their virtue? Of course not! We disregard those ready in their envy to accuse us and to say something like, Do not *speak in the name of the Lord* [Deut. 18:22], lest we *cast out your name as a wicked thing* [Luke 6:22], having already composed and published slanders and false accusations against you! Ignoring them for now, let us add to our discussion, looking to what our holy fathers have said, trusting in

that and reiterating it, and so persuading others of the same. For it says, *I believed, therefore I spoke. And we believe, therefore we also speak* [2 Cor. 4:13].

58. When every shameful passion lurking in us has been driven out and the intellect, as our argument has already shown, has returned perfectly to itself and recalled the soul's other powers, it tends the soul lovingly by cultivation of the virtues. Having established practical steps, the intellect ascends to what is greater and more perfect, cleansing itself with God's help. Not only does it then wipe away every trace of evil, but also everything accreted from matters indifferent, even what leans towards the better.

59. When the intellect has transcended even intelligible realities and ideas still not free from the imagination, and when in a godly and devout spirit it has cast off everything, it will stand before God as one 'deaf and mute' [Ps. 37:14]. Then the intellect takes the part of matter and is shaped into its highest form in perfect acquiescence. For, since nothing knocks at it from outside, inward grace transforms it to the better and, illuminating the intellect paradoxically with unspeakable light, perfects the *inward self* [2 Cor. 4:16]. When, according to Peter the chief Apostle [2 Pet. 1:19], *day dawns and the morning star rises in* our *hearts*, then, as in the prophetic oracle, will the true *human go forth to her* true *work* [Ps. 103:23], taking the path of light by which she ascends to *the everlasting hills* [Ps. 75:5]. Oh, what a marvel! In this light, the intellect separated from its original matter (or not, depending on how it has progressed) is made into a spectator of things beyond the cosmos. For the intellect travels not on the imaginary wings of discursive reason, which wanders about blind to everything, since it can gain no precise or certain apprehension either of absent objects of sense or transcendent objects of thought. Rather, it ascends on the unutterable power of spirit and, with spiritual and unutterable assistance, hears *unutterable words* [2 Cor. 12:4] and beholds unimaginable sights. Thereafter, even if absent from it, the whole intellect is bound up in this marvel. It vies with the tireless hymnists, truly like another angel of God on earth. Through its participation in all of them, the intellect

draws every form of creation to God, but now has a share also in God, who is beyond all, that it may be the perfect representation of his image [Gen. 1:26–7, Col. 1:15].

60. Therefore, the divine Neilos says that *the mind's state is an intelligible height, like the colour of heaven, to which the light of the Holy Trinity comes during times of prayer.*[9] And again, *If you would like to see the mind's condition, empty yourself of all mental images and then you will see it, like sapphire or the colour of the sky. To do this without dispassion is impossible, for it is necessary that God work with you and imbue you with his connatural light.*[10] The holy Diadochos says, *Through baptism holy grace accomplishes two good things for us, one of which boundlessly surpasses the other. Right there in the water baptism renews us and polishes what is 'in the image' – rubbing us clean from every smudge of sin. The other, which is the 'in the likeness' [Gen. 1:26] looks for our cooperation. When, therefore, our intellect starts to taste the goodness of the Holy Spirit with much feeling, then we need to know that grace is then beginning to paint, as it were, the likeness within the features of the image. So then, while we feel ourselves being formed according to the likeness, we come to know the perfection of the likeness from illumination.* And again, *But it cannot procure spiritual love, unless it has been enlightened in full assurance by the Holy Spirit. But the only way of possessing spiritual love is through being enlightened in full assurance by the Holy Spirit. For unless the intellect fully receives what is in the likeness [Gen. 1:26] through divine light, it can hardly have all the other virtues and remains without a share in perfect love.*[11]

61. In like fashion we hear St Isaak [the Syrian] saying that during the time of prayer a mind filled with grace sees its own purity *similar to the heavenly shade, which is called 'the place of God' by the elders of Israel, when he appeared to them on the mountain.*[12] Again, he says, *Prayer is purity of mind, which is cut from the light of the Holy Trinity with utter astonishment.*[13] Again, *Purity of mind, on which shines the light of the Holy Trinity during prayer.*[14]

62. Remember, though, that the intellect granted that light

conveys numerous indications of the divine beauty to its conjoined body, mediating between divine grace and the bulk of flesh, and having implanted a capacity for impossible things. Its disposition thereafter is godlike and unparalleled, impossible (or at least very difficult) to impel towards vice. Thereafter the Word [*Logos*] clarifies the principles [*logoi*] of beings and freely reveals the mysteries of nature, thanks to the intellect's purity. Through these inner principles, the Word draws up our intellection by inherent analogies to comprehension – which the Father of the Word has held fast in an immaterial caress – of supernatural things heard about in faith. Thereafter follow various miracles, as well as insight, foresight, and describing things happening far off as though they took place right before one's eyes. But the greatest miracle is this, that it is certainly not the aim of the supremely blessed saints to attain such powers; it is, rather, as if when looking at a ray of sunlight, one can also perceive tiny particles in the air way, although that is not one's purpose. So it is with those who commune purely with the rays of divine light, which by nature reveal all things as well: not only things that are and things that have been, but also things that have yet to come to pass. According to their degree of purity they acquire – albeit as something incidental – knowledge of these things. The saints' concern is the intellect's return and unification with itself; or, rather, though it sounds incredible, the return of all the soul's faculties to the intellect and their operation in keeping with both the intellect and God. In this way saints are restored to their original state and assimilation with their first state, grace restoring their ancient and inimitable beauty. To such a height as this does blessed grief carry the *humble in heart* and *poor in spirit* [Matt. 11:28, 5:3].

63. Since these heights are beyond us, thanks to our innate laziness, come, let us return to its foundation and say a little more about grief. Certainly, grief accompanies all manner of worldly, involuntary poverty. For how could someone not grieve who is in need, who unwillingly goes hungry, who is oppressed and dishonoured? Such mourning is inconsolable, the more so as one grows more destitute, or, rather, the further one falls from true knowledge. If, rather than subjecting pleasures and pains of the senses to reason, she abuses her cleverness and subjects reason to pleasures, she wrongly increases pleasures to no profit, and so comes to catastrophic loss. For she produces a clear sign and proof against herself, that she does not really believe in God's Gospel, in his prophets before that, or in those who learned through God and were sent to preach good news to the poor, all of which promised inexhaustible wealth through poverty, unutterable glory through insignificance, painless delight through self-control, and deliverance, through patient endurance of the tribulations that surround us, from the eternal anguish and affliction that awaits those who have loved a free and easy life now and have not chosen to *enter into life through the small and narrow gate* and *way* [Matt. 7:14].

64. Paul, that divine oracle, said well that *worldly grief works death* [2 Cor. 7:10]. Through this statement he showed us the *sin unto death* [1 John 5:16]. If the soul's true life is divine light flowing from godly grief (as was said above, by our fathers), then the soul's death will be the wicked darkness that comes to it from *worldly grief*. That is the darkness concerning which St Basil the Great said that '*sin, which subsists in the abandonment of goodness, forms an intelligible darkness through an accumulation of wrongs*'.[15]

65. The divine Mark, however, asks, '*How will someone who is surrounded with wicked thoughts see the substantial sin hidden by them? That sin is darkness and fog rising in the soul from evil notions, words and deeds. When will someone blind to the sin that envelops her supplicate God and be purified of it? Not being purified, how can she discover the place of pure nature? Not discovering that, how will she ever see the inner dwelling of Christ? We must, therefore, cry out as we persevere in prayer, and seek* not only *to gain this dwelling* but to *guard it* as well. *For there are some who have been destroyed after receiving it. For youths and late learners may both gain mere knowledge or chance experience of it, but pious and much-experienced elders barely gain its constant activity that comes with endurance.*'[16] To Paul, Basil and Mark, you might add Makarios, the confessor of heavenly knowledge,[17] and the whole chorus of Saints.

66. If you look carefully, you will find that just as this darkness of sin takes its subsistence from all our failures, *worldly grief* [2 Cor. 7:10] is likewise given birth and nourished by all our passions. Accordingly, *worldly grief* bears the image and is a sort of first fruit, prelude, and pledge of the endless grieving awaiting all who have not chosen the mourning which our Lord blessed. Blessed mourning not only confers a profit of consolation and bears as its fruit a pledge of eternal rejoicing, but it cements virtue as it renders the soul immovable towards evil. If someone has been impoverished and humbled, and has striven after godly humiliation, but has not added mourning in her advance towards better things, then she is easily turned around to long again for those things which she had left behind and yearn for what she originally renounced, and so make herself into an apostate. If, on the other hand, while being constant and attentive to a disposition for blessed poverty, she cultivates grief in herself, she will lose all inclination to turn back, doing well and not wickedly reverting back to what she has fled.

67. For *godly grief*, just as the Apostle says, *cultivates repentance that we will not regret* in the soul, *unto salvation* [2 Cor. 7:10]. Therefore, one of our fathers said that 'mourning both cultivates and guards'.[18] Mourning not only helps someone become all but immovable to evil and uninclined to revert to former sins, but it has the benefit also of making it as though those former sins never happened. For since she first mourns on their account, God considers them as involuntary, and we are not liable for involuntary actions. Someone who mourns her penury testifies that it was hardly voluntary and therefore falls into the Devil's traps along with the rich and those who desire wealth. Unless she changes and strives to escape those traps she will be cast down with them to the same eternal punishment. In just the same way, if someone sins against God but persists in mourning for her sins, then in all fairness those sins will not be considered voluntary. She will advance without stumbling in the company of those who have not so sinned along the way that leads to eternal life.

68. Here is the profit of mourning's initial phase, which is painful because it is conjoined with the fear of God. As mourning advances, it is marvellously joined to the love of God and bears fruit in sweet and holy consolation, as she who has been formed in mourning tastes the goodness of the Comforter. This goodness, because it is unutterable, is quite unbelievable among those who have not directly experienced it. For if one can hardly describe honey's sweetness to those who have never tasted it, how could anyone possibly convey to those who have not experienced it themselves the pleasure of holy joy and God-sent grace?

69. Moreover, the beginning of mourning seems to be something which, I admit, seems nearly unattainable: namely, a request for betrothal to God. Therefore, those who mourn because of their yearning for the unwedded bridegroom make a kind of romantic entreaty. They strike themselves and call with loud cries because the one to whom they want to be united is not and may never be present. Yet the end of mourning is perfect nuptial intercourse in perfect purity. Thus, the great Paul, having referred to married couples' sexual union into *one flesh*, continued: *I say this in reference to Christ and his Church* [Eph. 5:3–2]. For, as two humans become one, so are the people of God one spirit with God. Certainly Paul said as much elsewhere: *Whoever is joined to the Lord is one with him in spirit* [1 Cor. 6:17].

70. Where are those who claim that the grace indwelling God's saints is something created? Let them know that they are blaspheming against the Spirit himself, who, in giving grace, is united with the saints. As for us, let us present an even sharper image of the matter at hand. The beginning of grief resembles the return of the prodigal son [Luke 15:11–32], and it fills the mourner with the same dejection and induces her to use his words: *Father, I have sinned against heaven and before you, and I am no longer worthy to be called your son* [Luke 15: 18–19]. The end of mourning, however, resembles the highest father's running to meet his wayward son, and his embracing him. In that moment the Prodigal is struck by the wealth of his Father's incomparable compassion and because of it finds enormous joy and confidence. He is kissed and kisses in return, and they go inside together to feast, he and his Father, and to rejoice together in heavenly delight.

71. But *come, let us fall down* in blessed poverty *and weep before the Lord our God* [Ps. 94:6], that we may leave behind our former sins, make ourselves immovable towards evil, and attain to the Comforter. Being comforted in him we offer up glory to him, together with his Father without beginning and the only-begotten Son, now and ever and to the ages of ages.

Amen.

Kallistos, various writers who bear this name

The writers included in the *Philokalia* after Gregory Palamas all write in the shadow of Palamas, and endorse his theological point of view as much as hesychast prayer. If the *Philokalia* crests with Palamas, in the various writings ascribed to 'Kallistos', Symeon of Thessaloniki and Mark of Ephesos, it washes the shores smooth. With them we can see hesychasm being disseminated, defended and practised by monks beyond Athos and, soon, beyond the receding borders of the Byzantine Empire.

Kallistos Angelikoudis,
On Hesychast Practice

KALLISTOS ANGELIKOUDIS
(*c*.1325–*c*.1395)

Little is known about our first Kallistos, save for the monastic career his various monikers suggest and the spiritual texts ascribed to him, several of which are present in different editions of the *Philokalia*, one of which, *On Hesychast Practice*, is included here with a concluding section *On five kinds of stillness*. He is referred to in the 1782 *Philokalia* as 'Tilikoudis' and 'Kataphygiotis'; the former, probably a mistake for Angelikoudis, and the latter, after his *kathisma* or hermitage in Macedonia, dedicated to the Mother of God, under her title, 'Refuge [Kataphygion] of Christians'.

Kallistos makes 'stillness' (*hêsuchia*, from which come 'hesychast' and 'hesychasm') the framework and context of all ascetic practice. What had once been treated as the goal, or aspiration, of repentance, psalmody, vigil, prayer and other activities, is now the indispensable ingredient in their practice. One cannot repent, cannot pray, cannot sing psalms or collect one's thoughts without stillness. Hesychasm has become the very air one breathes, and prayer the rhythm of that breath.

Sources

Main text: Selections of Kallistos, *Homily* 22, in S. Koutsas, 'Callistos Angelicoudès: Quatre traités hésychastes inédits', Θεολογία 67–8

(1996, 1997): 67.518–28, 696–754; 68.212–46, 536–72. Numbers in brackets refer to Koutsas's divisions.

Appendix ('**On five kinds of stillness**'): *PHILOKALIA* (1782): 1105–7; *Philokalia* (1893/1982): vol. 4, 370–72

Alternative text: (as 'Kallistos Telikoudis') *PHILOKALIA* (1782): 1103–7; *Philokalia* (1893/1982): vol. 4, 368–72

On Hesychast Practice

[1] It is impossible to repent without stillness. Neither is it possible to attain purity in any way at all without withdrawal from the world. Neither is it possible, after seeing people and conversing with them, to be deemed worthy of communing with God and contemplation of him. Because of this, for those seeking to repent of their own failings, to be purified from their passions, and to attain and enjoy communing with God and contemplation of him – which is, after all, the end and goal of those who conduct their lives according to God, and a pledge (if I may put it thus) of God and the eternal inheritance – it is necessary to pursue stillness by every possible means. They therefore make a start by dedicating their whole soul and choosing to withdraw and flee from humans. From this, they derive their first principle, mourning in stillness. They reproach and blame themselves, so as to attain greater purity. This entails vigils, standing still in one place, self-control and bodily labour, the purpose of which is the humble flow of tears from eyes that look with humility, in compunction of heart. And so they apply themselves to purification, and attain it through ascetic struggle. The goal here is peace in our thoughts, joined, as we have said, with the shedding of tears.

Then the intellect begins, in accordance with its true nature, to look upon the natures of beings, to discern the very art of God, and to apprehend divine thoughts, in this way coming to behold God's power, wisdom, glory, goodness and all else that is contemplated about God, as it enters into the hidden mysteries of the Scriptures. So it comes to taste supernatural goods and enjoys things whose beauty belongs beyond the cosmos,

finally being established as a receptacle of God's love. Ravished
by love, it rejoices, and is glad, having run ahead to the goal
of the virtues, that is, the love of the Creator of all, without
suffering any delusion or suspicion in these matters. As subject
to change, it endures temptations, sinful impulses and inappropriate movements from many causes – among which it must
recover itself, standing far off from despair, and winged with
the divine hope of God's love for humankind, busying itself
with tears, prayer and the other aforementioned good works,
and, finally, so far as this is allowed, enjoying the divine Paradise of love. It sees nothing more – no form, no materiality, no
shape, nothing at all, to put it simply – just experiencing tears,
peace of thoughts and love of God. For in these things it is kept
free from delusion, and is rewarded with the salvation, granted
to the humble-minded and vigilant soul that prays in Christ
Jesus our Lord.

[2] Being seated in your cell, let your intellect be filled with
confidence in God's presence and humility: humility from its
sense of worthlessness and nothingness; but confidence on
account of God's unsurpassable love and the loving forbearance he has for humans. For thus is the soul led to honour
God, when, although knowing its sinfulness, it nevertheless
takes courage in God's love for humankind and acknowledges
its dependence on him. For this reason, the sacred Paul commands us, saying, *Let us approach the throne of grace with
confidence* [Heb. 4.16]. For truly, such confidence is a kind
of eye of prayer, its wing perhaps, or an unheard-of way of
cleaving to God; not, however, if one relies for such confidence
on one's own goodness – let us put any such thought far from
our mind – but, rather, when the soul has been given wings
of divine hope, by the thought of God's unspeakable love for
humankind, affection and forbearance. Pray, therefore, with
confidence based on humbleness of mind, being fed on good
hopes in God, in accordance with the things set forth in Jesus
Christ our Lord, as we have said.

[3] You must always pursue activities that calm your body
and wash your mind clean of annoyance. These are: moderate
food, light drink, brief sleep, standing as much as you can,

bending your knees easily in a humble position, cheap clothing, brief and necessary speech, sleeping on the ground, and everything else that can to some degree subdue your body. Along with these, you need to pursue as many activities as awaken your mind and arouse it to cleave to God. These are: reading of the Holy Scriptures and their interpretations by the Saints (and this only moderately!), reciting psalms with attention to their meaning, meditation on what is said in the Holy Scriptures and on the marvels to be seen in creation. Lastly, engage in verbal prayer – that is, until the grace of the Spirit manifestly moves you to prayer from your heart. For then prayer is a different feast and an occasion for another celebration – not prayers spoken verbally but from your heart, made active in the Spirit. But pass on to such things now.

Now you should pass on to such exercises: make prostrations as often as you can, and then sit down to pray. When you grow listless from praying, go and read a bit, as has been said, and return again to praying. And when next you grow listless from praying, rise to recite a section of the Psalter and so return yet again to praying. When you grow listless again, then spend a little time in meditation as we have said before and thus again cling to prayer. Finally, holy friend, make use of a little handiwork, which is an obstacle to listlessness, as we have heard from the Fathers.

[4] In all your godly activity, from dawn to dawn, let prayer take the lead. For we only pass over to the other activities mentioned because we are exhausted with praying. Then, when mercy comes to the soul and the Spirit's grace causes prayer to well up from your heart as though from a spring – at that point your mind engages in prayer and contemplation alone, having removed itself from everything else. It feeds, then, only on prayer and contemplation, as in the Paradise of divine love.

Prayer gives us the power to perform every good work. It gives birth to the weeping of repentance. It contributes supremely to the peace of thoughts, driving us to consider God alone, who is our supreme peace. Prayer itself is the birth-giver of God's love. Prayer itself alone purifies the rational faculty of the soul, bringing to our mind God as the source of purification, even for the angels. Prayer preserves the soul's desiring faculty pure for God, for, being absorbed in communing with God – who is by nature infinitely and abundantly good and beautiful – prayer focuses every desire on God. Prayer soothes the irascible faculty so deeply that it falls down before him, supplicates and invokes God and humbles the soul through prostration before Him. For no one can supplicate God and beseech him without humility or with a mind full of anger. For this reason, to speak briefly, holy prayer purifies and sets right all the soul's faculties, both practical and spiritual – especially when it is accompanied by the contemplation of God and divine longing in silent dwelling and conduct, as we have already said.

[5] While you are praying, turn inward and let your mind fix its attention on and see without disturbance the place of the heart from which tears flow. As you pray, let your mind descend into the heart while you breathe in gently through your nostrils, and let it stay there, as long as possible. For this is exceedingly beneficial, conducive to many tears, setting free the intellect, productive of spiritual peace and prayer. It leads to the discovery of prayer of the heart, with the help of God, by the grace of the life-giving Spirit in Christ Jesus our Lord.

Appendix: On five kinds of stillness

[1] You, who practise contemplation, and behold the mysteries, and are nourished by them, need to know that just as God and humankind are two, so it follows that there is a duality in what has been said about inner grief, whether you want to speak generically or specifically: there are practices that belong to mourning and, following behind them, ones that belong to tears. These have come to differ, each from the other, and their distinction is great, even though both are good, both given by God, and both harbingers of divine goodwill and the inheritance that comes with it. For mourning has its origin in divine fear and grief, while tears have divine love leading to God. Likewise, while mourning does not lead to much rejoicing, tears produce an abundance of joy. Finally, mourning belongs to beginners, tears to those on their way to perfection through grace.

[2] There are five practices that nurture stillness. First, prayer – that is, the ceaseless memory of Jesus, introduced through breathing into the heart without any conceptual thought whatever, which is achieved through all-encompassing control of the stomach, sleep and the other senses, within the cell, and with humility. Secondly, recitation of the Psalter, a little at a time. Thirdly, reading likewise from the divine Gospels, the divine Fathers and chapters on prayer – especially those by [Symeon] the New Theologian, Hesychios [of Sinai] and Nikephoros [the Monk]. Fourthly, meditation on God's judgement, or on calling to mind death, and similar matters. Fifthly, a little handiwork. And again returning to prayer – even if you have to force yourself – until your intellect has accustomed itself to casting away its own restlessness by remembering the Lord and to the effort of descending unceasingly into the heart. This activity belongs to the novice monks who desire to practise stillness.

[3] A novice, then, ought not frequently to come out of his cell, and should abstain from seeing people and conversation with them, save in the case of some great need. Even then, he should only do so rarely, with caution and careful attention. For not only among novices, but also among those already making progress, such activities as conversation and looking around are a cause of distraction. Now, this very prayer, practised with attentiveness and without any conceptual thought, does two things. First, through praying the words 'Lord Jesus Christ, Son of God' immaterially and silently, the intellect that has remembered the Lord in everything reaches up towards him. Secondly, through the words 'have mercy on me', it directs the intellect to itself, unable to refuse to pray for itself. Having progressed to love through unified experience it reaches out to the Lord himself, no longer needing the assurance of the second part of the petition [the request for mercy]. Therefore, the Fathers have not always handed down the prayer in its entirety. Certainly, some, such as Chrysostom, have it whole.[1] But Paul, for example, has *Jesus is Lord* – to which he added *in the Holy Spirit* [1 Cor. 12:3]. He means that when the heart receives the Holy Spirit's activity, through which it also prays – which pertains to

those making progress but not yet completely perfect – this is enlightenment. On the other hand, Klimakos says, 'Flog your enemies with the name of Jesus!' and 'Let the memory of Jesus be attached to your breathing',[2] but adds nothing else.

[4] Beginners are allowed to pray mentally sometimes with all the words of the prayer, sometimes only a portion, as has been said – not, however, constantly vacillating, lest from this practice they suffer division in themselves. From remaining steadfast in the aforementioned practice of pure prayer, even if he does not live purely otherwise (clearly because of the predispositions and thoughts which get in the way of prayer), the spiritual wrestler comes to be in a state of praying without compulsion by causing his intellect to remain fixed in his heart rather than forcefully drawing it in through inhalation and straightway breathing it back out; that is, it stays in the heart and remains there. This is, and is called, the prayer of the heart. A certain warmth in the heart precedes this kind of prayer, which keeps at bay the impediments to perfectly accomplishing superior and pure prayer, and so the intellect prays as it remains, unhindered in the heart. In such warmth and prayer, love for the Lord Jesus, whose name has been remembered, is born in the heart, from which sweet tears pour forth out of yearning for Jesus, who is thus constantly brought to mind.

[5] To be deemed worthy of these things and of everything which follows them (of which now is not the time to speak), we need to strive, as has been said, to keep the fear of God before our eyes, together with the memory of Jesus in our hearts and not simply outside them. We strive in this way so as to turn away easily not only from evil deeds, but even from impassioned thoughts, and come instead to make progress – having within the assurance of God's love for us. Only, do not seek God's manifestation, lest we receive the darkness which masquerades as light. For when the intellect, although not seeking it, sees light, let it neither accept nor reject it. Rather, let him ask one who has power to teach and let him in that way learn the truth. And if he finds someone to instruct him – not just from his knowledge of the divine Scriptures, but from the enlightenment he has himself experienced – well, then, thanks be

to God! If, on the other hand, he cannot find such a teacher, then it is better not to accept the vision, but to flee to God in humility, declaring himself unworthy of such a vision, just as he has been taught by the Fathers in their actions. It is true that, in some of their writings, they speak of the signs that distinguish real from illusory illumination. Nevertheless it is better to hear about such matters through a living voice, when the right moment comes; but now is not the time. For right now, more than anything else and before everything else, you need to learn this: someone who wishes to learn archery does not bend the bow without a signal. So too let the one who wishes to learn to cultivate stillness have as a signal his being always meek in heart. And he never gives trouble or is troubled in anything unless the matter at hand concerns piety. And even this might be accomplished good-naturedly, as he keeps away from all people and keeps silent as much as possible. But if he should ever meet someone, he ought immediately to repent, find fault with himself, and look to what follows, that, as he makes a beginning of calling upon Jesus in stillness and with a pure conscience, as we said, and as he advances in the way, he may have the grace of God resting in his soul. Not only this, but he must keep his soul perfectly unmoved by the demons and the passions that formerly troubled it and have it rejoicing with unutterable delight. Then even if they trouble his soul again, they cannot rouse it, for it is not attached to them and does not desire the pleasure they promise. For such a man's entire desire looks to the Lord who gives him grace. For his soul is warred upon by God's permission – but not God's abandonment. Why? So that his intellect not be exalted on account of finding this very good thing, but, being warred upon, it always holds tightly to humility, through which alone the intellect not only conquers its proud enemies, but is made worthy of ever greater gifts.

May we also be made worthy of these gifts, given by Christ, who humbled himself for us and now richly offers his grace to such humble people, now and forever and unto the ages of ages. Amen.

Kallistos I,
Fourteen Chapters on Prayer

KALLISTOS I, ŒCUMENICAL PATRIARCH
(PATRIARCH 1350–53, 1355–63; d.1363)

Our second Kallistos was a monk of Athos and disciple of Gregory of Sinai. He was made Patriarch of Constantinople ('Œcumenical Patriarch') in 1350. During his first tenure as patriarch, he presided at the Council of Constantinople (1351), which endorsed the teaching of Gregory Palamas and confirmed the orthodoxy of hesychast spirituality. He was deposed in 1353 because of a dispute with Emperor John VI Kantakouzenos, but after the latter's abdication returned to his throne in 1355 and remained there until his death in 1363.

Kallistos was a devotee of St Gregory of Sinai, even writing his biography; and a disciple of Gregory Palamas. Included in the 1782 *Philokalia* were *Fourteen Chapters on Prayer*, a selection from a larger work, consisting of 109 chapters. It is the text of 1782 that is translated here. In the second edition of the Greek *Philokalia*, further 'missing texts' were added by the editor, Panagiotis Tzelatis, but these seem to belong to Kallistos Angelikoudis (q.v.). *Fourteen Chapters on Prayer* rests on the comparison of prayer to playing the lyre. This may seem an odd image to use, since monks did not (and do not) generally play the lyre, but it is probably intended to put readers in mind of King David, the Psalmist, and his songs, which Christians have long used as prayers.

Sources

Text: Selections from Antonio Rigo, 'Callisto I Patriarca, I 100 (109) Capitoli sulla purezza dell'anima: Introduzione, edizione e traduzione', *Byzantion* 80 (2010): 333–407. Numbers in brackets refer to Rigo's divisions.

Alternative text: *PHILOKALIA* (1782): 1100–1102; *Philokalia* (1893/1982): vol. 4, 373–5

Fourteen Chapters on Prayer

1. If you wish to learn the truth, take as your model the lyre player. For he bends his head down and, engrossed in the music, he strums the strings with the plectrum. As the strings are struck skilfully one with another, the lyre lets out a melody, and the player's heart resounds with joy at its sweetness. [17]

2. Take as your model, too, the diligent tender of vines, and put your trust in what I say. For if, with sober intensity, you concentrate like the lyre player, in the depth of your heart, you will readily find what you seek. For a soul utterly seized by divine love cannot turn back. As the divine David says, *My soul cleaves to you* [Ps. 62:9]. [18]

3. The lyre seems to me, my beloved, to be the heart. Its strings are the senses: the plectrum the mind. When the mind works its spiritual power, ceaselessly moving the plectrum, it brings about the memory of God, from which a certain indescribable delight comes upon the soul, as divine rays are reflected in the pure intellect, as in a mirror. [19]

4. Unless we shut up our body's senses, the welling water – which the Lord gave to the famous Samaritan woman – will not spring up in us [John 4:4–26]. For she, seeking corporeal water, found the water of life welling within herself. For as the earth naturally holds water and pours it forth, so also the earth of the heart has this water naturally welling up and flowing abundantly, as if it were a native light. Adam lost this light through his transgression. [12]

5. Just as from an ever-flowing well, so this *living* and welling *water* bubbles up from the soul [John 4:14]. This same water, welling up in the soul of that God-bearing man Ignatios,

accustomed him to say, *In me there is no fire of love for matter; rather, there is water* working and *speaking*.[1] [33]

6. This bliss, indeed this triple bliss – I mean the spiritual watchfulness of the soul – is like welling water, and water that flows from the depth of the heart. Water that issues from a well fills it, while the welling water that issues from the heart, which is ever-movingly moved through the Spirit (so to speak), fills the whole *inner person* with divine dew and spirit, while it renders the *outer person* fiery [2 Cor. 4:16]. [37]

7. An intellect, purified from external things and keeping in check its senses through the practice of virtue, becomes immovable like the axis of the heavens. Looking down into the depth of the heart, as though gazing towards the centre, it seizes on rays of insight from the mind and, as it were, draws them up to form divine concepts, all the while keeping in subjection all the bodily senses. [34]

8. Let no one, therefore, who listens to the uninitiated, or who requires milk [cf. Heb. 5:12–14], partake of such things as are to be refused out of season. For the divine Fathers reckon such people as seek those things before their due season – for example, those who hasten to cross the borders of dispassion before it is appropriate – as doing nothing other than taking leave of their wits. For it is impossible for someone who does not know letters to meditate on written texts!

9. The motion roused in the soul by the Holy Spirit on account of spiritual struggles stills the heart and *cries out, Abba! Father!* [Rom. 8:15]. This same motion, though formless and shapeless, transfigures us with the radiance of divine light. It simultaneously fashions us by the blaze of the Holy Spirit (as is apparent) and alters and changes us by divine authority (as God alone knows). [45]

10. A mind purified through watchfulness is easily darkened unless it withdraws in every way from external things by means of the constant memory of Jesus. But one who has joined practical virtue to contemplation by the guarding of the mind, does not pay attention to noises or seek to shake off sounds, whether inarticulate or articulate. For the soul which has been wounded by divine *eros* for Christ cleave to him as a lover to his beloved. [46]

11. The passions of the flesh and its urges beset those who spend their lives in the world. At times, thanks to their reasons, they have some peace, in accordance with the passage: *Be still and know* ... [Ps. 45:11]. But this is a passing state and not a permanent one, and it is impossible to eradicate or annihilate the passions. [56] We know, however, that a solitary life uproots them. [57]

12. Concerning that welling water – one spring may have a faster motion, and another a slower calm. The former, therefore, cannot be easily muddied, on account of the speed of its movement. And even if it is muddied briefly, it is swiftly cleared by its swift motion. But when the current is diminished to near calm, not only is the water muddied, but it becomes stagnant – for it requires a certain cleansing movement. [74]

13. The demon attacks novices who are learning moral principles in one way, those engaged in monastic practice in another, and in yet another way those who busy themselves with contemplation. As regards the first [two], he attacks by means of noises and sounds, both inarticulate and articulate. As regards those engaged in contemplation, he crafts certain idolatrous fantasies, which seem to colour the very air as light would, and then he displays them like fire. He does this that he may through these contrary approaches mislead the athlete of Christ. [87]

14. If you want to learn how you need to pray, consider the purpose of attention – or, better, of prayer – and do not be deceived. For its end, my beloved, is ceaseless compunction, the heart's distress, and love for our neighbour. Its opposite is quite obvious: the thought of desire, whispers of slander, hatred for our neighbour and whatever else resembles these. [96]

St Symeon of Thessaloniki, *On the Sacred and Deifying Prayer*

ST SYMEON, ARCHBISHOP OF THESSALONIKI (*c*.1381–1429)

Symeon grew up in Constantinople during its twilight. He joined a monastery at some point, probably the Xanthopoulos Monastery, which was a haven of hesychast thought and the home of several Philokalic writers as well as many of the patriarchs of Constantinople in the fourteenth century. Symeon, however, was assigned in 1416 or 1417 to Thessaloniki (Thessalonica), which was already in a precarious position between Venetian, Byzantine and Ottoman forces. By 1422, the city was fully besieged and Symeon had to leave surreptitiously to ask the emperor for more forces, but he never got that far. Turning back at Mt Athos, Symeon returned to Thessaloniki and remained there until his death in 1429, not long before the city fell to the Ottomans in 1430.

During these years, Symeon was an active church leader and theologian; nonetheless he wrote extensively on matters theological. His longest work, *The Life in Christ*, includes dogmatic sections and then full commentaries on the whole cycle of liturgical services. In the course of this commentary, Symeon included an extensive treatise on prayer, from which Nikodemos and Makarios excerpted a brief section for inclusion in the *Philokalia*. This short excerpt, *On the Sacred and Deifying Prayer*, falls into two parts. The first explicates the transformative power of the 'Jesus Prayer', while the second enjoins it on all Christians, and not just monks. Symeon's broad-minded approach informed Nikodemos's own claim that the *Philokalia* was for all Christians too.

Sources

Text: Excerpts from Symeon, *On Prayer*, in *Patrologia Graeca*, vol. 155, cols. 536C–670C

Alternative text: *PHILOKALIA* (1782): 1160–62; *Philokalia* (1893/1982): vol. 5, 60–62

On the Sacred and Deifying Prayer AND That all Christians, whether priests, monks or laity, ought as much as they can to pray in the name of Jesus Christ

[296] *Concerning the sacred [and deifying] prayer.*

This divine prayer, the invocation of our Saviour, runs: 'Lord Jesus Christ, Son of God, have mercy on me.' It is both a supplicatory prayer and a vow, a confession of faith, bestower of the Holy Spirit, procurer of divine gifts, a purification of heart, expeller of demons, indwelling of Jesus Christ, a fount of spiritual concepts and divine thoughts. It is cleansing from sins, hospital for souls and bodies, provider of divine radiance, welling up of God's mercy, and awarder of divine revelations and initiations in humility. It is itself salvation since it bears in itself the saving name of our God, which is the only *name invoked by us* [James 2:7]: Jesus Christ, Son of God. And, as the Apostle says, *It belongs to no other for us to be saved* [Acts 4:12]. Now, the prayer is a supplicatory prayer because in it we seek divine mercy. It is a vow because we offer ourselves to Christ by invoking him. It is confession because when Peter confessed this, he was blessed [Matt. 16:16]. It is a bestower of the Spirit because *No one says Lord Jesus except in the Holy Spirit* [1 Cor. 12:3]. The prayer is a procurer of divine gifts because, says Christ, *For this reason I will give to you*, Peter, *the keys of the Kingdom of Heaven* [Matt. 16:19]. It is purification of heart because it sees God and calls him, and it purifies the one who sees [Matt. 5:8]. It is an expeller of demons because all demons were and are cast out in the name of Jesus Christ [Luke 10:17, Acts 16:18]. It is Christ's indwelling because

by our recollection of him Christ is in us and through our
memory of him he indwells and fills us with gladness: for it
says, *I remembered God and was glad* [Ps. 76:4]. The prayer is
a fount of spiritual concepts and thoughts because Christ is the
repository of all wisdom and knowledge, and he bestows both
on those in whom he dwells. It is cleansing from sins since,
on account of this prayer, *Whatever things you loose*, he says,
will be loosed in heaven [Matt. 16:19]. It is the hospital for
souls and bodies because, as it says, *In the name of Jesus Christ
rise and walk!* [Acts 3:6]. And *Aeneas, Jesus Christ heals you*
[Acts 9:34]. The prayer is a provider of divine radiance because
Christ is *the true light* [John 1:9] and he bestows his own radiance and graces on those who invoke him. It says, *And let the
radiance of the Lord our God be upon us* [Ps. 89:17]. And *One
who follows me will have the light of life* [John 8:12]. It is the
welling up of God's mercy because we seek mercy and the *Lord
is merciful* and has compassion on all who invoke him [Ps.
102:13, 110:4, etc.]. He *brings about justice* swiftly *for those
who cry out to him* [Luke 18:7]. The prayer is an awarder of
divine revelations and initiations for the humble because it was
given to Peter, a mere fisherman, through a revelation of the
heavenly Father. And Paul was snatched up in Christ and heard
revelations, too, and the prayer always accomplishes this [2
Cor. 12:1–4]. It is itself salvation because, as the Apostle says,
It belongs to no other for us to be saved [Acts 4:12], and Christ
himself is the Saviour of the world. For this reason, on the last
day *every tongue will confess* and proclaim, both those who
want to and those who do not, that *Jesus Christ is Lord, to
the glory of God the Father* [Phil. 2:11]. This is the sign of our
faith, since *we are and are called Christians*.[1] It is a testimony
that we are from God. For *every spirit that confesses that the
Lord Jesus Christ has come in flesh, is from God* – as we have
said – and any spirit that *does not confess is not from God, and
this is the spirit of the Antichrist* [1 John 4:2–3], which does
not confess Jesus Christ. Thus, all the faithful must ceaselessly
confess the name, for a proclamation of faith, for love of our
Lord Jesus Christ – from whom nothing must ever separate us –
for the grace from his name, for remission, cleansing, healing,

sanctification, enlightenment and, above all, salvation. For the apostles wrought marvels and taught in this same divine name. The divine Evangelist says, *These things have been written that you may believe that Jesus is Christ the Son of God* – you see the faith there! – *and that, believing, you may have life in his name* [John 20:31] – there you see salvation and life!

[297] *That all Christians, whether priests, monks or laity, ought as much as they can to pray in the name of Jesus Christ for a determined amount of time.*

Let every pious individual make this invocation as a prayer, constantly, both in his mind and with his tongue. Whether he stands, travels, sits, reclines, says or does anything, let him compel himself to this prayer. He will then find the greatest calm and joy, as those who practise this have learned by experience. But since this task is beyond the reach of those who live in the world and monks who *live in the din of a community*,[2] in each situation there must be a definite time set apart for the prayer. And all must hold this prayer as their exemplar, to recite as vigorously as they can, whether they be priests, monks or laity. Since monks have been commanded to do this and owe it as an inescapable debt, then, even if they are serving in a noisy place let them compel themselves constantly to perform this prayer as its debtors, and to pray ceaselessly to the Lord. Even if they fall into distraction and confusion – which is and is called 'captivity of the intellect' – let them not grow careless because the enemy has robbed them, but let them return to the prayer and then rejoice. Now, let priests be diligent in this task because it is apostolic, because it is a divine proclamation, because it accomplishes divine activities, and because it presents them with Christ's love. Let the laity living in the world perform this prayer as much as they can, as a seal for themselves, as a sign of faith, as a guard, sanctification and expulsion of every temptation. So then everyone, priests, monks and laity, should, upon rising from sleep, think of Christ first, remember Christ first, and so offer Christ this task as a first fruit and sacrifice of every thought. For we must remember, more than anything else, Christ who saved us and loved us so much, since

we *are and are called Christians*. We have been clothed in him
by divine baptism [Gal. 3:27], we have been sealed with his
oil, we have partaken of his holy flesh and blood, we are his
members [1 Cor. 6:15, etc.], his temple [1 Cor. 3:16]. We have
put him on and he dwells in us [1 Cor. 3:16]. For all this, we
really ought to love him and remember him always. So then, let
everyone have, as a kind of repayment plan, a set time and a set
number of recitations of this prayer, according to their ability.
Let this suffice for the present, since there are numerous texts
available for the instruction of those interested in the prayer.

St Mark of Ephesos, *On the Words of the 'Jesus Prayer'*

ST MARK OF EPHESOS, OR EUGENIKOS
(1392–1445)

St Mark is sometimes called one of the 'Three Pillars of Ortho-doxy', alongside St Photios of Constantinople (ninth century) and St Gregory Palamas, and for much the same reason: he was seen to set down doctrine in good order and opposed Roman doctrines seen by Byzantines as corruptions and compromises of the truth. Unlike Photios and Gregory, however, Mark voiced his opposition to Rome at a council held for the express purpose of reuniting Latin West and Greek East. This was the Council of Ferrara/Florence (1438/9), a last-ditch effort by the Byzantine emperor and his advisors to effect union with Rome and secure papal and western European aid against the im-pending destruction of the Byzantine Empire at the hands of the Ottoman Turks. Mark, well educated in philosophy and theology, a devout monk and devotee of Gregory Palamas, was appointed Bishop of Ephesos and charged with attending the council as the leading theological voice of Constantinople. There, he loudly opposed doctrines of purgatory, papal auth-ority, the 'Filioque' (an addition to the Creed to the effect that 'the Spirit proceeds from the Father *and the Son*') and other matters. When union was decreed and delegates signed off, Mark refused. Upon his return to Constantinople he was hailed by many as a hero who upheld the faith in the face of politically expedient corruption, thereby becoming an enemy of the em-peror and patriarch both. He was later caught in port fleeing to

Mt Athos and subjected to exile, though he eventually returned to Constantinople and died the leader of the Orthodox opposition to union with Rome. He was shortly thereafter hailed as a saint, a defender and martyr of orthodox faith, and his reputation ever since has been defined by this. He is, therefore, a rather polarizing and poorly understood person whose words and deeds are lobbed as grenades on Roman Catholic or Eastern Orthodox opponents.

However, the short text included (anonymously) in the *Philokalia* breathes a different air entirely. In this work, *On the Words of the 'Jesus Prayer'*, Mark meditates on the origin of each word in order, the connections that can be formed between them, the biblical passages which inspire them, and even the doctrinal work they can be seen doing. It is a study in what one might ponder while praying, and how one might connect this short prayer to the Church's rich theological and liturgical traditions, while making Scriptural passages into triggers that recall the prayer and so return the reader to it.

Sources

Text: Irenej Bulović, ʻΗ ἑρμηνεία τῆς εὐχῆς τοῦ Ἰησοῦ ὑπὸ τοῦ ἁγίου Μάρκου Ἐφέσου', *Κληρονομία* 7 (1975): 347–52

Alternative text: (Anonymous, in demotic) *PHILOKALIA* (1782): 1163–7; *Philokalia* (1893/1982): vol. 5, 63–8

On the words contained in the divine prayer – 'Lord Jesus Christ, Son of God, have mercy on me.'

What power is contained in this prayer – 'Lord Jesus Christ, Son of God, have mercy on me' – what gifts are given to those who undertake it, or to what worthy state it leads them, it is beyond our power to say. Rather, the words of the prayer were first discovered by our holy Fathers, who have not spoken individually or on their own account. Rather, they took their start from the divine Scripture itself and then from Christ's chief disciples. Or, to put it better, they laid up a fatherly inheritance which they have handed on to us also, so that from it even those who must can learn without experience the inspired divinity and, as it were, oracular power of this prayer. For we believe that everything which Christ, having spoken to his holy apostles, furnished for them to say or write, is oracular, divine, a Spirit-bearing revelation and a voice of God.

To begin with, that supremely divine Paul, as though speaking with us right from the *third heaven* [2 Cor. 12:2], says, *No one can say 'Lord Jesus' except by the Holy Spirit* [1 Cor. 12:3]. Reading between the lines, Paul marvellously reveals how lofty and far beyond most people is the invocation of the Lord Jesus. John the Theologian, who thundered out matters of the Spirit, began where Paul left off, and, in a sense joining his own words to Paul's, gave us the next part of the prayer: *Every spirit which confesses Jesus Christ has come in the flesh is from God* [1 John 4:4]. Having used an affirmation here, John has followed Paul in the order determined by the Spirit's grace and established the invocation and confession of Jesus Christ. Let the very peak and summit of theologians come third, to hand over the rest of the prayer under consideration. For, the Lord asked his disciples, *Who do you say I am?* Peter's zeal outstripped the others, as was his wont, and he answered, *You are the Christ, the Son of God* [Matt. 16:17] – just as the Saviour himself testified, having been revealed by the Father and the Holy Spirit [Matt. 3:17, 17:5].

Look with me now at these sacred disciples: they cling to one another as in a ring, and each takes his divine words from another, so that each begins by picking up where the other left off. Thus, Paul says 'Lord Jesus' and John 'Jesus Christ' and Peter 'Christ, Son of God' – end joins to beginning in a circle, like we said, so that it makes no difference whether one says 'Lord' or 'Son of God'. For both names reveal the divinity of the only-begotten Son of God, establishing him as equal in nature and honour with his Father. These three blessed men, the most trustworthy of all, have thus bequeathed to us the invocation and confession in the Spirit of 'Lord Jesus Christ, Son of God'. As it says somewhere in the divine account, *'Every claim* is *confirmed* through *three witnesses'* [Deut. 19.15, cf. Matt. 18:16, 2 Cor. 13:1].

Likewise, the order of the apostles who uttered these divine words is not without significance. For the mystic transmission of the prayer begins with Paul – chronologically last among the disciples – and the words proceed through their midst, with John, to the first disciple, Peter, who out of love drew near to Jesus more than all the others. I consider this a symbol of our own well-ordered progress and ascent, and our union through ascetic struggle and contemplation in love with God. Paul, who said, *I advanced further than all of them* [1 Cor. 15:10], expresses ascetic struggle; John expresses contemplation; and Peter, who was averred to love Jesus more than others [cf. John 21.15–17], expresses love.

Not only that, but it is possible to see these same divine words of the prayer clarifying our pious doctrine and driving off every heresy of false belief. First, 'Lord': which denotes the divine nature of Christ, overthrows the heresy of those who say that he was only a man, and not God. Then 'Jesus': which shows again the human nature of Christ, and overthrows those who say that he was only God and not man, and only appeared to assume humanity in a phantasm. Then 'Christ' – which shows the two natures, divine and human, existing in one person and one *hypostasis*, and overthrows the heresy of those who say that Christ had two natures separated the one from the other. And then 'Son of God': which shows that in Christ the natures are unconfused both earlier and after the union and overthrows the heresy of those who say that the divine and human nature in Christ cannot be distinguished. Thus, these four titles, since they are God's words and spiritual swords, overthrow and destroy the two pairs of heresies, which, though diametrically opposed, are equally wicked and equally impious.

The prayer's titles and their connections defeat those who follow the heretics listed below:[1]

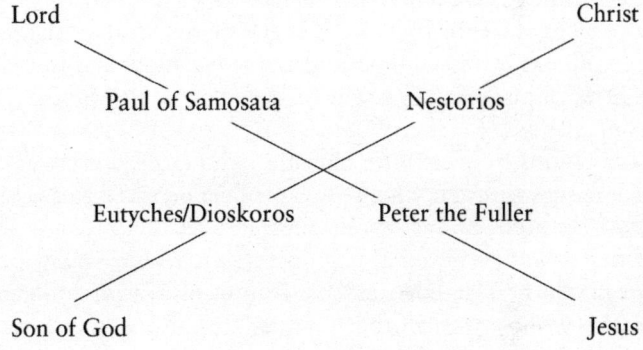

Lord · Christ

Paul of Samosata · Nestorios

Eutyches/Dioskoros · Peter the Fuller

Son of God · Jesus

These same divine words have been handed down to us and are rightly called a pillar of prayer and orthodoxy alike, sufficient for those who have advanced in Christ-like stature and been perfected in spirit. Those people cherish and welcome each of these divine oracles as a complete work of prayer, just as they were published by the holy apostles – that is the 'Lord Jesus', 'Jesus Christ', 'Christ, Son of God' – and, yes, sometimes the sweetest name of Jesus, by itself. Through this prayer they are filled with unutterable and spiritual delight, having left flesh and world, and attaining divine gifts. Initiates understand, as they say.

Now, there is added 'have mercy on me', which concerns infants in Christ and people still imperfect in virtue. This phrase shows the imperfect to be cognizant of their own state and in need of great mercy from God. So, for now, they imitate that famous blind man who, yearning to look up, cried out to the Lord as he passed by, *Jesus, have mercy on me!* [Mark 10:47]. Some people in charity make the object of the prayer plural. Hence, they present us with the prayer thus: 'Lord Jesus Christ, our God, have mercy on us.' Such people recognize love as the *fullness of the law and prophets* [Rom. 13:10, Matt. 22:40], since it embraces and recapitulates every commandment and spiritual practice. They lovingly draw their brethren into the prayer's communion and in this way exhort God to send down greater mercy to all in common. They inaugurate a shared mercy since, perhaps, divine mercy is accustomed to accrue to us through right faith in the matter of doctrine, and our fulfilment of the commandments in the matter of practice. The brief phrase of this prayer has been shown to be comprehensive of both.

One could, by following chronological order, discover the divine names through which we have been granted to contemplate the exact meaning of our doctrines, sitting in good order and succession as noted above, in the same way as we speak them in the prayer. For the Old Testament always proclaims God the Word as 'Lord', both before and after the coming of the Law. It says, *The Lord rained fire from the Lord* [Gen. 19:24] and *The Lord said to my Lord* [Ps. 109:1]. But the New Testament introduces the angel to give a name to his incarnation, and to say to the Virgin, *You will call his name Jesus* [Luke 1:31] – which, according to the divine Luke, he was called. Insofar as he is God, he is Lord of all, yet he desired in his economy for humankind to style himself our Saviour – which, after all, the name 'Jesus' signifies when translated. As to the name 'Christ', which reveals the deification of the nature which he took to himself, he forbade his disciples to call him by it prior to his passion, but after his death and resurrection Peter boldly proclaimed it. He said, *Let the whole house of Israel know that God made him Lord and Christ* [Acts 2:36].

This makes sense, for our nature, when it was taken by God the Word, was immediately anointed by the divinity which assumed it, and when this anointing happened, it became thereafter identically God after my Jesus' being glorified in his passion and resurrection from the dead. When did the acclamation of the title 'Christ' find its due season? Not merely when he appeared our benefactor, fashioning us in the beginning, and again refashioning and saving us, broken as we were; but when he leads our nature to heaven, glorifying us with himself and vouchsafing us a seat with him next to the Father. Indeed, when the Son of God and God began to be announced by the apostles, at first, in the early days of the Gospel, they reverenced the title and used it sparingly, but later they *shouted it from the rooftops*, in splendour, as the Lord himself had foretold them [Matt. 10:27]. Thus, the divine words of the prayer have been ordained logically and in the sequence of our faith's chronological elaboration, so that the divine wisdom of the words ordained and transmitted to us may shine out splendidly in all directions: from the orderly submission to the apostolic confessions and transmissions; from our pious doctrine blazing out; and from our recalling the seasons in accord with which we have variously benefited from God's providence, as we are introduced to piety by the corresponding phrases.

Now then, we have suggested these ideas about the words of the prayer so far as we are able, as though plucking the flowers of some grand and beautiful tree. Let others, to whom long meditation and discipline have given it, who, indeed, have penetrated the depths and drawn near to God, harvest the fruit that lies still within the words.

Glossary

activity: see *energeia*
autonomy: see *autexousia*
capacity: see *dunamis*
contemplation: see *theôria*
despondency: see *akêdia*
emotion: see *pathos*
free choice: see *proairesis*
imagination: see *phantasia*
intellect: see *nous*
justice: see *dikaiosunê*
leading faculty: see *hêgemonikon*
mind: see *dianoia*
moderation: see *sophrosunê*
passion: see *pathos*
righteousness: see *dikaiosunê*
stillness: see *hêsuchia*

akêdia: translated as despondency, but including meanings of
   listlessness and boredom mixed with anxiety and self-doubt.
autexousia, to autexousion: autonomy, self-governance;
   humans have moral responsibility over things 'up to us'
   (*ta eph' hemin*), though they may not have much choice
   in a given moment because of patterns of habit or ways of
   thinking. Thus, autonomy is not quite the same as 'free will'
   (see *proairesis*), but it is the capacity humans have by virtue
   of reason (see *logos*) to act in ways that can be praised or
   blamed.
dianoia: translated as mind, having the sense of discursive
   reason or ways of knowing that require time, development,

argumentation and the like. It is frequently opposed to the direct, intuitive knowing of *nous* (and its verbal form, *noesis*). Words derived from this (*ennoia*, *epinoia*, etc.) are generally translated as 'concept'.

dikaiosunê: justice, or righteousness; a word with biblical resonance (usually as 'righteousness') as well as philosophical ('justice'). In the latter tradition, *dikaiosunê* is a sort of comprehensive virtue indicative of the soul's parts and capacities functioning in harmony. It is also a way of describing individuals' behaviour in civil society, in which they contribute to the same kind of harmony at a macro-scale.

dunamis: capacity, often in the Aristotelian sense of what an entity is suited for by nature or divine purpose. When this capacity is put to use in practice, it becomes *energeia*, or activity.

energeia: activity, often in the Aristotelian sense of an entity's natural activity for which it is suited by nature or divine purpose, and so fulfils a creature's *dunamis*.

epithumia, epithumêtikon: desiring part of the soul in a Platonic psychology. Desire is inevitably aligned with the quest for pleasure (*hêdonê*) and the flight from pain (*odunê*), which bind humans to passion (see *pathos*).

hêgemonikon: leading faculty, originally a Stoic term for the guiding rationality of soul, this came to be used synonymously with 'rational part' or even 'intellect' (see *logistikon* and *nous*), but to describe the capacity of humans for rational self-direction more than contemplation or cognition.

hêsuchia: stillness, silence; this term underwent a crucial shift in meaning around the twelfth century. Before then, this word was commonly used to describe an eremitic monastic life, on one's own or with one or two companions. Those who practised this kind of monasticism were called *hêsuchastai*, or 'hesychasts'. *Hêsuchia* meant a predominantly silent existence. However, among later writers, the language of stillness and isolation came to be aligned with practices of continual prayer, so that eventually a 'hesychast' refers to a practitioner of continual and interior prayer, regardless of their living situation, and that practice came to be called *hêsuchia*. From this we get the term 'hesychasm' which refers to this mode of spiritual practice. The range of meaning encompassed by *hêsuchia/hêsuchastês* is, therefore, markedly different among earlier Philokalic writers and later ones.

logismos: thought, train of thought; frequently used negatively as harmful or distracting trains of thought. These are frequently suggested by demons, although not always.

logistikon: rational part of the soul in a Platonic psychology, so called because it is where *logos* operates (see *logos*).

logos: Word of God, spoken word, capacity for reason, an account or argument; this term is foundational to Christian thought right from the beginning in John 1:1: 'In the beginning was the *Logos*, and the *Logos* was with God, and the *Logos* was God.' Christian writers personalize *logos* as referring specifically to the second Person of the Trinity, the Son. But it is also the term for the rationality built into creation by God. Thus, beings have principles according to which they are made, and these are their *logoi*. But *logos* can simply mean reason or discursive reason, and creatures which have it (humans and angels both) are called *logikoi*. But reason is expressed in language, and so, again, *logos* may mean the spoken word, the written word, a treatise or sermon, and so on. At the same time, since reason allows for judgement, distinction and persuasion, *logos* can mean argument or even the criterion of a good argument.

Logos–logoi–logikos: this connection is at the very core of Greek Christian metaphysics, a way of conceptualizing human beings, the created world and its Creator under the same forms. We have often included *logos* in brackets when the English is not obviously related.

nous: translated as intellect, having the sense of rational, direct cognition, sometimes contrasted with discursive reason (see *dianoia*). Words derived from *nous* (*noeros*, *noêtos*, etc.) are translated as 'intellectual' or 'intelligible'. One exception is *noema*, which means something more like 'concept' or 'mental representation', either of an object perceptible to the senses (an idea of stone, for example) or one purely intellectual (an arithmetical proof).

pathos: passion, emotion, frequently in a strongly negative sense of an irrational emotional response to persons, events or objects, predicated on improper attachments to property or status. There are other meanings of *pathos*, too, though Philokalic authors tend to use the term for problematic emotions and attachments.

phantasia: imagination, mental representation, used sometimes to mean the soul's capacity to represent objects in the mind or to mean those objects themselves. The latter is basically synonymous with *phantasma*. If used negatively in context, we have sometimes rendered *phantasia* as 'fantasy'.

phronesis: moral wisdom; this is Aristotle's guiding virtue and has the connotation of good sense, sound thinking, unimpeded by mistaken values or judgements.

prosbolê: attack, provocation; a technical term for demons' initial suggestions, which, if entertained, grow into trains of thought (see *logismos*).

praktikê: practical virtue, which means virtue attained through repetitive practice and habituation. This is also used to delimit the earlier stages of ascetic life, in which passions (see *pathos*) are reduced and removed through regimes of psalmody, fasting, vigil and prayer. This paves the way to the later stages, dedicated to contemplation (see *theôria*).

proairesis: free choice; this is more restricted than moral responsibility and human autonomy (for which see *autexousia, to autexousion*), and refers to choices made through deliberation, with purpose, and in situations where it is possible to have chosen otherwise.

sophrosunê: moderation; though moderation is insufficient. *Sophrosunê* comprehends 'practical wisdom' and the agreement of knowledge and action in one's life. It can also include connotations of self-control or chastity – not simply in the sense of celibacy, but, rather, of total integrity of action.

theôria: contemplation, especially contemplation of the creation ('natural contemplation'), of angelic hierarchies and, ultimately, of God ('theology'). Sometimes this term is used to mean interpretation of a text or saying. More frequently, it or a derivative (*theôrêtikê*) describes the later stages of ascetic practice, dedicated to prayer and contemplation of God (see also *praktikê*).

thumos, thumêtikon: irascible or spirited part of the soul in a Platonic psychology. This can also be a term for strong emotion generally, though often in a negative way.

Frequently Cited Sources

THE PHILOKALIA

Makarios of Korinth and Nikodemos of Athos [the Hagiorite], eds., *ΦΙΛΟΚΑΛΙΑ ΤΩΝ ΝΗΠΤΙΚΩΝ ΠΑΤΕΡΩΝ* [*PHILOKALIA TŌN NĒPTIKÔN PATERÔN*], (Venice: Antonio Bortoli, 1782; in 5 vols., Athens, 1893; repr. Athens: Aster, 1982)

English translation: G. E. H. Palmer, Philip Sherrard, Kallistos Ware et al., *The Philokalia: The Complete Text*, 5 vols. (London: Faber & Faber, 1979–2023)

(Ps-)Dionysios the Areopagite: Pseudo-Dionysius, *The Complete Works*, trans. Colm Luibheid, Classics of Western Spirituality (New York: Paulist Press, 1987)

Evagrios of Pontos (or, Pontikos): *Evagrius of Pontus: The Greek Ascetic Corpus*, ed. and trans. Robert E. Sinkewicz (Oxford: OUP, 2003)

St Gregory Nazianzen, *On God and Christ: The Five Theological Orations and Two Letters to Cledonius*, trans. Lionel Wickham and Frederick Williams, Popular Patristics 23 (Crestwood, NY: St Vladimir's Seminary Press, 2002)

St Gregory Nazianzen, *Festal Orations*, trans. Sr Nonna Verna Harrison, Popular Patristics 36 (Crestwood, NY: St Vladimir's Seminary Press, 2008)

St Isaak the Syrian: Holy Transfiguration Monastery, *The Ascetical Homilies of Saint Isaac the Syrian* (rev. edn; Boston: Holy Transfiguration Monastery, 2020)

St John Klimakos: Saint John Climacus, *The Ladder of Divine Ascent*, trans. Lazarus Moore (Jordanville, NY: Holy Transfiguration Monastery, 1979)

SAYINGS OF THE DESERT FATHERS

The *Alphabetical Collection* (Name #): *Give Me a Word: The Alphabetical Sayings of the Desert Fathers*, trans. John Wortley, Popular Patristics 52 (Crestwood, NY: St Vladimir's Seminary Press, 2014)

The *Anonymous Collection* (N #): *The Anonymous Sayings of the Desert Fathers: A Select Edition and Complete English Translation*, ed. and trans. John Wortley (Cambridge: CUP, 2013)

The *Systematic Collection* (S #): *The Book of the Elders: The Sayings of the Desert Fathers. The Systematic Collection*, Cistercian Studies 240, trans. John Wortley (Kalamazoo, MI: Cistercian Publications, 2012)

Further Reading

ORTHODOX SPIRITUALITY (SEE ALSO 'FREQUENTLY CITED SOURCES')

Anonymous, *The Way of a Pilgrim: Candid Tales of a Wanderer to His Spiritual Father*, ed. Andrew Louth, trans. Anna Zarenko (London: Penguin Classics, 2019)

Igumen Chariton, *The Art of Prayer: An Orthodox Anthology*, trans. Eugenia Kadloubovsky and E. M. Palmer (London: Faber & Faber, 1997)

Nikodemos of Athos, *A Handbook of Spiritual Counsel*, trans. Peter A. Chamberas, Classics of Western Spirituality (Mahwah, NJ: Paulist Press, 1988)

STUDIES AND ESSAYS

Bingaman, Brock and Bradley Nassif (eds.), *The Philokalia: A Classic Text of Orthodox Spirituality* (Oxford: OUP, 2012)

Bolshakoff, Sergius, *Russian Mystics* (Collegeville, MN: Liturgical Press, 1976)

Hausherr, Irénée, *Spiritual Direction in the Early Christian East*, Cistercian Studies 116 (Kalamazoo, MI: Cistercian Publications, 1990)

Louth, Andrew, *Modern Orthodox Thinkers: From the Philokalia to the Present* (Chambersburg, PA: InterVarsity Press Academic, 2015)

———, *Selected Essays*, vol. 2, ed. Lewis Ayres and John Behr (Oxford: OUP, 2023)

Rigo, Antonio (ed.), *Da Teognosto alla Filocalia (XIII–XVIII sec.): testi e autori* (Bari: Edizioni di Pagina, 2016)

Russell, Norman, *Gregory Palamas and the Making of Palamism in the Modern Age* (Oxford: OUP, 2019)

Ware, Metropolitan Kallistos, *The Inner Kingdom* (Crestwood, NY: St Vladimir's Seminary Press, 2000)

Notes and References

INTRODUCTION

1. For the story of the relationship between the *Philokalia* and the *Dobrotolyubie*, see Andrew Louth, 'The Slav *Philokalia* and *The Way of a Pilgrim*', in *Mount Athos and Russia: 1016–2016*, ed. Nicholas Fennell and Graham Speake (Peter Lang, 2018), 99–116, and more briefly in *The Way of a Pilgrim*, trans. Anna Zaranko, intro. Andrew Louth (London: Penguin Classics, 2019), ix–xvi.

INTRODUCTION TO THIS BOOK

1. Gregory Nazianzen, *Oration* 38 ('On Theophany') 11, in *Festal Orations*, 68.
2. Scholion 12 to Maximos the Confessor, *Questions to Thalassios* 61: in Maximos the Confessor, *On Difficulties in Sacred Scripture: The Responses to Thalassios*, Fathers of the Church 136, trans. Fr Maximos Constas (Washington DC: Catholic University of America, 2018), 447.
3. Maximos the Confessor, *Commentary on the Lord's Prayer*, in this volume.
4. John Chrysostom, *Homily on Matthew* 20.1, in *Nicene and Post-Nicene Fathers*, First Series, vol. 10: *Chrysostom: Homilies on the Gospel of Matthew* (Peabody, MA: Hendrickson, 1994), 140.
5. Basil of Caesarea, *Homily on the Words, 'Attend to yourself'* 2, in St Basil the Great, *On the Human Condition*, trans. Nonna Verna Harrison, Popular Patristics 30 (Crestwood, NY: Saint Vladimir's Seminary Press, 2005), 95.
6. Gregory Nazianzen, *Oration* 27 ('Against Eunomius') 4, in *On God and Christ*, 28.

EVAGRIOS PONTIKOS

1. Makarios 'the Egyptian', a monk of Nitria; Evagrios was his disciple for a time, and included several sayings attributed to him in the *Praktikos*.

2. A triangular number is a number R_n, which is equal to $R_{n-1} + n$, beginning from $R_0 = 0$. Thus $0 + 1 = 1, 1 + 2 = 3, 3 + 3 = 6, 6 + 4 = 10$, $10 + 5 = 15 \ldots 21 + 8 = 28 \ldots 136 + 17 = 153 \ldots$ Greeks would not have thought of the series this way, however. Rather, they used the term 'triangular' because the component parts could be arranged into an ever-expanding equilateral triangle:

3. Hexagonal numbers are a subgroup of triangular numbers, and may be represented as $R_n = R_{n-1} + 4n + 1$, beginning from $R_0 = 1$. Thus $1 + 4(1) + 1 = 6, 6 + 4(2) + 1 = 15, 15 + 4(3) + 1 = 28 \ldots$ $120 + 4(8) + 1 = 153 \ldots$ Again, Greek mathematicians represented these figurally, with each new figure containing the previous ones.

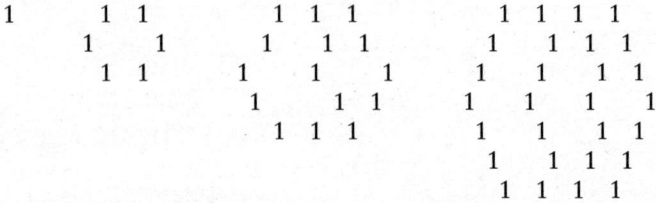

4. Evagrios means a 'circular' number, which is 'recurrent' – its last digit is the same in all powers (e.g. $5 \times 5 = 25$).

5. These are square numbers as we think of them – the product of an integer multiplied by itself. It may be represented as $R_n = R_{n-1} + 2n - 1$, beginning from $R_0 = 0$. Thus we have either $1^2 = 1, 2^2 = 4, 3^2 = 9 \ldots$ or $0 + 2(0) + 1 = 1, 1 + 2(1) + 1 = 4, 4 + 2(2) + 1 = 9, 9 + 2(3) + 1 = 16, \ldots 81 + 2(9) + 1 = 100$. Again, though, the Greeks conceived of these numbers figurally:

1	1 1		1 1 1			1 1 1 1
	1 1		1 1 1			1 1 1 1
			1 1 1			1 1 1 1
						1 1 1 1

6. Cf. Prov. 23:27 and Socrates' parable about the souls of hedonists in the *Gorgias* (493a–494a).

7. Evagrios's version does not correspond well to modern editions of the Greek New Testament.

8. Evagrios refers to the federation of monasteries founded by Pachomios (292–348), and centred in Tabenessi, in Upper (Southern) Egypt. These monasteries are considered prime examples of communal, or coenobitic, monasticism.

9. A disciple of Pachomios and later leader of the Pachomian monasteries.

10. In the LXX, the Philistines, as they are named in the Hebrew and English versions, are simply called *allophuloi*: 'of another race', or 'aliens'.

ST DIADOCHOS OF PHOTIKI

1. Some manuscripts have 'rational'.

2. Cf. Evagrios Pontikos, *Praktikos* 58; *Evagrius of Pontus: The Greek Ascetic Corpus*, 108; Maximos the Confessor, *Four Hundred Chapters on Love* 1.88, in this volume.

3. 'Martyrdom of conscience' refers to a very popular description of the ascetic life in Athanasios of Alexandria, *Life of Antony* 47, in Athanasius, *The Life of Antony and the Letter to Marcellinus*, trans. Robert C. Gregg, Classics of Western Spirituality (Mahwah, NJ: Paulist Press, 1980), 66.

ST MAXIMOS THE CONFESSOR, *FOUR HUNDRED CHAPTERS ON LOVE*

1. Dionysios the Areopagite, *Mystical Theology* 1.3, in Pseudo-Dionysios, *The Complete Works*, 136–7; Gregory Nazianzen, *Oration* 38 ('On the Nativity') 7 or 45 ('On Holy Pascha') 3, in *Festal Orations*, 65 and 163–4.

2. Three passages: Gregory Nazianzen, *Oration* 2 ('In Defense of His Flight') 38, in Philip Schaff and Henry Wace (eds) *Nicene*

and Post Nicene Fathers second series, vol. 7: S. Cyril of Jerusalem. S. Gregory Narzianzen (Peabody, MA: Hendrickson,
1994), 212–13; Oration 39 ('On the Lights') 11, in Festal Orations, 87; and Oration 25 ('In Praise of Hero the Philosopher')
17, in Gregory of Nazianzus, Select Orations, trans. Martha
Vinson, Fathers of the Church 107 (Washington DC: Catholic
University of America Press, 2003), 172–3.

3. Flavius Josephus (c.37–100 CE), a Jewish historian. See his
Jewish War 6.4.5–8.

4. Dionysios the Areopagite, On the Divine Names 4.23, in Pseudo-
Dionysios, The Complete Works, 90.

5. Evagrios Pontikos, Praktikos 58, in Sinkewiecz, Evagrius of
Pontus: The Greek Ascetic Corpus, 108; see also 1.88 above.

ST MAXIMOS THE CONFESSOR,
COMMENTARY ON THE LORD'S PRAYER

1. Cf. Eucharistic Prayer of the Liturgy of St John Chrysostom.

A DISCOURSE ON ABBA PHILEMON

1. Probably the Monastery of Al-Baramus in the Wadi Natrun,
west of Alexandria.

2. Arsenios was a monk of Sketis in Egypt in the late fourth century, renowned for his isolation and austerity. The question
comes from Arsenios 40, in Give Me a Word, 51.

3. The location is unknown.

4. John Chrysostom, On the Priesthood 6.3 in Philip Schaff (ed.),
Nicene and Post-Nicene Fathers, First Series, vol. IX: Saint
Chrysostom.

5. Basil of Caesarea, Epistle 2.2, in Basil, Letters, vol. I: Letters
1–58, trans. Roy J. Deferrari, Loeb Classical Library 190 (Cambridge, MA: Harvard University Press, 1926), 11.

6. Perhaps using a simple melody repeated for each verse and
interspersing short hymns or choruses between. See Johann von
Gardner, Russian Church Singing, vol. 1: Orthodox Worship
and Hymnography, trans. Vladimir Morosan (Crestwood, NY:
St Vladimir's Seminary Press, 1980), 32, 49–51.

7. The 'Apostle' is the book containing everything in the New Testament besides the Gospels (and Revelation), or the book containing the liturgical readings from this part of the New Testament.

8. Compare Diadochos of Photiki, *One Hundred Gnostic Chapters* 31, 59, 61, in this collection.

9. i.e. the Nicene Creed.

10. i.e. the Eucharist.

11. i.e. Constantinople.

12. Alluding to Evagrios Pontikos, *Foundations of the Monastic Life* 9, on which this whole passage is also modelled: in *Evagrius of Pontus: The Greek Ascetic Corpus*, 9–10.

13. Gregory Nazianzen, *Oration* 20 ('On Doctrine and the Office of Bishop') 12, in Brian E. Daley, SJ (trans.), *Gregory of Nazianzus*, The Early Church Fathers (London: Routledge, 2006), 104.

14. Basil of Caesarea, *Longer Response* 2.18–19, in his *Asceticon*: Anna M. Silvas, *The Asketikon of St Basil the Great*, Oxford Early Christian Studies (Oxford: OUP, 2005), 165–6.

15. Although he was a priest he was not involved with Eucharistic services.

16. The exclamation of the priest in the divine Liturgy, after the Lord's Prayer, marking the beginning of the preparation for Holy Communion.

ST SYMEON THE NEW THEOLOGIAN

1. John Klimakos, *Ladder of Divine Ascent* 29 title, in Saint John Climacus, *The Ladder* 221.

2. Lit. 'they allegorize badly'.

3. Gregory Nazianzen, *Oration* 38.7, in *Festal Orations*, 65.

4. i.e. death.

5. i.e. the set of church services beginning with Matins and culminating in the divine Liturgy.

6. i.e. a personal rule of prayer maintained in addition to communal services.

7. From the first Pre-Communion Prayer in the Byzantine Rite, ascribed to St John Chrysostom.

8. All of these refer to sections of the church office at which a monk would be present daily. The Six Psalms (3, 37, 62, 87, 102 and 142) are chanted at the beginning of Matins, after which the

Psalms of the daily setting ('*kathismata*') are chanted responsively. The Scripture reading probably refers to the Epistle and Gospel readings which come at the end of the first half of the divine Liturgy, and so the reference here to 'divine Liturgy' focuses especially on the Eucharistic Prayers and reception of the Eucharist – times which are considered especially reverent and demand greater attentiveness.

9. The last service of the evening, after which monks retire to bed.

10. A brief set of prayers which are said morning and evening, and at the beginning of almost all services. Their recital takes less than five minutes.

11. Eastern Orthodox Lent (forty days from Clean Monday to the Friday before Lazaros Saturday) and the Nativity Fast (also called St Philip's Fast, 15 November–24 December) are both fasts lasting forty days. The other two fasting periods – the Dormition Fast (fourteen days before the Feast of the Dormition of the Mother of God, 15 August) and the Apostles' Fast (Monday after All Saints' Sunday to the Feast of the Apostles, Peter and Paul, 29 June) – are both less than forty days, but they (or one of them) seem to be included with the two principal fasting periods here.

12. John Klimakos, *Ladder of Divine Ascent* 26.69, in Saint John Climacus, *The Ladder of Divine Ascent*, 172.

13. A *kanon* is a complex hymnodic form originating among Byzantine monastics and very popular by the tenth century. It gradually overtook the earlier hymnodic forms of *kontakia*. It is a series of hymns arranged according to nine 'odes' (or songs) found in Scripture. For each ode a melody is determined and a series of *troparia* (verses) sung, with a brief chorus between that is repeated throughout the *kanon*. In practice, the second *ode* is always omitted (usually not even composed), so a *kanon* is a series of eight stanzas of four to seven verses each.

14. A practice of reciting twelve psalms as a night-time service is attested among Egyptian monastics as early as the fourth century: John Cassian, *Institutes* 2.4–6. The practice was maintained as a service through the Byzantine period, with the rule being found at the back of Psalters. It is no longer in use.

15. This prayer refers, probably, to one made by the Martyr Eustratios prior to his death, included in Symeon Metaphrastes, *Martyrdom of Eustratius and His Companions* 32 (PG 116: 505B–C), and thence in daily morning prayers for Saturdays.

16. i.e. meat.

17. Cf. Ezek. 18:23; but really this is a quotation from the prayers of absolution, said over a penitent who has confessed.
18. Gregory Nazianzen, *Oration* 20 ('On Doctrine and the Office of Bishop') 4, in Daley, *Gregory of Nazianzus*, 100.
19. i.e. the altar.
20. i.e. a monk who is also an ordained priest.
21. The prayer book which contains the prayers and rubrics for most services. In fact, it is – and was – more common for the Gospel Book to be placed on the head of the one being ordained.

PS-SYMEON

1. Abba Moses 6, in *Give Me a Word*, 195.
2. John Klimakos, *Ladder of Divine Ascent* 27.33, in Saint John Climacus, *The Ladder of Divine Ascent*, 203.

ST ELIAS EKDIKOS

1. Maximos the Confessor, *Four Hundred Chapters on Love* 3.71, in this collection.
2. Elias follows Evagrios's distinction between contemplation of material beings and the principles according to which they exist ('second natural contemplation') and the contemplation of immaterial, rational beings and their principles ('first natural contemplation'). For a concise discussion, see David Brakke, *Demons and the Making of the Monk* (Cambridge, MA: Harvard University Press, 2006): 74–6 and notes.
3. This was a commonly believed legend about stags.
4. Evagrios Pontikos, *Praktikos* 68: 'The perfect man does not practise self-control, and the dispassionate man does not endure. Endurance belongs to one who still suffers and self-control to one still troubled' in *Evagrius of Pontus: The Greek Ascetic Corpus*.

NIKIPHOROS THE MONK

1. Evagrios Pontikos, *Praktikos* 91: in *Evagrius of Pontus: The Greek Ascetic Corpus*, 112.
2. Originally a term of praise for philosophy, but as that term came to be used for monasticism and spiritual direction, the epithet

was frequently transferred as well. Nikiphoros may have in mind Gregory Nazianzen, who uses the term for spiritual direction: *Oration* 2 ('A Defence of His Flight') 16, in Philip Schaff (ed.), *Nicene and Post-Nicene Fathers*, Second Series, vol. 7: *S. Cyril of Jerusalem. S. Gregory Nanzianzen* (Peabody, MA: Hendrickson, 1994), 208.

3. St Antony the Great (250–355/6), remembered as the first hermit and trailblazer of eremitic monasticism. The passage is from Athanasios of Alexandria, *Life of Antony* 59.1–6, in Athanasius, *The Life of Antony and the Letter to Marcellinus*, 75.

4. Not found in John's works; perhaps they are scholia.

5. St Theodosios of Palestine founded a lavra east of Bethlehem in 476. The monastery still stands and bears his name. The passage is compiled (quite strangely) from Symeon Metaphrastes, *Passion of Saint Theodosius the Coenobiarch* 12 and 40–41, in PG 114:469–553.

6. Arsenios, or, as he is commonly called, Abba Arsenios, was a famous monk of Sketis in Egypt at the turn of the fifth century. According to tradition he was tutor to Arcadius and Honorius, children of Theodosios the Great. He left Rome to become a monk and undertook a particularly austere lifestyle. The passage is from *Life of the Holy Arsenios*, 14, in F. Halkin, *Hagiographica inedita decem*, Corpus Christianorum, Series Graeca 21 (Turnhout: Brepols, 1989), 91–110. The story originates in the *Sayings of the Desert Fathers*, Arsenios 42, in *Give Me a Word*, 52.

7. *Life of the Holy Arsenios*, 16.

8. Paul was born near Elaia in the later ninth century. He was tonsured at a monastery on Mt Latros (Beşparmak, in southwestern Turkey) and given leave to live as a hermit. He eventually commissioned a chapel and soon a monastery, dedicated to the Mother of God of the Pillar. The passage is from *Life of St Paul the Younger* 20, in H. Delehaye (ed.), 'Vita S. Pauli Junioris', in T. Wiegand (ed.), *Milet*, 3.1: *Der Latmos* (Berlin: Reimer, 1913), 105–35.

9. St Sabbas (Saba), 'The Sanctified', lived from 439 to 532 in Byzantine Palestine. He founded several monasteries, the most important of which is Mar Saba in the Wadi an-Nar (Kidron Valley), east of Jerusalem. The passage is largely a paraphrase of Cyril of Skythopolis, *Life of St Saba*, in Cyril of Scythopolis, *The Lives of the Monks of Palestine*, trans. R. M. Price, Cistercian Studies 114 (Kalamazoo, MI: Cistercian Publications, 1991), 122.

10. Agathon was a monk of Sketis in the fourth century. The passage is Agathon 8 in *Give Me a Word*, 55.

11. Excerpts from Mark the Solitary, *Letter to Nicholas* 12–13, in this collection.

12. St John Klimakos ('Of the Ladder', *c.*579–649) was abbot of the Batos Monastery in Sinai, usually called St Catherine's. He composed one book, the *Ladder of Divine Ascent*, which became an enormously popular and influential work of spiritual direction in the Christian East. The passage is a composite of *Ladder of Divine Ascent*, 27.6, 27.22–3, 26.78 and 26:2.33, in Saint John Climacus, *The Ladder of Divine Ascent*, 198, 200, 173, 194.

13. Isaiah of Gaza (or, of Sketis, d. 489) was a monk in Gaza who initiated a style of intense, personal direction in Gazan monasteries which would influence many Philokalic writers. Nikiphoros quotes an epitome of Isaian material gathered into short *kephalaia* under the title *On Guarding the Intellect*, but the passage at hand can be found among Isaiah's *Discourses* 17.6 and 21.10, in Abba Isaiah of Scetis, *Ascetic Discourses*, trans. John Chryssavgis and Pachomios (Robert) Penkett, Cistercian Studies 150 (Kalamazoo, MI: Cistercian Publications, 2002), 137, 161.

14. Nikiphoros refers to Makarios the Egyptian, monk of Nitria and teacher of Evagrios, but the text comes from *Homilies* by an anonymous Syrian monk around the end of the fourth century, referred to by scholars as 'Pseudo-Makarios'. The passage is similar to one available in Pseudo-Macarius, *The Fifty Spiritual Homilies and the Great Letter*, trans. George A. Maloney, SJ, Classics of Western Spirituality (New York: Paulist Press, 1992), 168–9.

15. The passage is taken from Diadochos of Photiki, *One Hundred Gnostic Chapters* 57, in this collection. Diadochos's life is discussed there.

16. Isaak (*c.*615–700) came from Beth Qatraye (modern day Qatar) and was a member of the Church of the East. He was a great student of philosophical and theological learning, and a gifted teacher and preacher. He was made Bishop of Nineveh in 676 but abdicated after five months and retired to an eremitical life in what is now northern Iraq. Isaak wrote in Syriac, but this passage is taken from the Greek translation of Isaak's homilies, made within a century of his death, and extraordinarily popular among Byzantine Christians: *Homily* 30.9, found in *Homily* 2 (Greek 30.9) in *The Ascetical Homilies of Saint Isaac the Syrian*, 121.

17. John, Bishop of Karpathos (a Greek island east of Crete), writing probably in the seventh century. The passage is taken from his *Chapters for the Monks in India*, 52, in *Philokalia* 1:310.

18. Some of Symeon's writings appear in this collection, and his life is discussed there. This passage does not come from or correspond to any of the published works of Symeon.

19. Paraphrasing Gregory Nazianzen, *Oration* 39 ('On the Lights'), 14, in *Festal Orations*, 91.

ST GREGORY OF SINAI

1. Genesis calls the land Hevilath and says that there is good gold there. From Herodotus onward, Greek writers associated India (the Indus basin region, really) with gold, and so Byzantine authors associated the biblical Hevilath ('Euilat' in the LXX) with India. Gregory follows Kosmas Indikopleustis's (sixth century) account very closely here: *Christian Topography* 2.81.

2. Andrew of Caesarea, *Commentary on Revelation* 22.64 (on Rev. 20:11), in Andrew of Caesarea, *Commentary on the Apocalypse*, trans. Eugenia Scarvelis Constantinou, Fathers of the Church 123 (Washington, DC: Catholic University of America Press, 2011), 216.

3. The opinions of Antipater and Irenaeus as reported by Andrew of Caesarea, *Commentary on Revelation* 22.64 (on Rev. 20:11), in Andrew of Caesarea, *Commentary on the Apocalypse*, 216–17.

4. See John of Damaskos, *An Exact Exposition of the Orthodox Faith* 8, in St John of Damascus, *On the Orthodox Faith*, trans. Norman Russell, Popular Patristics 62 (Crestwood, NY: St Vladimir's Seminary Press, 2022), 78–9.

5. Elias Ekdikos, *Gnomic Anthology* II.27, in this collection.

6. The 'three giants' of Mark the Solitary, *Letter to Nicholas* 12, in this collection; Gregory refers to this doctrine at 122 below.

7. John of Damaskos, *An Exact Exposition of the Orthodox Faith* 64, in St John of Damascus, *On the Orthodox Faith*, 217.

8. Dorotheos of Gaza, *Instructions* 2.33, in Dorotheos of Gaza, *Discourses & Sayings*, trans. Eric P. Wheeler, Cistercian Studies 33 (Kalamazoo, MI: Cistercian Publications, 1977), 98.

9. Both in Symeon the New Theologian, *Discourse* 25.5, in Symeon the New Theologian, *The Discourses*, trans. C. J. deCatanzaro, Classics of Western Spirituality (New York: Paulist Press, 1980), 271.

10. Isaak the Syrian, *Homily* 77 (Greek 20.10), in *The Ascetical Homilies*, 537.

11. Gregory Nazianzen, *Oration* 39 ('On the Lights'), 20, in *Festal Orations*, 97.

12. Dionysios the Areopagite, *Celestial Hierarchy* 2.2, in Pseudo-Dionysios the Areopagite, *The Complete Works*, 149.

13. Probably a reference to Gregory Nazianzen, *Oration* 2 ('Apology for His Flight, etc.'), 7, in Philip Schaff and Henry Wace (eds.), *Nicene and Post-Nicene Fathers*, Second Series, vol. 7: *Cyril of Jerusalem. Gregory Nazianzen* (Peabody, MA: Hendrickson, 1994), 206.

14. Diadochos of Photiki, *One Hundred Gnostic Chapters* 86, in this collection.

15. Maximos the Confessor, *Four Hundred Chapters on Love* 2.94, in this collection. Maximos only mentions the first two motives.

ST GREGORY PALAMAS

1. A paraphrase of Abba Arsenios 13, in *Give Me a Word*, 42.

2. Dionysios the Areopagite, *On the Divine Names* 4.11, in Pseudo-Dionysius the Areopagite, *The Complete Works*, 80.

3. St John Chrysostom ('the golden-mouthed'), known for his fiery preaching and pastoral care as a priest in Antioch, was appointed Archbishop of Constantinople in 397. He came into conflict with Theophilos, Archbishop of Alexandria, and Epiphanios, Bishop of Salamis, as well as the Empress Eudoxia. At a synod in 403, John was condemned as a follower of Origen, whom Theophilos and Epiphanios prosecuted as a heretic, though he had been dead more than a century. John was condemned, and exiled to Cappadocia and then to Georgia, dying en route in 407. He was soon venerated as a saint and is commemorated in Orthodox Churches as the writer of the divine Liturgy and one of the Three Hierarchs, along with St Basil of Caesarea and St Gregory Nazianzen.

4. Aristotle, *Nicomachean Ethics* 8.8 (1159b).

5. Not Paul, but the Epistle of James 4:4.

6. Gregory Nazianzen, *Oration* 45 ('On Pascha') 18, in *Festal Orations*, 179.

7. Mark the Monk, *Against Those Who Believe Themselves Justified by Works* 197; modified: in Mark the Monk, *Counsels*

on the Spiritual Life, trans. Tim Vivian and Augustine Casiday, Popular Patristics 37 (Crestwood, NY: St Vladimir's Seminary Press, 2009), 136.

8. John Klimakos, *Ladder of Divine Ascent* 6.13, in Saint John Climacus, *The Ladder*, 67.

9. Gregory intends Neilos of Ankyra (fifth century), but unknowingly quotes Evagrios Pontikos, *Reflections*, I: *Gnostic Chapters* 4, in Sinkewiecz, *Evagrius of Pontus: The Greek Ascetic Corpus*, 211.

10. Evagrios Pontikos, *Reflections*, I: *Gnostic Chapters* 2, in *Evagrius of Pontus: The Greek Ascetic Corpus*, 211.

11. Diadochos of Photiki, *One Hundred Gnostic Chapters* 89, in this collection.

12. Isaak the Syrian, *Homily* 23, in *The Ascetical Homilies*, 245, quoting Evagrios Pontikos, *On Thoughts* (longer version) 39, in Sinkewiecz, *Evagrius of Pontus*, 180.

13. Isaak the Syrian, *Homily* 23, in *The Ascetical Homilies*, 245, claiming to quote Gregory Nazianzen, but the source is unknown.

14. Ibid.

15. Pseudo-Basil of Caesarea, *Ascetic Constitutions* 4 (PG 31:1353B).

16. This long quotation consists of selections from Mark the Monk, *Against Those Who Believe Themselves Justified by Works* 211, in Mark the Monk, *Counsels on the Spiritual Life*, 138–9.

17. Either Makarios the Egyptian (or 'the Great', fourth century), whose words and deeds are described in Desert literature; or Pseudo-Makarios, a Syrian writer of the same period whose *Spiritual Homilies* were very popular reading among Byzantine Christians. Gregory probably has the *Spiritual Homilies* in mind but would have assumed their author to be the Egyptian Makarios.

18. The Father is Abba Poemen: see Poemen 39, in *Give Me a Word*, 234.

KALLISTOS ANGELIKOUDIS

1. St John Chrysostom (d. 407); however, Kallistos is referring to medieval texts under Chrysostom's name.

2. John Klimakos, *Ladder of Divine Ascent* 21.7 and 27.61, in Saint John Climacus, *The Ladder of Divine Ascent*, 131 and 207.

KALLISTOS I

1. Ignatios of Antioch (d. *c.*135), *To the Romans* 7.2.

ST SYMEON OF THESSALONIKI

1. Athanasios of Alexandria, *First Oration against the Arians* 3.3, and John Chrysostom, *Oration 8 Against the Jews* 5.
2. John Klimakos, *Ladder of Divine Ascent*, 27.21, in Saint John Climacus, *The Ladder of Divine Ascent*, 200.

ST MARK OF EPHESOS

1. Paul of Samosata was Bishop of Antioch (260–68), and famously regarded not only as corrupt, but as an adoptionist. He stands in here as a proto-Arian: denying the divinity of Jesus.

   Nestorios was Archbishop of Constantinople (428–31), deposed and condemned at the Council of Ephesos (431); the great opponent of St Cyril of Alexandria. Nestorios is associated with a Christology that separates Christ's human and divine natures, against which Cyril advanced a strongly unitary Christology, according to which divine and human natures are one in the person of Christ.

   Eutyches (*c.*380–*c.*456) was a Constantinopolitan monk, a fierce supporter of Cyrilline Christology, a hero of the Council of Ephesos, but declared a heretic at the Council of Chalcedon (451). His opposition to Nestorios's Christology of 'conjunction' led him, it seems, to extremes of 'unionist' Christology. He was deposed in 448 but reinstated at a council (called the 'Robber Council' by Pope Leo the Great) by Dioskoros, then Archbishop of Alexandria (444–54). Dioskoros attempted to follow in his predecessor's, Cyril's, footsteps, but with less success. At Chalcedon his understanding of Cyrilline Christology was rejected in favour of Pope Leo's and he was himself deposed. Eutyches and Dioskoros became synonymous in Byzantine memory with 'monophysitism' – a Christology that, interested in the unity of divine and human natures in Christ, loses its proper regard for their distinction.

   Peter the Fuller was an openly anti-Chalcedonian Patriarch of Antioch (471–88). Mark here sets him out as one who denigrated the humanity of Christ in his emphasis on the divine nature, probably having in mind Peter's infamous addition of the words 'Who was crucified for us' to the hymn 'Holy God, holy strong, holy immortal': Chalcedonians understood this as a Trinitarian hymn, but Peter, following Antiochene custom and in accordance with Cyril of Alexandria's Christology, applied it to Christ.

INDICES

Index of Biblical Quotations

Index of Names

Index of Subjects